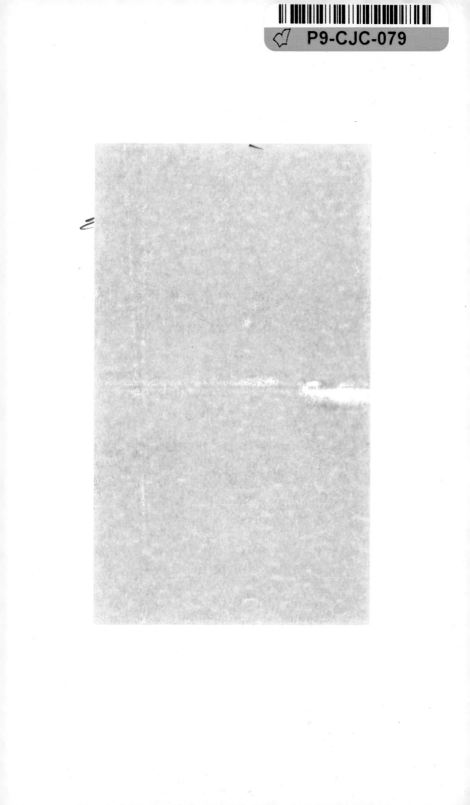

KOREA: THE SEARCH FOR SOVEREIGNTY

Also by Geoff Simons

IRAQ: From Sumer to Saddam

LIBYA: The Struggle for Survival

THE UNITED NATIONS: A Chronology of Conflict

UN MALAISE: Power, Problems and Realpolitik

Korea

The Search for Sovereignty

Geoff Simons

Foreword by
Tony Benn, British Member of Parliament

St. Martin's Press   New York

© Geoff Simons 1995
Foreword © Tony Benn, MP 1995

First published in the United States of America in 1995

Printed in Great Britain

ISBN 0–312–12531–3

Library of Congress Cataloging-in-Publication Data
Simons, G. L. (Geoffrey Leslie), 1939–
Korea : the search for sovereignty / Geoff Simons ; foreword
by Tony Benn.
p. cm.
Includes bibliographical references.
ISBN 0–312–12531–3
1. Korea—History. 2. Nationalism—Korea—History. I. Title.
DS907.18.S487   1995
951.9—dc20   94–39657
                                                    CIP

Contents

List of Figures

List of Tables

Foreword

Tony Benn, MP

Geoff Simons is a bold man to write about Korea as he has done in this important book. For the history of the last 50 years – as it has been endlessly explained to us by the authorities in Washington, London and in the tame media which they control – has offered only one explanation which every right-thinking person has been expected to accept uncritically. It is that South Korea is a model of democracy, and that North Korea is the last and worst of the old-style communist dictatorships, and an aggressor nation as well, now threatening world peace by developing its own nuclear weapons programme.

The Korean War, in the 1950s, was one of the most dangerous periods in the Cold War, and American, British and other troops were used to fight off the attack from the North against an apparently sovereign state. It was that war which, along with the Berlin blockade, the invasion of Hungary and the Cuban missile crisis, kept alive the arms race and encouraged the war hysteria that still goes on.

Against that background it is bold for anyone to challenge that established view and set this story in its historic perspective to allow us to examine the facts more coolly. For even the simplest summary of that history reveals aspects of this situation which must necessarily give the ordinary reader grounds for questioning what we have been, and still are being, told about Korea.

How many people know of the suffering of the Koreans under the Japanese occupation, of their longing for unity and independence, or of the price that was paid when that country was partitioned after the war? How can it be right that South Korea should still have a huge American base, which at one time and maybe still contains nuclear weapons, while the North is to be subjected to action by the US against it, even if the United Nations does not agree? Why is Israel with its own armoury of atomic weapons to be accepted, and supported by America, while other nations are prohibited from acquiring them?

In saying all this Geoff Simons should not be accused of being an apologist for the North Korean government, which has been guilty, like many of America's closest allies, of severe breaches of human rights. What he is drawing attention to in this book are the double standards that are the hallmark of the new imperialism that is run from Washington in the name of some 'New World Order', as proclaimed by the then President Bush after the collapse of the Soviet Union and when the Gulf War had proved the invincibility of US military power world-wide.

For this New World Order is little more than a coded message telling every nation in the world that America is now able to dictate to every other nation what it can and cannot do. Cuba is blockaded, against all the principles of international law, and Libya has been bombed in defiance of that same law. The people of Iraq are being starved by sanctions and the death toll rises year by year, while around the world some of the most authoritarian regimes are still supported by that same US administration. US airpower is available for use whenever the White House thinks it necessary in support of its global interests.

Queen Victoria followed a similar policy a hundred years ago to win and sustain the British Empire, and now we are back where we were then, though today it is all masterminded by the CIA.

To say all this is not to endorse the lack of democracy in North Korea or to advocate the spread of nuclear weapons, which are far too dangerous where they now are. But it is to warn those who get to read this book that the old American war machine that dominated Western policy from 1945 to 1990 is still at it, and we should think twice before we believe all that we are told.

Koreans are right to want to see their country re-united, and free from foreign troops and bases so that they can work out their own destiny as a genuinely independent nation. The dangers that face her stem, in large part, from the fact that she has been, and still is under the effective control of a foreign power, as has so often happened in the past.

Those who really want to see Korea, and the Koreans, develop along the lines of peace, human rights, and democracy would do well to remember that this can best be achieved through normalising its international and trading relations and allowing it to find its own way forward.

This is a well-researched and important book that will give its readers facts and an analysis that we are denied in our own press, and it will have to be taken seriously.

Preface

Some books represent real adventure, whether to read or to write. Every compulsive reader knows the signs: the disturbing encounter with new facts that shake preconceptions; the sudden evocation of delight or anger; the sweet empathy with a writer who calls compellingly across the chasms of time, space and culture.

Writing the present book was an adventure, not least because the research – performing its characteristic trick – spun off promiscuously in every direction. It was inevitably fascinating to explore an unfamiliar culture and its place in the world, but two stark impressions stand out above the rest. The first is how the Korean people, forced by geography to live under the shadow of powerful neighbours, have struggled with great fortitude over the centuries to protect their national identity.

Foreign invasions, military occupations, economic exploitation, genocide – all greatly intensified in the twentieth century when Korea was freshly colonised, ravaged in civil war, forced to endure a superpower onslaught, and to suffer the death and mutilation of millions. Throughout this entire period the national struggle for sovereignty was never extinguished. How ironic for the West that it is the communist regime of North Korea, rather than the traditional puppet in the South, that today most unambiguously represents Korean sovereignty. The South, against the instinct of many of its people, still has a foreign military presence; and implements only domestic and foreign policies that are congenial to Washington.

The second abiding impression is of the monumental arrogance and hypocrisy of the United States, perhaps the inevitable concomitants of unassailable military power. This is the country, keen to claim moral superiority over lesser states, that carried out chemical experiments on North Korean prisoners; that fire-bombed civilian targets during the Korean War, in violation of the Geneva Convention; that, in supporting the Israeli nuclear weapons programme, is one of the worst violators of the Nuclear Non-Proliferation Treaty. This is the country that, in contempt for Article 2(4) of the UN Charter, was prepared in 1994 to threaten a fresh war in the Korean peninsula.

The troubled history of Korea; the unending search for sovereign independence and national identity; above all, the dreadful tally of

human suffering, particularly in this century – all this should be remembered by the comfortable commentators in the West.

We need to see an end to the strategic posturing of powerful
states; an end to the age-old assumption that only hegemonic military power is entitled to claim virtue and to interpret the law; and,
more particularly, an end to the black comedy in which, as happened in 1994, an American secretary of state, Warren Christopher,
can announce with unconscious risibility that the United States –
with a 50-ship battle fleet off the coast of Korea, cruise missiles tar-
geted on Pyongyang, 20,000 nuclear weapons, and missiles that can
hit the planets – 'will not be intimidated by North Korea'.

GEOFF SIMONS

Acknowledgements

I am grateful to various people for providing generous support in the production of this book. Some of these, unstinting in their efforts, deserve particular thanks:

Tony Benn MP, who interrupted his own writing to supply the Foreword;

Tam Dalyell MP, who provided enthusiastic support and offered the generous prepublication commentary;

Alexandra McLeod, Librarian at the United Nations Information Centre, 18 Buckingham Gate, London SW1E 6LB;

Dr Bhupendra Jasani, Senior Research Fellow, King's College, University of London;

Dr Patricia M. Lewis, Director of the Verification Technology Information Centre (VERTIC), Carrara House, 20 Embankment Place, London WC2N 6NN.

Particular gratitude is due also to Christine Simons for maintaining her invaluable archive and for making many other contributions; and to Colette Simons for her many research initiatives.

I greatly appreciate the efforts of Elizabeth Lee (UN Information Centre) in supplying copious documentation; and the work of Emma Hillyard at the Korean Embassy in servicing my requests for information.

I remain especially grateful to Tim Farmiloe, Editorial Director at the Macmillan Press, for his enthusiastic and sympathetic support for this book and my other Macmillan titles.

Introduction

The dispute over North Korea's possible development of nuclear weapons began in the 1980s, took on a new dimension with the collapse of the Soviet Union, and began to assume crisis proportions in late 1993.[1] The crisis had escalated because of Washington's response to the refusal of Pyongyang, a signatory to the 1968 Nuclear Non-Proliferation Treaty (NPT) and the associated safeguards agreement, to allow IAEA (International Atomic Energy Agency) inspectors unfettered access to all North Korea's nuclear development facilities. The suspicion was created that plutonium was being diverted from peaceful nuclear projects to facilitate the development of nuclear weapons, a possibility that the United States had resolved not to tolerate. As the crisis escalated through 1994 there was mounting talk of the need to invoke punitive UN sanctions against North Korea, of the need to bring economic pressure to bear (on a state that the West depicted as already in terminal economic decline), and of the possibility of a new Korean war.[2]

One of the main purposes of the present book is to set details of the dispute *in the context of the post-Soviet world* (the so-called 'New World Order'), and *against the historical development of the Korean nation.* Today political opinions are too often shaped by sound bites, photo opportunities, one-liners, newspaper headlines, media caricatures, and other facile substitutes for thought and information. It is useful to remember that there is merit in political opinions that go beyond the simplistic knee-jerk reactions of ideological convenience.

An immediate impact of the collapse of the Soviet Union in the early 1990s was a massive reduction in Russian influence at the United Nations. The inevitable corollary was an increase in American influence, no longer constrained by the prospect of a Soviet veto in the Security Council. It soon became apparent that there was immense scope for corruption in this enlargement of US power.[3] The permanent and rotating members of the Security Council were variously bullied and bribed to support American strategic interests,[4] just as China was later offered Most-Favoured-Nation Trading status (in gross violation of President Clinton's earlier commitments on human rights) and the prospect of GATT membership[5] to buy Beijing's support for UN sanctions against North Korea.[6] Washington felt free to maintain punitive sanctions on Iraq, a *de facto* ban on the importation of food and medical supplies which was estimated by aid agencies in 1994 to be killing Iraqi children at the rate of 100,000 a year.[7] At the same time Washington felt under no obligation to pay its mandatory financial dues to the United Nations. At the time of the Gulf War (early 1991) the United States owed the UN some $451 million; in September 1992, $757 million; in early 1993, $845.7 million. In April 1994, at a time when Washington was beginning to exert serious pressure for the imposition of UN sanctions on North Korea, America owed the United Nations a total of $1,070 million.[8]

This is the broad context within which any major US foreign policy initiatives should be considered: a context in which Washington picks and chooses what international laws it observes, which legally derelict states it censures, which foreign nuclear weapons programmes it will oppose, and what methods it will use to suborn the UN Security Council (an odious practice that one international legal expert has suggested should be referred to the International Court of Justice[9]).

It is important also, in considering the particular case of North Korea, that various other matters be borne in mind. We need to remember that for many years the United States stockpiled nuclear weapons in South Korea, a military deterrent – and also a provocation – to the North. Washington seemed oblivious to suggestions that a withdrawal of its own nuclear weapons might contribute to an improved political atmosphere in the region.[10] Today there are (South Korean) claims that the US no longer maintains nuclear weapons in the peninsula, but Washington would be loath to agree to North Korean inspections of US military bases in the South.

There is also the circumstance that Washington itself has violated the Nuclear Non-Proliferation Treaty (Appendix 1) that the US is now so keen to invoke against Pyongyang.[11] The United States has shown no enthusiasm for implementing its obligations under Article V of the Treaty, namely that it will 'take appropriate measures' to make nuclear research available to non-nuclear states for peaceful purposes. More importantly, Washington has violated both the spirit and the letter of the Treaty in endorsing Israel's nuclear weapons ambitions (a massive provocation to the other states in the Middle East).

President Nixon at first delayed ratification of the Treaty because he believed that 'defensive nuclear weapons' should be made available to selected non-nuclear powers, those that supported US foreign policy. Once the Senate had ratified the Treaty, Nixon and Kissinger together issued a classified document, National Security Decision Memorandum (NSDM) no. 6, effectively undermining any impact the Treaty might have: 'there should be no efforts by the United States to pressure other nations . . . to follow suit [and ratify the Treaty]. The government, in its public posture, should reflect a tone of optimism that other countries will sign or ratify, while clearly dissociating itself [in private] from any plan to bring pressure on those countries to sign or ratify.'[12] In short, *the US government would lie in public about its support for the Nuclear Non-Proliferation Treaty.*

The American attitude to Israel's development and stockpiling of nuclear weapons is now abundantly clear. Thus Morton H. Halperin, a close Kissinger aide on the National Security Staff, commented: 'Henry believed it was good to spread nuclear weapons around the world. I heard him say that if he were the Israelis, he would get nuclear weapons. He did not believe that the United States should try and talk them out of it.'* During the 1960s Israeli nuclear developments at the Dimona site had been officially inspected by Floyd L. Culler Jr, a nuclear science expert and then deputy director of the Chemical Technology Division at the Oak Ridge National Laboratory; but in 1969, the year after the launch of the Non-Proliferation Treaty, Kissinger ended the Culler inspections.[13] Israel was given the green light for its development of nuclear weapons. Not only would Washington not object, it would agree the shipment of nuclear-linked products (for example, the krytrons used to trigger atomic bombs) to Israel.[14]

American support for Israel's nuclear weapons programme had another significant dimension. At a time when there was an international arms embargo on South Africa, 'the Israelis, the CIA, the Pentagon and the US State Department all united in a concerted three-year secret effort'[15] to ship to that country the materials and technology for the development of an artillery system able to deliver nuclear bombs. This meant that there was now significant American

---

*Washington has always helped Israel to acquire technically advanced weapons. For example, in June 1994 the US agreed to supply Israel with 25 F-151 fighter-bombers, highly sophisticated aircraft that would enable Israel to strike deep into Iraq and Iran without refuelling. The terms of the deal (valued at $2,400 million) meant that Israel was to be virtually given the aircraft (*The Independent*, 23 July 1994).

support not only for the Israeli nuclear weapons programme but also for the provision of a nuclear weapons capability to apartheid South Africa in its confrontation with the black states of southern Africa. In 1993 it was revealed that South Africa had come close to dropping an atomic bomb on Luanda.[16]

Today Washington remains equally selective in its approach to nuclear non-proliferation. The policy of duplicity and double standards introduced under the Nixon/Kissinger regime has persisted to the present day. No American president has been prepared to condemn Israel's clandestine development of nuclear weapons as a destabilising factor in the Middle East. Clinton 'will not tolerate' Pyongyang's alleged development of nuclear weapons, while remaining indifferent to how an Israeli nuclear arsenal serves as an obvious incitement to such states as Iraq, Syria, Jordan and Iran. In June 1994 the Indian premier, Narasimha Rao, announced that India would retain the option to develop nuclear weapons; the announcement provoked no American denunciation or threat of UN sanctions. Similarly, the position of Japan, now known to be stockpiling plutonium, remains deeply ambiguous. Japan has taken steps to convince the international community that it has no plans to develop nuclear weapons,[17] but at the same time we can discern a different message. Ichiro Ozawa, a key political figure behind the then premier Morihiro Hosokawa, has long advocated a more assertive Japanese role in international affairs; while at the same time there is mounting Japanese dissatisfaction with the country's post-Second World War 'pacifist' constitution. There are now signs that Japan is contemplating the development of nuclear weapons. In December 1993 Morihiro Hosokawa declared that 'owning nuclear arms is not entirely banned by the constitution as long as they are the minimum needed for self-defence'; and in early June 1994 the Japanese government prepared a statement which included the words: 'The use of nuclear weapons is not always illegal from the standpoint of international law.'[18]

These are the circumstances in which Washington seemed intent on moving towards sanctions against North Korea; even, if necessary, without China's commitment to refrain from using its veto in the Security Council. Now the United States, with the reluctant support of Japan and South Korea, was reportedly prepared to threaten Pyongyang with a ten-point programme of sanctions if it refused to open its nuclear facilities to IAEA inspection.[19] The Japanese premier, Tsutomu Hata, had agreed to cut air, trade and investment links with North Korea, and to stop the transfer of funds from the Korean immigrant community to Kim Il-sung's regime. It was left to the secretary-general of the opposition Socialist Party, the largest faction in the parliament, to protest that this was a premature decision. Said Wataru Kubo: 'We should be cautious about sanctions before the United Nations had even decided on anything.'[20]

The position was plain. The United States would continue to press in its characteristic way for a Security Council resolution (there was some hope that China would eventually yield), but if it proved impossible to dragoon the United Nations then Washington would contrive to apply economic and other pressures on Pyongyang in the absence of UN authorisation (much in the way that the US pressures other states into supporting its economic blockade of Cuba in violation of UN resolutions). Chapter 1 of the present book highlights some of the features of this post-Soviet 'New World Order', before charting the chronology of events in the 1990s that have led up to the present situation. Attention is also given to aspects of the nuclear non-proliferation issue that bear on the Washington–North Korean dispute.

Part II (Chapters 2–4) presents an outline history of the Korean nation, with particular focus on foreign incursions and the Korean struggle for national independence. Chapter 4 is of particular significance since the decades-long Japanese occupation of the Korean peninsula, a brutal part of Japanese colonialism in East Asia, prepared the way for the US-inspired geographical and ideological partition of the peninsula.

The consequences of partition – from the 'drawing of the line' to the current pressure for reunification – are considered in Part III (Chapters 5–7). It is suggested that, though the regimes of both North and South were authoritarian and owed their inception to foreign powers, the two parts of the peninsula were set to evolve in very different ways. An early distinction was that whereas the post-Second World War American military government in the South, via a procession of brutal proxies, preferred to retain Japanese-style repression for the preservation of large landlords, burgeoning capitalists and the military faction, the regime in the North introduced radical reforms – including land distribution to the peasants, workers' protection and feminist legislation – for the benefit of the mass of the people. This should be borne in mind in any consideration of the origins of the Korea War: it is not difficult to see why the communists in the North, having achieved a measure of popular consensus and not needing the protection of a foreign military occupation, should have regarded their incursion into the South as a legitimate attempt to liberate their compatriots from a US-imposed oppression.

It was inevitable that Washington, having decided (against earlier public declarations) to retain half of the peninsula as a strategic enclave in the Cold War, would depict the Korean War in rather different terms. The Southern regime, claimed Washington, enjoyed UN legitimacy – no real surprise since at that time the United Nations was a manifest toy of US Cold War strategies, a circumstance aided by a Soviet Union briefly absent from the Security Council in protest at the absurdity of US insistence that the Chiang Kai-shek rump be allowed to retain the Chinese seat on the Council. The hollowness of the Southern regime's claims to UN legitimacy has often been exposed.[21] And while Washington was denouncing the perfidy of the North Koreans, the United States was fire-bombing civilians in the North by the hundreds of thousands, and carrying out chemical experiments on North Korean prisoners regarded as 'expendables',[22] an activity depicted by one authoritative American academic as analogous to the behaviour of Nazi doctors in the death camps.[23]

Chapter 7 outlines some of the principal developments in North and South Korea in the decades following the Korean War. The two authoritarian regimes continued to develop in their characteristic ways, while at the same time there was mounting evidence of civil rights abuses under Kim Il-sung in the North and under the procession of US-sustained military dictators in the South. During this period various terrorist acts were attributed to the Pyongyang regime. Thus on 18 January 1968, some 31 North Korean commandos, disguised as South Korean soldiers and civilians, crossed the demilitarised zone (DMZ) and headed for Seoul in a vain attempt to assassinate President Park Chung Hee. On 24 January North Korean forces used a patrol boat to attack, board and capture the USS *Pueblo*, an intelligence vessel caught in North Korean waters; several of the American sailors were killed or wounded, and Secretary of State Dean Rusk called the seizure an act of war. The surviving crew members were not released until 24 December 1968, by which time the North Korean authorities had achieved 'confessions' and confiscated the *Pueblo*'s sophisticated electronic surveillance equipment.[24]

On 8 July 1985 President Ronald Reagan branded five nations (Iran, Libya, North Korea, Cuba and Nicaragua) members of a 'confederation of terrorist states' that was carrying out 'outright acts of war' against the United States. He declared: 'The American people are not ... going to tolerate these attacks from outlaw states run by the strangest collection of misfits, looney tunes and squalid criminals since the advent of the Third Reich.' The assumed terrorist status of North Korea was repeatedly reaffirmed thereafter, most recently in a US government document published in May 1994. In late 1993 a regional analyst was quoted as suggesting that North Korea no longer carried out terrorism: 'A lot of terrorism in the 1980s was attributed to Kim Jong Il [Kim Il-sung's son and heir apparent] but that has stopped. At some point you grow up.'[25]

It is interesting to look at the fortunes of Reagan's so-called 'outlaw states' (why were Iraq and Syria left out?): all, except North Korea, have received American attention in recent years. Iran survived the immense losses of the Iran–Iraq War (1980–1988) despite the US 'tilt' in favour of Iraq as a useful tamer of Moslem fundamentalism; Nicaragua was tortured into submission by years of US-orchestrated terrorism; Libya continues to be squeezed by escalating US-contrived UN sanctions (which, by banning air ambulances, have caused Libyan fatalities); and Cuba slides into destitution under the burden of the 35-year-long US economic blockade (maintained in violation of UN General Assembly resolutions).

With the collapse of the Soviet Union, recalcitrant states that persisted in their hostility to world capitalism were newly vulnerable. In the early 1990s the United States decided to pay some attention to the irritating problem of a communist regime's survival on the Korean peninsula.

Part I
New World Instability

1 The Mounting Tensions

NEW WORLD PRESUMPTION

With the collapse of the East European communist states in the late 1980s, the West was quick to herald the emergence of a new international order. President George Bush, in his State of the Union address to Congress on 31 January 1990, announced the 'new world of challenges and opportunities' and the 'need for leadership that only America can provide'. With the demise of the Soviet Union and Washington's military success in the 1991 US-led war against Iraq, there was growing talk of a New World Order set to shape the post-Soviet global scene. Bush himself was uniquely associated with the concept of the New Order; having contrived the killing, wounding or traumatising of many more than one million Arabs, he declared on 1 March 1991: 'There is a better climate now ... we are going to try to lead.'[1]

It seemed that Washington was well placed to define the contours of the New World Order. Recalcitrant (and weaker) states would be forced into compliance with the US interpretation of international law. Noam Chomsky, the leading American dissident and academic, nicely characterised the unambiguous message that Washington was keen to convey: in the New Order 'we are the masters and you shine our shoes'.[2] In the event the New World Order emerged as an unoriginal concept, at once simplistic and unworkable.

Throughout history the leaders of powerful states have been interested in imposing their individual versions of international order. *Pax romanus*, the papal distribution of lands between Spain and Portugal in the fifteenth century, the European colonial order in the nineteenth, the League of Nations – all were generated by powerful rulers who imagined that they would be able to hold eternal sway over their neighbours or over lands across the sea. George Bush was not the first leader in modern times to invoke the concept of a New Order: the same concept was proclaimed by Adolf Hitler and his National Socialists, defeated by an alliance of 'united nations' which even in war was laying the foundations for a successor organisation to the League. George Bush, in invoking his particular New World Order, seemed not to notice that the international order nominally protected by the Charter of the United Nations was subverted above all by the sovereign whims of powerful nations, and that in the post-Soviet world the primary culprit was the United States. If UN members, including the US, had been prepared to observe their obligations as signatories to the UN Charter there would have been no talk of a New World Order.

After the eviction of Saddam Hussein from Kuwait, the United Nations was assigned its role in Bush's New Order. The UN was thereafter to be prompted to provide a legal gloss, troops and other forms of support for Washington's foreign policy initiatives. Washington itself would not be required to observe international law or its obligations under the Charter;[3] and separate initiatives, operating in parallel with those involving the United Nations, could be taken in full knowledge that the Security Council would remain indifferent.[4] The Bush theory was that Washington was now in a position to interpret international law and the role of the United Nations as it saw fit, with any states that disagreed given no right of appeal; and that an international coalition of forces acting under nominal UN auspices would be available to demand compliance. The international policeman, writing its own laws and licensed to kill, would be instructed by Washington, supervised by American officers, and able to demand funding (by Japan, Saudi Arabia, Germany, and so on, after the Gulf War model) for mercenary troops. Said one authoritative financial editor of a leading American publication: the US will be 'the world's rent-a-cops', now able 'to pound our fists on a few desks' in Japan and Europe to 'extract a fair price for our considerable services', demanding that rivals to the United States 'buy our bonds at cheap rates, or keep the dollar propped up, or better yet, pay cash directly into our Treasury'.[5]

Now it seems that the neat plan has run into various problems. Not all Americans were sold on the idea. Thus Patrick Buchanan, a co-host of CNN's *Crossfire* and a syndicated columnist, remarked that talk of a 'new world order' sounds like 'the [Woodrow] Wilsonian gobbledygook we followed into the trenches of World War I – when, all the time, the hidden agenda was to pull Britain's chestnuts out of the fire'.[6] And even the prestigious Henry Kissinger, Secretary of State in the Nixon and Ford administrations, felt forced to comment that 'the new world order cannot possibly fulfill the idealistic expectations expressed by the president'. Kissinger, himself no stranger to the pragmatic use of lies, dictators and genocide to protect and extend American power, rightly perceived the likely complexities of the post-Soviet world.[7]

Another problem was that Bush's successor, President Bill Clinton, seemed to have little appetite for managing the clearly unworkable New World Order. When he addressed the UN General Assembly on 28 September 1993, Clinton declared that the United States 'intends to remain engaged and to lead'; just as on 28 May 1994, in affirming his renewal of China's 'most favoured trading' (MFT) nation status (and so reversing his earlier insistence on human rights progress), he again announced that the United States had a primary leadership role. Washington would *lead*, whatever that meant, but now there was no talk of a New World Order: indeed, the very term had come to acquire derisory connotations.

This is not to say that the United States will not continue to exploit its dominant position in the United Nations (though now it can no longer ignore the possibility of the Russian or Chinese veto in the Security Council); and the Pentagon will continue to plan for worldwide military interventions and to compute the likelihood of wars it will have to fight in the future.[8] In these latter scenarios North Korea is always granted a special place: a typical war-game scenario has North Korea invading the South with 300,000 troops and 5000 tanks; and more recently it has been assumed that the North will use nuclear weapons. President Clinton, happy for the moment (late 1994) with the role of Governor (rather than President) of the United States, may be content to stay with most of Bush's foreign-policy initiatives – such as intensifying the blockade of Cuba, maintaining the sanctions on Iraq, and squeezing the Libyan regime – but the US president has never been the only force shaping American foreign policy. There are always war factories to stimulate, the Pentagon to appease, war strategists to satisfy. Washington is generally unhappy without war or the threat of war, whatever the UN Charter might say.

In this complex and shifting situation it would be folly to imagine that Clinton's current diffidence will endlessly guarantee American passivity in the face of frequent foreign-policy humiliations. In the post-Soviet world, many US institutions, happily fledged in the Cold War, are uncertain what to do and where to turn. Muammar Gaddafi and Saddam Hussein may be tamed but Washington was not yet fresh out of useful bogeymen. They may be thin on the ground but the Washington strategic planners knew where to find the few that were left. As General Colin Powell, head of the Joint Chiefs

during the Gulf War, observed: 'I'm running out of demons – I'm
down to Fidel Castro and Kim Il-sung.'[9] New World Order or not,
there is plenty of mileage yet in the useful problem of Korea.

NUCLEAR PROLIFERATION

The use of atomic bombs to destroy the Japanese cities of
Hiroshima and Nagasaki in August 1945 evoked a wave of revulsion
that called forth a range of treaties to limit the possession and possible use of such weapons of mass destruction. An early seminal development was the holding of an international conference at the
United Nations headquarters to approve on 26 October 1956 the
Statute of the International Atomic Energy Agency (IAEA). The
Agency came into existence in Vienna on 29 July 1957; and on
14 November 1957 the UN General Assembly approved an agreement defining the Agency's relationship with the United Nations.
Subsequent treaties include: the 1959 Antarctic Treaty, banning
nuclear tests and the disposal of nuclear waste in that continent; the
1967 Treaty of Tlatelolco, aiming to introduce a nuclear-free zone;
the 1971 treaty banning the emplacement of nuclear weapons on the
seabed; and various treaties prohibiting the testing, development and
dissemination of atomic weapons. Of these treaties, and for the
purpose of the present book, the Treaty on the Non-Proliferation of
Nuclear Weapons (NPT) is of particular importance.

The IAEA, established in 1957 'under the aegis of the United
Nations', has an interest in the NPT (Appendix 1), the international
agreement signed in 1968 by the United States, Britain, the Soviet
Union, France and more than 100 other countries. The main treaty
objective is to prevent the spread of nuclear weapons to non-nuclear
states, so confining the possession of such devices to the Permanent
Members of the Security Council and one or two other (US-
approved) states (most notably, Israel). There can be little doubt
that the IAEA and the NPT were created and shaped to protect the
security and strategic interests of powerful nuclear states; in particular, the US. The Agency was designed by Washington as essentially
a strategic device to establish an international nuclear status quo
among the nations of the world. Thus in May 1954 the US began
secret talks with other uranium-producing states (Britain, Canada,
South Africa, France, Belgium, Australia and Portugal) as a prelude

to the drafting of the IAEA treaty. The IAEA, effectively run by the US, supported some nuclear schemes and opposed others, though it was soon obvious that the Agency would not be able to establish comprehensive global controls on the development of nuclear weapons. By the mid-1950s a number of developing states (India, Taiwan, Argentina and South Korea) had established their own national atomic energy commissions and there were suspicions that yet more states were becoming interested in the possibility of acquiring nuclear weapons.

By 1960 the non-proliferation debate had gained momentum, with various proposals advanced as draft resolutions in the UN General Assembly. Thus an Irish scheme proposed the total removal of all options for additional countries to join the nuclear club (then the US, the Soviet Union, Britain and France), while an ambitious Swedish proposal, the Unden Plan, urged the voluntary development of nuclear-free zones. On 4 December 1961 both resolutions were adopted, the Irish one unanimously and the Swedish one with a 58–10 vote with 23 abstentions (the Eastern bloc voting for, the Western against). Little then happened until in 1964 India submitted a special agenda item, 'Non-proliferation of nuclear weapons', to the General Assembly. Then the non-aligned members of the Geneva Disarmament Committee agreed a memorandum stressing that 'measures to prohibit the spread of nuclear weapons should ... be coupled with or followed by tangible steps to halt the nuclear weapons and the means of their delivery'. Such developments stimulated the United States to submit draft treaties to the General Assembly designed to protect the two-tier system in which some countries (those in the nuclear club) would be allowed nuclear weapons and the rest would not. The shortcomings in the resulting Non-Proliferation Treaty were glaringly revealed when, on the General Assembly vote (June 1968), a number of important countries abstained (Argentina, Brazil, France, India and several African states). It was widely perceived that the NPT had been drafted to protect the strategic interests of the atomic superpowers rather than to further the security of the world community of nations.

A central problem was that powerful states were free to pick and choose which Articles of the NPT would observe, which they would ignore, and which they would insist that other (weaker, non-nuclear) states would observe.[10] Thus Article VI, requiring the nuclear powers to cease the nuclear arms race, had no impact on the development of nuclear weapons; and the verification requirement specified in Article III was largely ignored by the major powers. Similarly, Article IV, framed as an inducement to developing powers wanting access to peaceful nuclear power, was never implemented: the nuclear powers had no intention of furthering 'the fullest possible exchange with the non-nuclear powers of equipment, materials and scientific and technological information for the peaceful uses of nuclear energy'. Such considerations and others soon made it apparent that the Non-Proliferation Treaty had been designed solely to protect the nuclear monopoly enjoyed by a few powerful states.[11]

There was thus no sense in which the Treaty was intended to enshrine the *sovereign equality* of UN members (as specified in Article 2 of the Charter). Some nations were fit to have nuclear weapons and some were not: the NPT was highly discriminatory in both conception and implementation, as it remains highly discriminatory in today's post-Soviet world. This should be remembered in any discussion of the obligations of non-nuclear signatories to the Treaty. In particular, for the purposes of the present book, North Korea's much-hyped derelictions should be set against how the nuclear powers (primarily the United States) ignore NPT Articles that they find uncongenial.

The relative failure of the Non-Proliferation Treaty is shown by the increasing number of states thought to possess a nuclear-weapons capability, by the failure of Washington to invoke the NPT in an even-handed way (US policy on Israel's nuclear weapons development remains a gross dereliction*), and the need continually to address issues that were nominally settled when the NPT was enacted almost three decades ago. President Clinton, to his credit, has urged a ban on the production of materials used to make nuclear weapons and has supported the moratorium on nuclear testing.[12] On 25 January 1994 the UN Conference of Disarmament began the quest for a total nuclear test ban in the context of the growing threat of proliferation (in such 'pariah' states as Iraq and North Korea). On 2 February diplomats began drafting an international treaty to ban nuclear tests. With the NPT itself due for review in 1995, the situation remains fluid: if the United States decides to

---

*America's active support for the Israeli nuclear weapons programme is a blatant violation of the Non-Proliferation Treaty (see Introduction, p. xvii).

resume testing then the other major nuclear powers will be quick to follow suit, and a boost will be given to international nuclear proliferation.

The course of global proliferation will in part be determined by US policy: it would be helpful if Washington were as keen to put pressure on client states as to threaten and isolate ideologically unsympathetic countries. At the same time it is now increasingly recognised – even with no possibility of a Soviet veto in the Security Council – that the US room for manoeuvre is limited (see 'The Wider World', below); and that the scope of even a revised NPT is unimpressive. States can remain outside the Treaty if they judge it in their interest to do so; and no clear benefits derive from membership. Equally important – and this should be noted in the context of the North Korean dispute – signatory states are free to withdraw from the NPT whenever they wish: under the terms of the treaty there are no legal penalties to punish withdrawal. Thus Article X(1) of the NPT reads:

> Each Party shall in exercising its national sovereignty have the right to withdraw from the Treaty if it decides that extraordinary events, related to the subject matter of this Treaty, have jeopardized the supreme interests of its country. It shall give notice of such withdrawal to all other Parties to the Treaty and to the United Nations Security Council three months in advance. Such notice shall include a statement of the extraordinary events it regards as having jeopardized its supreme interests.

This means that any signatory (in particular, for our purposes, North Korea) to the NPT is legally entitled to withdraw from the treaty at any time, subject to three month's notice and a statement. In the context of national sovereignty the withdrawing state is the only power entitled to judge its own 'supreme interests' and the significance of the 'extraordinary events' that it cites. *No other state, however powerful, has recourse under the Treaty to object to the decision or to take action against the state in question.* Any country that threatens military action against a state that declares its intention to withdraw from the NPT is in violation of Article 2(4) of the UN Charter.

Such considerations are important in examining US policy on possible nuclear developments in North Korea. In law, North Korea is entitled to withdraw from the NPT and thereafter to develop its own nuclear weapons. Such an event may or may not be desirable (according to one's political perspective), but it is not illegal; and in such circumstances the IAEA has no recourse. Whether or not the United States opts to apply military or other pressure – against the terms of the NPT and the UN Charter – is another matter. It is however abundantly clear that neither the NPT nor the IAEA will be invoked to punish US derelictions, not merely treaty violations or neglect of UN Charter provisions but also irresponsible mismanagement of the American nuclear programme: for example, in May 1994 the US government publicly admitted that it could not account for up to 1.4 tons of plutonium – enough to make 300 nuclear weapons – so acknowledging serious failures of its nuclear accounting system. There had already been formal enquiries into the possibility of US plutonium being used in the Israeli nuclear weapons programme. In any event the new findings opened the US government 'to charges of breathtaking irresponsibility'.[13] Similarly, a 22-month investigation by the General Accounting Office, the top congressional watchdog, exposed a dangerous laxity in US controls on nuclear-related exports (in the past five years some 1500 export licences granted for sales to countries of 'special proliferation concern' – including Iraq, Iran, India and Pakistan). More than half of the questionable licences involved Israel (*The Guardian*, 19 May 1994).

It is useful to bear such matters in mind when considering the US-North Korea dispute over the nuclear issue. In particular, it should be acknowledged that the United States, acting to protect its perceived strategic interests, is well prepared to ignore its treaty obligations and other requirements of international law.

THE CRISIS CHRONOLOGY

With growing evidence of North Korea's nuclear ambitions, there was increasing concern in the United States. Thus on 18 November 1991 the US Defense Secretary, Richard Cheney, and the Chairman of the Joint Chiefs, General Colin Powell, voiced alarm at what they chose to depict as the growing nuclear threat from North Korea. Cheney was scheduled to attend the annual US–South Korea security talks, at which principal agenda items would be North Korea's development of nuclear weapons and its refusal to open its nuclear facilities for IAEA inspection. Little attention was given to North Korea's evident perception of a nuclear threat from the South: the United States was believed to be storing some 60 nuclear bombs and 40 nuclear-tipped artillery shells at the Kunsan Air Base near Seoul.[14] President Bush had floated the possibility of withdrawal, but many military planners in Washington and Seoul saw such weapons as a legitimate means of pressuring North Korea to accede to US demands. It never seemed to occur to such strategists that a North Korea under nuclear threat may feel compelled to develop its own nuclear deterrent.

At the strategic talks in Seoul Cheney announced (19 November) that he wanted 'to serve notice on the North' that the United States and South Korea were united in their determination to resist aggression: 'We will of necessity focus on the major threat to security posed by North Korean development of nuclear weapons and its refusal to abide by the terms of the Non-Proliferation Treaty, to which it is a signatory.' The scheduled reduction of US forces in the South from 43,000 to 36,000 by the end of 1992 would go ahead, but no further cuts would be contemplated until North Korea came in line. Compared with South Korea's 750,000 men under arms, the US military presence could easily be represented as symbolic rather than substantive; but with the joint forces remaining under US command – 40 years after the end of the Korea War – it was difficult to avoid Pyongyang's charge that South Korea still operated as a US puppet regime.

On 21 November it was reported that South Korea's President Roh Tae Woo would announce during President Bush's planned visit in January that South Korea was now nuclear-free (that is, that the US nuclear weapons had been withdrawn). The move was seen as a significant gesture to Pyongyang: North Korea, it was argued, would no longer have an excuse for preventing IAEA inspection of its own nuclear facilities. However, it was still open to the North to see South Korea as sheltering under the US 'nuclear umbrella': with the possibility of air-launched weapons and sea-borne cruise missiles, the withdrawal of US nuclear weapons from the South had little military significance. At the same time Roh Tae Woo declared his hostility to military strikes against North Korea to destroy its nuclear plant. The hawks in the Pentagon were at least temporarily shackled.

President Bush arrived in Seoul on 5 January 1992 amid speculation that the growing North–South dialogue – not least on nuclear matters – would force the United States to contemplate direct talks with North Korea. Already the two regimes had concluded an agreement to work for a non-nuclear peninsula, with Pyongyang now suggesting that IAEA inspections might be allowed following direct negotiations between the US and North Korea. Marlin Fitzwater, the White House spokesman, noted the 'changed relationship' between the North and the South, and commented that Mr Bush 'will have a lot to say ... it will all be positive'. At the same time it was reported that Kim Woo Joong, chairman of the South Korean Daewoo conglomerate, was planning to visit Pyongyang to propose joint ventures in hotels and telecommunications. There were also signs that Bush intended to press South Korea to open its markets further to US goods: in two provincial cities, farmers and students demonstrated in protest, and further demonstrations were anticipated. Bush, seemingly oblivious to such events, none the less seemed prepared to adopt a placatory tone, especially on the North–South issue. A few weeks before, Cheney had been keen to denounce North Korea's '40-year history of aggression, terrorism and irresponsible weapons sales'; now Bush, avoiding the customary rhetoric, seemed to be flirting with the idea of *rapprochement* with the North. On 6 January widespread protests were held throughout South Korea in protest against US pressure to allow the import of rice: students and farmers set fire to US flags, and effigies of President Bush were burned.

There were now signs that North Korea was prepared to bend to international pressure. The IAEA announced that Pyongyang's ambassador in Vienna would soon declare his government's willingness to sign the mandatory Nuclear Safeguards Agreement as required for NPT signatories (Pyongyang had signed the NPT in 1985 but defaulted by not agreeing to safeguards). Now it was being suggested that Kim Il-sung's transfer of effective power to his son, Kim Jong Il, was being linked to attempts to stabilise the North Korea regime. The United States had already undertaken low-level talks with Pyongyang, and now it seemed likely that these would be upgraded. On 22 January 1992 a meeting was held in New York between Arnold Kantor, the US Under-Secretary of State for Foreign Affairs, and a delegation headed by Kim Young Sun, Secretary of the (North) Korean Workers' Party (KWP). With Pyongyang now having promised to sign the NPT safeguards agreement the following week in Vienna, there were still substantial US doubts about North Korean intentions. An American diplomat commented: 'They have to be whole-hearted about inspection. The incentive is something closer to normal relations with the US, but North Korea is still stonewalling as much as it can.'

On 30 January North Korea signed an agreement to open all its nuclear installations to IAEA inspection; but a senior Pyongyang official declared that ratification could take several months. The uncertainties still remained. Seoul pointed out that North Korea had rejected its idea of early pilot inspections, so fuelling suspicions that Pyongyang was simply playing for time. Only after ratification of the Agreement was North Korea required to submit to the IAEA an inventory of its nuclear materials, after which the inspections began. (Seoul had complained that the period between signature and ratification would allow unmonitored nuclear development.) On 4 May North Korea provided an initial report to the IAEA, and the first inspection took place soon after. The report gave details of nuclear material and design information, including: a research reactor at the Institute of Nuclear Physics, to which the IAEA had already gained access; a sub-critical facility at the Kim Il-sung University in Pyongyang; a nuclear fuel-rod fabrication plant and storage facility in Nyongbyon; an experimental 5-megawatt nuclear power reactor; and a radiochemical laboratory of the Institute of Radiochemistry being constructed in Nyongbyon. The report also gave details of a 50-megawatt nuclear power plant being built in Nyongbyon, a 200-megawatt plant being constructed at Taechow in the North Pyongan Province, three planned 635-megawatt reactors, two uranium mines, and two plants for producing uranium concentrate. Such details left no doubt that North Korea was highly committed to the development of nuclear power; but the question of nuclear weapons development was still open.

The first on-site IAEA inspections were undertaken in May 1992. Hans Blix, the Agency's Director-General, with a number of senior advisors, visited North Korea from 11 to 16 May at the invitation of the government. Talks were held with various high-level officials, including premier Yon Hyong Muk; Choi Hak Gun, the minister for atomic energy; and Kang Sok Ju, the first deputy minister of foreign affairs. The IAEA delegation visited several nuclear installations, and were assured by North Korean officials that the country's entire nuclear programme was devoted to peaceful purposes and that the safeguards agreements would be scrupulously respected. The officials also declared that, with a view to creating transparency and confidence, the IAEA personnel would be allowed to visit any site and installation, irrespective of whether it appeared in the initial report submitted by North Korea to the Agency.[15] A second inspections visit, by an IAEA safeguards team, was scheduled for July.

The atmosphere of apparent accord was not set to last. The Pyongyang authorities, for reasons that may be surmised, became increasingly reluctant to allow unfettered IAEA inspections of nuclear sites; and at least one international incident did much to sour the worsening climate. In December 1992, following President Boris Yeltsin's earlier announcement that Russia was stopping all military aid to North Korea, Russian special forces stormed a jet about to leave Moscow airport and arrested some three dozen senior weapons scientists, some of whom had been recruited to work on North Korean weapons development. It was reported that North Korea had selected the scientists from various Russian nuclear weapons research institutes, including the top secret Arzamas-16 and Chelyabinsk-70 facilities in the Urals. The Russian action followed Western pressure to prevent the exodus of senior nuclear specialists; today, despite all the talk of 'new freedoms', there are thought to be around 3000 such specialists banned from leaving Russia.[16]

In February 1993 North Korea rejected an IAEA request for further inspections, whereupon Hans Blix convened a meeting of the Agency's governors to discuss the deteriorating situation. By now the idea was being floated that if North Korea refused to comply then the dispute would be referred to the Security Council. This time the IAEA request had focused on two nuclear waste disposal plants in Yongbyon, 60 miles north of Pyongyang. The North Koreans claimed that the plants in question were military installations whose secrecy was important for national security, a claim that the government-controlled newspaper *Rodong Sinmun* supported by asserting that there were no hidden nuclear materials in the country. The IAEA, increasingly disposed to dispute this suggestion, had already examined plutonium samples from the Yongbyon facility which provided evidence that plutonium had been produced in larger quantities than had been so far admitted. David Kyd, an Agency spokesman in Vienna, commented that 'it does seem as if something is amiss'.

Now Pyongyang was warning that IAEA insistence on inspection would further damage international relations. Ri Tcheul, North Korea's permanent representative to the United Nations in Geneva, warned that the dispute was putting in jeopardy the safeguards agreement: 'If the IAEA continues to request a special inspection, then it forces [North Korea] not to implement her obligations under the agreement. If the IAEA blocks the way to negotiation or dialogue with us with coercive actions, it is quite natural for [North Korea] to take self-defensive measures.' On 22 February Kim Il-sung declared that his country faced an 'unprecedented' political and economic crisis. Some observers began to suggest the possibility of another Korean war. Thus a commentary in *Rodong Sinmun* stated that if a 'special inspection' or 'sanctions' were forced upon North Korea 'and the inviolable soil of our country is infringed upon by big powers, it would result in plunging the whole land of the North and the South into the holocaust of war'. With the Central Intelligence Agency (CIA) announcing that North Korea may produce a bomb 'this year' (1993), and other international experts agreeing that Pyongyang was about to acquire nuclear weapons, a 'race against time' was started to halt North Korea's nuclear weapons programme.[17]

The United States was now turning to the UN Security Council. The Council had been successfully manipulated in underwriting Washington's strategic attacks on Iraq and Libya. Perhaps the same trick could be worked against North Korea. After all, it was now useful to be able to depict Kim Il-sung as a much graver threat to peace than even Saddam Hussein. Thus Gary Milhollin, a nuclear expert, commented that the North Korean situation 'is far more serious' than in Iraq: 'North Korea has already produced enough plutonium and spare fuel for several bombs. They're right on the edge and going down to the wire. The Iraqis were three to five years away. North Korea could already have the bomb.' In the same vein the CIA chief James Woolsey warned that North Korea's bomb programme, 'our most grave current concern', could destabilise the region and pose a threat to Japan. In such circumstances Washington was increasingly keen to activate the Security Council; first for the imposition of mandatory sanctions on North Korea, and then what? The formation of fresh mercenary coalition to invade the North?

On 12 March 1993 North Korea announced that it was withdrawing from the Non-Proliferation Treaty, a decision it was fully entitled to take under Article X(1) of the treaty. The announcement immediately brought condemnations from South Korea, Japan and the United States. Pyongyang declared that it was withdrawing from the NPT in a 'well-justified self-defensive measure against the nuclear war manoeuvres of the secretariat of the IAEA'; US 'nuclear threats against North Korea' were condemned; and Washington was urged to suspend its joint military exercise being held with South Korea. Washington and Britain now suggested that the Security

Council would consider the question, though a fresh uncertainty was evident: China, a signatory to the NPT and a Permanent Member of the Security Council, could not be relied upon to tolerate firm Council resolutions against Pyongyang, as it had against Iraq and Libya. For the first time in the post-Soviet circumstances of the so-called New World Order it seemed that Washington no longer had total control of Council deliberations. China announced that the problems 'should be settled properly through consultations in a manner conducive to the universality of the Nuclear Non-Proliferation Treaty'. There was no support in this for mandatory UN sanctions and even sterner measures. A halt had seemingly been called to Washington's talk of effective UN action and to the demands of the American Right for military intervention.

The North Korean announcement of Pyongyang's intended resignation from the NPT did nothing to stabilize the situation. Fears were strengthened that North Korea was about to become a nuclear power, and US–South Korean military manoeuvres involving some 120,000 troops were launched. Pyongyang, interpreting the military activity as a deliberate provocation, announced that the country was going on to a 'semi-war footing' to deter an attack from the South. The North Korean decision on the NPT, albeit legal, was unprecedented: no other country had ever felt obliged to withdraw from the 154-signatory pact, though many had violated its letter and spirit in various ways.

Now North Korea, as either a cynical ploy or through genuine anxiety, was taking a number of military precautions and warning South Korea and the United States against any attack on the North. Kang Sok Ju, the North Korean First Deputy Minister of Foreign Affairs, declared: 'If those forces hostile to North Korea attempt to frighten us ... bringing pressure and sanctions, it is a foolish dream ... We will answer strong-arm actions with self-defensive measures and military sanctions.' At the same time Japanese Korean-language radio broadcasts were being jammed, a UN economic team scheduled to enter the country was barred, and the South Korean Yonhap news agency reported that foreign diplomats had been ordered to leave the North Korean capital. Unconfirmed reports said that Pyongyang had ordered troop reinforcements to the border between North and South; while Kwon Young Hae, the South Korean Defence Minister, ordered the South's forces to be put on alert as a 'precaution' against any military provocation from the North. South Korea's new President, Kim Young Sam, declared that North Korea was 'courting isolation from the international community'. Again there was growing Western talk of moves to involve the Security Council. At a Council meeting, most members were highly critical of Pyongyang's position; but, significantly enough, China blocked all attempts to make the Council issue any strong statement condemning North Korea. The United States, in a gesture of obvious bluster, declared that the United Nations might take punitive steps against North Korea if it refused to retract its decision to withdraw from the Non-Proliferation Treaty. There were no signs that China – with power of veto – would sanction 'punitive' measures; and in any case the projected withdrawal was legal within the terms of the Treaty.

An impasse had developed. North Korea was refusing to yield to international pressure; but the West, primarily the United States, was clearly frustrated in not being able to push punitive resolutions through the Security Council. Pyongyang had made it clear that it could not tolerate the inspection of every site selected by the US-dominated IAEA. Had the position of the principal parties been reversed there would have been no question of North Korean members of an international body – even linked to the United Nations – being allow untrammelled access to secret installations in the United States. In fact this scenario is not quite as fanciful as it might appear. The South Koreans have expressed their belief that there are now no nuclear weapons in their country, *but Washington still denies the North Koreans inspection rights over US bases in South Korea.* Perhaps there are still US nuclear weapons in the South. It is important also to remember that the IAEA Statute (signed by all Agency members) contains no provision for punitive action in the case of non-compliance. The benefits of membership can be withheld from the offending state and the matter can be referred to the United Nations. We should also note that Article XVII (Settlement of Disputes) requires differences not settled by negotiation to be referred to the International Court of Justice at The Hague. At no time has Washington shown any interest in observing this IAEA Statute provision.* Similarly, the Non-Proliferation Treaty contains no provisions for punitive action in the event of non-compliance. Hence no powerful state can cite the authority of the IAEA or NPT terms as a justification for unilateral action against a derelict state.

---

*Just as Washington resolved to ignore the 1986 World Court ruling condemning US terrorism against Nicaragua; and to ignore the World Court provisions in the 1971 Montreal Convention (the relevant tool for dealing with the Lockerbie outrage).

The IAEA had laid down 25 March (1993) as a deadline for North Korean compliance, and rumours began to circulate that if Pyongyang refused to accede then North Korea would be attacked shortly after that date (just as Saddam Hussein was bombed after his refusal to observe the deadline for withdrawal from Kuwait). It was reported that Les Aspin, the new US Defense Secretary, had inherited a set of contingency plans from the Bush administration for the bombing of North Korea's nuclear sites, but it seemed clear that officials in the Clinton administration had less of an appetite for military solutions to international problems; US official advocates of air strikes were slowly being replaced by opponents of such a policy.[18] At the same time the crisis was serious. On 15 March a North Korean diplomat warned that war could break out at any times; and Ri Tcheul, the North Korean ambassador to the United Nations in Geneva, announced that bullets and shells were being fired 'towards our side' in the joint US–South Korean ('Team Spirit') military exercises. Ri commented: 'If we respond to it, it will mean a war and this war cannot but be an all-out war. That is why we are stressing that a hair trigger situation has been created which could lead to an outbreak of war at any time.'[19]

Washington and Britain were continuing to press the Security Council to agree a resolution which could lead to economic sanctions against Pyongyang; Russia and France, as Permanent Members, would go along, but it still seemed likely that such a resolution would be blocked by China. Any resolution would stress the authority of the IAEA and the importance of the Non-Proliferation Treaty, and prepare the way for a progressive escalation of pressures on Pyongyang. President Clinton declared himself 'very concerned' about North Korea's actions and hoped that it might 'reverse its decisions'. South Korea, in a unilateral sanctions move, suspended investment in North Korea and maintained diplomatic pressure. Now it was being claimed that Pyongyang, quite apart from its nuclear derelictions, was currently testing weapons containing anthrax, cholera and bubonic plague.[20]

By 17 March there were signs of reduced tension in the peninsula. A senior government source in Seoul suggested that Pyongyang was willing to negotiate with the United States over North Korea's NPT withdrawal; and South Korea, as an evident placatory gesture, announced that it would not be asking the US troop reinforcements to stay once the Team Spirit manoeuvres had ended. Seoul had resisted American pressure to come down hard on Pyongyang, so allowing a reduction in tension; and the IAEA had agreed to an extension of the deadline to 31 March. Now there were rumours that Pyongyang would not withdraw from the NPT after all. The Team Spirit exercises ended without incident and North Korea lifted its two-week 'semi-war' alert, hailed by Kim Jong Il as a successful countermeasure. As the new deadline approached, there was no sign that Pyongyang would compromise. Diplomatic pressure was maintained but it remained clear that Washington would still not be able to pressure the Security Council into passing a sanctions resolution. Instead there were signs that the Council would wait until mid-June, when North Korea's NPT withdrawal would come into effect, before the question of punitive action would again be raised. *Rodong Sinmun* was still conveying the robust line of the North Korean leadership: 'If the US-led imperialists seek to violate our national sovereignty, and destroy our Socialist system with blockades or sanctions, we will respond with strong countermeasures.' Few observers believed that such bluster would have any practical consequences.

On 1 April, after Pyongyang had ignored the new IAEA deadline, Washington again urged North Korea to rescind its decision to pull out of the Non-Proliferation Treaty; but a condemnatory IAEA resolution in Vienna was opposed by China (and Libya), suggesting that any fresh appeal to the Security Council would be blocked. The Japanese foreign ministry spokesman, Masamichi Hanabusa, expressed the hope that China would 'change its position and make more efforts to persuade North Korea' and in the same spirit a senior Western diplomat observed that the main priority was to maintain the integrity of the NPT and that time was needed 'to permit those with influence in Pyongyang to exercise it'. On 12 May North Korea rejected the first appeal from the Security Council, a resolution* (vote: 13–0, with China and Pakistan abstaining) drafted without reference to sanctions in order to avoid the predictable Chinese veto. South Korea, noting the Chinese abstention, saw the vote as a diplomatic triumph, saying that Pyongyang could no longer rely on China's support. At the same time Washington maintained its diplomatic pressure, and by June there were signs that North Korea was prepared to compromise.

---

*Security Council resolution 825 (1993), calling on the DPRK to reconsider its withdrawal decision, to honour its NPT obligations, and to comply with the safeguard agreement as specified by the relevant IAEA resolution (25 February 1993).

Now it was being suggested that earlier North Korean intransigence had weakened Pyongyang's friendship with Beijing, and that in consequence North Korea was being forced to abandon its international isolation. (It was reported that a border clash in which several Chinese had been killed by North Korean troops had fuelled the growing tension between the two countries.) On 11 June 1993 Pyongyang suspended its threatened NPT withdrawal, announcing that it had 'decided unilaterally to suspend as long as it considers necessary' its withdrawal from the Treaty. At the same time there were doubts how long the suspension would last, and Pyongyang was insisting on various conditions: assurances against the threat and use of force, including nuclear weapons, support for peaceful reunification, peace and security in a nuclear-free Korean peninsula, mutual respect for each other's sovereignty, and non-interference in each other's internal affairs. Pyongyang's announcement, the upshot of US–North Korean talks, came a month after Pyongyang had successfully test-fired a Rodong-1 missile, based on the design of the Soviet Scud-C, which was judged able to carry nuclear or chemical warheads.

Despite North Korea's decision to suspend its NPT withdrawal, Washington continued to make threats. One leading editorial highlighted official suspicions that Pyongyang was still 'engaged in delay and deception';[21] and on 4 July the Secretary of State, Warren Christopher, announced that any North Korean attempt to build nuclear weapons would not be tolerated by the United States: We'll follow our intelligence closely, and we'll be very concerned about our vital national interest.' President Clinton was now on record as regarding the Korean peninsula as the 'scariest' place on Earth, with North Korean atomic weapons 'not something we can afford to let happen'.[22] On 11 July Clinton declared, during a visit to US troops in South Korea, that it would be 'pointless' for the North Koreans 'to try to develop nuclear weapons because, if they ever used them, it would be the end of their country'.[23] A few days later the US–North Korean talks in Geneva resumed, and despite some evident problems appeared to defuse the crisis: Robert Gallucci noted 'a step forward', even though Pyongyang had not yet agreed to the necessary IAEA inspections. On 3 August the IAEA announced that Pyongyang had allowed three Agency inspectors into the country, but there was still uncertainty about what they would be allowed to see.

It was increasingly clear that the problem had not been resolved. Pyongyang was successfully stalling IAEA inspections of the disputed sites, and Washington continued to vacillate between 'stick' and 'carrot'. By November it appeared that the Clinton administration was offering Pyongyang the inducement of normalised diplomatic and trade relations, and a peace treaty that would formally end the Korean war. At the same time Washington refused to cancel the provocative annual joint war games in the South and chose to highlight rumours that North Korea had massed 70 per cent of its military forces near South Korea as a possible prelude to invasion. Now nearly 2 million troops were dug in along the two sides of the 152-mile demilitarised zone (DMZ) and the United States had reportedly prepared plans for a cruise missile attack on North Korea's nuclear sites.[24] Now there was speculation that the US was contemplating a pre-emptive strike against the North.

On 15 November 1993 the joint US–South Korea 'Foal Eagle' war games began in the South, smaller than the annual Team Spirit exercises held in the spring but, to Pyongyang, equally provocative. (North Korea had declared that it would allow some inspections if the exercises, seen as a rehearsal for invasion, were cancelled.) In Washington, Warren Christopher, Les Aspin and Tony Lake, the National Security Advisor, were meeting to discuss the Korean issue, while American specialists on North Korea were accusing the CIA and the Pentagon of exaggerating the threat posed by Pyongyang. On 23 November, after Clinton had met Kim Young Sam in Washington, the South Korea president declared that economic sanctions on North Korea were 'not a particularly attractive option'; and there was fresh speculation that Washington might be prepared to offer Pyongyang concessions in order to resolve the crisis. A week later, James Woolsey, the CIA chief, was again warning that North Korea might be prepared to go to war to avoid the possibility of IAEA inspections of its nuclear facilities.

In early December Hans Blix, the IAEA head, commented that there was no longer any 'meaningful assurance' that North Korea was using its nuclear development for solely peaceful purposes – so increasing the pressure on the Clinton administration to press for UN sanctions.[25] This followed an earlier North Korean assurance that 'the inspection cameras and seals of the IAEA remain on the nuclear facilities': a comment that had little value 'in the absence of verification' (Blix). Japan now seemed more concerned with the dispute over the GATT Uruguay Round than with what Washington was depicting as a nuclear crisis: a senior Japanese diplomat commented that Washington was 'taking a more alarmist view of the nuclear problem than we are'.[26] And even the South Koreans seemed keen to reduce the level of tension: a senior Seoul official remarked that the debate in Washington could be used by the North 'as an excuse to end our discussion, or even to lash out. So we are trying to get some more time.'

On 7 December the UN Secretary-General, Dr Boutros Boutros-Ghali, released to the Security Council a further IAEA communication (3 December). The report noted further deterioration in the safeguards situation. Since the last report (11 October): 'no consultation between the Democratic People's Republic of Korea and IAEA and no inspections of any kind at nuclear facilities . . . have taken place. Surveillance equipment, such as cameras, have ceased to operate, seals have not been checked and many items, which for reasonable assurance against misuse, require visits and verification at determined intervals, have not been visited.'[27] The report included comprehensive details of Pyongyang's position, as expressed by Director Choi of the Department for External Relations of the DPRK Ministry for Atomic Energy: in short, the IAEA's provocative 'resolutions' are condemned, and North Korea urges fresh negotiations; and as expressed by Kang Sok Ju, the first Deputy-Minister for Foreign Affairs: 'If the International Atomic Energy Agency ignores our sincere proposal for negotiation to ensure the continuity of safeguards and distorts the fact as if the continuity of safeguards in the Democratic People's Republic of Korea has been broken, it would be considered to be a signal urging' the DPRK 'to quit the Non-Proliferation Treaty promptly.'[28] It seemed increasingly obvious that no progress was being made to break the stalemate. Clinton had remarked that 'all possible contingencies' had been examined, and that there was still hope that agreement could be reached: 'I hope that we are not headed towards a full-blown crisis. I hope we can avoid one, but I am not positive that we can.' Pyongyang was still offering only limited inspection access; and, despite evident policy confusion in Washington, the possibility of war over the Korean dispute seemed increasingly likely.[29]

Then UN Secretary-General Boutros-Ghali, in his first high-profile initiative over the Korean crisis, paid a Christmas visit to Kim Il-sung and Kim Jong Il. Boutros-Ghali and his wife Leah crossed the Korean military demarcation line on Christmas Eve and travelled with an entourage of eleven personnel to Pyongyang where gifts were given to the North Korean president and his son. At what the official North Korean news agency called a 'cordial and friendly' meeting, Kim Il-sung informed Boutros-Ghali that North Korea wanted a peaceful end to the dispute but would take 'decisive measures' to defend its sovereignty. Boutros-Ghali expressed the UN's real apprehension about any undermining of the Non-Proliferation Treaty, said he wanted to find ways in which the UN could improve the situation, and urged North Korea 'to look to the future and not to events of 40 years ago'. North Korean officials reportedly commented that Boutros-Ghali's mediation was not needed and that the United Nations had in fact acted as a belligerent party to the armistice that ended the Korean War. On 27 December Boutros-Ghali said in Beijing that 'patience' was needed to solve the Korean nuclear dispute: 'If I have a message, my message was: continue to negotiate with the American administration, continue the dialogue between the North and the South and continue to talk to the International Atomic Energy Agency in Vienna. And I can say the answer was positive on both sides.'[30] Now the Clinton Administration seemed to be admitting that there were no steps it could take to stop Pyongyang acquiring nuclear weapons and that this was a serious setback to American foreign policy.

Early in January 1994 North Korea, seemingly detecting the lack of resolution in Washington, began pressing for substantial economic and diplomatic concessions from the United States. Kim Il-sung again warned of 'catastrophe' if the US made further threats: 'Pressure or threats will have no effect on us . . . The US must see all the facts squarely and behave with prudence.' On 5 January Washington announced that agreement had been reached for inspections at seven North Korean nuclear facilities, but the deal sidestepped the two crucial sites at Yongbyon. A White House official admitted: 'It's one of those cases where the administration was huffing and puffing and backed down. There's nothing wrong with trying to come out of this without a war.' The Clinton U-turn was manifest. General Brent Scowcroft and Richard Haass, senior officials under Bush, denounced Clinton's 'crucial error' in compromising with Pyongyang, and argued that US pressure for full inspections must continue.[31]

The American concessions failed to defuse the crisis. North Korea was now reportedly buying 40 attack submarines from Russia's Pacific Fleet, according to American, South Korean and Japanese officials;[32] and, in a sudden stiffening of attitude, the Clinton administration announced that it might ship Patriot anti-missile batteries to South Korea, following a request from General Gary E. Luck, the senior American commander in Korea. Pyongyang responded by denouncing the US plan to send Patriot systems as an 'unpardonable grave military challenge' which could derail US–North Korean talks. It was now reported that technical upgrades to the Patriot missiles enabled them to defend five times more ground area than had been possible during Desert Storm. While Frank Wisner, the US Under-Secretary of Defense for policy, was declaring that the Patriot deployment 'is clearly not meant to increase tensions, the Chairman of the House Appropriations Defense Subcommittee declared that he expected 'a confrontation' with North Korea this year (1994) over the issue of nuclear weapons: 'I think it's so serious that we have to consider the ultimate, and that's military action.'[33] On 2 February William Perry, the US Defense Secretary, warned of a possible 'nightmare scenario' if Pyongyang's nuclear ambitions were not checked. At his confirmation hearing on Capitol Hill, Perry declared that the US goal 'must be to stop' the North Korean nuclear weapons programme. There was now a growing feeling in Washington that Clinton had done no more than demonstrate US impotence (Democrat Senator Charles Robb: 'We've created the impression we're militarily, politically and diplomatically impotent'). Pyongyang was still denying the IAEA inspectors permission to visit crucial nuclear sites, and the news of Patriot shipments had done nothing to whip North Korea into line. Now it was even being suggested that Pyongyang would delay the IAEA access to the agreed seven sites in an effort to wring further concessions from Washington.[34] However, after some procrastination the inspectors arrived in North Korea in early March and began their work. At the same time Seoul was suggesting that it might be prepared to abandon the provocative Team Spirit exercises if Pyongyang were prepared to allow full inspections to proceed. But the two sides, meeting at Panmunjom, made little progress. Song Young Dae, the Seoul delegate, reported that North Korea was insisting that the war games be abandoned, that the Patriot missiles be barred from Korean soil, and that President Kim Young Sam withdraw his allegations that Pyongyang was developing nuclear weapons. On 18 March, seemingly frustrated by the lack of progress, South Korea resolved to proceed with the Team Spirit exercises and expressed support for the plan to deploy Patriot systems in the South.

Again the situation was deteriorating. The Seoul–Pyongyang talks had collapsed in acrimony, and yet again there was widespread talk of war.[35] On 19 March Clinton ordered preparations for the joint US–South Korean military exercises and expressed his support for economic sanctions against Pyongyang. It was reported also that the IAEA inspectors had been allowed into the seven agreed sites but had not been permitted to take nuclear samples to determine whether nuclear material had been diverted to weapons development. The IAEA visit was judged a failure, a conclusion that was quickly conveyed to the UN Security Council. A UN source then announced: 'There will be a staged approach to this. The first step will be to give the North Koreans a timetable to allow full inspections. Exactly what form the sanctions will take has not been decided, but action is inevitable.' But Wu Jianmin, the Chinese foreign ministry spokesman, commented that the issue should be settled 'through dialogue and no parties shall take measures to exert pressure or take measures that will lead to the complication of the situation'. It still seemed unclear how Washington would be able to overcome China's opposition to mandatory UN sanctions.[36]

Yet again, having raised the stakes with talk of military exercises and Patriot deployments, Washington took steps to cool the rhetoric over the Korean crisis. Warren Christopher declared that the US would be proceeding 'very deliberately and prudently'; and President Clinton commented that the administration 'was not trying to ratchet up the tension'. There was further reference to the possible involvement of the Security Council, while the resumption of the Team Spirit war games and the deployment of Patriot missiles continued to anger Pyongyang. Chu Chang-Jun, the North Korean ambassador to Beijing, commented on 23 March that such events would only 'accelerate the speed towards war'. With tension again mounting. North Korea threatened to turn Seoul into a 'sea of fire' and Kim Young Sam put the South Korean forces on alert. At the same time the IAEA Board of Governors adopted a resolution declaring that the DPRK remained in non-compliance with the safeguards agreement and had aggravated the situation by not co-operating with the IAEA inspectors during their recent visit to North Korea. Finally the resolution called upon North Korea to allow the necessary inspections and to comply fully with the safeguards agreement.[37]

Now Russia called for an international peace conference to discuss the crisis as Seoul declared that its patience was running out and Washington hinted that it would send more troops to the area. Walter Slocombe, the Principal Deputy Under-Secretary of Defense, told a US Congressional hearing on 24 March that the Pyongyang rhetoric was 'very bitter and very threatening' and called North Korea 'the single greatest threat to stability in Asia today'.[38] The

Seoul stock market continued its two-week slide, despite what was widely judged to be a thriving South Korean economy. In the North the rhetoric mounted, with *Rodong Sinmun* declaring that if the situation were to worsen 'and a war breaks out, Japan will never be safe, either . . . The reckless military action of the Japanese reactionaries against the Korean people will result in digging their own grave.' Kim Young Sam visited Beijing to seek China's support but was told on 28 March that the crisis could only be ended through dialogue. It was again clear that Washington would be unable to push a punitive sanctions resolution through the Security Council. In the event, despite several days intensive manoeuvring at the United Nations, China refused to agree any Security Council resolution that even hinted at the possibility of sanctions against Pyongyang. The upshot was a moderate Security Council appeal to North Korea (Appendix 2), calling on North Korea to allow full IAEA inspections in accordance with the safeguards agreement and the Non-Proliferation Treaty; further the document 'requests' the DPRK and the ROK to renew their talks to implement their Joint Declaration on the Denuclearisation of the Korean Peninsula. It was declared that, in the characteristic phrasing on UN resolutions, the Security Council would 'remain actively seized of the matter' with a view to 'further Security Council consideration . . . if necessary in order to achieve full implementation' of the IAEA–DPRK safeguards agreement. There was however nothing in this moderate Council communication to pressure North Korea into compliance. The communication (31 March 1994) advertised above all the complete impotence of the Security Council (and US manoeuvring) in the face of China's veto.[39]

Washington still had the option of recourse to unilateral military action (as with the 1986 bombing of Libya, the 1989 invasion of Panama, and the 1992 imposition of the no-fly zone over southern Iraq) in circumstances where UN support was not forthcoming. It was useful rather than essential to cloak American strategic policy with UN authorisation; but now, despite Clinton's willingness to bomb Baghdad (27 June 1993) on the thinnest of pretexts, it seemed unlikely that he would have an appetite for unilateral military action against North Korea. William Perry, the US Defense Secretary, declared in a *Washington Post* (31 March 1994) interview that the United States would be prepared to go to war over the issue, and that already steps were being taken to ensure that in the event of an outbreak of hostilities the US Air Force 'can quickly get overwhelming air power' to the region, to allow 'massive air strikes on North Korean ground forces'.[40] But there were caveats also. Perry commented that though Washington would not flinch from 'strong action' to stop North Korea's nuclear weapons programme the United States was not contemplating a pre-emptive strike 'under these circumstances, at this time'.[41]

On 4 April North Korea announced that it was going to resume peaceful nuclear activities', temporarily suspended during the international negotiations. The new statement added:

> It must not go unnoticed that the UN Security Council unreasonably took issue with the Democratic People's Republic of Korea over its peaceful nuclear activities, while turning a blind eye to the countries which are hellbent on dangerous nuclear gambling under the patronage of the United States. This shows that the UN Security Council is playing into the hands of the United States in executing the latter's hostile policy of stifling the DPRK, applying double standards.

The statement caused fresh problems for Washington, but appeared not to overly concern Japan, itself stockpiling plutonium – to the apparent indifference of the IAEA. Thus Ichiro Ozawa, the power behind the Japanese ruling coalition, said that North Korea probably had a nuclear weapon; while Shigeru Hatakeyama, the Deputy Defence Minister, claimed that there was no evidence that Pyongyang had nuclear weapons. Shigeru played down the possibility that North Korea's Rodong missile could carry nuclear warheads, but commented that this could not be ruled out 'in the future'.

Now Seoul was softening on its terms for further negotiations with the North. On 15 April South Korea dropped its long-standing condition that the issue must be linked with the wider problem of North–South relations; and, with US Patriot missiles about to arrive in South Korea by sea, Pyongyang appeared to be moderating its rhetoric, while Park Young Su, the important official who had declaimed that Seoul would be turned into a 'sea of fire', was sacked. On 18 April the Patriots were conveyed on USS *Meteor* and USS *Comet* into Pusan harbour under conditions of tight security, and it was announced that between three and six batteries had been delivered (each battery including eight launchers and 64 missiles). At this time Kim Il-sung was celebrating his eighty-second birthday; some commentators speculated on why no Chinese delegation had been sent to Pyongyang for the occasion, and why plans for Kim's visit to China later in 1994 had been quietly dropped. But if Beijing was now pressuring Pyongyang to adopt a more moderate stance, this was not reflected in North Korea's current posture on the central issue. On 29 April Herr Hans-Friedrich Meyer, an IAEA spokesman, declared that Pyongyang's most recent response to Agency demands was still 'unsatisfactory'; and inspectors, invited by Pyongyang to supervise the replacement of fuel material in a reactor at Yongbyon, would not now be going. Pyongyang had refused to grant permission for certain radiation levels to be measured, even though this check was 'crucial to prove that the North Koreans have not diverted fissile material to military ends' (Herr Meyer).[42] Yet again, in their seemingly endless 'nuclear two-step', Pyongyang and Washington were manoeuvring for position.[43] Soon it was announced that an IAEA team would now be despatched to North Korea to carry out various inspection tasks, though there were still various unresolved questions.

In mid-May 1994 it was reported that fuel rods at the Yongbyon reactor were being extracted: a 'serious violation' of nuclear safeguards, according to the IAEA.[44] At the same time one American official was declaring that, according to IAEA inspectors, there was 'no diversion' of spent nuclear fuel for ulterior motives: the spent rods had been stored in cooling tanks of water, and there was no evidence of any attempt to take plutonium away for possible use in nuclear weapons.[45] But no one doubted that the problem remained. Pyongyang was continuing to limit IAEA activity in the country; a seemingly impotent Washington continued to vacillate between resolution and frustration; and there were no signs that China – despite Clinton's stark U-turn in agreeing a renewal of 'most favoured nation' trading status (in the absence of Chinese progress on human rights) – was about to agree punitive UN sanctions on North Korea. Now the problem had lasted for some years, and the two central questions remained unanswered: what was the precise significance of North Korea's nuclear development programme?; and what was the US-led international community to do about it?

TOWARDS SANCTIONS?

Knowledge of North Korea's nuclear development programme has long been in the public domain. In the early 1960s the Soviet Union was supplying nuclear technology to North Korea, and this type of aid continued in subsequent years. During the 1960s and 1970s, according to a Russian official at the Kurchatov Institute, the Soviet Union provided extensive nuclear reprocessing information to North Korean personnel working in Soviet plutonium separation laboratories; and supplied also an array of nuclear 'hot cells' to North Korea as part of a deal to build a research reactor in Pyongyang. By the early 1970s North Korean scientists trained in the Soviet Union 'were thoroughly familiar' with the process chemistry required for plutonium separation.[46] In the mid-1980s Washington claimed to have information about a nuclear reactor being built at Yongbyon, 90km north of Pyongyang; and by 1990 American spy satellites were reportedly photographing the construction of facilities that might be used to extract plutonium from spent fuel. In September 1989 the authoritative London journal *Jane's Defence Weekly* declared that North Korea 'could produce a nuclear device within five years and a deliverable weapon shortly thereafter'. A few months later, in February 1990, Professor Sakata Toshibumi of Tokai University in Tokyo claimed that computer analysis of photographs of Yongbyon, taken by the French SPOT earth-observatory satellite, tended to confirm the Western reports.[47] By now the existence of a North Korean nuclear development programme was undisputed, and soon it became possible to chart the organisation of the nuclear programme, the disposition of the various component elements (research, uranium mining, uranium processing and enrichment, and nuclear power facilities), and a provisional timescale (mid-1960s to mid-1990s) for the development of the DPRK's nuclear infrastructure.[48] The question was not whether North Korea had nuclear ambitions but precisely what these were: in particular, was there an intention to develop nuclear weapons?

On 4 May 1992 North Korea, observing its obligations under the Non-Proliferation Treaty and the associated safeguards agreement, submitted to the IAEA the inventory of nuclear material and facilities (see above, p. 13). The listing included developments and facilities at Pyongyang, Taechon, Pakchon, Pyongsan and Shin Po, with details of the major nuclear facilities at Yongbyon.[49] There was now mounting speculation about the real ambitions of the North Korean nuclear development programme. An issue of the prestigious *Strategic Survey*, published in May 1992 for the London-based International Institute for Strategic Studies (IISS), declared for 1991–2 that North Korea represented the most immediate nuclear-weapons proliferation danger. François Heisbourg, the IISS director, commented: 'If North Korea were to confirm its nuclear ambitions . . . then certainly the United Nations Security Council would have cause to come into the picture.' In early 1993 it was reported that analysis of plutonium samples declared by North Korea to the IAEA, together with satellite reconnaissance information supplied to the IAEA by Washington, suggested that North Korea might be developing a more elaborate plutonium production infrastructure than it had admitted to the IAEA.[50]

There were now also signs that Pyongyang was pulling back from its agreement with the South to ensure a nuclear-free Korean peninsula.[51] In April 1993 the 'Insight' team of the London-based *Sunday Times*, citing newly obtained classified documents, claimed that North Korea was building a heavily disguised underground A-bomb complex.[52] Again reference was made to information supplied by spy satellites and to the growing concern being expressed by the IAEA (now the Agency was referring the issue to the UN Security Council). A consensus was emerging that if the North Koreans did not already have nuclear weapons it would not be long before they did. The IAEA was claiming growing evidence that Pyongyang might be stockpiling plutonium for use in weapons manufacture, with the North Koreans underestimating the sophistication of the IAEA inspections that had so far been allowed.[53] Now a serious disagreement was evident between the different branches of the US intelligence community. Whereas the CIA was claiming that Pyongyang may already have enough nuclear material to make a bomb, the National Security Council and the intelligence arm of the State Department reportedly believed that North Korea was using its 'phantom bomb' as leverage to secure diplomatic gains. The dispute was all the more bizarre because all the intelligence branches had access to the same surveillance data – suggesting ideological tensions between the hawkish supporters of the CIA and the more placatory members of the State Department under the Clinton administration.[54]

In early 1994 the same questions were being asked that were first posed two or more years before: 'Does Kim Il Sung have the Bomb? The mystery deepens as the US presses for answers.'[55] It was again being emphasised that President Clinton had publicly vowed that the United States would not allow North Korea to acquire atomic weapons, but how this was to be achieved seemed no clearer that it had done months before. Again US–North Korea talks were being held under nominal UN auspices, but the problem seemed no nearer a resolution than when Washington had first publicly expressed its anxieties. In March 1994 commercially available satellite photographs were evaluated by Dr Bhupendra Jasani, a senior research fellow at King's College, University of London, and judged to have provided evidence that North Korea had an active nuclear weapons programme.[56] Such evidence, taken together with the findings of IAEA inspectors, make it likely that North Korea is engaged in nuclear weapons research. The question as to whether Pyongyang yet has a nuclear device that could be used for military purposes remains open. North Korea has expanded its capacity to produce plutonium and, like many other countries – including the five Permanent Members of the Security Council – it is bound to see the strategic advantage in having its own nuclear deterrent. And despite the various blocks on nuclear specialists travelling to North Korea, it is likely that the barriers are highly permeable, with plenty of skilled (and perhaps redundant) nuclear scientists prepared to work in North Korea for adequate remuneration. There is moreover an abundant international nuclear-physics literature in the public domain; and it is likely that Pyongyang – following decades of Soviet support – has already developed a sophisticated indigenous nuclear capability.

As tension mounted during May 1994, people began taking to the streets in South Korea. On 29 May, in demonstrations that received little publicity in the West, 50,000 students marched in Kwangju to mark the tenth anniversary of the suppression of the uprising against military rule; and at the same time they called for the resignation of President Kim Young Sam and for the withdrawal of the 35,000 American troops from their country.[57] At the same time Japanese newspapers were reporting that Pyongyang was about to test-launch its Rodong-1 missile (a Scud upgrade), and Hans Blix, the IAEA chief, was warning that North Korea was discharging fuel from the Yongbyon reactor at such a rate that the inspectors would be unable to verify whether any had been diverted for possible use in nuclear weapons. On 30 May the Japanese premier, Tsutomu Hata, declared Japan's willingness to provide economic assistance to North Korea in exchange for concessions on the nuclear issue. Kim Young Sam declared that the world was facing 'a critical challenge' by North Korea; and that the Seoul government 'should prepare itself for the possibility of an unexpected move by North Korea facing a crisis' stemming from economic difficulties. And it was reported also that China seemed to be on a collision course with Washington over the growing support in the Clinton Administration for UN sanctions against Pyongyang. Now it was clear why Washington had decided to ignore China's persistent human rights abuses. Said one UN diplomat: 'The prospect of the US being able to persuade China to endorse sanctions looks evenly balanced . . . China owes the US a favour for its renewal of Most Favoured Nation trading status.'[58]

On 1 June North Korea test-fired a missile over the Sea of Japan, not the expected Rodong-1 but (according to Japanese sources) an improved version of the Chinese-designed Silkworm anti-ship missile. In a clear attempt to play down the test, a Japanese official noted that the Silkworm missile 'is very old . . . with a range of only about 80 kilometres'. At the same time Kim Young Sam was travelling to Moscow to ask for Russian help in what Seoul was now depicting as the mounting crisis over the nuclear issue. On 2 June Pyongyang warned that it might yet withdraw from the Non-Proliferation Treaty, and that any attempts to curb its nuclear programme would bring 'devastating consequences menacing peace in Asia and the rest of the world'. Some 8000 fuel rods were now being removed from the Yongbyon reactor, stimulating fresh charges from Washington and the IAEA that soon it would not be possible to ascertain whether plutonium was being diverted for weapons production. Again there was talk of UN sanctions, branded by Pyongyang 'an act of war'. A North Korean foreign spokesman denounced the IAEA for 'groundless slanders . . . and a sinister political intrigue' and commented: 'In case pressure is put on us again, we will no longer fall victim to the unreasonable demand but will have to go our own way, unhindered by anything.' It was reported that Robert Gallucci, the US Assistant Secretary of State, would be meeting Japanese and South Korean officials to consider what steps to take.[59]

There were still signs that China was reluctant to move towards the imposition of UN sanctions on the Pyongyang regime. Thus Shen Guofang, a Chinese foreign ministry spokesman, declared that 'we do not favour the resort to means that might sharpen the confrontation'; and urged Washington and North and South Korea to 'remain calm' and to continue their dialogue. A North Korean delegation was reportedly in Beijing, with Seoul at the same time dispatching a high-level military chief for consultations in the Chinese capital. Now there were clear indications that President Boris Yeltsin would not support UN sanctions until a Russian-proposed international conference on the question had been convened.[60]

Washington continued to urge the need for effective UN action, while bellicose American comments were heard on every side. Republican congressmen were calling for military action and leading columnists were not baulking at the prospect of a new Korean war. Thus the journalist William Safire urged Washington to compel China, Russia, Japan and South Korea to isolate Pyongyang. President Clinton, he suggested, should declare: 'Together we can impose an immensely credible threat; if that doesn't work – if we are dealing with madmen – together we can make short work of the war.' In the same spirit an editorial in the London-based *Daily Telegraph* urged the need for 'a coherent, clearly stated policy – that the United States will not shrink from the risk of war'.[61]

On 3 June 1994 Washington rejected a further Pyongyang proposal for more talks on the crisis, and Robert Gallucci began discussions about sanctions proposals with Japanese and South Korean officials. At the same time it was reported that President Clinton was ordering up to 50 ships, 200 aircraft and 25,000 men to carry out naval exercises close to the Korean peninsula; and that the manoeuvres would involve the USS *Independence* battle group, plus Canadian, Australian, Japanese and South Korean forces.[62] No commentators bothered to point out that such a manifest military threat was in direct violation of Article 2(4) of the UN Charter.

Pyongyang continued to insist that it had no intention to develop nuclear weapons, though its denials may be no more credible than those of Israel over many years. However, whether or not Pyongyang has one or two nuclear weapons, one fact is now undeniable: it was the United States that first introduced nuclear weapons into the Korean peninsula. Thus one authoritative 1985 source puts the American stockpile of nuclear weapons then held at Kunsan Air Base in South Korea at 151: 60 aircraft atomic bombs, 40 8-inch artillery shells, 30 155mm artillery shells, and 21 atomic demolition munitions (ADMs or land mines).[63] It has been suggested that some of the B-61 tactical nuclear bombs, with yield options of from 100 to 500 kilotons, would be available for aircraft stationed in Korea (the Hiroshima atomic bomb had a 12-kiloton yield).[64] A later source (1993) points out that US forces have had tactical nuclear weapons in South Korea since 1958.[65]

In the 1990s the South Korean government has suggested at various times that there are no longer US nuclear weapons in the ROK (though they were almost certainly present in the battle group ordered by Clinton to manoeuvre off Korea in June 1994).

Washington has always refused to confirm or deny the presence of US nuclear weapons at its South Korean military bases, despite occasional hints from Seoul that reciprocal North–South inspections of bases might be an option. What is absolutely clear is that the United States can easily target cruise missiles (with or without nuclear warheads) on any part of North Korea; and that *the United States – exactly like Pyongyang – would be bitterly hostile to any 'enemy' suggestion that US sites with strategic military significance, in either the United States or South Korea, be open to North Korean inspection.*

THE WIDER WORLD

The problem of nuclear proliferation, though having unique features, is part of the wider problem of arms proliferation. It should be emphasised in this regard that the arms policies of the major suppliers – the United States, Britain, Russia, France and others (including North Korea) – are determined solely by commercial and strategic considerations. While the West is eager to condemn North Korea for its possible development of one or two nuclear weapons, Washington is keen to supply high-technology weaponry to a feudal and repressive Saudi Arabia (to protect Western access to cheap oil), and the British premier John Major rejoices in the supply of BAe Hawk aircraft to Indonesia to aid the genocide of the East Timorese people (to protect trade with Indonesia and possible access to oil in the East Timor Sea). In the same spirit, Britain leads opposition to UN efforts to prohibit the sale and supply of anti-personnel mines to trouble-spots throughout the world.[66] It would be naive to imagine that Western efforts to support non-proliferation (in circumstances where Japan's stockpiling of plutonium and Israel's development of its nuclear arsenal are ignored) are concerned with anything other than an attempt to freeze the West's global strategic advantage and to consolidate the capitalist control of the world economy.

Some states have been prepared to agree non-proliferation (of nuclear weapons) while at the same time criticising the Non-Proliferation Treaty for its discriminatory features. Thus Brazil and Argentina negotiated the Treaty of Tlatelolco (though delaying ratification) and entered into agreements to allow for the inspection and control of nuclear weapons. For example, the Nuclear Safeguards

Agreement (13 December 1991) was negotiated between Brazil, Argentina and the IAEA to facilitate comprehensive inspection procedures. Talks (some including Washington) have been held also between India and Pakistan to consider the possibility of an escalating nuclear arms race. This remains an unresolved dispute, just as the situation in Japan is fluid and uncertain: there is a powerful Japanese anti-war lobby and Japanese military ambitions are nominally blocked by the post-Second World War pacifist constitution, but there is pressure for Japan to develop nuclear weapons in the face of the North Korean 'threat' and Washington would welcome the emergence of Japan as an international military prop to the US-defined New World Order.

Many states have an interest in the international arms trade (including deals that support the development of nuclear weapons).[67] Several countries (India, Israel, Turkey, Afghanistan, Saudi Arabia, Greece and Japan) are importing more than $1 billion-worth of arms a year (South Korea imports arms on a substantial scale), and some of these states have a nuclear capability. There is a heavy arms traffic in all the unstable areas of the world. In the Middle East, North Korean Scud missiles have been shipped to Syria, a state that signed the Non-Proliferation Treaty but was reluctant to sign the associated safeguards agreement. In December 1991 the IAEA blocked a proposed Chinese sale of a small nuclear research reactor to Syria, provoking Damascus to declare that it would sign the safeguards agreement when Israel did. On 11 March 1992 it was reported that a North Korean cargo ship carrying Scud-C (Korean-built SS-1D) missiles bound for Iran had eluded US surveillance, to some American embarrassment. Pete Williams, a Pentagon spokesman, commented: 'I can't tell you precisely why we didn't see it all the time. It either followed a circuitous route or perhaps it hugged the coastline and wasn't picked out of the heavy coastal traffic in that area.' A year later, Washington announced that Iran was close to concluding a missile deal with North Korea that could threaten the peace of the region.[68] Now Israel was pressuring North Korea not to supply Rodong-1 (Scud-D) missile technology to Iran; and Washington was threatening that it would board and search North Korean ships on the high seas, a manifest violation of international law and technically an act of war. On 12 December 1993 it emerged that the Clinton administration had tried to conceal Russian involvement in a recent transfer of ballistic missile technology to the Middle East.[69]

In Asia there was now prodigious spending on weapons technology, much of it related to the development of nuclear devices. One observer noted 'future flashpoints . . . in Taiwan, Hong Kong and the Gulf of Tonkin, in Cambodia, Burma and the Philippines, in the Kurile and Spratly Islands, and in numerous other currently obscure but potentially explosive territorial disputes'; and he added that 'in this unfriendly neighbourhood North Korea has every right to feel nervous'.[70] In November 1991 the US Secretary of State, James Baker, had visited China in a vain effort the stop its export of missile technology to Pakistan and Syria; though pressure on Beijing was maintained thereafter using a variety of commercial and diplomatic levers. In 1993 the Clinton Administration was emphasising that the Asia–Pacific Economic Co-operation (APEC) body was the 'cornerstone' of Washington's relations with the Asia–Pacific region, but it was acknowledged that APEC had no brief to deal with such problems as North Korea's nuclear programme or Beijing's growing military ambitions in the South China Sea. By 1994 there were some signs that Beijing was prepared to pressure Pyongyang into allowing full inspection of its nuclear facilities, while the ubiquitous United States continued to agitate over this question and to involve itself in the mounting tenions between India and Pakistan over the Kashmir issue.

South Korea, trapped as ever in the dilemma of how to improve relations with Pyongyang while acceding to Washington's strategic and commercial wishes, continued to add to its own armaments potential. In June 1993 it was announced that Seoul was considering buying up to 12 Tornado fighter aircraft from the three-nation (Britain, Germany and Italy) manufacturers in a deal worth £360 million. The *Korea Herald* quoted South Korea's Defence Minister, Kwon Young Hae, as saying that while US-made weapons were necessary for US–Korean combined operations, 'diversifying the source of imports is inevitable unless current import terms, including price, are redressed'. In May 1994 Seoul decided to award a £39 million contract to BAe-Sema, a joint British-French company, to equip its destroyers with command and firing control systems. The decision had been delayed, reportedly while the Kim Young Sam government was conducting a colossal purge of corrupt officers in the armed forces: in 1993 some 39 generals, two former defence ministers and a former naval chief of staff were sacked, reprimanded or jailed for corrupt practices. Now it was thought that the new contract would be the start of a series of deals worth £200 million over a ten year period.[71] Despite Seoul's military build-up, there had been a gradual improvement in Chinese–South Korean relations. In September 1992, after diplomatic relations had been established, President Roh Tae Woo became the first South Korean head of state to make an official visit to Beijing. In July 1993 South Korea opened a consulate in Shanghai, and China opened a consulate in Pusan. It was expected that in view of the 'complementary nature of the economies of [South] Korea and China . . . the volume of trade and investment will continue to expand sharply in the future'.[72] Such matters are significant in circumstances where Beijing is increasingly being urged to put pressure on its North Korean ally.

Throughout 1993–4 the attitude of the Japanese government to the growing crisis over North Korea oscillated from one position to another, largely in response to US vacillations. Japan's own interest in nuclear technology has sometimes been a matter of controversy, but the possibility of a Tokyo-inspired nuclear weapons proliferation does not seem to have concerned the Washington policy-makers. On 8 November 1992 a shipment of 1.7 tons of plutonium left Cherbourg for shipment to Yokohama, a small part of the many tons of fissile plutonium that Japan is stockpiling from its own spent fuel and from nuclear materials shipped from La Hague in France and Sellafield in Britain.[73] Such shipments raise many questions: not least the issue of transit security, the significance of the Japanese stockpile of fissile plutonium (estimated to be at least 10 tons in the 1990s[74]), and what effects such matters might be reasonably judged to have on North Korean perceptions. Even Seoul, nominally in broad ideological accord with Japan (both under the US nuclear umbrella), has expressed anxiety about the possibility of Japanese nuclear weapons development. Thus the South Korean publication *Choson Ilbo* declared:

> The news that Japan has offered invitations to former Soviet Union's nuclear experts worries us very much . . . Should we now worry about Japan's possessing nuclear weapons? . . . The United States has allowed Japan to build up a military force as a way to stop communism from expanding. Now that communism is collapsing the United States has not stopped Japan from uncontrollably reinforcing its military . . . Thus we cannot help but be worried.[75]

In the same vein, Pyongyang has noted Japan's interest in stockpiling vast quantities of plutonium; and called upon South and North Korea to unite against the 'Japanese nuclear threat'.

There were now growing signs that Japan was becoming committed to its own development of nuclear weapons and missile systems that could be used to deliver them.[76] At a meeting of the Group of Seven (G7) industrialised nations in July 1993, the requirement for 'unconditional adherence' to the Non-Proliferation Treaty was reportedly downgraded to 'universal adherence' – which Japan celebrated as an acknowledgement of its right to a possible future arsenal. The *Asahi Evening News* commented that any call for the extension of the Treaty could be expected 'to generate mixed feelings in Tokyo . . . the treaty could deprive Japan of exercising a nuclear option'.[77] Noting these evolving Japanese attitudes, Selig S. Harrison, a director of a Carnegie Endowment project on Japan's role in international security affairs, declared in a contribution to *The Washington Post*:

> For the first time since the bombing of Hiroshima in 1945, Japan no longer rules out the possibility of producing its own nuclear weapons . . . American policymakers react with dismay to the prospect of a nuclear Japan. Yet the United States is indirectly helping Japan to accumulate a plutonium stockpile that could be used for weapons . . . South Korea, too, complains that the US policy discriminates in favour of Japan on nuclear issues.[78]

A further irony is that substantial financial aid is continuously channelled from Japan to North Korea to aid the Pyongyang regime. A flow of cash – often accompanied by food, machinery, cars and other items – is supplied by ferry from Niigata harbour in Western Japan to Wonsan in North Korea. The vessel, the *Mangyangbong-92*, built with $32 million in contributions from Korean residents in Japan, makes the journey two or three times a month and is supplied by the *Chosen Soren*, the General Association of Korean Residents in Japan. It is estimated that half of Japan's domestic intelligence organisation is now conducting surveillance of Pyongyang sympathisers among Japan's large Korean community. Washington had pressured Tokyo to block the supply of resources from Japan's 700,000-strong Korean community to North Korea; but Tokyo, seemingly concerned at the violence that might erupt, has been reluctant to move on this front.[79] It has also been reported that Japanese companies (including Anritsu Corporation, an affiliate of the NEC electronics giant) had been providing missile technology to North Korea, in violation both of Japanese law and of the international Co-ordinating Committee for Multilateral Export Control (COCOM).[80] In January 1994 *Jane's*

Defence Weekly reported that Japanese missile-guidance technology was being used in North Korean missiles.

Relations between Japan and South Korea, nominally favoured by a shared ideology, continue to be tested by Tokyo's reluctance to block the flow of cash (by 1994 estimated to be around $600 million a year) from Korean residents in Japan to North Korea, by the inferior legal status of Korean residents, and by the plight of 40,000 Koreans taken by the Japanese as forced labour during the Second World War and still incarcerated in Sakhalin. Only when such issues have been resolved 'will it be possible to wipe out the lingering after-effects of the grim past'.[81] The North Korean issue has prompted Seoul and Tokyo, under sustained US pressure, to support American calls for economic sanctions against Pyongyang; but there is plenty of evidence that North Korea's neighbours (China, Japan and South Korea) responded only with great reluctance to Washington's characteristic threats and blandishments.[82] It remained to be seen whether such a reluctant accord would yield the decisive action against Pyongyang that Washington was demanding.

NEW WORLD CALCULATIONS

There was also the persistent question of reunification, the familiar plank in many a Korean political programme. How would this option play in the US agenda? How would the concept of one Korea fit in the strategic framework of the so-called New World Order?

In December 1991 North and South Korea finally agreed a non-aggression pact which they dubbed a 'New Year's present' that would 'make history'. The agreement, signed on 13 December, provided for measures to prevent an accidental outbreak of hostilities, the total renunciation of efforts to overthrow each other's governments, and the installation of a telephone hotline between Seoul and Pyongyang. Other provisions included the acceptance by each country of the existence of the other's social and economic system, an end to 'slander and subversion', the reunification of families divided by the Korean War, and the replacement of the 1953 armistice with a peace treaty. Already the North Korean premier, Yon Hyong Muk, had committed his country to signing nuclear safeguards 'as soon as there is confirmation of the fact that the withdrawal of US nuclear weapons from South Korea has begun'.

All the signs were of a gradually improving atmosphere, a favourable political climate in which the overarching issue of reunification could at last be considered as a realistic option. Most Koreans entertained the dream, but even as long as half a century after the US-contrived partition there were still serious impediments to a merging of South and North. Hatreds remained; the Northern social system would be destabilised by untrammelled capitalism; in any democratic franchise system the Northern population (23 million) would be swamped by that in the South (44 million); and the South had little appetite to assume the burden of an impoverished North whose people may in the event stir up disruption in southern regions that still had a strong radical interest. There was (and remains) a widespread Korean hunger for reunification, but perhaps it is not a realistic short-term option.

Washington, for its part, continued to be irritated by the survival of North Korea as perhaps the only residual outpost of Stalinist communism. The US strategists, as always, assumed the overweening right to intervene in events on the other side of the world; and, far from adopting the imaginative unification ploy that would obviously result in the destabilisation of the North, Washington opted for a characteristic ideological posture that could only perpetuate North–South divisions and exacerbate the tensions in the region. There were plenty of signs of growing contacts between Pyongyang and Seoul,[83] even to the point that a Seoul consulting firm, Merit Communications, launched its *Korea Countdown* monthly newsletter in mid-1994 to prepare 'business and other leadership audiences' for the informed exploitation of the North Korean economy, once Pyongyang opened up.[84] Already the entrepreneurs were beginning to eye what would become (after the death of Kim Il-sung) the rich pickings in the North: the cheap labour, the educated workforce and the tempting real estate.[85] But now Washington was becoming increasingly impatient.

Through all the conflict-littered years of the Cold War (which had mercilessly punished Korea and stored up fresh problems for the future), the force behind US policy had always been a simple atavistic ideology rooted in American perceptions of commercial and strategic interest. In the post-Soviet world the same factors were clearly discernible, though mediated by US financial decline and the change in American leadership that this produced. It remained necessary to propitiate the military–industrial complex, to sustain the CIA[86] and other bodies created and sanctified by the crusade against an alien ideology that was now no more; to justify the prodigious allocation of people and treasure to the military sector; and to further tighten the grip of world capitalism on the global economy.[87]

This scenario has many ramifications; one of which is that recalcitrant states that pose a threat, however puny, to US hegemony can be picked off – by military onslaught, covert sabotage, economic strangulation or capitalist penetration. At this time (late-1994) many thousands of helpless children, women and men are dying every month in various countries (Iraq, Cuba, Libya, Haiti, and so on) through US-sponsored sanctions imposed either through US manipulation of the Security Council or in direct violation of specific UN resolutions (for example, GA Resolutions 47/19, 48/16 and 49/24 on Cuba). It was inevitable, in the post-Soviet world, that sooner or later Washington's calculating eye would focus on North Korea, one of the few recalcitrant states not recently punished by virtuous American strategists.

It was equally predictable that the strategic calculus would not take account of the copious suffering endured by the Korean people this century: there would be no attempt to quantify the miseries inflicted by Japanese tyranny, scorched-earth retreat, military occupation, civil war, the procession of US-spawned dictatorships – such suffering, a subjective matter, cannot be coded into Pentagon computers. Instead, the nice calculations would focus on how reluctant states could be bribed or threatened into agreeing punitive sanctions on what Washington argues is already an economically derelict state; on how to draft the requisite resolutions; on how economic strangulation might be progressively tightened; on how – if the North Koreans were reckless – the United States could take steps to ensure that, in Clinton's chilling words, 'it will be the end of their country'.

THE CRISIS IN ABEYANCE

On 30 May 1994 and UN Security Council issued a statement expressing grave concern that North Korea was continuing its 'discharge operations' at its 5-megawatt nuclear reactor at Yongbyon at a rate that would prevent the International Atomic Energy Agency (IAEA) from securing fuel rods for suitable measurement. The Council strongly urged the North Koreans to proceed with the discharge operations in a manner which preserved the possibility of fuel measurements; and asked the IAEA to maintain inspectors at the site to monitor the appropriate activities. It seemed unlikely that North Korea would accede to the Council demands. On 4 June South Korea ordered its armed forces to a higher state of vigilance and assessed their readiness for a possible war with the North. At the same time the United States continued to give every sign that UN economic sanctions against North Korea were still on the agenda. After talks with British premier John Major at Chequers, President Clinton declared: 'There is still time for North Korea to avoid the sanctions actually taking effect if we can work out something on the nuclear inspections. Sanctions are not any sort of act of war and should not be seen as such. I do not want a lot of sabre-rattling over this or war talk. This is peace talk.'[88] A report in a Chinese-funded newspaper in Hong Kong hinted that China might be about to alter its policy of opposition to UN sanctions.[89]

The Western leaders, meeting to commemorate the fiftieth anniversary of the D-Day operations, continued to focus on the problem of North Korea* On 6 June, in a televised interview from the aircraft carrier USS *George Washington* off the French coast, Clinton insisted that there was 'still time for North Korea to change its course'. China, despite Western hopes, continued to toast its 'ties of blood' with Pyongyang (recalling the Korean War), while at the same time it stepped up its economic co-operation with Seoul.

---

*The D-Day commemoration provided a fresh opportunity for Western pundits and politicians to rehearse a perennial propaganda theme: that 'new Hitlers' can be found wherever strategic or commercial interests are under threat. Thus Raymond Whitaker, Asia Editor of the London-based *The Independent*, can comment (7 June 1994) that North Korea is 'a modern tyranny that appears to be close to obtaining what Nazi Germany never had – nuclear weapons'; Clinton suggested that one of the messages of D-Day was that you should stand up to a tyrant at an early stage – as the Western powers should have done in the 1930s; and Lord Callaghan, in a BBC Radio 4 interview (4 June 1994), encouraged a comparison between Hitler and Kim Il-sung. The propaganda depiction of such leaders as Nkrumah, Nasser, Saddam and Kim Il-sung as 'new Hitlers' is ironic in view of the historical US support offered to historical Nazism. Consider how such US companies as ITT, Standard Oil and Ford helped to equip Hitler during the second World War (Charles Higham, *Trading with the Enemy*, 1983), how the CIA protected Nazi and Gestapo war criminals (Christopher Simpson, *Blowback: America's Recruitment of Nazis and its effects on the Cold War*, 1988), and the significance of Hitler's praise for the racist Henry Ford (*Mein Kampf*, London: Hutchinson, 1969, p. 583).

Washington, seemingly oblivious to China's repeated declaration of its relationship with Pyongyang ('as close as lips and teeth'), was yet again making it plain that the Clinton administration still regarded economic sanctions as a realistic option. Thus on 7 June in a televised interview Secretary of State Warren Christopher declared that progress was being made towards 'a unified international position that something must be done'; while at the same time Yun Ho-jin, North Korea's delegate to the IAEA in Vienna, was saying that Pyongyang would 'never allow inspections' of two nuclear wastes sites, and that the IAEA, relying on information supplied by American spy satellites, was 'acting under instructions of a super-power'. At the same time the director of the North Korean nuclear programme, Pak Yong-nam, was denying claims of IAEA director Hans Blix that it was now too late to check whether fuel had been diverted from the Yongbyon reactor.

On 8 June President Kim Young Sam of South Korea called a National Security Council meeting to assess the country's readiness for war; he commented: 'The target of North Korea's nuclear weapons is us. We have to stop North Korea from developing them at any cost.' But now the US campaign for (UN or other) sanctions against North Korea was running into fresh problems. Koji Kakizawa, the Japanese Foreign Minister, was now distancing Japan from the earlier assurance that Japan would join the United States and South Korea in imposing sanctions even if they were vetoed by China in the Security Council. Now even the US policy of tripartite sanctions, in the absence of UN support, seemed to have been derailed. Again efforts were made – this time by Han Sung Joo, the South Korean Foreign Minister – to enlist Chinese support for sanctions, deemed 'inevitable' by President Kim Young Sam; and yet again the efforts came to nought. Said Qian Qichen, China's foreign minister: 'Sanctions are not a sensible choice, as they would only aggravate the crisis.'

By now it seemed clear that the North Koreans had continued with their controversial removal of fuel rods from the Yongbyon reactor. Thus David Kyd, an IAEA spokesman in Vienna, announced that the fuel removal was 'virtually complete', and criticised Pyongyang's compromise offer of allowing later inspection of 40 fuel rods (out of 8000 removed) as 'not good enough' (the IAEA wanted to check 300 rods as they were currently being removed). Pyongyang was now saying that inspections would be allowed if US–North Korean talks were resumed – an offer rebuffed by

Washington, saying the North Korea had 'crossed the point of no return'[90] (a comment reminiscent of Washington's rebuff to Saddam's agreement, prior to the launching of the ground war, to withdraw from Kuwait in February 1991). On 8 June the US House of Representatives voted (415–1) in support of a non-binding 'sense of Congress' resolution urging sanctions on North Korea; and Warren Christopher, conscious of such support but seemingly paying no attention to the unambiguous Chinese position and Japanese vacillation, continued to assert that the US was making progress towards securing sanctions ('I think they can be achieved'). The Clinton administration was reportedly working on a draft resolution for circulation in the Security Council: an initiative that, despite Madeleine Albright's huddles with fellow diplomats behind closed doors, seemed an increasingly futile exercise. On 9 June former President Jimmy Carter announced that he had been invited to make a private visit to Pyongyang.

On 10 June the IAEA took the 'first crack'[91] at North Korea by voting to suspend technical aid,* whereupon Pyongyang asked the only two Agency inspectors in the country to leave. Some pundits took satisfaction in the fact that China had not voted at the IAEA meeting in Pyongyang's favour, and Hans Blix commented that 'something of a watershed' had been reached. Again there were signs that Washington was pushing for UN sanctions in the hope that China would refrain from blocking a Security Council resolution (Warren Christopher: 'I would distinguish between what they would prefer and also what they might abstain from if the other members of the Security Council were going along that route'). And again there was detailed press speculation about the mechanics of a new Korean war.[92]

---

*It seems that no attention was given to Article XVII (Settlement of Disputes) in the IAEA Statute, specifying that 'Any question or dispute concerning the interpretation of application of this Statute which is not settled by negotiation shall be referred to the International Court of Justice' [the World Court]. The reason why the US, as the dominant member of the IAEA, should be reluctant to take the specified course of referring the dispute to the World Court is plain. The US had virtually ignored the World Court since its ruling (27 June 1986) that in carrying out terrorist actions against Nicaragua, the United States was in violation of international law, that it should desist from its illegal actions, and that reparations should be paid to Nicaragua. Washington refused to acknowledge the authority of the World Court and ignored its ruling; just as later it was to ignore the proper role of the World Court in the dispute over the Lockerbie bombing outrage.

Russia was now reportedly joining with the United States in pressing for UN sanctions, with Robert Gallucci, the US co-ordinator for North Korean policy, reporting that now Japan also was on board: 'Japan believes it is time to show an appropriate response to North Korean actions, including sanctions at the Security Council.' Pyongyang announced that it might leave the IAEA, and South Korea declared that it would hold expanded war exercises in August, including a disaster relief exercise in Seoul. At the same time China 'defied international opinion' by exploding an underground atomic device at the Lop Nor site in the far west of China. Routinely condemned by the West for this action, China pointed out that it had carried out only one test for every 25 by the United States.[93]

The US talk of sanctions on North Korea continued, but there were few signs that useful practical progress was being achieved. The United States, South Korea and Japan again emphasised their determination to enforce sanctions and stepped up the pressure on China not to veto a Security Council resolution. On 12 June the US ambassador to Tokyo, Walter Mondale, commented to NBC's *Meet the Press*: 'We're working on a set of steps that will become a complete program'; while the Republican Senator John McCain, a keen advocate of an American military build-up in South Korea, declared that 'mild sanctions will send exactly the wrong signal to North Korea'. At the same time Japan's foreign minister, Koji Kakizawa, was announcing that Japan would play its part in enforcing UN sanctions within the limits of its constitution. Now there was talk of North Korea risking a UN embargo 'thumbscrew', steadily tightening UN sanctions,[94] though strong doubts were also being expressed about the likely efficacy of any such course. Thus Diane B. Kunz, an associate professor of history at Yale University, commented that an economic war, in the absence of accompanying military measures, would be no more than a 'comforting illusion'. A leader such as Kim Il-sung 'can only be stopped by military action or its credible threat'.[95] On 13 June Jimmy Carter arrived in Seoul on his private mediation mission, and passed into North Korea the next day. Already the visit was arousing controversy in the United States. Now the Seoul city government was preparing its citizens for the possibility of war with North Korea: in particular, the 15 million people who live in or around Seoul were being urged to collect 'war provisions', daily necessities that would last a month, including grains and other foods, fuel, lanterns, blankets, first-aid kits, drinking water and gas masks.[96] In one of its biggest ever civil defence drills, the South Korean government called up 6.6 million reservists. At the same time Pyongyang announced that it was withdrawing from the IAEA and would permit no further inspections of its nuclear facilities, while reiterating that it would regard the imposition of sanctions 'as a declaration of war'. Washington continued its work on a draft sanctions resolution for submission to the Security Council, amid hints that President Clinton might bow to mounting Congressional and Pentagon pressure for the United States to send troop reinforcements to South Korea.[97]

By mid-June some details of the US sanctions proposals were emerging. Washington was proposing a mandatory arms embargo plus a two-stage package of diplomatic and economic sanctions, the first phase being deliberately mild in the hope of avoiding a Chinese veto in the Security Council. On 16 June it was reported that Washington hoped to secure the resolution within a week. The British Foreign Secretary, Douglas Hurd, contributed by designating Kim Il-sung one of a brand of 'unpredictable tyrants with chips on their shoulders' who threatened post-Cold War peace. During the first phase of the sanctions package, in addition to the arms embargo, efforts would be made to secure the diplomatic isolation of Pyongyang. UN member states would be asked to reduce the presence of North Korean missions, to ban scientific and cultural exchanges, and to end arms purchases. UN development programmes would be terminated. The second phase – designed to tighten the economic noose – would involve the freezing of North Korean assets and the banning of asset transfers to North Korea by its overseas citizens. Now Jimmy Carter and his wife Rosalynn were in Pyongyang, meeting Kim Il-sung and other North Korean leaders; according to KCNA, Pyongyang's official news agency, Mr Carter, 'very glad to be invited', had long yearned to visit North Korea.

It now seemed that US efforts to secure a UN sanctions resolution 'within a week' were doomed to failure: the Russian Foreign Minister, Andrei Kozyrev, said that Moscow had not been consulted about the American draft resolution and would not support any motion drawn up without its agreement. Moreover, Russian proposals for an international conference to address the Korean crisis had been virtually ignored and it was now clear that Russian pride had been dented. Kozyrev, reported by the Interfax news agency, declared: 'We agreed unambiguously to work together on a draft resolution, which on the one hand would allow for sanctions and on the other hand the organisation of an international conference.' He added that Washington's initiative would 'seriously hamper the work of the UN Security Council'.[98] China was emphasising also that its friendship treaty with Pyongyang remained in force. Now, it appeared, Washington was getting nowhere: in the context of what White House spokeswoman Dee Dee Myers was depicting as Clinton's 'most crucial foreign policy issue', there appeared to be resolute Russian and Chinese hostility to the American posture, with Japan either vacillating or lukewarm on the sidelines. Kim Il-sung, seemingly unperturbed by the evidently vacuous US threats, commented in a meeting with Selig Harrison of the Carnegie Endowment for International Peace: 'We don't have any nuclear weapons or any intention of making them. It gives me a headache when people demand to see something we don't have. It's like dogs barking at the moon.' The talks between Kim Il-sung and Jimmy Carter continued in Pyongyang.

On 16 June North Korea offered what seemed to be an important conciliatory gesture by allowing the IAEA inspectors to remain at the nuclear facilities, though exactly what they would be allowed to inspect remained unclear. Jimmy Carter reported from Pyongyang that the inspectors would be allowed to monitor the Yongbyon nuclear site and that the UN surveillance equipment would be maintained in good working order. Kim, said Carter, had pledged to keep these commitments 'so long as good-faith efforts are being made jointly by the United States and North Korea to resolve the nuclear problem'. He commented that this was 'a very important step in resolving the crisis'.[99] Despite the seeming concessions, Pyongyang continued to denounce the US for amassing 'huge aggression forces' in South Korea.

There were now signs that Jimmy Carter's visit to Pyongyang had been a useful enterprise. In addition to Kim Il-sung's new commitments on inspection and surveillance, he was now offering to meet South Korea's President Kim Young Sam, an offer reportedly accepted 'gladly'. On 18 June Jimmy Carter returned to Seoul, declaring that the 'vigorous, intelligent and surprisingly well-informed' Kim Il-sung had promised also to freeze North Korea's nuclear programme during 'good-faith talks'. Carter commented that the pursuit of sanctions was 'counterproductive' in the 'particular and unique society' of North Korea: 'This is something that in my opinion would be impossible for them to accept. After observing their psyche and the societal structure and the reverence with which they look upon their leader, I am even more convinced that what I have just said is true.' Kim had further suggested that, as a permanent solution to the nuclear problem, the United States supply North Korea with a light-water reactor, which produces less plutonium than Yongbyon's graphite-moderated reactor. Many Western observers remained sceptical of the promises and suggestions. Other commitments and offers of talks had gone unfulfilled in the past.[100]

It soon emerged that Jimmy Carter and President Clinton were putting different interpretations on the significance of the Carter meetings with Kim Il-sung, Carter was shown on American Television assuring Kim that Washington had suspended its plans for UN sanctions, while Clinton moved quickly to deny that this was the case. There was now a widespread perception of 'an embarrassing breakdown in communications' between the two American leaders.[101] Washington hawks continued to denounce Carter for visiting North Korea, declaring that at best he had blurred the situation. In a televised discussion (CNN, 19 June 1994), Lee Hamilton, the chairman of the House Foreign Relations Committee, agreed with the former Secretary of State Laurence Eagleburger that Clinton should now move ahead with sanctions. The fundamental issue had not changed at all and the crisis was not over. Carter 'should have stayed at home' (Eagleburger), and it remained obvious that North Korea was 'not living up to its commitments' (Hamilton). Kim Il-sung was a 'murderer', but 'I don't know whether we'll go to war' (Eagleburger). The Clinton Administration should now escalate pressure on North Korea 'through sanctions and military pressure' (Hamilton). Tony Snow (of the *Detroit News*) commented that Carter's intervention had been 'unseemly' and that Kim Il-sung was 'not reliable'. For his part, Carter said that he had been 'distressed' to learn of any misunderstandings, emphasised that he had discussed the intended trip with Al Gore, and continued to emphasise the need for communications rather than sanctions. It now seemed clear that Clinton, despite his earlier robust support for sanctions, was now moving closer to Carter's position – a manifest shift in emphasis that was helping to defuse the crisis.

Having briefed the National Security Advisor, Anthony Lake, at the White House, and having spoken to President Clinton by telephone, Jimmy Carter said that he believed that the crisis 'is over'. There were now 'no unanswered questions' about Kim Il-sung's offer of an early summit and the important task was to press ahead to implement the agreements. Even the Clinton administration was now conceding that the crisis, if not resolved, was in abeyance. Carter refused to comment on the sanctions drive, but Paul Galluci, the Assistant Secretary of State, commented that 'there may be an opening' in the new situation and that the former President 'may have brought back something from which we can build'. No one doubted that Kim Il-sung had secured an important diplomatic victory: by dint of concessions conveyed through Carter he had blunted the US campaign for UN sanctions, at the same time enabling Clinton to abandon a policy that was going nowhere. Carter himself, often portrayed as a naive southerner, had grown in stature: he had allowed the Clinton administration to regain some dignity, and enabled Washington to step back from the escalating crisis. Whether Kim Il-sung would honour his new commitments, and whether anything useful would come from the proposed talks, remained to be seen. But at least the crisis was in abeyance.[102] President Clinton had reiterated after the Carter visit that the United States would continue to work for UN sanctions, but by now no one doubted that the steam had gone out of the campaign.

However, it quickly transpired that a crisis in abeyance was not a crisis forever extinguished. North Korea was soon attacking Japanese premier Tsutomu Hata when he claimed that Japan had the technical potential to build nuclear weapons. What more evidence was needed – from the Pyongyang perspective – that Tokyo had nuclear weapons ambitions? Nor did North Korea doubt that Japan's pursuit of a permanent seat on the UN Security Council was linked to its resurgent imperial ambitions in Asia. Even Yohei Kono, leader of the Japanese Liberal Democratic Party, commented that Hata had made a clumsy remark when 'every nation is making concerted efforts to resolve North Korea's suspected nuclear weapons development programme'. But some players in the game seemed to be admitting that the chance had been lost. Thus the former CIA director Robert Gates voiced a theory held by many with access to the best intelligence available in Washington: it was too late to stop the North Korean bomb but steps should be taken to prevent Pyongyang acquiring more than a few crude devices and selling its technology to such troublesome countries as Iran and Libya. In this spirit one characteristic editorial (*The Independent*, 22 June 1994) urged caution and suggested that the Clinton administration was wise 'to react coolly to Kim Il-Sung's charade . . . a firm American stance should continue to command international support'.

On 22 June the Pyongyang authorities indicated that they were ready to discuss an unprecedented summit between Kim Il-sung and South Korea's president, Kim Young Sam. The South Korean

Foreign Minister, Han Song Joo, commented that the prospects for a summit 'look better than ever', but added: 'That isn't saying much.' Now the movement towards talks seemed to be gaining momentum. North Korean premier Kang Song-san, speaking down the telephone hotline linking the North and South liaison offices at Panmunjom, confirmed Pyongyang' support for a meeting and agreed that preliminary enabling talks could take place the following week. President Clinton announced that Washington would suspend its efforts to isolate North Korea after securing Pyongyang's commitment to freeze its nuclear programme. The United States and Korea, he declared, would resume diplomatic contacts in Geneva the following month to consider 'the full range of security, political and economic issues' affecting Pyongyang's relations with the rest of the world. While the US and North Korea had stepped back from the escalating confrontation, there were still crucial problems to solve (Clinton: 'This is not a solution but an opportunity to find a solution'). The CIA was still suggesting that North Korea already had enough enriched plutonium to make a few nuclear weapons, and Washington remained reluctant to agree one of the Pyongyang demands brought back by Jimmy Carter – that the United States issue a formal declaration of 'no first use' of nuclear weapons in the Korean peninsula. Whatever demands Washington imposed on relatively weak states, it was keen to maintain its own unfettered nuclear option.[103]

The crisis had been defused but doubts remained about Kim Il-sung's real intentions. According to a report in the Russian newspaper *Isvestiia* (24 June 1994), the then KGB chief Vladimir Kryuchkov had sent a memorandum (dated 22 February 1990) to the Politburo indicating that North Korea had completed work on an 'atomic explosive device'. The memo claimed that research had been carried out at Yongbyon but the bomb had not been tested for fear of detection. This account, if authentic, served to confirm CIA suspicions and to expose recent Russian denials of Pyongyang's nuclear weapons competence as disingenuous. Many Western observers continued to urge a strong line against North Korea: if Pyongyang had 'the bomb' then this was no time to retreat from former firm commitments against the North Korean nuclear weapons programme. Thus the former Secretary of State James Baker, bewailing the policy failures of the Clinton Administration, commented: 'North Korea only understands one thing. We have to be forceful. Break off the talks. Let them know we mean it. And make people stand up and be counted at the UN . . . We led in the Gulf war. We led in Nato . . . We have to lead.'[104]

THE KIM IS DEAD! LONG LIVE THE KIM!

By July 1994 few observers doubted that ex-President Jimmy Carter's visit to North Korea had substantially influenced the course of events. But it was not yet clear what would transpire. Commitments had been extracted from Kim Il-sung, but would these be honoured? Agreements had collapsed in the past and there were enough sceptics around to declare that this would happen again. What exactly was the position of the IAEA inspectors allowed to remain in North Korea? Had Kim Il-Sung really ordered the freezing of the country's nuclear programme? Had enough plutonium already been extracted from the Yongbyon facilities, in ways that could no longer be checked, to manufacture one or more nuclear weapons? Was Kim Il-sung to be believed when he said that North Korea had no nuclear bomb ambitions? Such matters might be clarified in the projected talks, one of the manifest fruits of the Carter initiative.

On 27 June the North Korean authorities confirmed that they would begin talks with the United States on 8 July; the discussions, they declared, would address the question of a 'fundamental solution to the nuclear issue'. At the same time, following Carter's efforts, talks in Panmunjom between representatives from North and South Korea concluded with an agreement that Kim Young Sam would travel to Pyongyang to attend an unprecedented summit (25–27 July) with Kim Il-sung. Two days later the North Korean state radio was warning that the planned US–North Korean talks were being threatened by American military moves: the US Congress had voted to boost military spending in South Korea and US minesweepers had been despatched to the region. But it seemed unlikely that such events would derail the talks that all the parties now appeared to welcome. There was a changed atmosphere: Carter was announcing in Hiroshima that Kim Il-sung would welcome talks with Japan; and the United States, South Korea and Russia were reportedly working on a plan to provide Pyongyang with civil nuclear technology in exchange for 'nuclear transparency'. Nothing, it seemed, could prevent the projected talks. Kim Il-sung had spoken for North Korea; the authorities in Seoul appeared committed to a fresh dialogue; and the American Cold War hawks had much diminished influence under the Clinton administration. No one anticipated that the talks would be threatened by the death of the North Korean leader.

The death of the 82-year-old Kim Il-sung on 8 July 1994 threw all the diplomatic plans into confusion. Kim had reportedly died of a heart attack but Western commentators were quick to suggest that he had been assassinated – perhaps by communist hardliners resentful of Pyongyang's support for dialogue and conciliation.[105] Perhaps the peace talks would be aborted in the new situation of 'crisis'. Perhaps war was imminent: Seoul ordered a mobilisation of its forces and Pyongyang reportedly followed suit. The Western obituarists were in no doubt how to estimate Kim Il-sung: he was an 'absurd megalomaniac', a 'Stalinist dictator', a 'monster' who 'fed his people on a diet of lies'. In one commentary (*The Sunday Telegraph*, 10 July 1994) the writer remarked that 'it would take a heart of stone not to laugh with joy at the news' of Kim's death: 'Most of the world's greatest swine have died in harness and in bed' and Kim Il-sung was to be numbered among them. 'Thank God', declaimed the writer, 'for the existence of Hell.'

There was no disputing the dimensions of Kim Il-sung's personality cult, one of the most extravagant personal concoctions of the twentieth century. In this he was the secure god-king, the fount of all wisdom and genius, the omniscient and omnibenevolent father of a devoted and submissive people. For his sixtieth birthday he opened a museum where, in galleries extending for more than two miles, his life was creatively invented and embellished; for his seventieth, the *Juche* tower, comprising some 25,550 blocks of white granite (one for each day of his life), was built beside the Taedong river; 50,000 statues of Kim were spread around the land; Kim badges were worn by much of the population; and his copious written works were revered above all other books. Yet this bizarre cult of personality appears to have secured its main purpose: at least the acquiescence, at best the love, of much of the North Korean population. It seemed ill-judged for Western observers to report the 'organised hysteria' at Kim Il-sung's death. One report, depicting Kim as a 'monster', also concedes that the North Korean people 'seemed genuinely to love him'[106] (though this presumably does not apply to those incarcerated for political offences); and another, keen to describe the shortcomings of the regime, notes also that 'North Korea is not a state of robots, where smiles are rare'.[107]

The world – most of which had routinely dismissed Kim Il-sung as a deranged tyrant – was not forced to confront the aftermath of Kim's death. There was a broad consensus that his son and designated successor, Kim Jong Il, would become the new President of North Korea; but there were hints also of other possibilities. Kim Il-sung's younger brother, the 71-year-old Kim Yong Ju, was cited as a possible contender; as was Kim Jong Il's half-brother, Kim Pyong Il. Various pundits hinted at tensions within what had emerged as the ruling dynasty, within the structural paradox of a communist monarchy. It quickly emerged that Kim Jong Il, long prepared by his father for leadership, would be well placed to assume the mantle of Kim Il-sung; though how firmly he would be able to retain his power remained to be seen. There were plenty of Western observers prepared to announce that one psychotic monster had replaced another. It had long been alleged that Kim Jong Il had been implicated in the axing to death of two US soldiers in the demilitarised zone in 1976, in the 1983 bomb attack in Rangoon that killed members of the South Korean cabinet,* and in the 1987 bombing of a Korean Airlines plane in which 115 people perished. At the same time some observers were prepared to admit that the 'sadistic playboy' (*The Sunday Telegraph*, 10 July 1994), the 'short, fat nightmare' (*The Daily Telegraph*, 11 July 1994), might be more prepared to bring economic reform than his doctrinaire father had been. Seoul was reportedly sensing a 'softer line' as Kim Jong Il took power, and at one level was 'seeking to build bridges'.[108] At another level South Korea was persisting with its old repressive habits, cracking down hard on anyone who mourned Kim Il-sung's death. Thus in one incident 55 students were arrested after an informant told police that they intended to offer condolences to North Korea over Kim's death. The police action led to public protests and the petrol-bombing of nine police stations.[109]

On 13 July Radio Pyongyang began referring to Kim Jong Il as head of the party, the nation and the military – signifying to observers in Seoul and elsewhere that Kim Il-sung's 52-year-old son had effectively taken over as chief of the Korean Workers' Party (KWP), chairman of the Central Military Committee, and President of the country. This followed a closed plenary session of the KWP, but no official confirmation of Kim Jong Il's assumption of power was expected until after Kim Il-sung's funeral (19 July). The US–North Korean talks at Geneva and the preparation for the

---

*In an interesting development a South Korean Foreign Ministry official declared on 13 July 1994 that the Rangoon bomb blast which killed 17 of President Chun Doo Hwan's entourage had to be seen in context. The outrage had occurred, he asserted, after two South Korean provocations: the sinking of a North Korean fishing-boat, and the shooting of several North Korean soldiers in a border skirmish.

North–South summit had been postponed, but all the signs were that they would both resume after the funeral display of Kim Il-sung's body – later to be embalmed, at a cost of £200,000, by Russian specialists – and once Kim Jong Il had been safely ensconced in power.

The funeral was staged as a vast spectacle that Kim Il-sung would have approved. Western commentators, excluded from the event, were keen to strike the appropriate note: they spoke of 'orchestrated mourning', 'grief by numbers' and 'regimented sorrow'; and took some pleasure in the irony that the black and gilt inlaid coffin, draped with the flag of the Korean Workers' Party and set in an array of white crysanthemums, was carried by a Lincoln Continental limousine, a symbol of the hated United States. There was also abundant speculation that the two-day delay in the funeral (originally scheduled for 17 July) had been designed to enable Kim Jong Il to purge dissidents in the North Korean hierarchy.[110] It was suggested that the new Kim would need the support of his father's former colleagues to beat off challenges from rivals. Kim Pyong Il, Kim's half-brother and a graduate of a military academy, was said to enjoy support among the North Korean armed forces; and a question mark remained over the ambitions of Kim Song Ae, Kim Il-sung's widow and second wife. It was perceived by Western pundits as highly significant that by the time of the funeral both Kim Pyong Il and Kim Song Ae had 'done a disappearing act'. A South Korean, monitoring Pyongyang's television news output, observed: 'On Monday [11 July] Kim Song Ae was shown in 28 mourning scenes, but later in the week she had disappeared from what was basically the same footage.'

After a private funeral ceremony in the presidential palace, Kim Il-sung's body was brought out for a final display before an estimated two million North Koreans in Pyongyang. A ten-foot portrait of Kim, surrounded by white flowers, was conveyed on one Mercedes; a huge wreath on another; and 27 motorcycles spearheaded the stately parade of dozens of automobiles. The people wept in evident grief, shook their arms, and tore at their clothes – all in accordance with traditional Korean funeral custom which encourages public wailing by bereaved relatives. An official commentator, weeping with the rest, declared, of the dead god-king: 'You are leaving us, but with all our hearts we will follow General Kim Jong Il's leadership'; another noted that 'the whole country and the capital city of Pyongyang were enveloped in the bitterest grief ever in the history of the nation spanning 5000 years'; and women wailed into television microphones as Kim's body passed before them: 'Wake up ... Tell us you are only sleeping ... Come back ... Why can't you work a miracle?' It was later reported (*The Guardian*, 23 July 1994) that many North Koreans had died as a result of Kim's death: some of heart attack at the news, and some of heat-stroke after the lengthy mourning vigils.

In South Korea the tone was rather different. In June thousands of riot police had been deployed to crush anti-government protests by strikers and students. Hundreds of soldiers were used to replace railway mechanics and engineers who ignored a government ban on work stoppages and paralysed the railways; and riot police stormed university campuses and the Seoul headquarters of a Christian group, making nearly 400 arrests. On 17 June CNN television reported some 5000 South Korean students protesting against government policy, the likely impact of rice imports under the new GATT terms, and the continued American presence in the country. In the official accounts around 50 students and 110 riot police were injured, though it is likely that the actual casualties were much higher. The strikes and demonstrations continued into July, causing massive disruption to the rail and subway systems, millions of dollars lost in stalled exports, and public stampedes and transport overcrowding that left dozens injured (*Time*, 11 July 1994). Now the death of Kim Il-sung had served to exacerbate the tensions in the South. The Seoul authorities suppressed any attempts to mourn Kim's death and efforts by South Koreans to journey North to attend the funeral ceremony. On 14 July, Han Chan Woo, a South Korean student leader, reported on BBC Radio 4, declared that South Korea was no more than a 'colony' of the United States; and in the same vein the BBC reporter Philip Short commented that 'most Koreans' believed that the US presence was a 'humiliating burden' that should be shed. On the day of Kim's funeral (19 July) the Seoul authorities deployed 28,000 riot police, some wearing gas masks and wielding batons, to suppress any attempt in the southern capital to mourn the death of Kim Il-sung.

The South Korean government did not stop at suppressing its workers and students, and at cracking down on any attempts to show sympathy with the manifest national grief in the North. At a time when some Western pundits were claiming to discern a new air of North–South détente, Seoul was seemingly making efforts to worsen its relations with the northern regime. Rumours continued to circulate that Kim Il-sung had been assassinated by hardliners, and

that his heart attack might not have been fatal if the doctors had
not been delayed: the Seoul daily newspaper *Choson Ilbo* reported
that the specialists had been delayed by a mishap, possibly a heli-
copter accident, when Kim fell ill on 7 July and that he was dead
when they arrived the next day – a report that contradicted the
official Pyongyang line that Kim had died despite the strenuous
efforts of his doctors. Further, Seoul chose the day of Kim's funeral
to release documents, of Russian origin, to brand Kim Il-sung with
responsibility for the Korean War. Said one Seoul government
official: 'Obviously they were going to be upset by our branding
their former leader a war criminal.'[111] And even the delay in holding
the funeral, according to Seoul rumour, was a Machiavellian plot to
encourage South Korean students to hold campus memorial services
in honour of the North's dead leader. In one characteristic announcement the police declared their determination to arrest
whoever was responsible for building a small altar at a university in
Kwangju in honour of Kim Il-sung: no expression of regret at Kim's
death was to be permitted.

At the same time, while in one mode Seoul pundits and politicians
seemed keen to exacerbate tensions, there were some signs that a
new accord with the North might be possible. A South Korean government official had acknowledged (13 July) that the so-called
(Pyongyang-orchestrated) terrorist attacks of the 1980s sometimes
followed South Korean provocations; and analysts in Seoul were
now even prepared to suggest that alleged terrorist acts by the
North were invented for reasons of Cold War *realpolitik*: 'All those
stories were reported by South Korea's CIA in the old cold war
days. Many were just propaganda.'[112] And even the US State
Department seemed prepared to acknowledge that North Korea –
while maintaining contact with various terrorist groups and continuing to provide political sanctuary to terrorists – had not sponsored
any terrorist acts since 1987.[113] Perhaps the Pyongyang regime was
less odious than the ceaseless US and Seoul propaganda had suggested; and perhaps Kim Jong Il, Kim Il-sung's son and successor,
was 'not the fiend the world had been led to believe he is' (*Time*,
25 July 1994).

In Seoul and Washington, as in Pyongyang, various factions were
vying to assert their different interpretations of the Korean question.
It remained to be seen which of the factions would emerge as the
principal shapers of Korean political developments after the Kim Il-
sung era.

The escalation of political tensions over the Korea issue in the so-called New World Order focused world attention on many ideological matters: not least the overweening arrogance of the United States and the double (or multiple) standards it was prepared to apply in furtherance of its perceived strategic interests. US arrogance over Korea had been well advertised long before the controversy over Pyongyang's alleged nuclear ambitions. Thus David Watt, prestigious journalist and one-time scholar of All Souls at Oxford University, noted the 'American association with a right-wing regime [that of Syngman Rhee] notorious for its brutality', and commented:

> The superlative arrogance of MacArthur's suzerainty over the Far East was beginning to cause real alarm in America as well as in Europe long before the North Korean invasion [of 1950]. His conduct of the war itself was even more disturbing, for it implied irresponsibility . . . MacArthur no longer seemed to be under proper political control.[114]

The subsequent sacking of MacArthur by President Truman probably averted the disaster of a wider US–China war, but did nothing to dispel the manifest arrogance with which Washington sustained the procession of proxy South Korean dictators in the post-war years. This was the attitude that was allowed to shape Washington's approach to Pyongyang's possible development of nuclear weapons in the post-Soviet world.

We have seen that the United States, in protecting Israel's nuclear ambitions, is a principal violator of the Non-Proliferation Treaty; that in 'losing' some 1.4 tons of plutonium (enough to make 300 atom bombs) – a lapse admitted by the US government in May 1994 – Washington had demonstrated massive irresponsibility; and that, in sustaining export policies condemned by its own congressional General Accounting Office, the US government had demonstrated its cavalier indifference to nuclear proliferation. And we have noted that Japan, arousing no American comment, is currently accumulating substantial stockpiles of plutonium that at any time could serve as the basis for a nuclear weapons programme. There are other matters also that should be considered. On 17 July the German authorities expressed their alarm at the discovery of weapons-grade plutonium from Russia on the black market. In one estimate some 330 lb of such plutonium might now be available via 'nuclear mercenaries' operating in Europe. The German Chancellor, Helmut Kohl, has expressed his 'deep concern' at the lack of safety and control at Russian nuclear installations.[115] In China the free-market revolution has similarly put nuclear security in doubt: 'crime and corruption are rampant. The military, which controls arms manufacture and export and has access to nuclear materials, is not exempt.'[116] And in a further revelation it has emerged that Saudi Arabia planned to acquire nuclear weapons by massively funding Saddam Hussein's nuclear programme – to the tune of up to $5 billion – as part of an agreement in which Iraq would share its nuclear technology with Riyadh.[117] There were no signs that Washington would move to denounce the manifest nuclear ambitions of its principal Middle Eastern ally and oil supplier.

This then is the framework of Washington's '*multiple standards*' on the question of nuclear weapons proliferation. At one extreme, successive US governments have been prepared to protect or ignore the nuclear ambitions of their allies. Thus, in the case of Israel, 'one of America's most important allies – a beleaguered ally surrounded by avowed enemies constantly threatening war – has secretly amassed a large nuclear arsenal while Washington looked the other way'.[118] Similarly the one-time nuclear ambitions of South Africa and Saudi Arabia were either ignored by US governments or clandestinely supported by the CIA and other agencies. With a middle category of states – such as India, Pakistan and Brazil – Washington has been prepared to discourage nuclear proliferation, but only in a desultory fashion that fell far short of passionate denunciation and threat. In the case of Iraq, copiously armed by the West,[119] the United States was prepared to wage war and still maintains punitive sanctions – at present (late 1994) killing Iraqi children, through disease and starvation, at the rate of 100,000 a year – for various reasons, not least to crush Saddam's nuclear ambitions. With North Korea, Washington worked hard to secure a Security Council sanctions resolution; strove to achieve extra-UN sanctions and other anti-Pyongyang measures, after China had stymied Washington's UN efforts: and during this entire period repeatedly threatened military action.

In this context whether or not a state is a member of the IAEA or a signatory to the Non-Proliferation Treaty is – in the *de facto* world of *realpolitik* – a quite secondary matter. Both the IAEA Statute and the Treaty were framed to protect the military hegemony of the established nuclear powers; and such powers are always cynically selective in how they interpret the Statute/Treaty clauses that define their obligations. North Korea, within the terms of the Treaty, is legally entitled to withdraw from the agreement if it so chooses – yet Washington creates an international crisis when Pyongyang declares it might do so. Similarly, when Washington claims that North Korea is in violation of its obligations under the IAEA Statute, the US government ignores the Statute's stipulated provision for recourse to the International Court of Justice. Instead Washington preferred to exert pressure for UN (or non-UN) sanctions; military reinforcements were despatched to South Korea; and a US battle fleet massed off the Korean coast.

The question of Pyongyang's nuclear ambitions remained unresolved. On 27 July 1994 the defector Kang Myong-do, claiming to be the son-in-law of the North Korean premier, Kang Song-san, told a press conference that North Korea had already produced five atomic bombs and that it planned to complete five more before openly declaring itself a nuclear power. Pyongyang, said Kang, was merely playing for time.[120] Because of his claimed links to the higher echelons of the North Korean political hierarchy, some Western observers inclined to accept Kang's assertions. North Korean radio denounced his claims, denying that he was a relation of the premier and describing Kang Myong-do as 'good-for-nothing ignorant human trash'. And, in an unusual gesture of support for Pyongyang, the IAEA publicly discounted Kang's claims: 'The statement made by the defector is not judged to be plausible.' It could not be concluded – on such insubstantial grounds – that Pyongyang possessed nuclear weapons.

At the same time the possibility that North Korea had nuclear ambitions could not be discounted; though it remained important to estimate any Pyongyang derelictions, if such there were, in full appreciation of the historical and political context. We need to recall the unique circumstances and ravages of the Korean past; why the West, principally the hegemonic United States, cynically and selectively invokes clauses in flawed treaties to put pressure on ideologically unsympathetic states; and the way in which Western pundits and politicians, buttressed by unassailable military power and a global propaganda machine, reserve the sole right to adopt moral postures and to interpret the law. We need to remember that Article 2(1) of the UN Charter enshrines the principle of 'the sovereign equality' of all members of the United Nations. It is important to emphasise that there is no licit way in which vast military power can be used by a government to abrogate the sovereign rights of smaller states.

Part II
The Historical Frame

2 Beginnings

THE LAND

Korea hangs like a shrivelled appendage from the great body of Asia. In vivid metaphor the Korean peninsula has been a lumpy phallus, a cultural bridge linking giants, the sandwich filling trapped between the great powers of China and Japan.

Korea has not always been a peninsula. During the ancient glacial phases of the Pleistocene epoch, the earlier period of the Quaternary age that began around two million years ago, the level of the seas was lowered as great moving masses of ice accumulated on the land. One consequence was that the relatively shallow Yellow Sea to the west of Korea dried up, so merging Korea with the continental land mass of east Asia. The East Sea, today's Sea of Japan, became a land-locked lake, while many islands – not least Cheju and the islands of Japan – became joined to the Asian continent. The glacial invasion did not extend far into mountainous Korea but the severe lowering of the temperature had a profound effect on the flora and fauna of the region.

Today the mountainous peninsula of Korea, with an average width of about 150 miles, extends south-east for some 600 miles. More than 3000 islands, most of them small and uninhabited, surround the irregular 5400-mile coastline. The total land area of Korea, dwarfed by the great mass of China, is around 85,250 square miles, three-fifths the size of Japan, two-thirds the size of Italy, and not much smaller than the combined land area of England, Scotland and Wales. The Korean population, today in excess of 65 million, is in the same order as the populations of the major powers of Europe.

Korea is topographically defined by the chain of flat-topped mountains that stretch down from the Asian continent. The crests are largely plateaux, the result of centuries of erosion, with the highest mountains those in the Paektu-san range to the north-east of the western lowlands. Mount Paektu, at 9003 feet Korea's highest peak and to some optimists a symbol of political unity, holds in its vast crater a two-mile wide lake, the Pool of Heaven (Chonji). Only about one-fifth of the peninsula is lowland terrain suitable for settlement and cultivation. Most of the plains, some of them alluvial, are no more than narrow strips of land surrounded by hills and lofty plateaux. The Taebaek Mountains, the peninsular backbone, form the main watershed feeding the meandering rivers and streams that help to make much of Korea a beautiful land.

ORIGINS

It is impossible to say exactly when people began to live in the Korean peninsula, though there is general speculation that pale-olithic communities first inhabited the area some 50,000 years ago. Paleolithic remains from several areas have been reported but some of the claims are of questionable value. For example, the Japanese archaeologist Nobuo Naora described paleolithic finds at Tonggwanjin in the Tumen River area in Hamgyong province (Figure 2.1) in 1940, though this report was viewed with some scepticism. Stone and bone artefacts, along with fossils of mammoths and other mammals, were discovered at the Tonggwanjin site but it is possible that the artefacts belong instead among the many neolithic items found in the area. However, more recent excavations have yielded finds that provide insights into the paleolithic development of the region.

Significant sites, recognised as paleolithic, have been explored at Kulpori (confirmed by geologic stratigraphy) in Hamgyong province, at Sangwon in South Pyongan, at Sokchangni in South Chungchong, at the Commal Cave, Pojanni, in North Chungchong province, and elsewhere. The broad range of identified sites suggests that paleolithic communities occupied most parts of the Korean peninsula, living both in caves (for example, Chommal, Kumunmoru in Sangwon, and others) an in built dwellings (as at Sokchangni). There is much evidence that the paleolithic people were hunters, fishers and gatherers using primitive stone tools for killing prey, for preparing food, and for working on stone and wood to produce further artefacts. The remains of a hearth have been found at the Sokchangni dwelling site, suggesting the use of fire for warmth, cooking and other purposes. This site, discovered in 1964, has been radio-carbon dated to 29,000 BC.

The paleolithic cultures, characterised by the chipped stone tools of the Old Stone Age, gave rise to the neolithic communities of the New Stone Age in which polished stone tools and pottery were

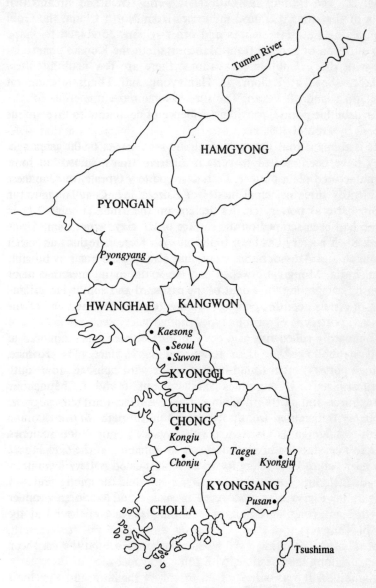

Figure 2.1 The eight provinces of modern Korea

made for the first time. Neolithic man appeared in Korea about 4000 BC, one fruit of the cultural flowering occurring in northern Asia at that time. Cultural influences from North China, the Gobi region, the Eurasian steppes and other regions combined to shape the diffusion of peoples from Manchuria into the Korean peninsula. As with the paleolithic excavations, there are few neolithic sites, notably those at Kulpori in Hamgyong and Tongsam-dong on Yongdo Island off Pusan. The sites become more numerous for the later neolithic period, providing evidence of communities throughout Korea by around 3000 BC.

It is thought that the early neolithic inhabitants of the peninsula may have been related to certain Siberian tribes, known to have manufactured plain pottery. Distinctive pottery types have been used to identify three principal modes of Korean life. *Comb ceramic* (or comb pattern) pottery carries designs on the artefacts as though a comb had been scraped on the surface of the clay before the pot was fired. Such pottery has been found in such Korean regions as South Pyongan and Amsadong in Seoul, and also in such areas as Siberia, Manchuria, Mongolia, Sweden and the southern Japanese island of Kyushu, suggesting the extent of the eastward and southward migration of Asia's neolithic peoples. *Mumun* (undecorated red or brownish-red) pottery is of various types though many such artefacts have an outwardly rolled rim or a cow-horn or nipple-shaped appendage with symbolic rather than functional significance. The Korean *mumun* pottery, often found in association with polished stone agricultural artefacts, resembles similar items found in Mongolia, Manchuria and northern China. *Burnished red* (painted) pottery, probably transmitted from northern China through Manchuria into north-east Korea, is associated with advanced agricultural societies able to manufacture bronze artefacts, as indicated at the Cho Island site near Najin. Here many forms of sophisticated pottery have been found, including footed basins, jars, bowls and steamers.[1] Painted designs have also been uncovered in such areas as Nonpodong in North Hamgyong, at Chitamni in Hwanghae, and at the Kyodong site in Kangwon.[2]

Most of the neolithic dwelling sites in Korea are on the banks of rivers or along the coastline, with fish a principal food of these early communities. It was easiest of all to collect shellfish; and the shell-mounds – refuse heaps – are a useful source of knowledge about neolithic people. Items found in abundance suggest the harvesting of oysters, abalone, clams, snails and sea scallops, while such fish as cod, flounder, bigmouth and sea perch were also available.[3] The discovery of stone sinkers suggests that nets were used to catch fish; and there is evidence also that neolithic people fished with rod and line. As well as the various types of bone fish-hooks, such items as stone arrowheads, spear points, two-edged axes and daggers, fishbone needles and shell ornaments and scrapers have been found in the excavation sites. The early neolithic communities relied solely on fishing, hunting (the bone of deer and wild boar litter the sites) and gathering (shown by the presence of acorns), but eventually there was resort to agriculture. Stone hoes were used to break the soil, stone sickles to harvest, and millstones to aid food preparation.

Soviet archaeologists in Manchuria revealed a bronze culture as early as the end of the second millennium BC, with Korean archaeologists disposed to include the Northern Tumen and Yalu River regions in this culture zone. However, it is judged that the Korean peninsula did not enter the metal age until the fifth century BC.[4] The bronze culture of Manchuria, northern China and Siberia was introduced into the Taedong River basin in north-eastern Korea at a time when iron was already replacing bronze in some parts of China. The bronze culture of the northern tribes, although deriving from China, soon developed distinctive features and became the predominant culture in Korea until the later establishment of the Chinese garrisons throughout the peninsula. Evidence for the spreading of an iron culture into Korea is the discovery of two types of coins: *ming-tao* (knife money) and *fu-chien* (spade money), used in China during the Period of Warring States (403–221 BC) and found also in southern Manchuria and in such Korean regions as Pyongan province in the north-east and Cholla province in the south. A Chin dynasty sword, bearing an inscribed date of around 222 BC, has been discovered at Pyongyang.

A wide range of bronze artefacts, often termed Scytho-Siberian, has also been found throughout much of the Korean peninsula. These, deriving from the culture of the Eurasian steppe, include horse trappings and animal-shaped belt clasps; similar items have been unearthed in Japan, as has a type of bell found in Korea in association with such artefacts. The horse-shaped belt clasps and other equine features suggest a nomadic people well equipped to encourage cultural dispersal. Various peoples moved into the Korean peninsula, often as refugees fleeing the wars in China, bringing with them their cultural conventions which in turn were modified by the communities already settled in the region. Thus the predominantly bronze

artefacts – daggers, spearheads, axes and others – evolved from their
Chinese origins through Korean metamorphosis: as one example, the
Chinese mirror with a single knob on the reverse side acquired a
second knob. Living practices also developed, shaped in part by the
impact of the new groups in the peninsula on the established
communities.

Many of the early Korean tribes lived in pit dwelling dug in circu-
lar or rectangular form from 10 to 30 feet in diameter and about
3 feet deep. Posts were set to support a straw thatch to provide protection from the weather, with stones or clay used to serve as
flooring. A hearth was often located near the centre of the dwelling
and pits set in the floor contained tools and grain supplies. Some
effort was made to separate living areas from parts of the dwelling
in which cooking and other activities took place. There were communal facilities for making cloth (a simple type of spinning was fa-
cilitated by spindle-whorls), for smelting iron ore, for shaping pots
on a wheel, and for treating rice in steamers. Most of the dwellings
have been located in relatively low areas, but a few also in the
mountains (in later times the *sansong*, the citadels of refuge located
near to every large settlement). The mortuary *dolmen*, found
throughout the peninsula and dating to around 800 BC, are further
significant construction achievements: for example, the northern
dolmen at Hogadon comprises seven-feet-high vertical stone slabs
supporting a covering slab 18½ feet wide and nearly 30 feet in
length. The dolmen, often set in groups, imply high levels of engineering competence and social organisation. They are associated with
interred ceremonial daggers and with the *menhir*, phallic symbols
suggesting fertility cults.

The early peoples of Korea, in common with neolithic communities elsewhere, held a variety of animistic beliefs, convinced that all
the objects of the natural world possessed souls. Mountains, stones,
rivers and trees were accordingly viewed with reverence as divinities,
to be cajoled and supplicated to aid human beings in their endless
struggle against the evil spirits of darkness. Stones set around a
human corpse were intended to protect it from baleful supernatural
forces, while the head of the deceased would be laid in the direction
of the sunrise: the sun would bring good fortune but nothing but
evil could be expected from the night. It was inevitable in this
context that music and dance would evolve to underwrite the spectrum of belief. Later neolithic ceremonies in Korea communities included *yonggo* (to invoke a sympathetic spirit), *tongmaeng* (for

ancestor worship), and *muchon* (for Heaven worship). Many artefacts, with deep symbolic significance, were used to support the
ritualistic ceremonies.[5]

The basic social unit in Korea throughout the neolithic period, as
elsewhere in the world, was the clan. Here consanguineous social
groupings were bound together through totemistic conventions, with
individual clans associated with particular objects in the natural
world. Thus the Hyokkose Pak clan had the horse as its totem, the
Kim clan of Alchi and Aryong the chicken. In the later phases of
neolithic development the clans were grouped in sophisticated as-
semblages for the settling of social problems. The *Hwabaek* (Council
of Nobles) convention in Silla (see below) is thought to have derived
from the ancient clan tradition. The early clan system was an effective economic unit, self-sufficient and jealous of its territorial claims.
If the land claimed by a clan community was violated then the
chaekhwa ('responsibility for damages') principle required that the
offender make compensation in some form.

The lineaments of neolithic Korean society were shaped by the
practical demands of the real world, by the day-to-day predicament
of small tribal units struggling for survival. At this time many
peoples competed for hegemony and there was no unified Korean
state. There were legends about how and when the first Korean
society came to be established but centuries would pass before the
secure establishment of a Korean nation throughout the peninsula.

MYTH AND OLD CHAO-HSIEN

The origin of the semi-Sinicised state of Chao-hsien (variously
Choson, Chosen, and so on, in English texts), the earliest name by
which the Korean area is known, is heavily shrouded in myth. In
one fanciful account the son of the divine creator descended to earth
in 2333 BC to organise the founding of Korea. It is interestingly co-
incidental that the progenitor of the Japanese imperial line was said
to have descended to earth in a similar fashion; and that the alleged
date is close to that of the supposed founding of the Hsia, the first
Chinese dynasty. This looks suspiciously like an attempt to claim a
prestigious antiquity for Korea.[6]

The legend involves the mysterious melding of a bear, an animal
revered throughout north-east Asia and by the Ainu of North

Japan, and a tiger, common in Korean art and folklore. The two beasts enter a cave from which, after a mysterious metamorphosis, a young woman emerges – to mate with the son of the divine creator. The fruit of this union is the boy Tangun, who subsequently becomes the founder of Korea, ruling over the tribes of the peninsula and teaching them the arts of civilisation.

In an alternative account Chao-hsien was founded in 1122 BC by Kija (Chi-tzu in Chinese), a scion of the royal line of the Shang dynasty. According to the Shang books and the Korean histories that derive from them, Chi-tzu was the uncle and counsellor to the last of the Shang emperors, Chou Hsin. Wu, the first sovereign of the succeeding Chou dynasty, demanded Chi-tzu's continued service; but Chi-tzu, regarding the new imperial line as an unwelcome usurpation, felt unable to comply and suffered ill-treatment as a consequence. Soon after offering Wu advice on the conduct of government, Chi-tzu journeyed with 5000 of his followers to the Korean peninsula to found the kingdom of Chao-hsien. He is said to have brought with him the skills of poetry, music, medicine and trade; and also a system of polity based on the 'Eight Laws', framed to bring order to barbaric tribes. This tale has been compared to the occidental account of how Aeneas fled from Troy and subsequently founded Rome.

There is debate about the truth of the Chi-tzu story.[7] It does however serve to advertise the importance of the Chinese legacy to the civilisation that was to evolve in the Korean peninsula.

THE CHINESE IMPACT

Through the period of the Later Bronze Age the settlements in the Korean peninsula experienced significant political development. One of the most important developments was the emergence of walled-town states, their existence recorded in Chinese accounts: Puyo in the Sungari river basin, Yemaek along the Yalu river, Imdun in the Hamhung plain on the north-east seacoast, Chinbon in Hwanghae province, Chin to the south of the Han river, and Chao-hsien in the Liao and Taedong river basins. Of all the walled-town states, Old Chao-hsien, set around Pyongyang, was the most advanced. Its early leaders were called *tangun wanggom*, to signify both their descent from the divine creator and, through the adoption of the Chinese term for king (*wang*), their monarchical status.

By the time of the fourth century BC Chao-hsien had combined with other walled-town states to form a confederated kingdom, an extended political unit of substantial military power. Chao-hsien was then confronting the Yen faction, a powerful contender from northern China, across their Liao river boundary. Yen assertions that Chao-hsien was arrogant and cruel are recorded. The scene was set for another wave of Chinese influence in the Korean peninsula.

The development of Chinese culture inevitably encouraged the colonisation and assimilation of surrounding peoples, including many of those who lived in the peninsula. The so-called Spring-and-Autumn (*Chun-chiu*) period, from the eighth to the fifth century BC, saw the emergence of iron technology to challenge the essentially bronze culture. The consequent development of effective iron weapons was one of the factors that encouraged the eastern drive of the Chinese, clearly evident during the Period of the Warring States (403–221 BC). The powerful Yen faction, one of the Warring States, invaded the Korean peninsula at the end of the fourth century BC, wereupon Chao-hsien was forced into inevitable decline.

The Yen forces, under the command of Chin Kai, advanced rapidly to secure the region as a new acquisition for the Yen domain. A commandery was established at Liao-tung which then came under Chin control, but soon after Chin had unified China, around 206 BC, the region fell to Liu Pang, the founder of the Han dynasty. Lu Wan, having been installed as the king of Yen, turned against Han, so initiating fresh political upheavals in China and a new flight of refugees to the east and into the Korean peninsula. One such refugee was Wiman, who moved into Old Chao-hsien with a thousand followers and persuaded King Chun to entrust him with the defence of the north-west border. In due course, having established a new power base, Wiman usurped Chun around 190 BC, forcing the erstwhile monarch to flee south where he dubbed himself a new Han ruler.

Myth had conveyed the idea that the most influential Korean factions owed their origins to Chinese incursions. Subsequently the Yen invasion stimulated new waves of Chinese traffic in officials, administrators, traders and military personnel. Then Wiman, the ruler of a migrant Chinese population, helped to shape the development of a society that continued also to be influenced by its roots in Old Chao-hsien: the old confederated kingdom, itself owing much to early Chinese influence, had evolved an indigenous culture that was at least partially resistant to the new phase of Chinese incursion.

Chao-hsien, substantially strengthened, was now able to subdue its neighbouring states: after the capitulation of Chinbon and Imdun, Chao-hsien controlled a territory stretching several hundred miles, with all the effects on trading patterns that this new hegemony implied. At the same time Chao-hsien faced the possibility of developing ties with the Mongolian Hsiung-nu, then expanding into the region of Manchuria. Such developments were increasingly disturbing the rulers of the Han dynasty in China, worried by fresh threats to trade and the danger of new military incursions. The growing tensions came to a climax when the Chinese envoy She Ho, who had formerly killed a Chao-hsien commander and fled back to China, was himself killed by Chao-hsien soldiers. This further affront to Emperor Wu of Han, already conducting military campaigns on various frontiers of the empire, was the only excuse he needed. In 109 BC he launched a formidable military assault on Chao-hsien, partly to establish a secure base in his struggle against the Hsiung-nu and partly to curb the expansionist ambitions of Chao-hsien itself.

The conflict – at times inconclusive and vacillating – lasted for a year, until Chao-hsien resistance finally collapsed, compelled to acknowledge the superior Chinese power but defeated also by divisions within the Chao-hsien ruling class: a peace group gradually eroded Chao-hsien resolve, until as a climax Wiman's grandson, Wei Yu-chu, was killed by his own subjects. After a year of conflict the Chao-hsien capital Wanggom-song, at the site of modern-day Pyongyang, was yielded to the Chinese and the Chao-hsien state dissolved. The robust Korean resistance was forced to acknowledge, not for the last time, the power of the giant to the north.

Emperor Wu had been quick to respond to the killing of She Ho, moving promptly to raise two powerful armies at least in part comprising criminals under death sentence. An army under Hsun Chih was ordered to march overland, one under Yang-Pu to journey by sea across the Gulf of Liao-tung. But the two-pronged assault, whatever the military justification, in the event proved to be fraught with dissension and incompetence, the powerful forces hampered by rivalries between the commanders and the uncertain loyalties of the soldiers. Yang-Pu's forces arrived first and attempted to invade the Chao-hsien capital, then ruled by Wei Yu-chu, but they were repulsed and fled in disarray. Hsun Chih at first fared no better: after a clash with Chao-hsien troops, well acquainted with the mountainous terrain, his soldiers were forced to retreat.

However, the initial setbacks were no more than a temporary embarrassment for the Chinese. Emperor Wu sent an envoy with reinforcements, and Wei Yu-chu realised the inevitable superiority of the Chinese numbers. The envoy was invited into Wanggom-song and received with apologies. Wei Yu-chu, indicating his willingness to acknowledge Chinese hegemony, agreed to despatch his heir to China as a token of good faith. But the suspicions remained, not least because the heir-apparent was accompanied by 10,000 troops in his entourage. Fighting again broke out, with rivalries between the Chinese commanders giving Wanggom-song a brief reprieve. Hsun Chi, concerned that Yang-Pu was about to make a separate agreement with the Chao-hsien leadership, arrested him and seized his army. At the same time the political uncertainties were feeding the tensions among the Chao-hsien ruling class in Wanggom-song. In 108 BC Wei Yu-chu was assassinated by his own people and Chao-hsien finally succumbed to the Chinese. Emperor Wu, dismayed even in victory by the confrontation between the two Chinese generals, exacted appropriate punishment: Yang-Pu was stripped of all honours and titles and Hsun Chih was condemned to public execution. The campaign was over. Chao-hsien, the first sovereign state to occupy a substantial part of the Korean peninsula, no longer existed.

Emperor Wu (Wu Ti, the Martial Emperor) had now brought the region under Han control, and to facilitate Chinese jurisdiction four commanderies were established; Lo-lang from (in modern-day geographical terms) Pyongan Province and Hwanghae Province to Kyonggi Province; Chen-fan in the region of Chungchong Province and Cholla Province; Lin-tun in Kwangwon Province; and Hsuan-tu in the area of Hamgyong Province.[8] The hub of the Chinese administration was Lo-lang, which survived as a centre of Chinese culture in the Korean peninsula for 400 years. Here a walled city was built on the southern bank of the Taedong river, bringing an unprecedented architecture to the peninsula and brick-paved streets for the chariots of the powerful. Han culture flourished, spreading a knowledge of sophisticated iron and bronze artefacts, delicate goldwork, textiles and ceramic wares, unprecedented art and philosophy, and new skills in trade and government throughout the region, even across the Straits of Korea to Japan. But the richness and vitality of Chinese culture did little to win the allegiance of the contending Korean tribes: the four Han commanderies were opposed by local people from the beginning and soon the Chinese interlopers were forced to make major adjustments to each of the administrative zones. Only 25 years after their creation, the Chen-fan and Lin-tun commanderies were abolished as separate units, with the regions under their nominal control transferred to the jurisdiction of Lo-lang and Hsuan-tu. In 75 BC, less than a decade later, the Han were forced to move the base of the Hsuan-tu commandery far to the west in east-central Manchuria, with various Hsuan-tu responsibilities transferred to Lo-lang. But even Lo-lang, at the heart of the Chinese presence, was beset by problems: tensions were growing among the ruling gentry and the local Korean tribes were constantly threatening the Chinese administration. In AD 30 the Lo-lang governor suppressed a rebellion by Wang Tiao, a member of the Lo-lang gentry, but the event helped to destabilise the administration. The Chinese established a new commandery, Tai-fang, south of Lo-lang, in a region formerly under the jurisdiction of the Chen-fan commandery, but by now the Chinese presence was under mounting threat. In 313 the Lo-lang and Tai-fang commanderies collapsed under pressure from the emerging Korean kingdoms. A new phase of Korean independence was about to dawn.

The Korean tribes, despite the broad Chinese hegemony in much of the peninsula, had never been totally subdued. In the southern regions, far from the Manchurian border, various Korean factions came under the influence of Chinese culture but still vied for local autonomy. All the tribes were rooted in earlier Chinese incursions, but by now many had developed striking indigenous features: the vigorous efforts to preserve local spheres of influence led to the collapse of the Chinese commanderies, the growth of strong Korean kingdoms, and ultimately to the unification of the peninsula as a single Korean state.

One of the most influential peoples of the region, the Puyo, emerged in the Sungari river basin in Manchuria. This group variously confronted the Chinese in their expansionist ambitions, gave rise – at least in part – to the emergence of the Koguryo people in northern Korea, and in due course came into conflict with the Koguryo, itself determined to resist Chinese invasion.

The Puyo are first reported about the fourth century BC, with frequent references appearing in Chinese records from the start of the first century AD. At that time the Puyo were regarded, along with the Hsiung-nu and Koguryo, as a likely threat to the Hsin dynasty (AD 8–23) of Wang Mang in China. At the same time the Chinese calculated that an agreement with Puyo would protect them from the expansion of other powerful regional factions. The Puyo similarly perceived that a Chinese alliance might offer them protection, not least from the Koguryo. There were still sporadic outbursts of violence between the Chinese and the Puyo but relations were generally cordial. In AD 49 Puyo envoys were sent to China, at the end of the Later Han dynasty the Kung-sun house formed marriage ties with Puyo, and when the Chinese general Kuan-chiu Chien invaded Kuguryo in AD 244 he was pleased to receive provisions from Puyo. Four decades later, in 285, the Puyo state was in jeopardy following an invasion from the Hsien-pei ruler Mu-jung Hui. The Chinese ruler of Chin offered support to the Puyo royal house but in 316 the Chin kingdom itself was driven south by nomadic tribes. Puyo, now isolated, struggled to survive as an independent political state but in 346 the Hsien-pei ruler Mu-jung Huang invaded the confederated kingdom to take the Puyon monarch, Hyon, and 50,000 of his people prisoner. Subsequently, with the collapse of the Hsien-pei state, Puyo passed under the control of Koguryo and disappeared from the pages of history.[9]

Koguryo was supposedly founded in 37 BC by Chumong from Puyo, who had moved with his followers to a region centred on the middle Yalu and Tung-chia river basin. Here Chumong consolidated a new state based in part on the indigenous Yemaek people, known to have settled in the area by about the fourth century BC. The Chinese had attempted to establish control of Koguryo by means of the Hsuan-tu commandery, designed in part also to resist the encroachments of Chao-hsien, but this was no more than 'a mere exercise in map drawing'.[10] In the latter part of the first century the Koguryo state felt strong enough the invade the Chinese region of Liao-tung, crossing the Liao river to attack Chang-cheng. Chinese expeditions sent into Koguryo territory were never able to achieve the total subordination of a hunting people well equipped to move over mountainous terrain. By the fourth century Koguryo had succeeded in creating a strong state extending over much of Manchuria and the Korean peninsula.

The expansionist ambitions of Koguryo derived in part from the character of the land in which they lived. The mountainous areas offered poor resources, so food and raw materials had to be obtained elsewhere. This encouraged Koguryo to expand into Chinese territory to the west and to Korea's eastern coast area inhabited by the Okcho and Ye tribes. The conflict with China was inconclusive but the Okcho and the Ye, centred on Hamgyong and Kangwon, were subdued and reduced to slaves. Now Koguryo had a further reliable supply of food, cloth, artefacts and necessary raw materials, all dutifully carried through the mountains by the conquered peoples. Moreover, the securing of the eastern lands made it easier for Koguryo to resist Chinese encroachments in the west.

Elsewhere in the peninsula other tribes, later to be important in the emergence of a unified Korean state, were contending for power. In the south were the Han tribes (not to be confused with the Chinese Han), divided amongst themselves but able to avoid total subordination by the Chinese commandery system. While the Koguryo were a hunting people the Han preferred to focus on agriculture: rice grains, along with shells and animal and fish bones, have been recovered from the Han shell mounds at Kumhae of about the first century AD. From the Chinese *Wei-chih*, which describes the conditions in third-century Korea, we learn that the Han tribes cultivated 'five cereals' (hemp, millet, rice, wheat and pulse), planted the mulberry tree, husbanded cows and pigs, and made silk cloth. By contrast the Koguryo depended solely on the tribute paid by subject tribes.

The Han tribes had three principal branches: the Ma Han, the Chin Han and the Pyon Han. There were 55 Ma Han tribes, with more than 100,000 households, living in the region of present-day Chungchong Province and Cholla Province; the Mokchi were the dominant Ma Han tribe until the rise of Paekche (see below). The tribes practised two important sacrificial ceremonies to the spirits one in the spring after planting and one at the time of the autumn harvest. The great chief (*sinji*) and the lesser chiefs were appointed by the tribes themselves or by Chinese officials when able to exercise administrative hegemony.

There were twelve Chin Han tribes, occupying much of the Naktong region and considering themselves to be descendants of Chinese refugees from the state of Chin (255–205 BC). The Chin Han lived in walled cities, used oxen and horse carts, and developed their agriculture in a fertile land. They also produced iron, their most famed product, which was used as currency and which stimulated a brisk trade with the other Han tribes, the Yemaek, and the Japanese Wa communities. Iron was also sent as tribute to the Chinese commanderies. The Chin Han have been depicted as a joyous people, fond of the lute and of drinking, dancing and singing; and as uniquely considerate to their dead, keen to bury large feathers with the corpses to help them fly away. One of the main tribes of the Chin Han was the Saro, out of whom the important state of Silla (see below) was to grow.

The Pyon Han lived around the lower reaches of the Naktong river in the area of South Kyongsang Province; as with the Chin Han, with whom they were in close contact, there were twelve Pyon Han tribes. The Chin Han and the Pyon Han together formed some 40–50,000 households. The Pyon Han communities worked together in the Kaya League and, as with the Chin Han, enjoyed trading and other connections with the Japanese Wa.

As the tribes expanded and jostled throughout the Korean peninsula it was inevitable that they would come into conflict. Expansionist ambitions varied from one culture to another but even the agriculturally rooted tribes were quick to see the advantage of acquiring new strips of fertile land in a difficult mountainous terrain. The contending tribes struggled for supremacy, not least over the Chinese interlopers, until the emergence of the three principal kingdoms of Koguryo, Paekche and Silla. The contentious period of the Three Kingdoms was the prelude to the final unification of the Korean peninsula.

THE THREE KINGDOMS PERIOD

The Growth of Koguryo

One of the consequences of the Chinese expansion into eastern Manchuria and northern Korea was to stimulate a degree of unity among the regional tribes. Koguryo, the fruit of one such alliance, had emerged in the mountains of south-eastern Manchuria by the first century and comprised, according to a third-century description, a union of five tribes: the Yon, Chol, Sun, Kwan and Kye. The Yon tribe was dominant for a time, until supplanted by the Kye in alliance with the Chol, a tribe known for supplying brides for the Koguryo rulers. The tribal leaders had an element of local autonomy and also served as part of the central government. The high officials emerged as a leisured upper class, suitably clad in silks and brocades and decorated with silver and gold artefacts. The Koguryo kings took care to sacrifice to the shrine of the mythical founder Chumong in the capital; and to worship also Chumong's mother, the daughter of the river god.

Koguryo exploited local tensions in the region to further its expansionist aims. At the start of the Wang Mang dynasty in China in AD 9 both Koguryo and Puyo sent envoys, whereupon China demanded the mobilisation of forces against the Hsiung-nu, a constant threat to the Chinese empire. When Koguryo refused, the Chinese were unable to impose their will, encouraging Koguryo to move into the power vacuum left by the withdrawal of the earlier Chinese Han dynasty from the northeast. Koguryo was now able to demand Okcho tribute formerly conveyed to Puyo and the Chinese. By the end of the second century the Chinese position in the peninsula had become untenable. Koguryo and the other Korean states took their opportunity to seize land and to consolidate their regional hegemonies.

However, the overall situation remained far from stable. In 342 the Mu-jung clan in the Manchurian state of Yen invaded Koguryo in the region of the Yalu river basin. The Koguryo capital was sacked and burned; 50,000 men and women, including the Koguryo queen dowager, were carried off; royal mausoleums were desecrated; and the bones of the king's father were taken for ransom (finally paid in 355). Koguryo survived as a state but its ambitions were blunted; now it was forced to pay tribute to the Chinese states of Yen and Chin, and to direct its expansionist ambitions south into the peninsula. The Yen threat to the survival of Koguryo ended in 370 when the Yen state fell to the Chin, but the Koguryo relief was short-lived: now Koguryo was faced with a fresh invasion, this time from Paekche (see below).

After the death of the Koguryo ruler in battle in 371, the powerful Sosurim took the throne, to rule for more than a decade. He entered into peaceful agreements with the Chin state, which is said to have exported Buddhism to Koguryo in 372. Sosurim, concerned at Koguryo's military failures when confronted with Mu-jung and Paekche invasions, then set about building up the army. The policy was successful: in 391 the great conqueror Kwanggaeto (also known as Hotae) inherited a vast military machine and immediately began to expand the frontiers of the Koguryo state. He led frequent campaigns to the south: rolling Paekche out of the Han valley, threatening Silla and land held by the Japanese; defeating the Ilou tribes in the northeast; and expanding Koguryo east into Manchuria. The victorious campaigns of Kwanggaeto were recorded on the stone memorial stele at the Koguryo capital of Kungnaesong (present-day Tung-kou, in Manchuria), erected the year after his death by his son, Changsu (r.413–391). The memorial declares that Kwanggaeto conquered 64 walled cities and 1400 villages. By now, Koguryo had become a large imperial state, extending through most of the northern half of Korea and a large part of Manchuria.

In 494 the Puyo people in the north were brought under Koguryo control. The national capital was consolidated at the site of present-day Pyongyang, and in addition there were two secondary capitals: the old capital of Kungnaesong and the erstwhile Paekche capital of Hansong. Koguryo was now at the height of its powers (Figure 2.2), its security built on the high competence of a professional military class. The long campaigns in Manchuria had created hardy legions of experienced veterans, all adequately funded from the guaranteed taxes on the peasants and nomad tribes. A seventh-century Chinese record, *The History of Sui*, tells how a standard Koguryo land tax was levied in terms of bushels of grain and bolts of homespun cloth.

Koguryo now controlled a vast subject empire; at the time of the collapse of the Koguryo state, the population comprised some 690,000 households, mostly conquered people captured in battle. Every phase of territorial expansion had served to increase the size of the slave population, which in turn demanded a comprehensive system of administrative control. Fortified bases were built throughout the empire, staffed by military personnel with civil administrators above them. Ten ranks of officials (the highest, *taedaero*) at Pyongyang were responsible for the internal and external affairs of the Koguryo state. The high officials and military leaders, generally deriving their position from the old tribal class hierarchies, now directly served the king, so weakening the old tribal system in which local chiefs enjoyed a substantial measure of autonomy in their own lands. The highest ranking official positions, invariably staffed by nobles, were rotated every three years, in part to prevent the emergence of powerful cliques that might threaten the monarch. In addition, the security of the Koguryo state was protected by a harsh penal system: rebels were burned to death by the common people, with public decapitation the penalty for robbery and murder. As befitted the requirements of an empire built on military conquest, the penalties for military defeat were equally severe: those individuals who survived a military defeat, or who surrendered a fort to the enemy, were decapitated.

Religious observance evolved through the life of the Koguryo state. Many of the tribes preserved an element of animism and ancestor worship, but also came under increasing pressure to worship

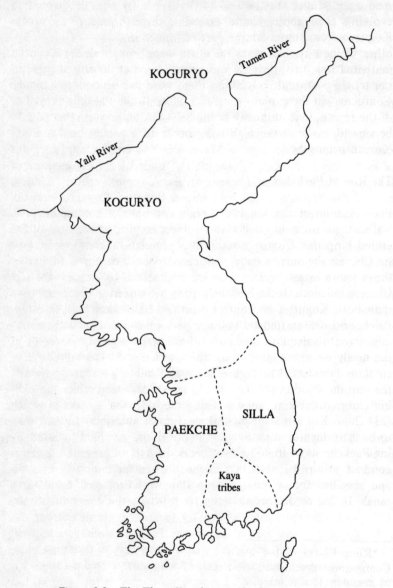

Figure 2.2   The Three Kingdoms in the fourth century AD

Chumong, seen as the divine ancestor of the entire Koguryo people. And again China impacted significantly on the credal systems now evolving throughout the peninsula: in 372 Buddhism reached Koguryo from the north, at a time when Confucianism and many other Chinese-rooted branches of learning – astronomy, medicine, mathematics, jurisprudence and others – were having a growing impact. In particular, emphasis should be given to the importance of Confucius* in the evolution of the philosophical and ethical systems of the region. One authority proposes that Confucian theory 'should be viewed as the ideological background for the early history of the Korean peninsula'.[11]

The Rise of Paekche

Paekche, one of the Ma Han tribes, developed to incorporate the walled-town states in the Han river basin and to constitute a confederated kingdom. First organised in BC 16, the kingdom of Paekche (in Chinese the name means 'hundred crossers'), with its frontage on the western coast of the Korean peninsula, remained subject to Chinese influence throughout its history.[12] With less military prowess than both Koguryo and Silla (see below), Paekche (also known as Paichi and Kudara) none the less felt able to take important military initiatives to safeguard its frontiers and extend its sway. Thus in 246 the newly emerging state of Paekche was able to resist military incursions launched by the Lo-lang and Tai-fang commanderies. In the ensuing conflict the Tai-fang governor, Kung Tsun, was killed, his troops unable to subdue the Paekche force led by King Koi (234–286). Koi (also depicted as the founder-king, Kui) was known to be instrumental in shaping the political lineaments of the developing Paekche state. In 260 Koi appointed six ministers (*chwapyong*) to conduct affairs of state, created sixteen grades of official rank, and specified the colours of dress that would define the particular ranks. In 262 he decreed that corrupt officials would be made to pay

---

*Kung Fu-tzu (551–479 BC). As with other creeds and philosophies, Confucianism developed a substantial corpus far wider than the writings of its founder. It was adopted as a state philosophy by the Former Han dynasty (202 BC–AD 25), and its influence ebbed and flowed thereafter. Confucianism inevitably influenced the attitudes and practices of the Korean peoples, as it influenced the peoples in all of Eastern Asia.

three-fold compensation and would be permanently barred from public office.[13]

In 369 the Paekche king Kun Chogo (346–375) took various military initiatives to extend the realm of the state, and two years later swept north to Pyongyang, killing the Koguryo king Kogugwon in the ensuing battle. Now Paekche controlled all the present-day provinces of Konggi, Chungchong and Cholla, as well as substantial areas of Hwanghae and Kangwon. At the same time Kun Chogo began negotiations with the Eastern Chin state and with the Japanese Wa people. He was succeeded by Kun Kusu (375–384), whose successor, Chimnyu, implanted Buddhism as a virtual state religion.

Despite the 369 victory, Paekche was usually the loser in conflict with its powerful northern neighbour and in later years with the rising state of Silla. In 475 Paekche was forced to move its capital southward, further away from Koguryo, to the modern town of Kwangju; and in 538 a further shift was necessary, this time to the southern region of Puyo (the same name as the Manchurian tribe). Paekche frequently sought alliances with Silla or Japanese forces to resist the growing power of Koguryo, but the strategy offered no long-term security. In 433 Silla concluded a useful alliance with Paekche, and established marriage ties four decades later, after the transfer of the Paekche capital to Ungjin (Kwangju) in 475. Silla honoured its alliance with Paekche, on occasions conducting joint military operations against Koguryo, until it set its eyes on greater ambitions. In due course the alliances shifted with, for a period, Paekche making common cause with Koguryo in assaults on Silla. But Paekche's doom was finally sealed by a fresh Chinese invasion: it was the Tang dynasty that would finally consign Paekche to history. A desultory effort at a Paekche restoration finally collapsed in 663.

Silla: Prelude to Unification

Silla, founded in BC 57 but not coming to prominence until the fourth century AD, began as a weak and backward state. It acquired political significance when Saro, one of the twelve Chin Han tribes, absorbed the surrounding states to create a broader union. Silla (also known as Hsinlo, Sinra and Shiragi) occupied difficult mountainous terrain: less fertile than the lands of Paekche and Koguryo, and lacking Paekche's abundant harbours. It had also never been occupied by the Chinese armies that had encroached on much of the peninsula, and so had derived few benefits from the advanced Chinese culture of the region. In its early days Silla was content to survive, rather than expand, in contention with its more powerful neighbours. It is interesting that the people of Silla – hardened by frugality, simplicity and all the other impositions of a harsh environment – would come to supplant the great states to the west and north, favoured by more fertile lands and the benefits of an advanced culture.

By the middle of the fourth century Koguryo was expanding to the south and Japanese invaders had entered the peninsula to establish bases in the Pyon Han region. Paekche, in alliance with Japan, threatened Silla from the west; on many occasions the very survival of the Silla state seemed uncertain. However, the unity of the Silla people provided a secure basis for the consolidation of the state and exhibited a high degree of resilience in confrontation with external threats.

The state of Saro had taken the lead in developing a confederated structure with the other walled-town states of the Chin Han region. In one account the appearance of King Tarhae (AD 57–80) from the Sok clan marks the start of this significant political development. The regional expansion of Silla continued until, by the time of King Naemul (356–402), a substantial confederated kingdom had been established. It is clear that the solid political structure, showing a manifest democratic element, had derived from traditional tribal practices. The tribal chiefs held crucial conferences (*hwabaek*) at which problems were discussed and resolved, unanimous consent being required for a solution. And the *hwabaek* system prevailed throughout the period of Silla's expansion: kings were appointed by the conference and other important matters of state were settled.

The revered founder of the Silla state, Hyokkose, was given the title of *kosogan*; his successor, Namhae, dubbed *chachaung*. Later the rulers (the third to the eighteenth) were called *nisagum*, (the nineteenth to the twenty-second) *maripkan*, and thereafter *wang* (the Chinese title of king). There is debate about the etymology of the terms, though they all seem to denote chief or paramount chief. *Chachaung* seems to denote a shaman, interested in communion with the spirits. In any event it is significant that the rulers were not hereditary but depended upon *hwabaek* decisions, so suggesting the persistence of ancient practices.[14] However, as Silla expanded its domain the chiefs of defeated tribes were not allowed a role in the *hwabaek*; and it was mandatory that the appointed king be a victor. The conquered tribes were permitted to retain their tribal structures but now they were entirely subordinate to the monarch of the confederated kingdom. It is significant also that the *hwabaek* appointment of a king, dependent upon conference unanimity, did nothing to erode the weight of the hereditary principle elsewhere in the structure of state power. This is most clearly shown by the 'bone-rank' (*kolpum*) status system.

The *kolpum* institution, one of the defining Silla features, operated to assign political and other privileges according to a person's bone-rank (that is, his hereditary bloodline). The 'first bones' class, the highest social stratum of Silla, comprised *songgol* (sage- or hallowed-bone) and *chingol* (true-bone). Both men and women were eligible for membership of this class, though favoured individuals were drawn only from particular clans, such as the Pak, Sok and Kim; there was no way that a lower-class person could become a 'first bone'. Kingship, though not hereditary, moved only among the 'first-bone' clans; and the *hwabaek*, the only authority for appointing the king, was comprised entirely of 'first-bone' members.

The royal house of Kim had both *songgol* status, for a period the necessary qualification to be considered for kingship, and *chingol* status, not formerly a kingship qualification. Towards the end of the Three Kingdoms Period the *songgol* bone-rank ceased to exist and *chingol* was allowed as a kingship qualification. This meant that the Pak lineage, as well as the Kim, was readmitted to the kingship stakes.

Below the first-bone class there were other bones strata: six grades of 'head rank' ('head-rank six' down to 'head-rank one'). The higher 'head-ranks' denoted the general aristocracy, with the lower 'head-ranks' signifying the ordinary people (*pyonggin*) or the common people (*paeksong*): that is, the general populace with few privileges and little political power.[15] The central aim of the solid state structure was to preserve the security of the system and the political power of the aristocratic clans.

The right to kingship was assigned to the house of Kim during the reign of King Naemul; and soon after, during the reign of Nulchi (417–458), the important hereditary principle of father to son succession was introduced. Thereafter, under either King Chabi (458–479) or King Soji (479–500), the main six clans were reorganised into administrative zones (*pu*) to facilitate government control. In 433 a fresh alliance with Paekche served as a bulwark to

Koguryo pressure; and Silla and Paekche thereafter carried out a series of joint military ventures. During the reign of King Chijung (500–514) important agricultural advances were made, with the introduction of ploughing by oxen and the extension of irrigation. King Pophung (514–540) consolidated the centralisation of the aristocratic Sillan state, and during this period the Pak clan emerged as a source of Sillan queens.

A code of law was introduced in 520, instituting the 'bone-rank' system, delineating what was now a seventeen-grade office-rank structure, and specifying the proper attire for officials (the highest officials, ranks 1–5, wore purple robes; ranks 6–9 wore scarlet; ranks 10 and 11 blue; and ranks 12–17 yellow). In 536 the era name *Konwon* ('Initiated Beginning') was adopted, signalling the decision that Silla was to have equal status in the international community. Around this time Buddhism was adopted as the state religion.

Now Silla felt confident enough to expand its domain, becoming in the sixth century the dominant kingdom in the Korean peninsula (Figure 2.3). King Chijung had already conquered Usan, the eastern island of Ullung in 512, and King Pophung subjugated much of the Kaya region two decades later. King Chinhung (540–576) extended the territorial expansion already begun by his predecessors: in alliance with King Song of a briefly resurgent Paekche in 551, Silla took substantial land from Koguryo in the region of the Han river basin, thereafter expelling Paekche from the lower Han region. A furious King Song confronted Silla but was killed in battle in 554, so finally marking the rupture of the Silla-Paekche alliance that had lasted for more than a century. Silla now stood alone against the combined forces of Paekche and Koguryo, an alliance that launched frequent attacks against the expanding Sillan state. In one such encounter the Koguryo commander Ondal, a famed warrior, was killed.

Silla was now consolidating its conquests as events to the north again moved to affect the political evolution of the Korean peninsula. The Sui dynasty had succeeded in unifying the Chinese empire but was coming under threat from the Tu-chueh (Turks). Koguryo, seeing the need to resist Sui advances into the peninsula, saw advantage in forming links with the Tu-chueh, while at the same time Paekche was building its contacts with the Japanese. There thus emerged an alliance between Koguryo, Paekche and the Tu-chueh in confrontation with an east–west axis comprising Sui, Silla and Japan. These fresh alliances grew out of the mounting tensions in

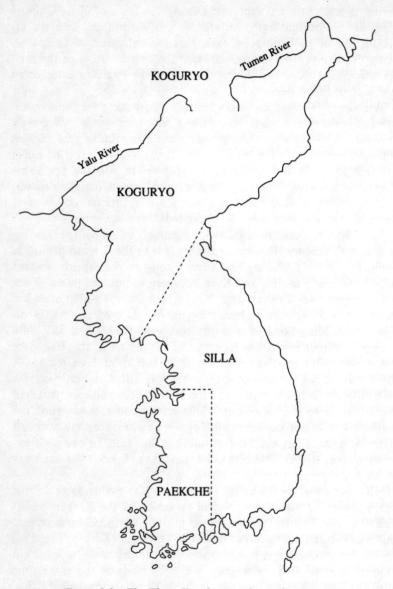

Figure 2.3   The Three Kingdoms in the sixth century AD

the region and heralded the storm that was soon to break over north–east Asia, a vortex of political turmoil that would bring in its train the unification of the Korean peninsula.

The Tu-chueh attacked Sui in 597, a prelude to a Koguryo incursion west of the Liao river and a brief Sui response. In 607 the Sui, having discovered a Koguryo envoy in the camp of the Turkish khan, launched a fresh series of attacks against Koguryo. After one desultory initiative, the Sui Emperor Yang in 612 launched a vast army which came to grief against the Koguryo forces: the famed Koguryo commander, Ulchi Mundok, lured the Sui army into a trap, and only 2700 Sui soldiers out of an original force of some 300,000 men managed to find their way home. A final Sui campaign (614) was no more successful, and the cost of the incursions into Korea is often cited as a principal reason for the collapse of the Sui dynasty. The successor to Sui, the Tang dynasty (618–905), soon developed its own plans for the conquest of the peninsula.

A power struggle ensued in Koguryo (642) when a military strongman, Yon Kaesomun, emerged to wield absolute power. His stance quickly exacerbated tensions between neighbouring states, including both Silla and Tang who formed what would eventually prove to be a decisive alliance. In 645 the Tang Emperor Tai Tsung launched a large army into Liao-tung and a naval force aboard 500 ships. The Chinese overran many fortified cities but were eventually frustrated by the walled-town of Ansi-song (the An-shih fortress, situated at present-day Ying-cheng-tzu). After an unsuccessful 60-day siege the exhausted Tang forces withdrew to China, taking thousands of prisoners with them. Subsequent Tang invasions also ended in failure.

In 667, after vast preparation and the emergence of a leadership crisis in Koguryo, Tang launched a new assault on the peninsula: General Li Chi commanded one of the Chinese armies, while General Hsueh Jen-kuei swept to the east, inflicting a crushing defeat on Koguryo forces. Chinese naval forces disembarked downstream from Pyongyang to join a Silla army under General Kim Inmun. The combined Tang-Silla forces advanced to the Koguryo capital and prepared for a lengthy siege, but the city capitulated during the winter of 668. Koguryo resistance to Chinese power, a bulwark against invasions from the north for over 70 years, was now at an end. Pyongyang – and with it all the Koguryo records – was destroyed in the siege, and the state of Koguryo was no more.

Tang then moved to establish administrative control over the entire peninsula. The land of the former kingdom of Paekche was divided into five governorships, with a Chinese military commander, fronted by Prince Yung, assigned control of the area around Ungjin. The Chinese also attempted to subsume Silla within the sphere of new administration for the peninsula, going so far as to designate the Silla capital the Kyerim Governorship with Silla's King Manmu (r.661–680) allowed to continue as 'governor' of his own kingdom.[16] Manmu was also induced to sign a covenant of peace dictated by the Chinese commander Liu Jen-Kuei, whereupon the sacred document was assigned to Silla's ancestral temple. Liu, based in Pyongyang with a force of 20,000 soldiers, was also intended to supervise nine governorships established through the former lands of Koguryo and to consolidate Chinese control over the entire peninsula. The Silla response was to organise military resistance to the Tang occupation.

Silla aided the burgeoning Koguryo rebel movement, settling the Koguryo king, An Sung, in the land of former Paekche and launching military attacks on the Tang forces in the region. By 671 Silla had occupied much of the former Paekche territory: the fortress at Sabi, the Paekche capital, was overrun, allowing Silla to establish the province of Soburi and to seize control of all the lands of the former Paekche kingdom. Tang responded by nominating Kim Il-mun, Manmu's younger brother, the new king of Silla, but this ploy achieved nothing. The Silla forces were victorious in a series of battles against the Tang in the area of the Han river basin, and in 676 the Chinese armies were forced into comprehensive retreat. The war between Silla and the Tang dynasty lasted for six years, with Silla able to resist and counter every substantial Tang initiative and to preserve the growing measure of national independence.

The Silla state did not succeed in unifying all the lands formerly controlled by the Three Kingdoms. Much of Manchuria, once under the sway of Koguryo, remained beyond the reach of Silla's armies; and it was there that refugees from the former Koguryo established the new kingdom of Parhae. Silla and Parhae confronted each other in the northern parts of the peninsula, so limiting the extent of the Silla unification. It was however Silla's unified rule of the bulk of the peninsula that laid the basis for the subsequent course of Korean history.

3 The Unified State

The unification of the Korean peninsula – achieved after centuries of foreign incursion and warfare between the kingdoms – lasted, with few interruptions, from the seventh century AD to 1945. For most of that period the integrity of the Korean state survived, despite frequent internal disruptions, more foreign invasions, masssive exploitation by occupying powers, attempts at genocide, and the constant cultural pressures exerted by more powerful states on the Asian continent and beyond the seas.

Japan and the other states saw Korea as a natural bridge to the continental land mass, or to Japan itself; and China had always perceived Korea as lying within its legitimate sphere of interest. When Japan and China, or later Russia and the West, were in dispute with regional powers for land or trade or strategic advantage, Korea was often one of the fields over which they contended. The history of the Korean people, like that of many nations, is largely about the absorption of foreign influences, the resistance to military aggression, the response to foreign occupation . . . the constant search for sovereignty. The political unification of a state does not always entail sovereign independence.

THE SILLA UNIFICATION (7th–10th CENTURY)

The expansion of Silla and its successful response to Tang invasions meant that the unified Korean peninsula was now set for progressive sinicisation rather than the ravages of a hostile military occupation. There are clues as to what would have happened if Silla had succumbed to Chinese aggression. The Korean people had already suffered under the Han occupation of much of the peninsula; and the Tang forces had already deported 200,000 Koguryo and 13,000 Paekche prisoners of war to China as slaves. The Lo-lang and Taifang commanderies had suppressed the local populations, exploiting the regional resources and retarding cultural development. The Silla unification, in curtailing the Tang excesses, was a process of great historical importance.[1]

Now most of Paekche's 760,000 households and Koguryo's 690,000 households were brought under Silla administration. Some of the land and peoples were distributed to Silla nobles, with some defeated chiefs being allowed to administer their erstwhile domains as fiefs or emolument estates (*sigup*). During the early phase of the unification, which at that time did not embrace the entire peninsula (Figure 3.1), the nobles did little to manage their newly acquired lands, being content merely to take tribute from subject peoples. In 687 civil and military officials were given paddies as a prudent hedge against conspiracy and rebellion. In these circumstances the aristocracy emerged as an increasingly wealthy class. Chinese documents record that the Silla prime minister owned 3000 slaves, troops and many domestic animals (horses, cattle and swine). The newly emerging aristocratic class posed some threat to the ancient families rooted in the bone-status (*kolpum*) system (Chapter 2), but it proved resilient: the *kolpum* structure survived but, with the growing administrative demands of the Silla domain, was forced to absorb increased sinicisation.

The Silla unification, while blocking the ravages of Tang excess, was still obliged to acknowledge China as a suzerain nation. This involved paying tribute to Tang but enabled Silla to function as an independent state and to develop a characteristic culture, albeit heavily influenced by China. The administrative burden on the Silla state encouraged the adoption of the Tang model; before unification Tang methods were used extensively throughout the peninsula, and during the reign of King Kyongdok (r.742–764) the administrative machinery came to mirror that of China in most details. Central government included a ministry of management, with boards, bureaux, departments and other subdivisions similar to those of the Tang.

To aid local government the country was divided into nine districts, in turn divided into counties and prefectures; at the lowest level were the country districts and wards. Military garrisons, some staffed by survivors form Koguryo and Paekche, were established at strategic points throughout the country. Silla officials were generally selected according to *kolpum* status, unlike the Tang convention of selection by examination. At the lowest level of the Silla hierarchy the farming population had the status of slaves ('ward' was originally a Chinese term used to denote slaves). The Silla class system had survived all the political vicissitudes of centuries. The capital of the state from beginning to end remained at Saro (present-day Kyongju), suggesting the resilience of the traditional structure; and

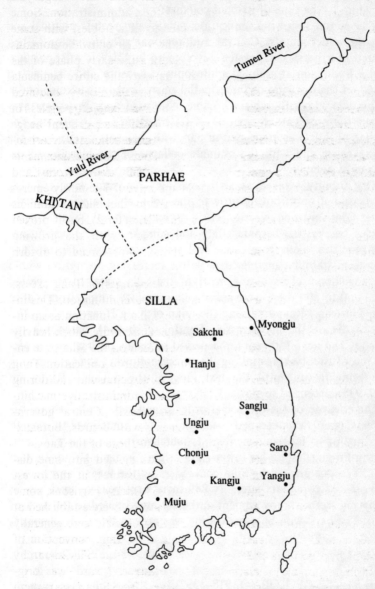

Figure 3.1   Unified Silla in the seventh century, showing the capital, Saro, and nine provincial capitals.

the *kolpum* system endured from Silla's expansion as a contending kingdom to the time of its final collapse.

The period following unification saw Silla's greatest political and artistic achievements. Central and regional administration, albeit rooted in a harsh class system, evolved to high levels of sophistication.[2] Buddhism stimulated philosophy, literature and art, with a focus on the doctrine of the essential oneness of humankind; but in Silla's later days Buddhism became associated with lavish extravagance, the profligate dissipation of state and private resources.[3] The decline of Silla was associated in part with the gross privileges of the ruling class, and with the ultimate collapse of the hitherto robust *kolpum* system.

The nobility evolved as an increasingly parasitic class, enjoying privilege but contributing little to the political development of the state. The *hwarang* warrior class, upon which all Silla's former glories had rested, became effete and complacent. The institutions and practices taken from China had proved unable to guarantee any long-term stability, unable to settle the increasing disruption within the key 'bone' clans at the heart of the Silla state. In the period from 750 to 800 there were six revolts or palace coups; from 800 to 890, fourteen.[4] Revolts during the reign of King Hyegong (765–779) led to his death; his assassin, Sondok (780–784), ascending the throne. The next 150 years, the period of Silla's decline, saw a succession of twenty kings taking the throne following struggles among the 'bone' clans, until the last king of the dynasty, Kyongsun (927–935), ascended to power.[5]

The collapse of the old social order stimulated revolts among the lower classes. Serfs escaped from the estates, sometimes turning to banditry or to independent lives as merchants. One such merchant, Chang Po-go, despite his lower-class origins, became strong enough by 839 to put one of the Silla contenders on the throne, but he was assassinated two years later. By 889 there were peasant uprisings in many regions with government authority now limited to the area of Saro. The hard-won Silla unification was now in terminal collapse.

THE STATE OF KORYO (918–1392)

One of the most successful of the rebel leaders was the monk Kungye, the son of a Silla king by a concubine. In 901, as the Silla state ran into dissolution, he founded the rival state of Later Koguryo in the north-central region of the peninsula. His aim was to build a new state modelled on the theory and practice of Silla government, but towards the end of this reign the regime degenerated into tyranny. Kungye's successor, the officer Wang Kon, came to power in 918 and set up his capital at Kaesong on the west coast. At the same time he decided to abbreviate the ancient name Koguryo to Koryo, from which is derived the Western name for Korea (in the past, Corea). In 935, with Later Paekche having overrun the Silla capital, the Silla king surrendered to Wang Kon. The remnants of the Silla administration were absorbed by Koryo, with the Later Paekche finally destroyed a year later. In 936 Wang Kon (also known as Taejo, the Korean pronunciation of Tai Tsu, the 'Grand Progenitor') again unified Korea as a single state.

The Koryo government was shaped first by Wang Kon (918–943) and later by two of his successors, Kwangjong (949–975) and Songjong (981–997), though minor revisions were carried out throughout the eleventh century. The Silla 'bone-rank' system had disappeared in the turmoil of the Silla collapse, leaving the Koryo kings free to intensify the sinicisation of the peninsula. A secondary capital was established at Pyongyang, the old Koguryo capital, with lesser capitals set up at the old Silla capital Kyongju in the east and at the site of modern Seoul. Now the institutions of central government included three boards, like those of the Tang, with a Bureau of Military Affairs, six traditional ministries, and many subordinate administrative organs. With Pyongyang, Kyongju and modern Seoul designated respectively the 'western', 'eastern' and 'southern' capitals, the rest of the country was divided into provinces, prefectures, subprefectures, districts and smaller administrative regions.[6] The state of Koryo was now governed by salaried officials, selected by examinations introduced in 958 on the Chinese model.

Wang Kon attempted to push Koryo's borders northward but soon ran into confrontation with Khitan (Figure 3.1). In 993 the Liao dynasty, founded in Khitan in 947, invaded Koryo, forcing it on to the defensive; a second Liao incursion resulted in heavy losses, the sacking of Kaesong, and the imposition of Liao suzerainty over the Koryo state. A third invasion, in 1018, was repulsed, allowing Koryo to achieve permanent control over all of the peninsula up to the lower Yalu river. Koryo then spent a decade (1033–1044) building a defensive wall from the mouth of the Yalu eastward to the coast of the Japan Sea north of modern Wonsan. Now all but the north-eastern corner of present-day Korea had been unified under a central Korean government.[7] Again unification served as a prelude to further political turmoil.

The Yi family (later to establish a lengthy dynasty) had been in-laws to the Koryo royal family through many reigns and by the time of King Injong exercised much power in the royal court. The ambitious family head, Yi Chagyom, then resolved to take the throne. In 1126 he attacked the palace and destroyed it; but was killed by an associate, Tak Cungyong, after which the entire Yi family was banished. This new tumultuous phase had led to the burning of many palaces and the destruction of much of Kaesong, but the turmoil was far from ended. In 1135 a faction led by Myo Chong, a priest learned in *yin-yang* and geomancy, organised a rebellion in Pyongyang but was defeated after a year of conflict. With this further bout of turmoil at an end, the leisured classes could again settle down to their normal hedonistic pursuits. King Uijong (1146–1170), Injong's successor, was closely associated with the nobles' way of life. Dubbed 'Lord of Tranquillity and Literature Appreciation', he habitually caroused, feasted and composed poems, engaging pursuits that did little to protect the stability of the state.

The central government of Koryo was frequently threatened by the military bureaucracy. In 1170 a palace coup attempt, known as the uprising of *Kyongin* (the Korean cyclical name for the year), was made by Chong Chungbu, a military official: as a royal pleasure party was passing through the gates of Pohyon Palace the followers of Chong Chungbu drew their swords and began attacking the civil officials accompanying the king. This led to further massacres of officials in the capital and elsewhere over a period of years, but Chong Chungbu and most of his military successors were killed in the ensuing coup attempts and power struggles within the military. This event in turn provided the opportunity for fresh peasant revolts, one of the most significant of these lasting for a year and a half (1176–1177) in Chungchong Province. In 1182 government slaves in North Cholla Province seized Chonju, with uprisings taking place at the same time in Cholla, Hwanghae and Pyongan. Over the next two decades there were dozens of rebellions throughout the peninsula, often involving thousands of peasants and slaves. In 1198 public and private slaves conspired to 'abolish the status of the unfree peoples', to burn the slave registers, and to kill civil and military officials. Local groups of slaves revolted and then joined other groups to swell their numbers. In 1203 Buddhist monks at temples in North Kyongsang Province rose in sympathetic revolt.[8]

The Koryo government succeeded in crushing the revolts but not in healing the divisions among the ruling class. After many coup attempts one of the military plotters, Choe Chung-hon, established his supremacy in 1196, deposed the king, and installed his own candidate upon the throne. Choe Chung-hon died in 1219, whereupon his son, Choe U, and the rest of the Choe family maintained their supremacy until 1258, consolidating their power but not usurping the throne. Through all the turmoil, peasant rebellions and palace coups, Koryo had largely retained its position as an independent state. Now it had to face a further threat, the hazard of a new merciless invasion from the north.

THE MONGOL INVASIONS (1231–1258)

Throughout its history the Korean peninsula has always been crucially affected by political developments on the Asian land mass. Thus at times when China was experiencing its own turbulent disruptions the resulting confusion gave scope for Korean leaders to take their own political initiatives. It was during the chaos that accompanied the end of Tang and the Five Dynasties (907–960) that Wang Kon managed to overthrow Silla and established the Koryo dynasty. Chinese authority in the peninsula had abated, giving Wang Kon scope for action; but following the Sung unification of China in 960 Koryo was quick to offer tribute, a prudent measure that for a time allowed Koryo to live in peace. But the Sung regime was not the only threat from the north.

In 994, during the reign of King Songjong, Koryo was forced to acknowledge the dominance of Khitan (Figure 3.1), a prelude to more invasions during the reign of King Hyonjong (1010–1031) and the occupation of Kaesong, the Koryo capital. An ambitious Buddhist carving project, designed to ward off such foreign incursions, lasted for almost 60 years through the reigns of four kings.[9] After Khitan, the Koryo state faced a fresh threat, this time from the Jurchen in Manchuria. In 1108 a Koryo force of more than 100,000 men under General Yun Kwan attacked the Jurchen with the aim of securing the northern frontier. The onslaught was repulsed and the Jurchen moved into northern Korea to seize Koryo fortresses. After many further incursions into the peninsula the Jurchen finally established the Chin Dynasty (1115–1234) and united with the Sung to subdue Khitan. Koryo submitted to the northern regimes as a means to a peaceful existence, but the Koreans still had to cope with the impact of the Mongol invasions.

The Mongols arose as nomads in the steppe region of north-central Asia to the north of the Gobi desert. As part of their vast expansionist ambitions they swept down to occupy Manchuria and north China in 1234, at the same time seeing various strategic advantages in further expansion to occupy the Korean peninsula: the occupation of Koryo would facilitate the crushing of the Sung and an invasion of Japan.

Koryo had already assisted the Mongols in the destruction of a Khitan army that had fled from Manchuria across the Yalu river, and had been forced to contend with Khitan forces pushed south by the advancing Mongol armies. In 1219 a combined Mongol–Koryo army forced a Khitan surrender at Kangdong Fortress, east of Pyongyang; after which the Mongols demanded annual tribute from Koryo. But when it emerged that the demands were excessive, Koryo refused to pay and the scene was set for a Mongol onslaught throughout the entire peninsula. The killing of the Mongol envoy Chuku-yu travelling back from Koryo in 1225 was a further incitement to the Mongol forces massing in the north. In 1231 the Mongols began their first invasion of the Korean peninsula.

The Mongol hordes poured across the Yalu river, by now Korea's northern frontier, and swept down the peninsula. A Koryo force under Pak So offered stubborn resistance at Kuju (modern Kusong) but the Mongols led by Sartaq abandoned the siege and moved towards Kaesong. Soon the Koryo capital was surrounded and surrender was inevitable. The entire Koryo court submitted to the Mongols and this initial phase of the conflict was at an end. Military governors (*darahaci*) were stationed in Koryo to supervise the activities of the Koryo authorities and much of the peninsula came under the direct rule of Karakorum, the Mongol capital. The main Mongol armies now withdrew, encouraging Choe U to consider fresh resistance to the Mongol occupation. In 1232 he moved the Koryo capital from Kaesong to Kanghwa Island, where he with an assortment of princes, officials and military personnel established a new Koryo court. The Mongols perceived the move as a rebellious act but were powerless to take decisive action: Choe U had exploited the Mongol fear of the sea.

This fresh phase of Koryo resistance provoked further Mongol invasions of the peninsula, though one withdrawal was forced when, later in 1232, Sartaq was killed in the battle at Choin-song (Yongin). Six invasions took place over a 30-year period, bringing the Mongols down to the southern boundaries of the peninsula. The famous *Koryo-sa* (History of Koryo) describes in 1254 the impact of the Mongol invasions: 'This year men and women seized by the Mongol troops reached the enormous number of 206,800 and innumerable people were massacred. All the districts through which the Mongol troops passed were reduced to ashes.' Such events, endlessly repeated, were common throughout the vast Mongol domain. At the same time the Koryo court, safely ensconced on Kanghwa Island, were enjoying their relative security. Palaces and pavilions were built, Buddhist festivals were enjoyed, and royal feasts were commonplace. It was still possible, despite the Mongols, to convey goods and taxes from mainland, though there was no thought of returning to liberate the peninsula. Prayers were offered and the Buddhist carvings remade to replace the earlier ones burned by the Mongols. Royal life in Kanghwa was much as it had been in Kaesong. However, in due course the inevitable court tensions developed again, and rivalries threatened the security of the royal house.

In 1258 Choe U was assassinated and the Choe family, the long-term power behind the throne, was stripped of its privileges and position. One dramatic consequence was a complete change in government policy: King Kojong, with his nobles and high officials, now abandoned their island redoubt and surrendered to the Mongols, the Koryo prince himself travelling to the Mongol court to apologise for earlier Koryo recalcitrance. When he returned he was allowed to ascend the throne as King Wonjong (1260–1274) to rule over what was now no more than a Mongol vassal state. Wonjong's successor, Chungnyol Wang, who had married a Mongol princess, a daughter of Khublai Khan, ascended the throne in 1274 and Mongol–Koryo relations were further consolidated. For many generations the descendants of this line became the monarchs of Koryo.

The rule of the Koryo kings throughout the peninsula had been reinstated, but at the price of total subservience to Mongol power. The abject surrender of the Koryo court had done little to reestablish the reputation of the aristocracy in the minds of the people, already crushed by the ravages of the Mongol occupation. The Koryo regime, in its hasty flight to Kanghwa, had merely instructed the peasantry to take refuge in their mountain fortresses as base points for the struggle against the invaders. The Mongols had responded by burning the ripened grain fields and slaughtering the entire populations of whichever forts fell to their attacks. In these circumstances the population declined, the survivors sliding into destitution, while the Kanghwa court continued to exact tribute from the accessible parts of the peninsula. Thus the puppet Koryo court, now sustained solely by Mongol power, enjoyed no popular support. Its power already drastically curtailed by the foreign overlords, the Koryo regime was ill-equipped to survive a Mongol departure.

The ancient title of *chong* for the Koryo king had been downgraded to *wang*, to signal an element of subservience. The king was now obliged to used *ko*, the subservient 'we', instead of *chim*, the kingly or imperial 'we'. Mongol officials and military personnel were stationed throughout the country to guarantee Koryo obedience to Mongol orders. And the Mongols insisted that Koryo aid the planned Mongol subjugation of Japan (just as, conversely, Japan would demand Korean support in its imperialist ambitions in the twentieth century). In the Mongol effort to subdue Japan in 1274, Koryo offered support by supplying 30,000 labourers, 5000 troops, and 900 warships, in addition to vast quantities of military supplies. Such impositions on an already impoverished peasantry can barely be imagined. At the time it was said: 'The farmers are all eating grass and the leaves of trees.'[10] In a second unsuccessful Mongol invasion of Japan in 1281 the Korean people were required to supply 10,000 soldiers.

The last century and a half of the Koryo dynasty saw the advent of the Japanese marauders (*Wako*), intent upon raiding the peninsula and the Chinese coasts. Much of the Korean coastline was ravaged, with even Kaesong threatened. By the middle of the fourteenth century rice and wheat were being carried off in great quantities, coastal people were being abducted or fled inland, and the transportation of Koryo grain taxes by sea was blocked. Such depredations eroded further the authority of the Koryo regime; and with the collapse of the Mongol empire, Koryo's only protector, the dynasty was doomed to extinction. In 1370 Koryo acknowledged Ming suzerainty, provoking a division in the Korean court between the pro-Ming faction and those who wished to retain links with the weakened and retreating Mongols. The pro-Mongol group won but the victory was short-lived. General Yi Songgye revolted during a campaign against the Ming armies and seized Kaesong in 1388 to install his own puppet on the throne and to take control of the government. Four years later he usurped the throne: in 1392, after nearly five centuries of rule, the Koryo dynasty was at an end.

THE YI DYNASTY (1392–1910)

The Yi Dynasty, the longest in Korean history, was established at Seoul and later forced to confront Japanese and Manchu invasions (see below). From the seventeenth to the nineteenth centuries the Yi rulers developed a policy of isolationism – so converting Korea into the 'Hermit Kingdom'. The isolationism broke down in the second half of the nineteenth century under trading and other pressures from Japan, Russia and the Western powers. The dynasty collapsed with Japan's annexation of Korea in 1910, the prelude to decades of merciless colonialism (Chapter 4).

The founder of the Yi Dynasty, Songgye, did not come from a famous Koryo family, though the Yi family had gradually acquired status in military circles. Yi Chachun, the first member of the lineage to become prominent, was offered a position in the Mongol Sangsong commandery, which in due course allowed King Kongmin to capture the commandery from the weakened Mongol forces. Chachun was thereafter appointed the military commander of the north-east region. Yi Songgye, the second son of this man, was 59 when he deposed his puppet in 1392 to establish the new dynasty. He had won advancement in battles against bandits, the Japanese marauders and the Mongol Tungning commandery in Manchuria. He had also overcome the rivalry of Choe Yong, the only military threat to the establishment of a new ruling dynasty in the Korean peninsula. Songgye named the new regime Chao-hsien, after the most ancient Korean kingdom (Chapter 2). Now Yi Chao-hsien (Yi Choson) was destined to see Korea into the modern age, into an abject period of colonialism and territorial division.

There now began a period of rich cultural development, though massively influenced by Chinese literature and scholarship: Yi Chao-hsien was to become 'a far more perfect replica of Ming China than Silla had ever been of the Tang'.[11] Songgye, despite his military credentials, was also the leader of a new literati class, a circumstance that would shape the development of the dynasty over the centuries. A wide range of cultural activities, their seeds already evident in

Korean society, was encouraged: including such pursuits as
Confucian studies, the writing of histories, the development of fine
arts, and progress in science and technology.[12] It is of interest that
in 1392, at the very end of the Koryo dynasty, a National Office for
Book Publication was established to cast type and to print books.
Thus the facility for movable-type printing, developed under the Yi
Dynasty, was introduced in the later Koryo period.* There were developments also in such areas as the cultivation of the cotton plant,
medical knowledge, and the manufacture of gunpowder (Choe had
persuaded the Koryo Court to establish a Superintendency for
Gunpowder Weapons in 1377).

Two of the principal innovations of the new Yi Dynasty were the
redistribution of farmlands and the advancement of Confucianism at
the expense of Buddhism. Songgye moved quickly to confiscate
lands owned by former landlords and to distribute these to deserving
government officials. Military personnel were not allowed to own
land, their supplies deriving from state cultivations specially designated for the purpose. Buddhism was discouraged because of its
hostility to the virtues of manual labour, a prime requirement of the
new regime. A famous historical Confucian text, the *Choson
Kyonggukjon* by the renowned scholar Chong Tojon, was recommended as the basic philosophical guide for the rulers of the new
kingdom. At the same time many innovations were introduced in
such areas as state administration, the shape of the government bureaucracy, state examinations, taxation policy, social discrimination,
and facilities for transportation and communications.[13]

Songgye had two main wives: one, of the Han clan, gave him six
sons; the other, of the Kang, two sons. He selected Yi Pangbon,
Queen Kang's eldest son, as the crown prince but Songgye was
opposed in this choice by many of his ministers. The scene was set
for another phase of characteristic power struggles around the
throne. Prince Yi Pangwon (1367–1423), suspecting that the princes
of the Han line were to be deposed, organised his forces to attack
the two Kang princes, killing them on the road. Then Pangwon, yet
another power behind the throne, deferred to one of his brothers, Yi

---

*There is a Koryo record of cast metal type used in the year 1234 for the
printing of the work *Prescribed Ritual Texts of the Past and Present*. This
follows the invention of movable type in the eleventh century by Pi Sheng
of the Sung Dynasty.

Panggwa (1357–1419) who took power when the ageing Songgye abdicated in 1399. But Panggwa (r.1399–1400) reigned for a mere four months: another prince, Panghan, staged an unsuccessful coup and was exiled by Pangwon who then assumed the throne as Taejong (r.1400–1418), a strong-willed ruler who encouraged cultural advance and introduced various reforms. Upon Taejong's abdication, his 22-year-old son was canonised Sejong (r.1418–1450) and began a brilliant 32-year rule.

A principal innovation of King Sejong was the Hall of Assembled Scholars (*Chiphyonjon*) where the finest intellects of the day contributed to the accumulation and dissemination of knowledge: many books were published and particular attention was given to agriculture ('the basis of government', according to Confucian doctrine) and to the related disciplines of mathematics, measurement and meteorology.[14] Chinese types of water wheel were used until supplanted in 1430 by a more efficient Japanese design. Yi scientists also developed improved firearms, musical instruments, metallic type, astronomical instruments, an improved armillary sphere (a celestial globe carrying depictions of stars on its surface), improved clepsydras, copper rain gauges, and many other devices.

Work was also carried out in medicine, leading to, amongst other texts, the 25-volume *Tongui pogam* (Treasured Mirror of Korean Medicine); in history; in Confucian ethical philosophy; in printing technology; and, most importantly, in the requirements for a refined Korean alphabet. The clumsy *idu* system of employing Chinese characters phonetically for Korean writing had yielded *kugyol*, unsuitable for writing Korean sounds. In 1446 Korean scholars produced a new refined alphabet called *chongum* (correct sounds) and later *onmun* (vulgar script or vernacular writing). Sejong officially adopted the new alphabet (known today as *hangul*, 'Korean letters') in 1446 by royal decree. *Hangul* has been depicted as 'the most scientific system of writing in general use in any country'.[15]

King Sejong died in 1450, leaving eighteen sons. His eldest son, Hang, was in poor health when he ascended the throne on his father's death, and he lived for only two more years. His son, the crown prince, later given the temple name Tanjong (r.1452–1455), was twelve years old when he became king. Hang, canonised Munjong, had placed his trust in members of the Hall of Assembled Scholars, and in particular in his closest officials, such as Kim Chongso (1390–1453) and Song Sammun (1418–1456). But these various advisors were unable to prevent the power struggle that erupted on Munjong's death. The lord of Anpyong (1418–1453), Sejong's third son, was one of the various contenders for power. The lord of Suyang made a bid for power in 1453, which led to the deaths of Kim Chongso, Hwangbo In and other officials who had been favoured by Munjong: a purge that enabled the lord of Suyang, canonised Sejo (r.1455–1468), to ascend the throne two years later. The young King Tanjong, though keeping the support of the Hall of Assembled Scholars, was kept under guard in the palace. Subsequent efforts to depose Sejo were ruthlessly suppressed (the individuals concerned were executed, as were their sons and grandsons. Key state officials, including Song Sammun, were killed, and thereafter known as the Six Martyrs; whereupon six other high ministers, the 'Six Ministers Who Lived') (*Saengyuksin*), resigned in protest. The young Tanjong was subsequently exiled, reduced to commoner status, and then killed, aged seventeen.

Sejo was succeeded by a son, canonised Yejong (r.1468–1469), who took the throne at eighteen and died a year later. His mother, the Queen Dowager Yun, managed to place another son on the throne; this one, canonised Songjong (r.1470–1494), managed a long reign, successful military campaigns, and the stimulation of many cultural achievements. He was succeeded by Yonsangun (r.1494–1506) who presided over further power struggles, purges of the literati, and various score-settling events (including the disinterring of corpses so that they could be hacked to pieces). Such events led to the deposing of Yonsangun, and his replacement by the eighteen-year-old Prince Yok, Songjung's second son. Yok, canonised Chungjong (r.1506–1544), acquiesced in further purges, spates of blood-letting that continued after his death. In 1545 King Injong ruled for eight months, whereupon the throne was taken by Hwan, canonised Myongjong (r.1545–1567). The bloody purges continued, bringing executions, dismissals and banishments. The demoralised state was ill-prepared to withstand a further phase of foreign invasions – by the Japanese and the Manchus (see below).

The invasions hastened the decline of the Yi Dynasty, shown, according to one commentator, by the dramatic reduction in the amount of land controlled by the state.[16] In only a few years government-controlled land decreased to about a quarter of earlier figures, the result not of what some today may see as prudent privatisation but of war forcing the tillers from the fields and massive public and private corruption. Private individuals enriched themselves at the expense of the public good, a sure sign of a society in decline: private avarice and the vast increase in the extent of tax-exempt land both contributed to a weakening of the government and the associated state bodies. Even during the reign of Yongjo (1725–1776), considered a time of rejuvenation, the government found it difficult to pay officials and to provision the army. Kwanghaegun (1609–1622) had initiated payment in rice as a means of increasing state resources, and thereafter other mechanisms for payment in kind were introduced: for example, the farming community was taxed in cloth, a further burden on the impoverished peasantry.

As the position of the ordinary people deteriorated, they viewed with increasing hostility the relative affluence of government officials and other favoured individuals. One consequence was a growing receptivity to the mix of Christianity and 'Western learning' conveyed to Korea by envoys from China. Korean scholars were at first attracted to Western skills in astronomy, mathematics and armaments, but before long there were also Korean converts to Christianity, banned in 1786 by an increasingly alarmed government. In 1801 the government rounded up the converts and executed their leaders, including the famous scholar Chong Yagyong (1762–1836). Chinese and French missionaries continued to enter the country, leading in 1839 and 1866 to further phases of suppression.

The Korean government perceived also a fresh threat from beyond the seas. In the late eighteenth century, French and English ships began to visit the Korean coast, a prelude to insistent Western demands for trade and diplomatic relations. By the second half of the nineteenth century there were frequent incidents involving European and American ships. A new phase of foreign influence, unprecedented in Korean history, had begun (see below).

THE JAPANESE INVASIONS (1592–1598)

The Korean peninsula suffered many Japanese invasions throughout the sixteenth century, ranging from the marauder (*Wako*) incursions through much of the century to the great invasions of the 1590s. In 1544 Japanese pirates attacked Saryang in South Kyongsang Province; in 1555 the coast of Cholla Province; and in 1589 the town of Hungyang in South Cholla Province. Now the *Wako* were ranging much more widely than had their predecessors, attacking not only Korea but many other countries in eastern Asia. The severe depredations brought by these 'latter-day *Wako*' caused official relations between Korea and Japan to be suspended. These troubles were however minor compared with what was to come.

Toyotomi Hideyoshi (1536–1598), the son of a Japanese peasant soldier, had risen to be one of the outstanding warrior rulers of the day. He built on the pioneer work carried out by Oda Nobunaga (1534–1582) for the unification of Japan, overcoming all challenges to his authority to bring to heel the contending feudatories throughout the country. By 1590 the whole of Japan was at peace for the first time in more than a hundred years, so bringing to an end the phase known in Japanese history as *Sengoku Jidai* ('the age of the country at war'). Hideyoshi's internal campaigns lasted a mere eight years, during which time he reformed the government administration and the coinage, began a national land survey, and built the Osaka fortress and the luxurious Juraku Mansion at Kyoto.[17] Of Hideyoshi, a foreign missionary wrote in 1586:

> He is so feared and obeyed that with no less ease than a father of a family disposes of the persons of his household he rules the principal kings and lords of Japan; changing them at every moment, and stripping them of their original fiefs, he sends them into different parts, so as to allow none of them to strike root deep.[18]

The domestic triumphs of Hideyoshi were to stand in marked contrast to the failures of his foreign adventures. He had been tantalised by the thought of extending his domain to the Asia land mass, reportedly announcing at the shrine of Minamoto Yoritomo, 'I mean to conquer China. What do you think of that?' He is also said to have boasted to Jesuit missionaries that he would subdue the Chinese and force them to adopt Christianity. The subjugation of the Korean peninsula was seen as the means to a greater end.

Hideyoshi began by demanding the co-operation of Chao-hsien in his planned campaign against China, but the Korean ruler sharply rejected the proposal dubbing the ambitious plan akin to 'measuring the ocean in a cockle-shell' or 'a bee trying to sting a tortoise through its armour'. The Korean king wrote to Hideyoshi in 1591, reminding him of Korean history and repudiating his reckless folly:

> You stated in your letter that you were planning to invade the supreme nation (China) and requesting that our Kingdom (Korea) join in your military undertaking ... We cannot even understand

how you have dared to plan such an undertaking and make such a request to us ... For thousands of years, from the time of yore when Chi-tzu, the founder of the Kingdom of Korea, received the investiture from the Chow dynasty, up to our own time, our kingdom has always been known as a nation of righteousness ... we have reverently adhered and attended to all duties and obligations due from a tributary state of Chung-Chao (China) ... We shall certainly not desert 'our lord and father' nation ... Moreover, to invade another nation is an act of which men of culture and intellectual attainments should feel ashamed ... your proposed undertaking is the most reckless, imprudent, and daring of any of which we have ever heard.[19]

The Korean king had decided that the threat of 150 million Chinese across his northern border had to be taken more seriously than the threat of 25 million Japanese across the seas. But his letter, an unambiguous reprimand, had done nothing to discourage Hideyoshi's imperial ambitions: the campaign would be launched, whatever the Korean government might decide. Korea would be subjugated as a prelude to the crushing of the Ming Dynasty in China.

In April 1592 a vast Japanese force (of anything from 150,000 to 250,000 men: the source texts vary) – comprising the combined armies of Konishi Yukinaga, Kato Kiyomasa, Kuroda Nagamasa, Mori Yoshinari, Ukida Hideie and others, all under the command of Hideyoshi (who none the less remained safely in Japan) – landed in the south-east of Korea at Pusan, once the Japanese fief of Karak. The Japanese forces (including, in one account, 5000 battle-axes, 100,000 long swords, 100,000 spears, 100,000 short spears, 500,000 daggers, 300,000 firearms and 50,000 horses) ruthlessly overwhelmed the southern part of the peninsula in a short campaign, occupying the capital at Seoul within a few weeks of disembarking. The invading armies then moved north to occupy much of the peninsula: the advance from Pusan to the Yalu river had taken less than six months.

However, Hideyoshi has miscalculated. He had assumed that Japanese pirates would be able to keep his oversea supply lines intact; and he had not reckoned with the scale of the predictable Chinese response. The Japanese craft were basically small coastal vessels, ill-equipped to deal with large Korean ships furnished with cannon and directed by the famous Korean admiral Yi Sunsin (1545–1598). At a time when Japanese commanders were demanding a constant supply of equipment and other provisions, the Japanese vessels were being sunk in great numbers. In addition, following a request from its Korean tributary state and doubtless with an eye on its own security, Ming China launched a huge force south to confront the Japanese in the peninsula.* At its peak the Chinese forces numbered around one million men, an enormous army for the times, compelling the Samurai swordsmen, against all their martial traditions, to demand more guns from Japan.

The Japanese were now short of supplies, and troubled by cold and epidemics. They were also harassed by the Korean guerrilla bands (*uigen*, 'righteous armies') that had risen to impede the Japanese occupation. The Chinese, although successful in pushing the Japanese forces well south of the Yalu river, had suffered their own defeats and were happy to begin peace talks. At the same time Yi Sunsin continued to attack the Japanese supply convoys to good effect. The heavy Korean vessels carried fortified superstructures of curved metal plates or spiked wooden panels and were in consequence dubbed *Kwi-son* ('turtle' or 'tortoise' ships) and were more or less immune to Japanese attacks.

The peace talks dragged on for three years, with China now demanding that Japan admit its vassalage to the Ming. Hideyoshi, frustrated at his thwarted ambitions and increasingly resentful of the Chinese imperial demands, launched a second invasion of the peninsula in 1597. A fresh army of around 140,000 men was despatched to confront the Koreans and Chinese, who by this time had consolidated an effective military alliance. Again the invasion came to nothing: the Japanese were quickly forced to abandon initial gains, before being pushed back to the southern coastal regions of the peninsula. As the Ming sent fresh new forces into Korea, Hideyoshi (in one account[20]) issued a death-bed injunction for the invasion of Korea to be abandoned. The Japanese armies withdrew and began the long struggle to return home, constantly harassed by Yi Sunsin's 'turtle ships'. It is recorded that while directing his attack on the evacuation fleet in 1598, Yi Sunsin was killed by a musket ball; like Nelson he had died in command at the moment of victory. Hideyoshi, dying the same year, had left a devastated landscape in Korea, a desolate people, and a memento in Kyoto in the form of a mound of pickled ears and noses from 40,000 enemy corpses.

---

*General Douglas MacArthur, when contemplating his own sweep to the Yalu river during the Korean War (Chapter 6), should have remembered the Ming response to a similar threat.

The war had lasted seven years, including the pauses to allow peace negotiations. The Japanese withdrew with massive losses, having failed to accomplish any of their imperial objectives. As in the modern Korean War (1949–1953), the whole of the peninsula had been a battlefield. The various armies, Japanese and Chinese, had ravaged the land, with crops burned, cities and villages laid waste, and the ordinary people slaughtered by the thousand. The starving survivors were preyed upon by thieves and corrupt officials while civil order disintegrated. Official documents had been lost or destroyed, making it impossible for the government to exact labour service or to assess and collect taxes. Ming China had suffered under the burden of military mobilisation, a circumstance that led to the accession of the Ching (Manchu) dynasty. In Japan, a Tokugawa hegemony emerged to supplant the Toyotomi family. Hideyoshi's imperial adventures had fallen far short of his grandiose ambitions; but inadvertently he had thrust the Korean Yi dynasty into irreversible decline, destabilised the Chinese Mings, and guaranteed the overthrow of his own family in Japan.

THE MANCHU INVASIONS (1627–1637)

With the final departure of the Japanese in 1598, peace was restored in the Korean peninsula and efforts began to restore and rehabilitate the country. Soon however a new threat loomed in the north. In 1609 Korea sent an envoy to Japan to establish normal relations. From that time until the end of the Tokugawa period (1867) there was peace between Korea and Japan; but a mere two years after the normalisation of relations Ming China was advising Chao-hsien to prepare her military forces against a possible Manchu invasion.[21]

After the collapse of Mongol power, the Ming had managed to reassert control over the Jurchen in Manchuria, but with the destabilisation of the Ming Dynasty the Jurchen again rose up and began to threaten the Chinese border regions. When the Ming defence forces in Manchuria were sent south to resist the Japanese invasions, the Jurchen had seized their opportunity. In 1616 the Manchu chieftain Nurhachi arose to unite the Jurchen and to found the Manchu Dynasty of Later Chin. Three years later Chao-hsien sent 20,000 men to support the Ming opposition to the expanding Manchu forces, but the combined Ming–Korean army was defeated at the great battle of Saerhhu Mountain. Nurhachi thereupon freed 5000 captured soldiers with a warning to the Korean king: 'The Mings sent troops to rescue you from the Japanese, and therefore I do not feel aggrieved at your aiding the Mings against me. I return you the prisoners. King, beware!'

Despite this warning, Chao-hsien decided to maintain its allegiance with the weakened Ming dynasty even though the land route to Peking was now controlled by the Manchu and tribute missions to China had to go by ship.[22] This posture could not be tolerated by the Manchus, now with their eye on Peking, and so they resolved to neutralise what might emerge as a Korean threat at their rear. The Manchu invasion of Chao-hsien began in 1637, stimulating the Ming emperor to attempt to provide assistance to the beleaguered Korean forces but contrary winds reportedly prevented the arrival of the Chinese fleet. The Korean government fled to the supposedly safe island of Kanghwa, but the Manchus, showing more maritime initiative than had the Mongols, brought boats, reached the island, and captured the queen, the prince and high officials, publicly proclaiming their capture and courteous treatment to induce King Injo (1623–1649) to surrender his own fortress on the island. Injo thereupon capitulated to the Manchu emperor, Tai Tsung in a public ceremony before the Manchu encampment.[23] The Manchus were quick to specify the terms of the surrender:

> The Emperor then ordered the King to give him the patent of investiture and the seal which he had received from the Ming, to offer his allegiance, to give him two of his sons as hostages, to adopt the (Manchu) new year (calendar), and to send each year tribute (*kung*) with a congratulatory address (*piao*). In case of war, he would have to raise an auxiliary force and furnish supplies to the army. He was not to erect fortresses (or walled cities) at his pleasure, or give refuge to fugitives.[24]

At the same time there is evidence that Chao-hsien remained reluctant to abandon its allegiance to Ming China (a Korean officer reportedly commented: 'How can we think of casting off our allegiance to China? ... though we live in a distant corner of the world, we have manners'). Indeed, in 1638 the Manchu emperor was forced to reproach the Korean king for his evident reluctance to take up arms against the Ming Dynasty. With the final triumph of the Manchus in China in 1644, Emperor Shih Tsu returned the king's son, held as hostages, and reduced the demanded tribute for the year. Such treatment was well calculated to erode some of the Korean hostility to the Manchu occupation.

The Manchu invasion had been relatively brief and less destructive than earlier foreign incursions. Moreover, under the Manchus, now in China designated the Ching Dynasty, the Korean people enjoyed two centuries of freedom from further foreign intervention. Even China itself was separated from Chao-hsien by a 300-mile fortification, the 'wall of stakes', built about 60 miles from the Chao-hsien frontier at the Yalu river. Between the wall and the Yalu lay a depopulated wasteland, a natural barrier to any invasion of China. But the mutual isolation of the two states did little to diminish their shared culture. Thus a Chao-hsien writer was able to comment that the 'Chinese themselves praise us saying "Korea is little China"'.[25]

The Japanese and Manchu invasions, though different in duration and scale, had contributed to a common end: the progressive decline of the Yi Dynasty. This irreversible process was to be further stimulated by mounting pressures from beyond the seas, by the growing impact of – for the first time in Korean history – non-Asian powers. Western attitudes and learning had filtered down the peninsula from China, but from the seventeenth century onwards the Western impact was to be direct and inescapable.

THE WESTERN IMPACT (17th–20th CENTURY)

A Spanish Jesuit, Gregorio de Cespedes (1551–1611), made the first recorded visit of any European to the Korean peninsula: in 1593 he arrived, not to serve the Koreans but to minister to Hideyoshi's Japanese invaders. Later he had contact with Korean prisoners of war in Japan and then returned to Spain after a stay of a year and a half.

In 1627 the Dutch ship *Ouderkress* reached the coast of Korea, and when three sailors went ashore for water they were captured. Two of them were killed in 1636 during the Manchu invasion. The third, Jan Janse Weltevree (given the Korean name Pak Yon), was an expert in cannon casting and so was assigned a post in the military. He later married a Korean girl and seemed content to remain on the peninsula. In 1653 he was sent to interview the survivors of the Dutch ship *Sparwer* (Sparrowhawk) that had been driven on the rocks of Cheju

Island on the night of 15 August of that year. Hendrick Hamel, one of the Dutch mariners, later wrote an account of his travels.

The survivors of the shipwreck were first interned on Cheju and then transferred to Seoul the following year. After fourteen of the men died, the remainder were assigned to the army in Cholla Province. In 1666 eight of them, including Hamel, escaped in a skiff from the southern port of Yosu and reached Japan. At this time there was little European impact on Korea. Various Western influences had percolated down from China and from Japan across the sea. But Korean technology, drawing heavily on Chinese influence, was already well advanced, particularly in the sphere of military development. Hamel describes in his *Journal* the military posture of the country ('Every province has its General, and every place its military officer; there is scarcely a village without at least its commanding corporal'); and he mentions two-masted naval vessels with banks of 30–32 oars and armed with cannon.

Over the next century and a half, despite the increased numbers of European ships in Asian waters, there was little Western contact with the Korean peninsula. There was growing European traffic with China and this sometimes led to contact with the Korean coast. In 1797 HMS *Providence* touched the coast, as did in 1816 the vessels *Lyra* and *Alceste*, conveying Lord Amherst on a mission to China. Captain Basil Hall, of the *Lyra* carried out an eleven-day survey of the south-west coast of Korea; in 1832 the vessel *Lord Amherst*, owned by the British East India Company, tried to trade in the region; and in 1845 HMS *Samarang* carried out survey operations in the area.[26]

In 1846 a French warship appeared off South Chungchong Province to demand an explanation for the killing of three French missionaries. Two French frigates, *Gloire* and *Victorieuse*, sent later the same year to collect the official reply, found themselves stranded by a falling tide with the crew having to be rescued by a passing English ship.[27] However, the Korean authorities did offer their reply, albeit sent through Peking to signal Korea's subordinate status. The reply (a 'Royal Proclamation in Korea'), the first official despatch from a Korean government to a Western power, contrasted how the gracious rulers of Korea had treated shipwrecked men with how Christian missionaries had crept surreptitiously into Korea. In any case, the reply concluded, all such questions should be referred to China; but China, now experiencing growing pressure from Western states, was unwilling to accept legal responsibility for Korea's actions.

At the same time there was evidence of growing American interest, not so much in the fate of missionaries but in the opportunities for trade. In 1845 US Congressman Zodoc Pratt introduced a House resolution to authorise the sending of diplomatic and trade agents to Japan and Korea so that 'the American people will be able to rejoice in the knowledge that the "star spangled banner" is recognised as ample passport and protection for all who, of our enterprizing countrymen, may be engaged in extending American commerce'.[28] The resolution served as a prelude to mounting American penetration of the region. Nor was the United States the only interested Western power. In 1861 Lord John Russell took steps to secure British participation in trade carried out between the Japanese island of Tsushima and the Korean port of Fusan, while at the same time putting pressure on Russia to abandon a naval station on Tsushima. In 1865 a Russian warship arrived at Kyonghung in Hamgyong Province. Now the French were urging Japanese envoys to use their influence to open up Korea to French trade, even though Japan had not dealt officially with Korea since 1763.

The Korean government was now becoming increasingly disturbed by the growing Western interest in the region. Thus the Tai-wun-kun, the father of the Korean child king, declared in his decree of 1866: 'The barbarians from beyond the seas have violated our borders and invaded our land. If we do not fight we must make treaties with them. Those who favour making a treaty sell their country.' In March 1866 Korean hostility to the West was further signalled by another onslaught on French missionaries: dozens were killed, only three escaping with their lives, and all organised Christianity in Korea was thus obliterated. A French warship was immediately sent to Korea and French outrage was quickly made apparent. Henri de Bellonet, the French chargé, sent a note to Prince Kung of the Chinese Foreign Office (so misjudging the character of Korean subservience) in which he deplored 'this act of savage barbarity'. The note continued:

The government of His Majesty cannot permit so bloody an outrage to go unpunished. The same day on which the King of Corea laid his hands upon my unhappy countrymen was the last of his reign ... In a few days our military forces are to march to the conquest of Corea, and the Emperor, my august sovereign, alone, has now the right and the power to dispose, according to his good pleasure, of the country and of the vacant throne.

Because China had said many times that it had no power over Korea, 'we declare, now, that we do not recognise any authority whatever of the Chinese government over the kingdom of Corea'. China responded by urging the French to ascertain the facts of the case before sending an expedition, at the same time hinting that China would in no way assume legal responsibility for Korean acts.

The French expedition, a mere 600 men, was duly despatched to achieve 'the conquest of Corea'. The troops landed on Kangwha Island, succeeded in capturing the main city, but were then defeated in an attack on a fortified monastery: only half of a contingent of 160 delegated soldiers returned uninjured. It was not long before the French perceived the futility of trying to subdue Korea with such a small body of soldiers. The remnants of the expedition returned to France and another brief episode in the long chronicle of military folly was over. There were no further thoughts of military reprisals against Korea.

In 1868 an American merchant ship, the *General Sherman*, sailed up the Taedong river on a trading expedition, became grounded, and was then set on fire following an argument between the American seamen and Korean officials. The entire crew was killed, whereupon Admiral Bell, the American squadron commander, requested that a reprisal mission backed by 1500–2000 troops be sent. But no military action was taken, despite an earlier American suggestion (1866) that a joint enterprise with the French be launched against Korea. Instead Commander Shufeldt of the *Wachusett* and Commander Febiger of the *Shenandoah* sailed to Korea to make enquiries and to chart the river leading to Seoul. However, the *General Sherman* affair remained unsettled and was influential in the American decision to send a punitive expedition three years after the event. An American force reached Kanghwa Island at the end of May 1871, disembarked and captured several forts, before being resolutely attacked and forced to withdraw. The Americans, like the French before them, had been roundly defeated.

The West, mainly interested in expanding its trading opportunities, had so far failed to conclude any useful treaties with Korea. Part of the problem was the ambiguous connection between Korea and China; and part the incomprehension generated by the collision of different cultures. Japan, in a position to exploit Western methods but sensitive also to Asian attitudes, succeeding in negotiating the first treaty with Korea on the basis of Western legal assumptions. Japan herself had been prised open by the United States in

1854, expanding the opportunities for trade and setting Japan to reform on the Western model. The Meiji Restoration overthrew the Tokugawa Shogunate in 1868 and the establishment of an imperial government accelerated the introduction of Western civilisation; here signalled in part by the suppression of peasant uprisings and workers rights.

Korea was now sensitive to how Japan had been opened up to Western penetration and so resolved to maintain her own protective isolation, a policy that took as much note of historical Japanese expansionism as of modern Western incursions. The clique government in Japan, eager to perceive provocation, saw the Korean attitude as an incitement to action. The Saigo Takamori party favoured an immediate invasion of the peninsula, a posture much encouraged by a Korean edict forbidding trade with Japan and adding further insult by refusing to acknowledge the new forms of address contained in official Japanese documents. But Saigo, dubbed by one admirer 'a stupid hero' (*muchi no eiyu*), had little further opportunity to develop his ambitions.[29] The party was suppressed in 1873 and nothing of Saigo's Korean scheme survived. At the same time the Japanese government was looking for a pretext to carry out its own onslaught on Korea. Two years later it found the excuse it needed.

In 1875 the Japanese gunboat *Unyo Kwan*, engaged in surveying the Korean coast, was fired on near Kanghwa Island. The Japanese stormed the attacking fortress, overcoming all resistance and killing the defenders. Reinforcements were quickly sent from Japan, whereupon Korea was forced to agree the Treaty of Kanghwa (1876), designed to open up the 'Hermit Kingdom'. Korea's tributary relationship with China was abolished and Korea was pronounced an independent state, but subject to many Japanese-imposed conditions. Korea had been opened up by force just as the Americans had abolished Japan's isolation a few years earlier.

The prising open of Korea as a new trading opportunity stimulated Western commercial ambitions. Thus the United States, Britain, Germany, Italy, France and other Western nations emerged increasingly on the Korean scene between 1882 and 1886.[30] The United States, sensitive to the Japanese success in achieving the 1876 treaty with Korea, realised the benefits that a treaty of its own might bring. On 8 April 1878 a resolution was passed in the United States Senate to appoint a commission to negotiate a treaty with Korea through the good offices of Japan (it was realised that Japan had now supplanted China as Korea's dominant 'partner'). This specific resolution became submerged in the Committee on Foreign Affairs but the Navy Department decided none the less to send Commodore Shufeldt, now of USS *Ticonderoga*, to Korea and other Asian countries. A principal aim was to negotiate the opening of Korea to American commerce. However, Japan refused to co-operate and a subsequent letter from Shufeldt to the Korean government was rejected because it was addressed to 'Corai' (Korea) instead of Chao-hsien, and also because 'it is well known that our foreign relations are only with Japan, neighbouring to us, which have been maintained for three hundred years, and that other foreign nations are not only situated far from us, but there has never been any intercourse with them'. It was clear that Korea was still trying to preserve an element of its 'hermit' status behind Japan's protection, where formerly China had served the purpose; and that the Japanese, for their part, were keen to monopolise Korean trade.

However, American resolve was undimmed. Shufeldt met the Chinese consul during a brief visit to Nagasaki and through him was invited to meet Li Hung-chang, the Chinese Viceroy who commanded much influence in Peking. At conversations in China, Shufeldt persuaded Li to encourage Korea to negotiate with the United States, though in subsequent talks Li seemed less keen on the idea. Finally, following representations from Li, word came that Korea was willing to agree a treaty with the United States. In 1882 Shufeldt and Li, with a Korean representative in attendance at Tientsin, negotiated a treaty covering such matters as peace, amity, commerce and navigation. There would be 'perpetual peace and friendship'; moreover, 'If other Powers deal unjustly or oppressively with either Government, the other will exert their good offices, on being informed of the case, to bring about an amicable arrangement, thus showing their friendly feelings.' There were also provisions for the exchange of diplomatic and consular representatives, protection of navigation and American citizens, the opening of trade, and the granting of most-favoured-nation treatment.[31] Shufeldt declared that America had accomplished 'the feat of bringing the last of the exclusive countries within the pale of Western Civilization'.

The conclusion of the US–Korean treaty to highlight the residual ambiguities in the Korea–China relationship, already severely eroded by the growing Japanese ambitions in the region. Shufeldt had no interest in a deal that might be emasculated by Chinese pressure on Korea; though the Korean government saw advantage in preserving the traditional Chinese connection. The growing confusion was compounded by mounting instabilities in Korea itself: in particular, a rebellion (the so-called '*émeute* of 1882') by soldiers and others incensed at the installing of Japanese officers in the Korean army, an event which gave China the excuse to invade with 5000 men and instal a sympathetic government that would abolish all Japanese-style reforms. The *émeute* of 1882 was a great blow to Japanese ambitions. Japanese officers were killed and the Japanese legation, a fruit of the 1876 treaty, was burned down. Japan responded by sending troops to the peninsula but they were powerless against the Chinese army. The Treaty of Chemulpo, agreed on 30 August 1882, secured some compensations for Japan, but her reputation had suffered greatly. A pro-Japan attempt at a coup, supported by Japanese troops still stationed in Seoul, was defeated; and this '1884 incident' caused the position of the Japanese in Korea to deteriorate still further. At the Li–Ito Convention (1885), the Japanese proposed that both Japanese and Chinese troops withdraw from Korea; and that each side would inform the other if it decided to send troops to the peninsula.

The Koreans, sandwiched between great powers and now increasingly vulnerable to world commercial pressures, knew only instability and uncertainty. The government was weak, constantly under the aegis of foreign might; the old official class, now increasingly impotent, was still in power; and there was mounting civil strife. In 1894 the Tonghak rebellion (*Tonghak*: 'Eastern Learning', contrasted with *Sohak*, 'Western Learning'), rooted in a religious movement with racial and cultural components, brought further chaos. The scene was set for the disappearance of Korea as an independent state.

TOWARDS ANNEXATION

The Korean government, seemingly helpless before the Tonghak rebels, desperately sought Chinese assistance. The Ching authorities responded quickly and Chinese troops again moved into the peninsula. At the same time Japan, still smarting under the humiliation of the *émeute* of 1882, decided to exploit the confusion and send forces to Korea. In the face of the various foreign troop contingents the Tonghak rebellion was crushed, but by now the Japanese army had occupied Seoul and weakened further the authority of the Korean government. The Chinese, increasingly alarmed at the Japanese presence in the peninsula, suggested the withdrawal of all troops from Korea; in this, they were supported by the United States, Britain, Russia and the other powers, now worried by the prospect of a permanent Japanese occupation.

Japan noted the proposals but did not respond. The Meiji and his oligarchs were satisfied that a highly successful military initiative had been launched. Not only the capital of Korea but other strategic cities had been overwhelmed in a brilliantly conducted blitzkrieg. Chinese ships tried to cut the Japanese supply lines and were promptly sunk by the Japanese navy. Emperor Meiji and the Japanese General Staff moved to Hiroshima to be within a day's carrier-pigeon flight of the front; and was so intense in his conduct of operations that his courtiers, concerned about his health, arranged for a favourite concubine to travel 500 miles from Tokyo to give him solace.[32]

China, realising the weight of the Japanese presence, sued for peace; and was ignored. Japan declared its right to 'protect' Korea, and also Taiwan and the Manchurian Kwantung Peninsula; Japanese troops were already in Manchuria, signalling the scale of the Meiji's imperial ambitions. Under pressure from the Western powers, Japan temporarily relinquished her rights to Kwantung, but military conflict with China in Korea was now unavoidable. The Sino-Japanese War began in August 1894, a decisive contest between the increasingly militarised Japan and the old Ching Empire. The Chinese were driven out of Korea and Korean 'independence' announced to signal the severing of the traditional Chinese–Korean connection. By the Treaty of Shimonoseki (1895), the Chinese agreed to pay a large indemnity to Japan, to grant trade privileges, to cede vast areas (including Taiwan) to Japan, and to acknowledge the independence of the Korean state.

While the Chinese were being finally evicted from the peninsula, the Japanese moved to oust the Korean Min government and to instal a pro-Japanese faction. Kim Koengjip and his supporters were placed in office and urged to carry out approved reforms. The Taewongun was allowed to lead the 'progressive', even though he had formerly supported Tonghak calls for the expulsion of the Japanese. However, once the substantial changes – the so-called 'reforms of 1894' – were well under way, the Taewongun was removed and Pak Yonghyo placed in the cabinet. In January 1895 the king announced the 'Fourteen Articles of Hongbom', designed to introduce a wide range of government reforms: not least the separating of government and palace expenses, the exclusion of the royal family from government affairs, tax reforms, the establishment of a civil and criminal law code, and the advancement of qualified men irrespective of background. The Articles extended and reinforced the reforms already introduced the previous year. Now some of the Japanese oligarchs decided that there was yet more to be done. Thus General Miura Goro, a *samurai* minister stationed in Korea, began plotting against the only surviving recalcitrant element in the Korean court, Queen Min.

On 8 August 1895, with the Korean Imperial Guards held at bay outside the palace, Miura's men chased the queen and her ladies through the corridors and hacked them to pieces. Then the mutilated bodies were doused in oil and burned in the palace courtyard. The Japanese authorities made some show of trying Miura for his manifest atrocity but the Japanese judges acquitted him 'for lack of definite evidence'. Miura remained an esteemed advisor to the Japanese government for the next 30 years.[33]

The Japanese had emerged victorious from the Sino-Japanese War (1894–1895) and had imposed their will on the Korean peninsula, but now they were disturbed by moves among the great powers; in particular, by the joint initiative by Russia, France and Germany (the so-called Three-Power Intervention). This initiative, coming rapidly on the heels of the Shimonoseki treaty (April 1895), was stimulated primarily by Russian anxieties at Japanese advances in Korea and Manchuria. In the event the Three-Power coalition was sufficiently weighty to force Japan to sacrifice most of its recent gains in the Korean peninsula. A 'second partition' of the Far East was now set in train, with the major powers struggling to secure trade and diplomatic advantage in Korea (Table 3.1) and China. One consequence was that the assassination of Queen Min, far from securing Japanese influence, resulted in the establishment of a pro-Russian government in Korea. A pro-Russian faction connived with Karl Waeber, the Russian minister in Seoul, to seize the king and transfer him to the Russian legation where he was forced to reside for about a year. In a series of conventions (1896, 1897 and 1898) it was agreed that neither Russia nor Japan would meddle in Korean affairs, with Russian agreeing not to restrict Japanese commercial enterprise in the country. The tensions temporarily abated but were soon brought back by the mounting confusion over the question of Manchuria.

Russia had avoided involvement in plans to relieve the foreign legations in Peking at the height of the Boxer rebellion (1900), where

Table 3.1   *Concessions and concessionaires in Korea, 1896–1900*

Year	Rights or privileges granted	Concessionaires
1896	Building of Inchon–Seoul railroad	American
1896	Exploitation of Kyongwon and Chongsong mines in North Hamgyong Province	Russian
1896	Exploitation of gold mines at Unsan in North Pyongan Province	American
1896	Building of Seoul–Uiju railroad	French
1896	Exploitation of forests in the Yalu River basin and on Ullung Island	Russian
1897	Exploitation of Tanghyon gold mines in Kumsong County of Kangwon Province	German
1898	Building streetcar lines in Seoul	American
1898	Building of Seoul–Pusan railroad	Japanese
1900	Exploitation of the Unsan gold mines in North Pyongan Province	German
1900	Exploitation of the Chiksan gold mine in South Chungchong Province	Japanese

Source: Takashi Hatada, *A History of Korea*, 1969

Japanese troops had been involved; but was prepared to exploit the spread of the troubles to the north-east provinces as an excuse to move into Manchuria. In 1901 Russia negotiated terms with China that suggested a new status for Manchuria as a Russian protectorate, a quite intolerable outcome for Japan. The Japanese government duly protested, forcing Russia to deny any territorial ambitions and helping to cement relations between Japan and Britain, itself worried that a permanent Russian presence in Manchuria would threaten its own commercial position in China. Subsequent Japanese–British talks (July 1901) were hampered by British insistence on protection for its interests in India and by British reluctance to give full support to Japan's position on Korea; there was no British enthusiasm for involvement in a specific Russo-Japanese dispute. After some delay, Britain dropped its demands over India, and the problem over Korea was side-stepped by careful drafting. The resulting treaty, signed on 30 January 1902, recognised that 'Japan, in addition to the interests which she possesses in China, is interested in a peculiar degree politically as well as commercially and industrially in Corea'. There was no provision for automatic help if Japan became involved in a war with Russia. The Anglo-Japanese Alliance did specify that either country would remain neutral if the other was active in hostilities in the Far East region; and that an attack by two powers or more on either party would necessitate military assistance by the other.[34]

Tensions were now mounting between Russia and Japan over the control of Manchuria and Korea. Talks had produced a Russian agreement to withdraw its forces from Manchuria, the operation to be staged at six-month intervals. The first was duly carried out in October 1902, though there were suspicions that the troops had been simply moved elsewhere in the region. The next scheduled move did not take place and there were signs that Russia was considering an advance. At fresh talks, held in St Petersburg through the second half of 1903, the Russians demanded a promise of territorial integrity for Korea, a promise that Japan would not fortify the Korean coast, and agreement that Manchuria was outside the Japanese sphere of interest. When Japan's reply (January 1904) was ignored she declared war.

The Russo-Japanese War (1904–1905) lasted less than eighteen months, with the largest land battles that the world had yet witnessed. The Russians were driven back across the Yalu river into Manchuria and thereafter the fighting was focused in the region before Port Arthur and astride the northern route from Port Arthur and Dalny to Liaoyang and Mukden. The Japanese, commanded by General Nogi Maresuke, lost 60,000 men at Port Arthur, including Nogi's two sons; but the Russian defenders were eventually overwhelmed and Port Arthur fell on the last day of 1904. At the Battle of Mukden, which lasted from 23 February to 16 March 1905, the Japanese were equally victorious. Here sixteen Japanese divisions, involving some 400,000 men, were thrown into the conflict. Japanese casualties alone numbered more than 40,000.

The Japanese victories at sea were equally decisive. There were some significant Russian successes, including the sinking of two Japanese battleships in two days by mines, but the most important engagements resulted in Russian defeats. A Russian squadron based at Vladivostok was largely ineffectual and a naval initiative launched from Port Arthur was repulsed by Admiral Heihachiro Togo (1847–1934), ennobled (*Koshagu*, 'Marquess') in 1907 as one of Japan's great war commanders. In October 1904, 40 Russian ships assembled in the Baltic and sailed for the Far East; Great Britain, as Japan's ally, viewing the progress of the fleet with concern. Seven months later, on 27 May 1905, the Russian fleet commanded by Admiral Rozhdestvensky was engaged by Japanese ships under Togo to the east of the islands of Tsushima. The ensuing Battle of Tsushima (or, for the Japanese, *Nihonkai kaisen*, the Battle of the Sea of Japan) produced one of the most comprehensive naval victories in history. Only two of the vessels of the Russian naval fleet avoided being sunk or captured. The Japanese suffered some 600 casualties and lost three torpedo-boats. The British took some satisfaction in the fact that most of the Japanese officers had been trained by Englishmen.[35]

Before the end of the war the Japanese had already tightened their grip on Korea, forcing the government to accept Japanese financial and diplomatic advisors and to make other concessions. Now the decisive military victory had served to consolidate the Japanese hold on the peninsula. In November 1905, Korea was forced to transfer control of its foreign affairs to Ito Hirobumi, the head of the Japanese mission sent to demand compliance. The Americans, at Japanese request, mediated the Treaty of Portsmouth at New Hampshire (signed 5 September 1905), so establishing Japan's war gains: not least the transfer to Japan of Russian assets in southern Manchuria and the recognition of Japanese supremacy in Korea.

In 1907 Japan presented the Korean king with fresh demands, sufficiently humiliating to force his abdication. His successor, the Crown Prince, was prepared to bow to Japanese pressure. Ito, having lost influence in Japan, resigned his position in Seoul in 1909 and during a journey in Manchuria later that year was assassinated by a Korean. Now the Meiji government had the only pretext it needed. After all Korea's struggle for independence, nothing could now stop its total annexation by Japan.

4 The Japanese Colony

In the early twentieth century the Korean peninsula was absorbed into the expanding Japanese empire. At that time Korea was the imperial prize, offering natural resources, abundant human labour and a platform for further territorial expansion. For centuries the Korean people had been buffeted by powerful neighbours who sometimes stimulated cultural advance but as often brought repression and exploitation. Now the prospects for national independence seemed bleak, the search for sovereignty increasingly desperate.

ANNEXATION

The first steps towards the Japanese annexation of Korea were taken in the second half of the nineteenth century. It was already obvious that Japan was attaching increasing importance to the control she had established in the politically critical region of Manchuria, 'the meeting ground of the conflicting needs and policies'[1] of three great nations, Russia, China and Japan. The Sino-Japanese Treaty of Shimonoseki (1895) forced China to pay an indemnity to Japan, ceded Chinese control of Taiwan to Japan, and recognised the independence of Korea, a necessary condition for its subsequent unopposed absorption by Japan. Pressure from Russia, France and Germany temporarily eroded these Japanese gains; but the likely incorporation of Manchuria and Korea into the Russian empire was prevented by the Russo-Japanese War, whereupon the US-brokered Treaty of Portsmouth (1905) served to consolidate and expand the familiar Japanese claims. Britain and the United States welcomed such developments. Russian ambitions would be blocked by an increasingly Westernised Japan; in this *realpolitik* world the welfare of Korea was of no account.

The British knew of, and approved, Japan's intention to create a protectorate over Korea, Thus Lord Lansdowne, in a despatch (6 September 1904) to the British ambassadors in Russia and France, commented that Korea's 'close proximity to the Japanese Empire, its inability to stand alone, and the danger arising from its weakness' meant that it 'must fall under the control and tutelage of Japan'. In like spirit, President Theodore Roosevelt's Secretary of War, W. H. Taft declared to Count Katsura, the Japanese premier and foreign minister, that 'the establishment by Japanese troops of a suzerainty over Korea ... would permanently contribute to permanent peace in the East'.[2] In a cable (29 July 1905), Roosevelt commented to Taft: 'Your conversation with Count Katsura absolutely correct in every respect. Wish you would state to Katsura that I confirm every word you have said.'[3] In the Portsmouth Treaty (Article II) Russia agreed 'not to interfere or place obstacles in the way of any measure of direction and protection, and supervision which the Imperial Government of Japan may deem necessary to adopt in Korea'. For its part, Korea vainly hoped that its nominal independence would survive, but without powerful foreign protectors the government was powerless in the face of Japanese ambition.[4]

In October 1905 Japan increased the pressure on the Korean emperor and his advisors to allow complete Japanese supervision of Korean affairs, including control of the country's foreign relations. On 15 November Marquis Ito Hirobumi announced to the Korean emperor that the Korean department of foreign affairs was to be abolished; that future diplomatic affairs were to be handled by a council in Tokyo; that the Japanese minister in Seoul was to be termed the 'General Superintendent' or 'Director'; and that the Japanese consular representatives in Seoul and in the Korean ports were to be termed 'Superintendents'.[5] The Korean emperor, dismayed at the proposals, reminded Ito that Japan had formerly pledged to 'preserve the independence and integrity of Korea'; and declared the proposals 'beyond my slightest apprehension'. Japan, ignoring this response, assumed direct control of Korean affairs, formalising and expanding the three Articles proposed by Ito.

A Japanese financier, Megata, had now assumed control of the Korean finance ministry. Japanese control was established over the entire Korean telegraph and postal systems, while the Japanese Army had already taken over large areas surrounding Seoul, displacing 15,000 Korean families in the process. A Japanese corporation headed by Nagamori acquired all Korean 'waste lands', comprising more than half of all the national territory, including all the underdeveloped mineral resources. Japanese agents, enjoying military protection, scoured the country to discover and seize valuable properties on the pretext that they were needed by the Japanese armed forces. Japanese money-lenders set up their trade in every Korean city, lending money at 12 per cent monthly interest rate and confiscating property in the event of default. Already, Koreans were abused by Japanese soldiers, forbidden access to particular areas, and subjected to summary military justice.[6] There were already some years to go before the formal annexation of Korea.

In June 1907 the Korean emperor sent a secret mission to an International Conference being held at The Hague to complain about Japanese policy on his country and to request Western support. When this initiative became known, the Japanese response was predictable. Japanese delegates managed to block Korean access to the conference chamber, and there were urgent calls in Tokyo for 'decisive measures', including a demand from the influential gangster Toyama Mitsuru, 'asserting and confirming' that the sovereignty of the Korean emperor 'should be delegated to our nation'.[7] It was now time to force the abdication of the Korean king.

On 16 July the Japanese government publicly announced that it was determined to 'go along with the opinion of the people' and adopt 'a strong line of action' towards Korea. The next day, Viscount Hayashi, the Japanese minister of foreign affairs, journeyed to Korea to consult with Ito; while, before his arrival, the pliant Korean cabinet called upon the emperor to sign with his own seal the proposed Articles (formalised 17 November 1905) which he had still not agreed (five of the eight-strong cabinet had signed). The Korean cabinet also suggested that the emperor accept the appointment of a regent, and that he go to Tokyo to apologise personally to the Japanese emperor.[8] Such moves, it was thought, might serve as an alternative to abdication. On 19 July 1907 the Korean emperor, still stubbornly refusing to agree the Articles, abdicated in favour of the crown prince. Evidence that he acted under duress is perhaps his statement to the contrary: 'In abdicating my throne I acted in obedience to the dictate of my conviction; my action was not the result of any outside advice or pressure.'[9]

The Japanese were now in a position to tighten their grip still further. With the Korean imperial authority now nominally in the hands of an inept crown prince, said by some to be feeble-minded, there was little difficulty in securing imperial assent for a total restructuring of Korean-Japanese relations. On 24 July 1907 a new seven-clause agreement (Appendix 3) was signed, removing from the Korean government any last vestige of power to make independent decisions or to exercise government functions. The earlier Japanese moves had merely placed Japanese officials in every sphere of Korean government and administration, with Koreans allowed to operate under condition of 'advice'. Following the 24 July agreement the functions of government were placed squarely in Japanese hands. On 29 November two-thirds of the offices of the Korean royal household were abolished, with a separate accounting bureau established for royal affairs. A Japanese Directorate of Police was set up for the entire country, and all provincial forces were run by Japanese officers. Korean soldiers, regarded as mercenaries, were not seen as 'a perfect instrument of national defence'; and so, on 1 August 1907, the Korean army was disbanded.[10]

As late as the end of 1907, Ito was still prepared to deny that a total annexation of Korea was being considered. He himself was said to prefer civilian to military rule, an attitude that generated factional opposition in Tokyo. This led to the selection of a successor Resident-General who would be more amenable to pressures from Tokyo. Thus Katsura commented to Yamagata Aritomo, the President of the Privy Council: 'An influential person is not necessary. I recommend Sone [Arasuke], because it will be easy to direct him as we wish.' In the event there were subsequent pressures for Sone's resignation as the Resident-General in Seoul, on the ground that he was insufficiently supportive of the (Japanese) Unite Japan and Korea Society (that is, was not sufficiently committed to the idea of annexation). Nor, it seemed, could Ito be relied on in this regard, though his acquiescence was sought: according to Black Dragon* testimony, a henchman of Yamagata 'was invited to Ito's residence for dinner and there he obtained Ito's approval' for annexation.[11] The need for a pretext for the final subjugation of Korea was soon supplied.

Ito had now been replaced by Sone as the Resident-General in Seoul: whatever his views may have been on the question of annexation, he was not popular with either the military factions in Japan or the Japanese forces in Korea. It was ironic in these circumstances that it was Ito himself who, albeit by default, was to provide Japan with the pretext for annexation.

In October 1909 Ito was despatched to Manchuria to discuss the possibility of a *rapprochement* with the Russian ambassador to China. At Harbin railway station, as the two men greeted each other, a young Korean, An Joong Keun, pushed his way through the crowd and shot and killed Ito.[12] Many questions were raised. How could

---

*The Black Dragon Society (*Kokuryukai*), a Japanese secret society with political ambitions and gangster connections, traditionally interested in extending Japan's frontiers.

An Joong Keun have outwitted the vigilant Japanese police? How could he have acquired a gun and travelled all the way to Harbin? How did he know where to intercept Ito? One rumour suggested that Ito's bodyguard had deliberately let the assassin through. And more questions were asked when An Joong Keun died under police interrogation. In some accounts more than one Korean was involved in the assassination.[13] Were the Japanese involved in the affair?

Japan was now moving towards the formal annexation of Korea. At Ito's funeral a 'Korean Problem Friends Society' was created, which quickly drew up a memorandum demanding annexation. Uchida Ryohei, the influential Black Dragon boss, then delivered a pro-annexation petition, via the Unite Japan and Korea Society, to the Japanese prime minister. On the advice of Resident-General Sone, the petition was rejected; whereupon, in July 1910, Sone was replaced by Count Terauchi, the minister of war during the Russo-Japanese conflict and an advocate of the view that the Korean nation should be either absorbed or decimated.[14] In nice accord with this approach, the Japanese-run Seoul press declared:

> The present requires the wielding of an iron hand rather than a gloved one in order to secure lasting peace and order in this country ... Japan is in this country with the object of promoting the happiness of the masses. She has not come to Korea to please a few hundred silly youngsters or to feed a few hundred titled loafers ... She must be prepared to sacrifice anybody who offers obstacles to her work. Japan has hitherto dealt with Korean malcontents in a lenient way ... there are some persons who cannot be converted by conciliatory methods. There is but one way to deal with these people, and that is by stern and relentless methods.[15]

The total Japanese control of Korea, already a *de facto* reality, now only waited on what could be represented as a *de jure* solution to the 'Korean question'.

In August 1910 the Korean emperor effectively abolished the monarchy, so bringing to an end the reign of the Yi Dynasty that had lasted from 1392. The treaty of annexation – to extinguish Korea as an international personality – was signed on 22 August, after approval by the Meiji and the Korean emperor, by Viscount Terauchi and Yi Wan-yong, the Korean prime minister. The members of the Korean royal family, now with no vestigial shred of power, were granted annual allowances sufficient for their life-styles, with the Japanese committed thereafter to awarding peerages and grants to those non-royal Koreans deemed meritorious. The treaty, with other relevant documents, was promulgated on 29 August 1910, the Korean emperor 'constrained to believe it wise to entrust Our great task to abler hands'; and the Meiji wanting no more than 'the maintenance of permanent peace in the Orient and the consolidation of lasting security to our Empire'. The expansionist Japanese politician Okuma Shigenobu spoke for most of his compatriots when he observed: 'For many years we have tried to control Korea, even at the cost of blood, and now we have accomplished peaceful annexation. It is like a dream.' Nor were the other great powers disposed to dispute Japan's claim, preferring to believe that a problem that had long disturbed the Far East was now settled. The views of Koreans were seldom canvassed.

The impact of the annexation was devastating for every aspect of Korean life. The currency was converted; transport and communications were controlled in their entirety by the Japanese government; and all Korean farmlands became the property of the Japanese Oriental Development Company, which at the same time retained the ancient system of feudal land-tenantry. Korea was now a helpless captive state. The Korean people, long accustomed to oppressive rule, were now forced to confront yet more decades of naked exploitation on an unprecedented scale.[16]

THE CAPTIVE STATE

Japan moved swiftly to impose a brutal military regime on the entire peninsula. Opposition movements, if not crushed, were forced into exile: one faction based in Manchuria, later to be headed by Kim Il-sung; another in Hawaii under Syngman Rhee. In Korea the Japanese took over land and property, vastly increasing the levels of poverty and homelessness. Thousands of Koreans voluntarily migrated to Japan in the search for work; or, even more pitifully, were forced to go there as virtual slave labour. Koreans, whether in their own land or in Japan, were regarded as racial inferiors and possessed none of the political rights enjoyed by the Japanese; and, as a subject people, were forced to endure a thorough programme of enforced 'Japanisation'. Harsh measures were undertaken to wipe out the indigenous Korean culture, with Japanese pronounced the official language in the 1930s. Korea and Taiwan now provided the most obvious examples of Japanese colonialism and would serve as models for the other lands to be occupied with the expansion of the empire in the years to come.[17]

Japanese historians and archaeologists conducted projects in the peninsula with the aim of demonstrating that Korean history was a part of Japanese and that there was an evident Korean backwardness that only Japan could rectify. Korean intellectuals, massively hampered in their work, none the less managed to emphasise the importance of national independence; and, in the early days of the occupation, to support various surviving Korean-language publications, including the daily *Tonga Ilbo* and *Choson Ilbo*, albeit published under the meticulous scrutiny of the Japanese censors. However, such publications lacked funds: in due course the poverty of the Korean people and official Japanese attitudes compelled their closure.[18] At the same time an underground literature, dedicated to the ultimate goal of Korean independence circulated in many of the towns and cities. It seemed unclear, in the early days of the occupation, how such independence would ever be achieved.

The Japanese authorities made it clear that any move of the Korean people towards independence would be met with 'severe punishment'. According to statistics published in the *Annual Statistical Bulletin* of the Japanese Governor-General of Korea, between 1911 and 1918 there were 330,025 cases of summary conviction under the military regime. In August 1911 the 'Korean Educational Ordinances' were introduced to inculcate obedience in the racially inferior Korean populace, but their impact was limited because of the low attendance figures for many Japanese-run Korean schools: in the early 1930s, with education wholly designed for the rearing of colonial slaves, only 20 per cent of children were attending school.[19] Even the churches, seldom a hotbed of nationalist fervour, were monitored by the Japanese for any sign of ideological deviation.

One Christian tract exhorting all Koreans to expel the devil within them was banned on the ground that the aim of the tract was clearly to denounce the Japanese military occupation. A Japanese official charged: 'When you say devil, you are referring to the Japanese, and you are encouraging the Koreans to rise in rebellion against them!' Thereafter, all religious publications were prohibited from using the word 'devil'. In the same spirit an issue of the missionary weekly *The Christian Messenger* was suppressed because reference to 'the new life' that broke in the spring was obviously an incitement to Koreans to rise up and establish a nationalist regime. In 1911 there were rumours that the Korean Christian Churches, an evident embarrassment to the Japanese authorities, were to be placed under the direct administration of Japanese churches. There then occurred what became known as the 'Christian Conspiracy Case': some 135 leading Korean Christians were arrested on the charge that they had conspired to murder the Japanese Governor-General. Under the harsh strictures of military law, nine of the accused were exiled and 106 were jailed for periods from five to ten years; three of the suspects were tortured to death in prison.[20]

In the light of these events, Dr Arthur J. Brown, Secretary of the Presbyterian Board of Foreign Missions, hastened to Korea to collect evidence which clearly showed a Japanese campaign to suppress Korean intellectuals and political leaders. Similarly, Dr Charles W. Eliot, the President of Harvard University, conducted his own investigation in Japan and concluded: 'The standing of Japan among Western nations would be improved by judicious modifications of her preliminary proceedings against alleged criminals.' And Dr W. W. Pinson, Secretary of the Board of Missions of the Methodist Episcopal Church South, produced his own report of the case which included the words: 'it is clear that the gendarmes have thrust their sickles in among the tallest wheat. These men do not belong to the criminal or irresponsible class of society ... These are not the type of men to be guilty of such a plot as that with which they are charged.'[21] Syngman Rhee, linked to some of those arrested, escaped the scene of danger following the intervention of Bishop Harris, a representative of the Methodist Church in North Asia. Such events, grave in themselves, were minor compared with what was happening throughout the entire Korean peninsula.

In the 1920s Japan itself was experiencing developments that would significantly affect its colonial policy in Korea. Disruptions in the increasingly industrialised Japanese economy had created a severe crisis in food supply. The 1918 rice riots, caused by massively inflated rice prices, had already increased the demand for Korean rice, a circumstance that would be exacerbated in the years to come. This meant that the Korean consumer was forced to suffer while rice was exported to satisfy the growing demands of the Japanese home market. Thus through the 1920s, with the Japanese annual per capita rice consumption reaching over 1.0 *sok* (about 80 kg), the per capita consumption for Koreans had declined to half as much. In short, the highly industrious Korean farmers were starving in order to feed the Japanese. Furthermore, the need to finance expensive irrigation projects in Korea – to further increase the export of rice to Japan – put yet more financial burdens on the oppressed Korean population, which in turn stimulated the growth of opposition movements.[22]

The character of Japanese investment in Korean industrial activity also signalled the colonial relationship of the two countries; in particular, how the heavy-industry sector was stimulated through the 1930s to fuel the Japanese military machine for the aggression against China. For the same reason, the Japanese invested heavily in Korean mining projects. In 1936 Korean gold production had risen to 17,490 kilograms worth 59,350,000 yen, more than half the value of the total Korean mining output. This escalating gold output enabled Japan to purchase oil, scrap iron, machine tools and other resources, from the United States and elsewhere, essential for the Japanese war on China. When the US–Japanese war began in 1941, Japan quickly shifted its mining emphasis to the materials now more directly relevant to its war needs, such as iron, tungsten, graphite, magnesite and molybdenum.[23] The mounting pressures on Japan directly impacted on its Korean colony, increasing the levels of repression and the scale of the exploitation.

The campaign to expunge the Korean national identity was intensified under the slogan 'Japan and Korea are One Entity' (*Nat-Sen ittai*) and with a banning of all forms of cultural expression that might be considered to have a nationalist element. Such newspapers as *Tonga Ilbo* and *Choson Ilbo* were closed down, as were other publications, such as *Literature* (*Munjang*), that used the *hangul* alphabet. In October 1942 leading members of the Korean Language Society were arrested, imprisoned and tortured; Yi Yun-jae and other Korean linguists died under interrogation by the Japanese police. The Chindan Hakhoe, Korea's leading historical society, was forced to close; and the use of the Korean language was now regarded as a subversive activity, even in the home. Japanese was used throughout the school system, and Korean writers were prohibited from producing works in their own language. Koreans – Christians and others – were required to worship at Japanese Shinto shrines, while Kim Kyo-sin and his co-publishers of the *Korea Bible News* (*Songso Choson*) were imprisoned. Now the Japanese were insisting that Koreans adopt Japanese family and personal names.[24] Such policies were designed to obliterate all remnants of Korean national consciousness to facilitate the increased exploitation of the peninsula.

Korean farmers were instructed to deliver their rice harvests directly to specified government locations, while Koreans in every labour sector were required to donate all kinds of metal objects to the Japanese war effort. And with Japan's own manpower coming under increasing strain, the forced mobilisation of Korean workers – effectively slave labour – was expanded to work the mines, the munitions factories and the forward Japanese bases in hazardous areas. In all, following the annexation of their country, some 700,000 Koreans were rounded up and transported to Japan as forced participants in Japan's 'divine mission'. Shinto shrines were set up in Korean schools and other public places, with children forbidden to utter words in the native language. Korean adults were forced to recite an oath of allegiance to the Meiji before being allowed to purchase the necessities of life.

The Japanese seizure of Korean land had resulted in the impoverishment of much of the Korean population. There was now a substantial number of large-scale Japanese landowners, with a number of pliant Korean landowners of the former privileged *yangban* class allowed to maintain their positions. Most of the peasants were now no more than marginal tenant farmers, having lost any rights to eventually own the land they worked. They typically worked at subsistence level on minuscule plots, often compelled to work as well on the land of others. According to figures supplied by the Japanese Governor-General, 44.6 per cent of all farm households, some 1,273,326 out of 2,728,921, were unable to earn enough to live on. Near to half of the entire Korean population, mostly unable to secure loans, were starving to death, forced to eat roots or the bark of trees in order to survive. Even the Japanese authorities conceded that at times more than a half of all Korean farm households were starving.[25]

One consequence was that many Korean farmers fled to Manchuria in the hope that they would secure a better life. Thus there were 560,000 Korean immigrants to Manchuria in 1927, rising to 800,000 in 1931, and to 1,450,000 by 1940. This vast influx of foreigners inevitably generated tensions with the indigenous population, in some cases leading to interracial outbreaks of violence, such as the Wanpaoshan incident on 2 and 3 July 1931. Many Chinese feared that the thousands of Korean immigrants into Manchuria were the vanguard of a Japanese takeover, a circumstance that the Japanese Kwantung army exploited to good effect.[26] At Wanpaoshan near Changchun a dispute developed between Chinese and Korean farmers over an irrigation canal being dug for Korean settlement. Gunfire was exchanged and both sides suffered casualties. Exaggerated tales of Koreans being brutalised in Manchuria appeared in the Korean press, followed by accounts of Chinese officials forcing Koreans off their Manchurian farms. Thus the Wanpaoshan episode was used by the Japanese authorities in Korea to whip up violent anti-Chinese riots in Korean cities. Western missionaries reported how Chinese shops had been attacked by Korean mobs while Japanese police stood by.[27] More than 16,000 Chinese residents in Korea, out of a Chinese population of around 90,000, fled the rioting. In such a fashion the Japanese authorities encouraged the exacerbation of tensions that would fuel the forthcoming Japanese onslaught on Manchuria.

The exploitation by the Japanese of Korean farmers was paralleled by their treatment of Korean industrial workers. Koreans had been driven into mines and factories in Korea and Japan through the 1930s and early 1940s as forced labour required in the mounting war effort. By 1944 there were 350,000 Koreans in Korean mines and 600,000 in the factories, all under close Japanese supervision and with no industrial rights. Nearly a half of factory workers and more than a third of mine workers toiled for more than twelve hours a day, while Korean workers typically received less than a half the pay of the equivalent Japanese workers, themselves exploited by a semi-feudal employment system. Similarly Korean women and children were paid less than half their Japanese counterparts, making it difficult to achieve even the most basic subsistence levels. In these circumstances the workers were often diseased or disabled, subject to common industrial accidents where there was no legal worker protection.

Korea was ravaged as a captive state for nearly four decades. The Korean people, repressed and brutalised, were stripped of much of their culture while their land was stolen and their buildings confiscated. Driven from their farms, the peasants either starved in a near-subsistence economy or were coerced into mines and factories to swell private wealth or to fuel Japanese imperial ambitions. In the event the Japanese failed to extirpate Korean culture, and were eventually evicted from the peninsula; but not before long decades of struggle and the deaths of countless martyrs to the independence cause.

The Japanese themselves have given some indication of the embarrassment caused to them by this brutal colonial period. Thus in July 1982 the Japanese Ministry of Education issued a number of text book 'corrections' approved by a screening committee. The forced deportation of 700,000 Koreans after 1910 to work in Japanese mines and factories was now termed 'the implementation of the national mobilisation order to Koreans'; the Japanese aggressions against China through the 1930s were now to be dubbed 'advances of the Imperial Army'; while a military initiative undertaken by the Japanese fleet against Chinese forces was to be merely 'a battle which broke out between Japan and China'.[28] Outrage at these revisions was voiced in China and Korea, and also in other South-East Asia countries that had suffered under Japanese colonial occupation. In May 1990 the Japanese prime minister and Emperor Akihito apologised to the South Korean President, Roh Tae Woo, for Japan's occupation of the peninsular from 1910 to 1945. There were moreover hints in November of that year that North Korea could expect compensation of some 700 billion yen ($5.1 billion) for the ravages of the Japanese occupation. On 10 August 1991 Mr Kaifu, while in China, remarked of the recent imperial past: 'There was an unfortunate period, for which Japan should reproach itself.'[29]

There are no signs that Japan would have been willing to depart from Korea and its other colonial possessions unless forced to do so. The principal deciding factor was the defeat of Japan in the Second World War. It is important to remember the contribution of the stubborn Korean independence movement to the historic military outcome of 1945.

THE INDEPENDENCE STRUGGLE

There were many factions in the Korean independence movement. Some were active as guerrilla bands (the 'righteous army') immediately after the 1910 annexation. Some struggled to survive, in the teeth of Japanese military control, within the Korean peninsula; some organised from across the northern frontier or from overseas. Two of the main factions – those headed by the pro-West Syngman Rhee and the communist Kim Il-sung – would come to symbolise the division of Korea through the period of the Cold War and beyond.

The March First Movement

As soon as the Japanese had secured annexation, they began a comprehensive land survey of the Korean peninsula to define the character of land ownership and related matters under the new regime. Soon after the nine-year land survey was complete various disturbances took place throughout Korea: these became known as the March First Movement (or the *Manse* or *Mansei* Revolution, signalling 10,000 years, i.e. Long Live Korea). The First World War had recently ended and President Woodrow Wilson's doctrine of national self-determination, coupled with the seismic upheavals in Russia, was stimulating the struggles of oppressed peoples throughout the world. Now Koreans at home and abroad were convinced that justice would replace force in political affairs, and that Korea would soon be able to achieve its freedom. Then the death of the former ruler of Korea, Yi Taewang, in January 1919, possibly at the hands of his Japanese physician, gave a further impetus to nationalist agitation.

On 1 March 1919, two days before Yi Taewang's funeral, an independence proclamation signed by 33 prominent Koreans (landowners, capitalists, religious leaders, intellectuals and others) was announced. The March First Movement derived its principal impetus from this bold statement, an effective Declaration of Independence; it begins with the words:

We herewith proclaim the independence of Korea and the liberty of the Korean people. We tell it to the world in witness of the equality of all nations and we pass it on to our posterity as their inherent right. We make this proclamation, having back of us five thousand years of history and twenty millions of a united loyal people. We take this step to insure to our children, for all time to come, personal liberty in accord with the awakening consciousness of this new era. This is the clear leading of God, the moving principle of the present age, the whole human race's just claim. It is something that cannot be stamped out, or stifled, or gagged, or suppressed by any means.[30]

The Declaration, against the inclination of many nationalists, did not call for violent struggle, preferring to suggest instead peaceful public demonstrations and appeals to foreign powers for their assistance. Thus the celebrated Committee of Thirty-Three added a threefold injunction to the Declaration for the guidance of the Mansei agitators:

1. This work of ours is on behalf of truth, justice, and life, undertaken at the request of our people, in order to make known their desire for liberty. Let no violence be done to anyone.

2. Let those who follow us show every hour with gladness this same spirit.
3. Let all things be done with singleness of purpose, so that our behaviour to the very end may be honorable and upright.

Dated the 4252d Year of the Kingdom of Korea, 3d Month, 1st Day.[31]

A nationwide organisation was developed with a local committee for every Korean township (*myun*). The demonstrators were urged to carry homemade Korean flags which could be displayed to commemorate the emperor's death; and to parade in the streets, shouting '*Mansei*: *Mansei*: May Korea live ten thousand years:' Further, the assembled crowds were instructed not to insult the Japanese, not to throw stones and not to use their fists – 'for these are the acts of barbarians'. The movement was initially developed without the knowledge of the Japanese, despite the nationwide network of spies and secret agents.

The Declaration was solemnly read out in public at 2.00 p.m. on 1 March, after which the leaders called in the Japanese police and requested that they deal with the matter calmly.[32] The leaders were promptly arrested and agitations broke out in many towns and villages throughout the country. More than two million Koreans were directly involved in the demonstrations, in more than 1500 separate meetings, in 211 of the country's 218 county administrations. The demonstrations spread also to Manchuria, to the Russian Maritime Territory, and to other regions.[33] There was worldwide recognition of the scale of the movement. The publisher of the *Bee* in Sacramento noted 'The Greatest Example in World History of an Organized Passive Resistance for an Ideal'; and an editorial in the Los Angeles *Times* (6 April 1919) declared: 'In our opinion this Proclamation will stand on a plane of exaltation with our own Declaration of Independence ... It is the voice of a prophet crying in the wilderness ... May God grant a mad world the grace to stop and listen to that voice.'

The Japanese authorities, astounded at the scale of the demonstrations, reacted with force, mobilising not only the military police but also the army and navy. The Japanese themselves recorded the scale of the subsequent repression: 46,948 demonstrators arrested, 7509 killed and 15,961 wounded. It is likely that these figures were conservatively estimated, with the actual numbers in all the categories much higher than those officially reported. The Japanese troops fired indiscriminately into assembled crowds, while many other atrocities were recorded: for example, in the Cheam-ni village near Suwon 29 people were forced at gunpoint into a church which was then set on fire to burn them alive.

In the face of ruthless Japanese suppression, the March First Movement collapsed: despite the scale of support, the movement had not been organised to cope with the extremes of hostile military action. It had proved totally unrealistic to arrange a 'calm meeting' with the Japanese; and there was no sign of the foreign support demanded by the leaders of the movement. The popular protesters had proved totally powerless to withstand the sheer brutality of the Japanese response. Thousands of men, women and children had been beaten, shot, bayoneted or burned alive. A representative of the Board of Foreign Missions of the Canadian Presbyterian Church in Korea produced an official report to note the scale of the torture being perpetrated by the Japanese authorities: 'I read affidavits ... which make one's blood boil, so frightful were the means used in trying to extort confessions from prisoners.' Other witnesses spoke of the sickening 'odor of burned flesh'; of how 'the beating goes on, day after day', the victims beaten with rods into unconsciousness, then revived with cold water for the process to begin again.[34]

The Japanese had sent an extra force of some 6000 troops to the peninsula to crush the uprising. Order had been restored throughout the country, but it was soon clear that the independence movement had not been wholly obliterated. Within Korea many activists went underground while nationalists began to organise beyond the northern frontier and overseas. The March First Movement had fired the enthusiasm of nationalists in Korea and in the many Korean communities elsewhere. One of the most significant fruits of the 1919 'Mansei Revolution' was the founding of the Korean Provisional Government.

The Korean Provisional Government

After the suppression of the First March Movement the independence efforts were focused in various overseas locations. At the peak of the 1919 demonstrations there were about 600,000 Koreans in south-eastern Manchuria, with around 200,000 in the Maritime Provinces and about 6000 in Hawaii and the United States. It proved impossible for any single nationalist organisation to unify the activities of these various groups. Hawaii was remote from the

Korean scene, while the Korean communities in Manchuria were far removed from the lines of international communication. Shanghai, despite its small Korean population (about 400 in early 1919), seemed to offer various compensations for the shortcomings of the other locations. The Chinese at that time, more than a decade before the Wanpaoshan incident, appeared to be sympathetic to independence movements and well disposed to the Koreans. Thus it was that the Shanghai Korean community finally decided to set up the Korean Provisional Government, a nationalist government in exile.

On 10 April 1919 the Shanghai Korean nationalists, drawing on the pantheon of eminent Korean agitators outside Korea, elected their officials. Only Yi Shi-yong, appointed as a putative Minister of Justice, was in Shanghai at the time; all the other 'ministers', with their various political preoccupations, were working abroad. They included: An Chang-ho, for a while ensconced in California and now head of the Korean National Association in Hawaii and Los Angeles; Kim Kyu-sik, working as the 'chief delegate' at Versailles; and Choe Chae-hyong, busy organising Korean forces in Siberia, but killed in May 1920 by the Japanese. Syngman Rhee, happy to remain in Washington, was elected Prime Minister of the Provisional Government. In fact there are signs that he viewed the Shanghai group with condescension, as did a number of the elected ministers. Syngman Rhee preferred his propaganda activities in the United States and Choe Chae-hyong never reached Shanghai. Similarly, Mun Chang-bom – with Yi Tong-hwi forming military groups north of the border – declined his new role, preferring to support the Korean communists (see below). And Yi Tong-hwi, once in Shanghai, suggested that the Provisional Government should be set up in Siberia.

The Shanghai activists organised committees, liaised as far as possible with their distant associates (including Syngman Rhee in the United States), and began publishing *Independence News* (*Tongnip Shinmun*). Before long the unwieldy committee system was nearing collapse and Syngman Rhee was urging reform of the government structure. Furthermore, nationalist groups within Korea had met secretly in Seoul, produced a provisional constitution, and created a government structure of their own, in which Yi Tong-hwi was designated premier, An Chang-ho Director of the Bureau of Labour, and Syngman Rhee the Chief Executive. Such tensions between the various factions were never wholly resolved.

Now Syngman Rhee was calling himself President, eager to command whatever provisional government emerged from outside or inside Korea. An Chang-ho thereupon sent Syngman Rhee a telegram, pointing out that since the Shanghai government had a Prime Minister and the Seoul government a Chief Executive there was no presidential post. An demanded that there be no further 'abuses', commenting: 'If you act as president without amending the constitution, you are violating the constitution and opposing the principle of unity.' Syngman Rhee responded by saying that he was using the title of president to pressure other states to recognise the Provisional Government. The deed was done (Rhee: 'I cannot alter it now'); and if An were to argue, Rhee declared, the squabble would not help the movement. To An Chang-ho, Rhee concluded: 'the responsibility will rest with you'.[35]

The crisis in the nationalist leadership continued for some time, not helped by Syngman Rhee's continued absence from Shanghai. An Chang-ho managed to secure a reorganisation of the government structure and was designated Acting President in the absence of Syngman Rhee who was by now accepted as President. But there were still tensions to resolve; not least because of the paradox that the liberal leaders in both Seoul and Shanghai still felt a residual loyalty to the Korean royal house. Moreover, the leaders clashed over general strategy. What was the proper balance between peaceful propaganda and armed struggle? Syngman Rhee, comfortable with his role in the United States, used 'diplomacy' as a means of achieving the important goal of US recognition. By contrast, Yi Tong-hwi believed that only the used of armed force against Japan would secure Korean independence, at one time suggesting that the putative Ministry of Military Affairs be transferred to Manchuria. And An Chang-ho favoured a middle road: the possibility of armed struggle could not be discounted but it would be a long time before Japan, as one of the world's most powerful military states, would be pushed out of the Korean peninsula. The various tensions and differences soon led to the virtual collapse of the provisional government. In 1921 both An Chang-ho and Yi Tong-hwi resigned from the organisation, leaving the nationalists in Korea and elsewhere to operate within an increasingly fragmented framework.

Military groups continued to operate out of Manchuria, intent upon deploying force to attack the Japanese and their collaborators. Such factions, communist and others, were dismissive of the vestigial Provisional Government and increasingly hostile to the efforts of the pro-West Syngman Rhee who seemed cavalier in his use of nationalist funds for his own purposes. Rhee, contemptuous of military action as likely to do no more than encourage further suppression of the Korean populace, remained convinced that his 'diplomacy' was the best way to secure invaluable American support for Korean independence. In fact some US senators were enlisted to the cause: Senator Seldon P. Spencer used a resolution to ask the Secretary of State whether the Shufeldt Treaty (1882) might be used to promote Korean independence*; and the following month (July 1919) Senator George W. Norris invited discussion of the 'Korean problem' on the Senate floor. Thereafter Senator Spencer read details of Japanese injustices against Korea into the *Congressional Record*; Senator James D. Phelan submitted a resolution sympathetic to Korean independence; and a subsequent contribution of Senator Norris occupied some fourteen pages of the *Record*.[36] In December 1920, Syngman Rhee, presumably bolstered by American support, arrived in Shanghai to find a much weakened government and to engage in further argument with the Shanghai leadership. Rhee's arrival in Shanghai added to the strategic and other confusions, leading to further resignations from the government. By now dozens of the erstwhile government supporters were prepared to accept the militant leadership of the communists.

With Syngman Rhee's predictable departure from Shanghai, Kim Ku took over the leadership of the provisional government to preside over an increasingly moribund organisation. After a decade's desultory activity, and prompted by the Japanese attack on Chinese troops in Mukden on 18 December 1931, Kim Ku decided to embark upon terrorist activity. To some extent he had no choice if anything of the Provisional Government was to survive: with the Japanese expansion into Manchuria, and the eventual creation of the pupper state of Manchukuo, the nationalists faced extinction if they did not fight back. On 8 January 1932, Yi Pong-chang, a Korean living in Tokyo, threw a hand grenade in the direction of the emperor's carriage; the grenade exploded some distance away, wounding two horses but the emperor was unhurt. A Shanghai publication, *Minkuo Jihpao*, subsequently lamented Yi Pong-chang's failure to kill the emperor; whereupon the Japanese, now in Shanghai, raided the newspaper and closed it down. Kim Ku and others continued with their terrorist campaign but to little effect. The conflict between China and Japan

---

*Earlier Korean invocations of the treaty to prevent annexation had fallen on deaf ears.

escalated inexorably, leading to the ultimate cataclysm of the Second World War. This, more than anything, forced the eventual Japanese withdrawal from the Korean peninsula.

The Communist Contribution

The communist faction within the independence movement had always been contemptuous of the Shanghai nationalists and the other supporters of the so-called Korean Provisional Government. From the communist perspective the Provisional Government remained aloof from the mass struggle of the Korean people, preferring to base its campaign on good relations with the United States and other capitalist states, not least the corrupt and discredited Kuomintang regime in Chiang Kai-shek's China. It was remembered that the Western powers had been highly sympathetic to Japan's colonisation of Korea: Britain had negotiated an alliance with Japan, and the newly established hegemony of Japan over Korea was consolidated in a treaty (the 1905 Treaty of Portmouth) mediated by the United States at Japanese request. Moreover, Syngman Rhee, in any estimate one of the leading figures in the Provisional Government, was denounced on many counts. His long sojourn in the United States had made his comfortable connection with American politicians more important to him than the rights of the Korean people; he, like many other members of the Provisional Government, remained distant from the nationalist struggles being waged within Korea itself and from the anti-Japanese initiatives being launched out of Manchuria. Syngman Rhee's betrayal of Korean interests seemed complete when in 1920 he petitioned President Woodrow Wilson to place Korea under the mandate of the League of Nations, so seemingly implying that Koreans were not fit to run their own affairs. By 1921 more than 100 Koreans in Shanghai had withdrawn from the Provisional Government and joined the communists.[37] The conflict between the Korean communists and nationals, later exploited by foreign powers, was set to continue through the century, leading inexorably to the post-Second World War division of the country.

The Korean communists, already active before the 1918 Bolshevik revolution, took heart from the manifest success of the activists in Russia. Now it seemed that the Korean activists would be able to develop a proven revolutionary ideology for the ultimate liberation of their own country. In November 1918 those Korean activists who had been exiled to the Far Eastern region of the newly constituted Soviet Union created the Korean Socialist Party at Khabarovsk, the first Korean socialist organisation. A short time later, with the development of the inevitable factionalism, the party split into two groups: each termed the 'Communist Party of Koryo', with one based in Irkutsk and the other in Shanghai. Neither the 'Irkutsk group' nor the 'Shanghai group' was, according to later communist orthodoxy, a truly communist party rooted in approved Marxist orthodoxy; in due course what would come to be recognised as the official ideology was generated elsewhere.

In early 1921 the 'Proletarian Fellowship Society' and the 'League of Men of Advanced Ideas', later to merge as the 'Proletarian Union', were created in Seoul – despite the Japanese secret police and their vast network of spies and informers. The Proletarian Union then linked with the Irkutsk group in May 1923 to form the 'Society for the Study of New Ideas', in November 1924 renamed the 'Tuesday Society'. Other radical groups were the 'Seoul Youth Society' established in January 1921, and the 'North Star Society' (later the 'North Wind Association') created in January 1923 and including Korean students in Tokyo. Reading circles were established to develop Marxist–Leninist thought in application to the Korean problem; and at the same time – again despite the ubiquitous Japanese repression – many organisations of workers, peasants and youth were established. Thus in April 1920 the 'Workers' Mutual Aid Society of Korea', Korea's first mass labour organisation, was founded in Seoul in April 1920, with linked groups subsequently established in most parts of the country. In 1924 the 'Korean Federation of Workers and Peasants' was created, later split into separate worker and peasant federations. At the same time the 'Korean Federation of Youth' was formed. All these groups were radical in character, substantially influenced by the impact of Marxism–Leninism as a perceived tool to rid Korea of the hated Japanese occupation.

Between 1920 and 1925 there were more than 330 substantial industrial strikes and countless lesser strikes and protests, involving tens of thousands of workers; significant among the large industrial stoppages were the general strike in Pusan in September 1921 and the strike of hosiery workers in Pyongyang in August 1923.[38] In the same period there were 570 peasant disputes involving some 30,000 peasants; and frequent student protests, stimulated by the radical reading circles and in defiance of the Japanese authorities, were held in support of mass protest. In April 1925 the Communist Party of Korea – deriving partly from the Irkutsk group and the Shanghai group – was formed, to be dissolved three years later. As always, factionalism among the radical groups divided the independence movement, rendering it permanently vulnerable to the omnipresent Japanese suppression. Thus the communist Kim Il-sung, eventually to emerge as President of North Korea, commented of the early factionalism: 'None of the bitter failures and sacrifices in the former communist movement and anti-Japanese national-liberation struggle was unrelated to the crimes of sectarians.'[39]

The Communist Party – an ostensible merger of the Tuesday Group, the North Wind Association and other groups – had quickly run into factional difficulties. In addition to the main component groups, fresh factions (for example, the 'Seoul Group' and the 'Manchurian Communist Youth Groups') quickly coalesced around particular issues or particular personalities. When the Japanese military police arrested activists from this or that faction, there were fresh arguments and recriminations within the movement, invariably leading to a regrouping of the factions and yet more fragmentation of the independence struggle.

One debilitating consequence was that the factions competed among themselves for popular support, constantly striving to win workers, peasants and youth organisations to their individual sectarian causes. In early 1927 the 'Singan Society' – temporarily uniting communists, socialists, nationalists and religious activists – was created to oppose the Japanese occupation. The Society stimulated various anti-Japanese initiatives, including nationwide student campaigns, but it too succumbed to sectarianism and was dissolved in May 1931. There was a desperate need for the groups to work to a common purpose, united under a leadership able to sustain and develop the solidarity of the independence movement.

On 15 April 1912 Kim Il-sung was born into a peasant family with clear revolutionary credentials: Kim Il-sung's father, Kim Hyong Jik, had long been active in the anti-Japanese campaign and had helped to steer many nationalist agitators towards the communist cause. On 17 October 1926 Kim Il-sung – as a fourteen-year-old schoolboy at Hwasong Uisuk School in Huatien County, Manchuria – formed the Down-with-Imperialism Union (DIU) as a tool for combating the Japanese occupation of Korea. The formation of the DIU has been depicted by apologists as a historical declaration of the emergence of a new generation of Korean communists. From January 1927 Kim Il-sung, then a student at the Yuan Middle School in Kirin, developed the DIU organisation, in August converting it into the Anti-Imperialist Youth League. At the same time he was laying the foundation for the Young Communist League, a vanguard communist youth organisation.

In 1928 Kim Il-sung helped to organise the student campaign against the Japanese Kirin–Hoeryong railway project, a scheme designed to extend Japanese communications and so project their military power from the Korean border north into Manchuria. According to a Japanese report, more than 2000 students of middle schools and higher educational institutions in Kirin gathered around the provincial general assembly and then marched down the road in four columns, shouting radical slogans and carrying banners with such inscriptions as 'Withdraw the Kirin – Hoeryong railway:', 'Down with Imperialism:' and 'Down with traitors to the nation:'. Later a petition was presented at the office of the provincial governor. The demonstrations continued over the following days when the students organised themselves into groups, erected platforms in various city locations, made speeches, scattered leaflets, and pasted up posters on walls and electricity poles.[40]

The official report said nothing about the scale of the clashes between students and police, or about the number of ensuing casualties. The then Korean newspaper *Tonga Ilbo* reported that the Japanese police had fired on the students, causing 148 wounded; it also commented that the student campaign was expected to continue. The new generation of students was less 'tainted' by nationalist influence, and had no connection with the divisive sectarian groups that had crippled the independence movement in the past. Moreover, the new alliance was based on the so-called Juche idea, a doctrine rooted in the creative application of existing revolutionary theory to the particular circumstances of the Korean struggle.

In October 1929 Kim Il-sung was arrested by the Japanese police and confined to Kirin prison; there he spread revolutionary propaganda among the prison inmates before being released in May 1930. In June he was advocating the Juche-orientated approach for the liberation of Korea; and in July helped to create the first unit of the Korean Revolutionary Army (KRA) with the core members of his communist organisation. All the efforts of the Japanese seemed powerless to prevent this significant development. KRA groups were despatched from Manchuria into Korea, launching attacks against the Japanese military police and spreading propaganda among the people. At the same time revolutionary groups were established in rural areas to support the local people, to deepen their political knowledge (or to spread propaganda), and to win support for the revolutionary cause.

Thus the Young Communist League, the Anti-Imperialist Youth League, the Peasants' Union, the Children's Pioneers and other organisations became active in various parts of the country. Various publications began to circulate, despite Japanese attempts at suppression, such as *Bolshevik Nongu* (Peasant Fellowship) and a *Reader for Peasants*. To convey political messages various plays were performed (including *The Mountain Shrine* and *The Landlord and the Farm Hand*, written by Kim Il-sung) by touring groups that then encouraged discussion on the topics raised. Revolutionary songs and operas were written, performed in rural areas, and became popular.

In September 1931 the Japanese launched their invasion of Manchuria, threatening the guerrilla bases in particular and heralding a chronology of pivotal events that would contribute to the demise of the League of Nations. In early 1932 Kim Il-sung formed a guerrilla unit and gradually expanded its ranks, at the same time giving advice on how other units could be created elsewhere. Using this experience, he founded the Anti-Japanese People's Guerrilla Army (AJPGA) in Antu, Manchuria, on 25 April 1932. Its aim, according to Kim Il-sung, was 'to overthrow the colonial rule of Japanese imperialism in Korea and bring national independence and social emancipation to the Korean people'. In March 1933 he led guerrilla units across the Tumangang river and advanced into the Onsong district on Korea's northern border. There Kim Il-sung called a meeting of underground revolutionary leaders to develop a plan for the expansion of the liberation struggle through the Korean peninsula. In March 1934 the AJPGA was reorganised into the Korean People's Revolutionary Army (KPRA), signalling a new stage in the revolutionary struggle and the growing communist impact on the Japanese forces in Korea. There was now a systematic organisation of divisions, regiments, companies, platoons and squads – a far remove from the small guerrilla bands that had struggled for survival two years before. Frequent Japanese attacks, none decisive, were launched against the revolutionary army, with severe 'scorched-earth' tactics used against villages thought to be sympathetic to the revolutionary cause. In response the communists mobilised entire communities to resist the Japanese onslaughts, creating and expanding a range of paramilitary organisations (the Red Guards, the Children's Vanguard, the Youth Voluntary Army, the Shock Brigade and others) to counter the frequent military attacks.

The Japanese replied with increased repression to crush what the communists called the revolutionary advance of the people. Now the

Japanese military police and their Korean collaborators wielded virtually unlimited powers, including 'the right to summary punishment'.
Under this provision some 453,000 Koreans were arrested, imprisoned
and abused between 1932 and 1935: a response that still failed to
prevent public protest, strikes and underground work for the Korean
struggle. From 1931 to 1935 more than 900 strikes involving over
70,000 workers were staged. Thus in 1934 the miners went on strike in
various regions, supported by workers in the major metal-working
factories; in October 1934 more than 600 workers at the Hungnam
Smeltery staged a general strike; in March 1935 some 1700 workers at
the Kyomipo Iron Works downed their tools in demand of better
treatment and higher wages; and in July around 1200 workers of the
Nampo Smeltery, supported by local peasants, went on strike to
demand a 50 per cent wage rise, better treatment, an eight-hour
working day, collective bargaining, and other reforms. Many of the
protests quickly developed beyond the demand for improved industrial conditions; the workers were now demanding political rights and
an end to the Japanese domination of their country. By now the peasants too were moving in concert with the industrial workers: according to official Japanese figures, between 1931 and 1935 there were
more than 350 mass tenancy disputes involving about 18,000 peasants,
with protests in various parts of the country, including Hwanghae,
South Pyongan, North and South Cholla, and North and South
Kyongsang provinces. And there were also anti-Japanese school
strikes, reading circle protests, and an increased circulation of anti-
Japanese and anti-war leaflets among Korean students.

Kim Il-sung was now directing KPRA units into wider areas of
Korea and North and South Manchuria. Substantial battles were
fought (for example, at Taipingkou, Lao-heishan, Shantungtun,
Chingkoutzu, Wanlikou and Pipadingtzu), often prior to linking up
with guerrilla groups operating in the area or as a prelude to efforts
at political education. KPRA units operating in Korea launched
attacks on Japanese forces in the Musan area and in the regions of
Puryong, Chongjin, Pungsan and Kapsan. The political education of
the people, wherever the KPRA ventured, was undertaken to
prepare the ground for what was assumed would be the eventual liberation and unification of the peninsula under a communist regime.

In the second half of the 1930s, as the Japanese imperial plans
became ever more ambitious, the repression and exploitation of the
Korean people were intensified. In Europe the emergence of powerful
fascist states with active support from international capitalism set the

scene for further invasions (of Abyssinia and Spain) which, with the Japanese expansion into Manchuria, would set the seal on the League of Nations. In these circumstances the anti-Japanese struggle in Korea became more intense in the context of widening world crisis.

On 5 May 1936, following a vigorous campaign by Kim Il-sung, the founding of the Association for the Restoration of the Fatherland (ARF) was announced. This new organisation was intended as a standing anti-Japanese national united front body, conceived in broad terms to maximise popular support. The organisation adopted the Programme, Statutes and Inaugural Declaration (Appendix 4) drawn up by the elected chairman, Kim Il-sung. He commented that the founding of the ARF 'was an event of epochal significance in consolidating the mass basis of revolution ... It became possible firmly to organise and mobilise all the anti-imperialist forces in the struggle to liberate the country.' Soon after, the communists began shaping the organisation, the Korean Communist Party, that would come to power in the northern half of the peninsula in the immediate post-Second World War world; but there were still many obstacles to overcome. In the early 1940s Kim Il-sung, under mounting pressure from the Japanese army, was forced to withdraw into the Soviet Union. (It was here that he met his first wife, Yong Sok, among the ex-patriot community. Kim's first son, Jong Il, later to be dubbed the 'Dear Leader', was born in Russia despite the legend that Yong Sok gave birth atop Korea's sacred Paekdu mountain.) But now the Japanese would soon be evicted from the Korean peninsula. It is ironic that it was the United States – the major capitalist power that had sanctioned Japanese hegemony over Korea four decades before – that was to play the major part in the defeat of Japan and so liberate Korea and bring Kim Il-sung and his communists to power in the North.

THE RACIST ENTERPRISE

The Japanese colonial policies, like colonial policies throughout the world, were rooted in racist assumptions; the Japanese were not alone in assuming the inferiority of conquered peoples.[41] One consequence of the Japanese occupation of Korea was that Koreans, often driven from the land and denied employment, flooded to Japan in search of work. By the early 1930s around half a million Koreans had gone to Japan for this purpose; by 1940, over one million. In addition to the 'voluntary' immigrants were the 700,000 Koreans 'mobilised' as virtual slave labour to work in Japan's mines and factories.

Once in Japan, the Koreans remained massively disadvantaged by their colonial status. They were not allowed to become Japanese citizens or to enjoy the normal civil rights of ethnic Japanese. Most of the Korean immigrants, with few skills, worked as labourers; and even in such disparaged and lowly employment for much lower wages than their Japanese counterparts. The Koreans were confined to impoverished ghettoes with little opportunity for child education, high levels of morbidity, and short life expectancy. They were regarded with derision by the Japanese and branded as criminal and subversive. The great reservoir of racist prejudice exploded in the unrest that followed the Great Kanto Earthquake of 1 September 1923.

The earthquake, occurring at a time of day when lunch was cooking over fires, was the worst in Japan in modern times. Strong winds spread the flames, and Old Tokyo and much of Yokohama were destroyed; about 100,000 people were killed. In the miserable days after the upheaval the bewildered and suffering Japanese looked for a scapegoat – and found it in the despised Korean communities in their midst. The hapless Koreans, who had themselves suffered many casualties in the earthquake and its aftermath, were charged with starting fires and causing explosions. Further, they were accused of looting, of taking advantage of the disruption to thieve and ransack the devastated buildings. And the Koreans were accused not only of exploiting the appalling results of the earthquake but of causing it. The Koreans had offended the spirits of Japan's ancestors by their disreputable behaviour; or they had provoked the great catfish Namazu that lives in the waters of the archipelago – and so the outraged spirits or the outraged catfish had shaken the islands and caused the earthquake. The Koreans were wholly to blame.[42]

At a time when the sympathy of the world was directed at Japan on account of the scale of the devastation and the resulting human losses, the Japanese authorities took the opportunity to kill thousands of the hated Korean immigrants in their midst. In Tokyo alone some 800 Korean residents were invited by the Japanese to military headquarters for their own protection, and every one of them was bayoneted or shot to death. Mass slaughters of Koreans also occurred in Osaka and Nagoya, either at the behest of the Japanese military police or by rioting Japanese mobs while the police stood by. The government even went so far as to encourage the rumour that the Koreans were poisoning the wells, and for a while every Korean in Japan went in fear of arbitrary eviction, assault and murder. Over a few days some 100,000 Koreans had been thrown out of their homes and deprived of their property.[43]

After the persecution and slaughter of the Koreans had run for several days, the Japanese government called a halt, by then too late. The military police were not reprimanded for committing mass murder, nor were the rioting Japanese crowds condemned for their outrages; no effort was made to return the evicted Koreans to their former homes. The government had clearly been prepared to tolerate, for a crucial period, the onslaught on the Korean communities; and there was moreover some evidence of anti-Korean incitement at the highest levels of the Japanese government. It has been suggested that that Rentaro Mizuno, the Home Minister in the Japanese cabinet, might have incited the anti-Korean police actions, On 2 September, in the immediate aftermath of the earthquake, he had a long conference with the Tokyo chief of police. Here Rentaro Mizuno made it quite clear how he expected the police to deal with the riots, the looters and other recalcitrant elements. It is hard to imagine that the subsequent actions of the police in Tokyo and elsewhere took place without the knowledge of a Home Minister known to detest the Koreans.[44] Nor could the mock courts have functioned without the tacit approval of the ubiquitous Japanese authorities.

Japanese householders had formed themselves into vigilante groups to 'protect' their ruined homes from 'invaders'; then they had started roaming the streets in search of Korean victims. The Koreans were tried before mock courts for their imagined crimes: always found guilty, they were then forced to their knees and beheaded. As the passions had continued to rise, the vigilante mobs became less discriminating. Suspects were stopped in the street and given a simple verbal test that only ethnic Japanese could pronounce correctly. In such a fashion the Koreans were detected (Koreans, particularly children, are often indistinguishable from Japanese), whereupon – whether men, women or infants – they were tortured, beaten to death or decapitated, for the sole reason that they were Koreans.[45]

The scale of Japanese racism was manifested through the entire period of the occupation of Korea; and in particular through the years of the Second World War when there was abundant scope for a promiscuous racism directed not only at non-Japanese Asians but also at Japan's white-race military opponents (which the white races reciprocated in ample measure).[46] In the 1930s the Japanese developed the so-called Greater East Asia Co-prosperity Sphere, a foreign policy initiative nominally designed to enable 'all nations and races to assume their proper place in the world' but one that was rooted in Japanese assumptions of racial hierarchy.

The Co-prosperity Sphere was intended to unite all the regions where Japan had established an undisputed hegemony (that is, China, Manchukuo, Korea and Taiwan) into an effective family in which Japan would remain the family head. Local customs in the various subject states might be permitted provided that they did not disrupt the larger goals of the Co-prosperity Sphere, and there would be due acknowledgement of 'common Oriental cultural ideals'; but at the same time the new bloc would be developed according to Japanese aims, Japanese would become the common language of the bloc, and Japan would take steps to 'assimilate other races into Nipponism'. A totalitarian control of the channels of information, facilitating the endless dissemination of propaganda lauding Japanese culture and Japanese military power, would guarantee the desired levels of indoctrination. There was no suggestion, in this ambitious scenario, that Japan would ever need to relinquish its role as the 'leading race'; Japan, it was made clear, had nothing to learn from other Asians.[47]

For four decades Korea was enmeshed in the humiliating and repressive matrix of Japanese racism. The Second World War was to shatter the Japanese imperial framework that had for too long allowed the extremes of racist prejudice to be inflicted on subject Asian states. But there can be little doubt that racist assumptions, hopefully attenuated and diminishing, have survived to the present day. With the population of Japan now in excess of 120 million, there are barely three-quarters of a million Koreans living in the country, many of them descendants of the forced labourers driven into the mines and factories following the 1910 annexation. By the 1990s many of these were residents of at least two generations' standing, but they are still not permitted to become Japanese citizens; worse, the Korean residents are required to submit themselves to regular finger-printing, a requirement that underlines the residual assumption that Koreans are likely to be criminal or subversive.*

---

*The dispute over the nuclear issue (Chapter 1) reportedly caused a fresh wave of racist attacks by Japanese against ethnic Koreans in Japan. The Korean community reported more than 120 verbal and physical attacks between April and June 1994, many on schoolgirls (*The Independent*, 22 June 1994; *Time*, 27 June 1994).

THE SECOND WORLD WAR

Korea and the Koreans were involved in the Second World War in many ways that are often ignored by commentators with a Eurocentric or American focus. In the war against Japan the United States gave consideration to the significance and geography of Korea in the conflict, just as Japan itself was to exploit the people and resources of the colony in various ways. As part of the long-standing War Plan Orange for the defeat of Japan, the American war strategists had considered the use of Korea for advanced US bases.[48] The idea was reconsidered during World War Two, and rejected. Similarly, American fleet admirals and war planners recommended taking harbours in North China and Korea to complete the encirclement of Japan, with the US Joint Chiefs rejecting such plans as needless diversions.[49] In the last phases of the war the Japanese fleet still had access to Korean ports and so to some much-depleted Korean resources, but this did nothing to delay Japan's comprehensive defeat by the United States and its allies.

Japan too gave thought to how it might exploit its Korean colony to best effect. Raw materials mined in the peninsula contributed significantly to the Japanese war effort, as did the rice shipments produced by the impoverished Korean peasants. It was also useful for the Japanese to call on Koreans to supplement the hard-pressed Japanese forces. At first a volunteer system operated, with Koreans simply being exhorted to present themselves for service in the armed forces. Then college students were instructed to report for military service, and from 1943 all Koreans were liable to conscription. Those who refused were forced as virtual slave labour into the mines and factories.[50] Others followed instructions but performed their military tasks without commitment, in some cases escaping to join the anti-Japanese forces. Even so, there were many Korean contingents that served a useful purpose in promoting the Japanese war aims.

It remained necessary for the Japanese planners to indoctrinate their Asian allies with the wisdom of the Japanese strategy and the superiority of the Japanese race. The corollary – that the white anti-Japanese forces were necessarily racially inferior and not deserving of respect – had to be promoted as effectively as possible, a task with which Japan's Korean collaborators were in full compliance. The Japanese spread their propaganda in various ways: endless propaganda was disseminated to advertise the bestial nature of the enemy, prisoners of war were humiliated by their Japanese and

Korean captors, and every opportunity was taken to broadcast Japanese triumphs. On 4 March 1942, the Chief of Staff of the Korean army, who was commanded by General Itagaki (later to be dubbed one of the Japanese 'major war criminals'), sent the following telegram to the Japanese War Ministry:

> As it would be very effective in stamping out the respect and admiration of the Korean people for Britain and America, and also in establishing in them a strong faith in victory, and as the Governor-General [General Minami, another 'major war criminal'] and the Army are both strongly desirous of it, we wish you would intern 1000 British and 1000 American prisoners of war in Korea. Kindly give this matter special consideration.[51]

On the following day General Itagaki was informed that 1000 'white prisoners of war' were to be sent to Fusan. He later commented: 'It is our purpose by interning American and British prisoners of war in Korea to make Koreans realise positively the true might of our empire as well as to contribute to psychological propaganda work for stamping out any ideas of the worship of Europe and America which the greater part of Korea still retains deep down.'[52]

In August 1942 a batch of 'white' prisoners captured in Malaya was paraded in Seoul and Fusan before a crowd of 120,000 Koreans and 57,000 Japanese. The appearance of the emaciated and brutalised men created the desired impression. Thus Itagaki's Chief of Staff reported the remarks of two Koreans in the crowd: 'When we look at their frail and unsteady appearance, it is no wonder they lost to the Japanese forces'; 'When I saw young Korean soldiers, members of the Imperial Army, guarding the prisoners, I shed tears of joy.'[53] However, the systematic indoctrination of Koreans was not always completely successful. For example, Koreans attached to Japanese units were less eager to fight to the death, as shown when American and Australia forces overran Japanese resistance west and south of Sanananda in New Guinea: of the 350 prisoners taken, most were Chinese or Korean labourers. Similarly, when US forces crushed Japanese contingents on Makin in the Gilbert Islands most of those who surrendered were Koreans. The co-opting of Korean labourers rarely generated enthusiasm for the Japanese cause.

The Japanese Imperial Army also rounded up Korean women and girls to serve as 'comfort women' for the Japanese forces. Estimates suggest that as many as 200,000 women were confined as sex slaves for Japanese troops for most of the duration of the war. The women, abducted from Korea and other Asian countries, were brought to frontline brothels and then individually required to service a dozen or more Japanese soldiers a day. The first 'comfort station' was established in Shanghai in 1932, and the practice continued – using mostly Korean women, but also women from China, Taiwan, the Philippines, Indonesia, the Netherlands and Japan itself – until Japan's final defeat in 1945.

In 1992 a Japanese government report, acknowledging the existence of the 'comfort women', said that there was no evidence of coercion, but on 4 August 1993 Yohei Kono, the chief cabinet secretary to the Japanese government, declared that 'the government of Japan would like to take this opportunity to extend its sincere apologies and remorse to all those ... who suffered immeasurable pain and incurable physical and psychological wounds as "comfort women"'. Moreover, the government would 'consider seriously' how it could express its remorse.* A statement from the South Korean Foreign Ministry expressed appreciation of the fact that the Japanese government 'now acknowledges that coercion was involved'; now, said a South Korean ministry spokesman, the issue would be dropped from the agenda at future diplomatic meetings.[54] Korean 'comfort women' were doubtless among the 10,000–15,000 Koreans in Hiroshima and Nagasaki when the atomic bombs were dropped.[55]

Despite the Japanese mobilisation of Korean men and women in the peninsula to serve the war effort, the internal struggle against the occupation continued. Kim Il-sung's Korean People's Revolutionary Army (KPRA) expanded its activities as a prelude to a general offensive throughout the country. Soon KPRA units had crossed the Tuman-gang river and advanced to the areas of Kyonghung and Kyongwon. Without the intervention of Soviet and American forces in the peninsula, it is likely that the whole of Korea would have fallen to Kim Il-sung in August 1945. The Japanese were now in retreat on all fronts, and on 15 August offered unconditional surrender, a few days after the dropping of the atomic bombs on Hiroshima and

---

*In July 1994 it was reported that more than 22,000 ex-PoWs and PoW widows, including 15,500 Britons, were to sue the Japanese government for £332 million compensation for cruel treatment during the Second World War (*The Guardian*, 1 July 1994).

Nagasaki. Kim Il-sung had been mobilising Korean anti-Japanese forces for two decades and had been active in the theatre of operations for the full duration of the Second World War. Syngman Rhee had preferred to remain in the United States for most of that period: he returned to Korea on 16 October 1945 when it was safe to do so.

There was however no immediate prospect of the emergence of a revolutionary government throughout the Korean peninsula. The great powers had their interests in the region and these would always be considered before the independence of the Korean people. A wartime report produced by the US Council on Foreign Relations had proposed four options for post-war Korea: (a) it might continue as part of the Japanese empire; (b) be controlled by China; (c) be controlled by the Soviet Union; or (d) be independent. An analyst had commented that he 'felt Korea incapable of self-government'; and taking note of this the report proposed that Korea be placed under some sort of international control. At the same time the report was generally inconclusive; but if 'the group was perplexed over the solution of the Korean problem' there was still agreement 'that Korea was not capable of self-government at the present time'.[56]

Now the situation was plain. The Japanese occupation of Korea – a miserable episode in the long Korean history – was at an end; with Soviet forces in the north of the peninsula (the Soviet Union having seen strategic advantage in a late declaration of war on a defeated Japan) and US forces in the south, there was now a new occupation of the Korean peninsula. The Korea that would emerge from the ruins of 40 years of independence struggle and the Second World War would be shaped largely by great powers interested more in the pattern of global politics than in the continuing predicament of a small state.

Part III
The Fruits of Partition

5 The Divided Nation

The defeat of Japan in 1945 led to the surrender of her occupation forces in the Korean peninsula, as elsewhere. The surrender was offered to the Soviet forces in the north and to the American forces in the south. It is ironic that it was Roosevelt's urging of Stalin to become involved in the Far East war after the defeat of Germany that gave the Soviets access to Manchuria and Korea. Had Roosevelt not encouraged Stalin to declare war on Japan, there would have been no Russian troops in the Korean peninsula, no Korean divide, and no Korean war.[1]

PRELUDE TO PARTITION

The Allies considered the Korean question during the Second World War, but it was not a high priority. Europe loomed large in their deliberations, and when Far Eastern matters were discussed it was inevitable that China and Japan would be given most attention. The 'forgotten nation'[2] of Korea was a peripheral issue: decisions would have to be taken in due course but the Korean problem was not a pressing one.

In March 1943 President Roosevelt and the British Foreign Secretary Anthony Eden, in discussions on the Far East, agreed that an international trusteeship would be established for Korea, with the likely trustees being the United States, the Soviet Union and China.[3] The idea reflected Syngman Rhee's earlier suggestion that a League of Nations trusteeship be established over the entire peninsula, a proposal that had been condemned by many Korean nationalists. In the fresh Allied discussions on Korea there was of course no requirement that the Koreans be consulted. Far Eastern topics were again considered at the Cairo Conference (22–26 November 1943) when Roosevelt met with British Prime Minister Winston Churchill and China's Generalissimo Chiang Kai-shek. Here it was decided that the war against Japan would continue until its surrender, that the Allies would forgo territorial gains, and that the 'three great powers, mindful of the enslavement of the people of Korea, are determined that in due course Korea shall become free and independent'.[4]

155

The question of trusteeship was again discussed when Roosevelt, Churchill and Stalin met for the Teheran Conference (28 November–1 December 1943). Stalin here agreed with Roosevelt's suggestion that the Koreans might need 'forty years' as a 'period of apprenticeship before full independence might be attained'.[5] And at the Yalta Conference (4–11 February 1945), attended by Roosevelt, Churchill and Stalin, Roosevelt suggested that a trusteeship for Korea might comprise representatives from the United States, the Soviet Union and China. Now Roosevelt felt that Korea might take 'twenty to thirty years' to prepare for self-government. Stalin commented 'the shorter the time, the better', and then asked whether there would be foreign troops stationed in Korea. When Roosevelt replied in the negative, Stalin said 'Good'. Roosevelt then commented that in the case of Korea he proposed not to involve the British, and he wondered whether they would be offended. When Stalin replied, 'They will be offended. In fact, the Prime Minister might kill us', Roosevelt burst into hearty laughter before removing his glasses and wiping his eyes.[6] At the foreign ministers' Moscow Conference (December 1945) the United States and the Soviet Union agreed on the creation of a Korean provisional government, to be followed by a temporary international trusteeship with American, Russian, British and Chinese representatives. But the Moscow Agreement was never implemented: at the time of its signing, *de facto* administrations were already emerging in North and South Korea.

The question of eventual Korean independence had been discussed at a series of conferences: principally, Cairo, Teheran, Yalta and Moscow. Korea was not discussed at the Potsdam Conference (17 July–2 August 1945) but the Cairo Declaration was reaffirmed, so underlining the commitment that Korea would be independent 'in due course'. The possibility of partition, of dividing the Korean peninsula for administrative or strategic reasons, was seldom if ever mentioned in the wartime discussions. Soon all the deliberations on trusteeship and eventual independence were to be overtaken by events.

DRAWING THE LINE

On 8 August 1945 – the day the atomic bomb was dropped on Nagasaki, and two days after the atomic bomb had destroyed Hiroshima – the Soviet Union entered the war against Japan, so honouring the agreement concluded at Potsdam. By 12 August, Soviet troops had moved into north-eastern Korea, a development that fuelled the growing alarm among American strategists. Already the United States was moving to secure a *de facto* division of the peninsula which in the years ahead, against all earlier talk of Korean independence, would consign the Korean people to military occupation and cement the creation of two Koreas as pawns in the Cold War.

On 10–11 August 1945, during a night-long session of the State–War–Navy Coordinating Committee in Washington, D.C., John J. McCloy, the Assistant Secretary of War, directed two young colonels, Dean Rusk and Charles H. Bonesteel, to withdraw to an adjoining room and to decide where to draw a line on the map to divide Korea.* (Rusk became a key figure in US Asian diplomacy and Secretary of State under Kennedy and Johnson; Bonesteel was later to command US forces in Korea.) Allowed 30 minutes for their historic task, the two men decided to draw a line at the 38th parallel – because, as Dean Rusk later declared, this placed Seoul, the Korean capital, in the US zone. Rusk acknowledged also that the line was 'further north than could be realistically reached ... in the event of Soviet disagreement', since it would take some weeks before American forces could land in the peninsula.[7] Since the unopposed Soviet forces could have taken the entire peninsula, Rusk was 'somewhat surprised' when the Soviets acquiesced in the US-defined partition. In fact the American decision to divide the Korean peninsula grew out of US strategic calculations made years before: 'The decision on the thirty-eighth parallel ... was based on years of planning ... .'[8] The Washington strategists had long been interested in protecting US assets in the Far East and in enlarging the sphere of US influence; in such a grand design Korea was one of the many elements that could not be ignored.

---

*The partition of Korea by the simple expedient of arranging for non-Koreans to draw a line on a map is reminiscent of how Sir Percy Cox, a manifest non-Arab, drew lines on maps in 1922 to carve up the Arab Middle East (see Geoff Simons, *Iraq: from Sumer to Saddam* (London: Macmillan, 1994) pp. 175–6). Just as Cox's line-drawing stored up massive problems for the future, so the Rusk–Bonesteel efforts served to cement the US strategic calculations that would lead to war.

On 15 August 'General Order Number One', drafted to define the procedure for the Japanese surrender, was waiting for President Truman's approval. As with the earlier drafts, the document contained the specific reference to the 38th parallel. Thus the second clause (of five) declared that 'The Japanese commanders and all ground, sea, air, and auxiliary forces within Manchuria, Korea north of 38 degrees north latitude, and Karafuto surrender to the Commander-in-Chief of the Soviet Forces in the Far East'; with the fifth clause declaring that 'The Imperial General Headquarters, its senior commanders, and all ground, sea, air, and auxiliary forces in the main islands of Japan, minor islands adjacent thereto, Korea south of 38 degrees north latitude, and the Philippines surrender to the Commander-in-Chief, US Army Forces in the Pacific.'

The full document was transmitted for the approval of the British and the Soviet Union, while at the same time the wording was read out over the telephone to General Douglas MacArthur. When Stalin's reply was received it was clear that he was not satisfied with the wording on the Kurile Islands and Sakhalin, but the question of Korea and the 38th parallel was not raised. After some changes had been made to the text the General Order was despatched for execution. The Soviets had seemingly accepted the demarcation of the Korean peninsula.

The 38th parallel had been selected because it 'maximised the territory' that could possibly be claimed by the United States at that time.[9] For the Korean people the artificial division of the peninsula was a disaster: 'the principal external factor that brought division and tragedy to the Korean people in the years ahead'.[10] From the Korean perspective in August 1945, there was no need for a US-contrived partition of the country: an ostensible embryo Korean government, rooted in the rural 'people's committees', already existed throughout the peninsula at the time of the Japanese collapse. The popular movements had gained credibility through the long years of struggle against the Japanese occupation and had established their political/administrative organs throughout Korea. The Americans created the partition, established a fresh military occupation (which for a while the erstwhile Japanese military police assisted), and began destroying the popular people's committees – in order to instal and develop a puppet right-wing regime in South Korea that would be congenial to US strategic planners and American business interests.

THE AMERICANS IN KOREA

The character of the American occupation of South Korea was soon made clear to the Koreans and others who had assumed that the defeat of Japan would have brought Korean independence. On 7 September 1945, General Douglas MacArthur, the Commander in Chief of the Pacific US Army Forces, issued his Proclamation No. 1:

> By virtue of the authority vested in me as Commander in Chief, United States Army Forces, Pacific, I hereby establish military control over Korea south of 38 degrees north latitude and the inhabitants thereof, and announce the following conditions of the occupation:
>
> All powers of government over the territory of Korea south of 38 degrees north latitude and the people thereof will be for the present exercised under my authority. Persons will obey my orders and orders issued under my authority. Acts of resistance to the occupying forces or any acts which may disturb public peace and safety will be punished severely.
>
> For all purposes during the military control, English will be official language ...

There was now no mention of the Cairo pledge to make Korea free and independent 'in due course'. In fact the US military authorities now seemed more hostile to the Koreans than to the Japanese. Thus Lieutenant-General John R. Hodge, the American commander of the US troops in Korea, dubbed Korea an 'enemy country of the United States', duty bound therefore to 'abide by the terms of capitulation'. In the same spirit, Major-General Archibald V. Arnold, the first of Hodge's three Military Governors, reported the serious problem of finding Koreans to work for the Military Government who had the 'American version' of integrity and efficiency to handle matters. He added that Koreans would be given their country when they were fit to run it: 'I have told them that it might be one year, ten years, or fifteen years.'[11] Until that time the American occupation forces would not only continue to employ Japanese officials and pro-Japanese Korean officials *but would also preserve the laws enacted under Japanese imperialist rule.* Thus on 2 November 1945, through 'Military Government Ordinance No. 21', it was announced that 'all laws which were in force, regulations, orders and notices or other documents issued by any former government of Korea having the force of law' would continue in full force and effect.

The Korean people, having suffered decades of Japanese oppression, were now being forced to endure a new military occupation. Japanese imperial ambitions had been crushed but Japanese officials remained in power in South Korea and Japanese laws were protected. The people's committees, virtually the only popular political organs in the south, were now being rooted out and forcibly dissolved. As under the Japanese, any dissenting views were banned. On 17 October, Lieutenant-General Hodge announced: 'The Military Government Office is the sole government of Korea. If there is any person who complains of the orders or deliberately slanders the Military Government, he shall suffer punishment.'[12] The United States Military Government in Korea (USAMIGIK), not a single member of which spoke Korean,[13] had on 10 October declared itself to be the only government in South Korea, and had called for an end to pronouncements from what it dubbed 'irresponsible political groups'. The Advisory Council, formed by the American authorities on 5 October, included many 'well-known collaborators',[14] quisling elements that had directly aided the Japanese suppression of the Korean people. Thus one of the US-appointed advisors was Kim Song Su, a pro-Japanese landlord who had urged Korean youth to shed much blood for Japan in the Second World War. Other members of the fascist Hanguk Democratic Party, formed on 9 September when the US army entered Seoul, were appointed to fill the posts of the President of the Supreme Court and the Public Procurator General, and as judges and procurators at all levels of the judicial hierarchy.

The Japanese occupation had been transmuted, with few changes, into an American occupation: military control, the suppression of democratic movements, foreign repression, the denial of national independence – all the elements that the Korean people had been forced to endure for almost half a century – had been preserved under the new regime. The American authorities boasted of how they had involved Koreans in the administration of their own affairs, but most of the officially appointed Koreans had come to prominence by upholding the Japanese occupation. John Gunther, a biographer of General MacArthur, noted that the Koreans who 'rallied around Hodge' included 'those associated with Japan, fascist elements, professional assassins'.[15] In these circumstances the Korean people came to believe that 'the liberators had become the oppressors'.[16] In 1947 the US Assistant Secretary of State admitted that 'Many Koreans feel they are worse off than they were under the Japanese'; an opinion poll showed that a majority of South Koreans preferred Japanese occupation to American;[17] and a one-time member of USAMIGIK commented that the condition of the Koreans in the American area 'became much worse during the American occupation than it was before'.[18]

It now seems clear that the United States government had no concrete policy on Korea following the Japanese collapse,[19] beyond that of partition and military control in the South. There were signs that Washington was prepared to withdraw from Korea, provided that the southern zone could be made secure for capitalism. Thus on 20 October 1945 the State–War–Navy Coordinating Committee declared that 'the present zonal military occupation of Korea should be superseded at the earliest possible date by a trusteeship for Korea'; there was always the problem, in Western perceptions, that Korea was not fit 'to exercise self-government'. In these circumstances, if Washington was to withdraw its military forces, the only realistic option was 'a period of trusteeship during which the Koreans will be prepared [that is, made ready] to take over the independent administration of their country'.[20] At the same time the Americans had created conditions that made it difficult for Washington to order a speedy troop withdrawal: the southern puppet regime, in due course headed by Syngman Rhee (see below), was fragile, disposed to perpetuate the unpopular dictatorial rule that the Americans had taken over from the Japanese, and inclined to make frequent bluster about marching north[21] to 'liberate' the other half of the peninsula – one of many details that the West ignores in its assumptions about the causes of the Korean War (Chapter 6).

In 1945–6 there were mounting political pressures in Washington, following the ending of the Second World War, for the withdrawal of American troops around the world. In these circumstances the US military occupation of South Korea has been represented as a temporary expedient, pending the creation of the appropriate political conditions in the region. Already the US had moved, via the Moscow Agreement (Appendix 5), to prepare the way for a trusteeship for Korea that would reduce the burden on the United States. Under the terms of the Agreement a Joint (US–Soviet) Commission was created, nominally to prepare the way for the four-power (United States, Soviet Union, Britain and China) trusteeship. In reality the Moscow Agreement did no more than consolidate the partition.

This meant that Washington, having cemented partition (a *de facto* divide that came to acquire *de jure* status), was prepared to contemplate withdrawal. There was growing pressure from the US Congress, reluctant then to agree continued high levels of military spending, for withdrawal; but this could not happen until the regime in the south had achieved a degree of stability. At the same time Washington perceived the advantage of an international underwriting of its strategic and commercial interests in the region: a requirement that came to be met through the mechanism of the United Nations (see below), then as now completely dominated by the United States.

The Soviets, having been virtually invited into Korea through Roosevelt's Potsdam negotiations, and having been presented with the US-contrived partition of the peninsula, came to have analogous interests in North Korea to those of the United States in the south. Moscow did not have the option of manipulating the newly hatched United Nations; but nor, from one perspective, did it need to. Most of the evidence suggests that – in the days after the Japanese defeat – the northern regime enjoyed considerably more popular support than did the south.

THE SOVIETS IN KOREA

The movement of Soviet troops into northern Korea was initially welcomed by many Koreans; as indeed the arrival of American troops in Seoul was at first welcomed as heralding the expulsion of the hated Japanese. The Soviets in the north had reason to expect a good reception: they had joined the anti-Japanese coalition, albeit belatedly, and shared the ideology of the communist-orientated people's committees that had been established not only in much of the north but also throughout most of the peninsula. The ideologically orthodox writers and commentators stressed how warmly the Soviet liberators were welcomed by the Korean population; while others, doubtless from their own equally interested perspective, emphasised the Soviet brutalities and the resulting discord. Thus Kim

Chang-sun, who later defected to South Korea, reported as an eye-witness that pillages and rapes by Soviet troops sprang up in every place, with 'the entire North Korean land ... filled with terror and fear'.[22] Other sources, some sympathetic to the Soviets, agree that rape and looting did take place and were only stopped in January 1946 when the military police were deployed.[23] Anna Louise Strong, reporting from North Korea in 1947, commented that the Soviet troops were 'tough babies from the German front', against whom the Koreans had 'some complaint'.[24]

Once the Soviets were inside northern Korea they quickly established a military command structure. Bureaux of local commanders (the so-called *komendatura* bodies) were set up to confiscate Japanese military equipment and to establish local order. Soon groups of Korean 'people's police', working with units of the Red Army, were patrolling the towns to suppress residual pockets of pro-Japanese resistance. From the beginning the Soviet authorities, highly sympathetic to the popular people's committees, encouraged the development of local self-rule councils and police units.[25] On 15 August 1945, Colonel-General Ivan Mikhailovich Chistiakov, commander of the Sixth Guard Army which had fought at Stalingrad and Kursk, issued an appeal to the Korean people:

> People of Korea: The Soviet army and the armies of the allies have chased the Japanese robbers from Korea. Korea has become a free state, but this is only the first chapter in the history of new Korea ... the happiness of Korea can only be achieved through heroic struggle and indefatigable labour of the Korean people ... Citizens of Korea: Remember that happiness lies in your hands. You obtained freedom and independence, and now your fate depends only on yourselves. The Soviet army created all conditions for the free creative labour of the Korean people. The Korean people must become the creator of its own happiness ... Restore the businesses and factories which have been destroyed by the Japanese: Open new productive enterprises: The command of the Soviet army guarantees the protection of the properties of all Korean enterprises ... Workers of Korea! Show heroism and creativity in your labour: ... Long live the liberated Korean people![26]

Now the Soviets were encouraging the emergence of popular organisations based on the workers and peasants. The first municipal people's committees were set up at Pyongyang and the big ports of

North Korea in the province of Hamgyong and elsewhere. On 16 August, soon after the founding of the local people's committee in Unggi, the first coastal city to be liberated (12 August), Lieutenant-General Zakarov (later an admiral) witnessed a 5000-strong liberation meeting. On 31 August 20,000 Koreans demonstrated to celebrate the Red Army's liberation of the town. When Chongjin was liberated on 16 August, a people's committee was promptly established, and on 29 August 50,000 Koreans paraded in celebration. A Russian publication describes the ensuing scene: 'thousands of people with red banners, with revolutionary songs, marched out in broad columns to their heavy work [of clearing away the ruins of the town], as on a holiday'.[27] Now the people's committees were being formed throughout the region, with massive worker involvement and enthusiastic Soviet support. Sometimes the committees, or preparatory bodies, were created before a town had been liberated: thus in Hwanghae, before Soviet control was established, a body was created to prepare a provincial people's committee. At the same time branches of what would become the Communist Party were being set up in parallel with the people's committees and other popular worker/peasant organisations. The Committee for the Preparation of Korean Independence (CPKI) had branches in many towns and cities.

The presence of the Red Army and Soviet officials in North Korea generated many of the problems that the Americans were experiencing in the South. Despite the initial popularity of the liberators, there were inevitable tensions between the foreigners and the indigenous people hungry for real independence. Sometimes the Red Army requisitioned local food supplies, so contributing to Korean hardship; while Soviet authors described how the Red Army was distributing food, consumer goods, fuel and other supplies to the Korean population. Kim Chang-sun comments that the initial period of Soviet rule was a period of 'excitement and confusion'; noting that 'lawless hoodlums were rampant'; and that while the Japanese had been removed the Red Army now committed acts of plunder.[28] In a few cases, though never on the scale practised by the American authorities in the south, the Soviets retained Japanese officials in post, usually a brief expedient.

The important overarching differences between the Soviet and American occupations was that whereas the Americans governed South Korea with direct military power the Soviets assigned the governing power to the North Koreans, 'maintaining indirect control without a military government of their own'.[29] This important distinction signals the greater accord that the Soviets had with the bulk of the North Korean people, despite all the tensions and dislocations in the post-war period. When the people's committees had been established in all the provinces of the north, the Soviet authorities issued their policy stipulations (14 September 1945):

1. the early establishment of a government representing the working people, peasants, industrial workers, and other Koreans opposed to the Japanese;
2. land distribution to the farming population;
3. placement of the Japanese-owned industry under the control of a worker's committee;
4. immediate purge of all pro-Japanese Koreans;
5. public control of all educational and cultural institutions.

The directives made clear the type of Korean regime that the Soviets intended to establish in the north. Rightists would not be tolerated; and now in fact could easily be condemned as Japanese collaborators. When unacceptable individuals (for example, Cho Man-sik) were purged it was convenient to brand them as wartime stooges of Japanese imperialism. When, on 28 September 1945, Hyon Chun-hyok was assassinated it was assumed that his bourgeois-democrat convictions had allied him too closely with the rightists. Deviation from the Soviet scheme would not be tolerated.

The Soviets were attempting to impose their version of order on a complicated and confused situation, having been forced to deal with numerous communist and nationalist factions competing for power. Five major factions have been identified: the indigenous nationalists (non-communists), the Korean communists, the returnees from China (the Yenan faction), the returnees from the Soviet Union, and the Kim Il-sung faction (the Kapsan group).[30] On 8 October the Soviets convened the so-called Temporary Five-Provinces Committee (later named the Five-Provinces Administrative Bureau) at Pyongyang, an attempt to amalgamate in one organisation the People's Political Committee from five northern Korean provinces and the various communist factions returning from Siberia, Manchuria and China. The Administrative Bureau was to be the embryonic government of North Korea, that has been represented as – forgetting about the imposition of the US-contrived partition – the first step towards the emergence of a separate North Korean state.[31]

THE ROLE OF SYNGMAN RHEE

In the conventional wisdom Syngman Rhee (1875–1965) was a corrupt rightist who became increasingly repressive and authoritarian. This portrayal is substantially accurate but there are complications that are often ignored. At times Rhee seemed to be advocating the eventual nationalisation of banking, public utilities, the railways, coal mining, textile manufacturing and other industrial sectors[32] – despite American assumptions that a Rhee government in Korea would necessarily protect US business interests. In December 1946 Rhee annoyed Lieutenant-General Hodge in bypassing him to lobby Washington for the withdrawal of American troops and the early establishment of a Korean government. There were also signs that even in the early days the Americans were worried by Rhee's autocratic approach to political questions, despite their own repressive methods in South Korea. And, while actively supporting the League of Korean Students which was petitioning Washington to repudiate the Yalta Agreement (that allowed the 'devilish' division of Korea), Syngman Rhee was prepared to declare to Seoul reporters: 'The United States is responsible for the division of Korea.'[33]

Such attitudes should be set in the context of Rhee's virulent anti-communism and his hatred of the Soviet Union, a posture that was sometimes sufficiently strident to alarm Washington in the early days of the Cold War. Despite some American misgivings, Rhee returned to Korea on 16 October 1945 after his long sojourn in the comfort of the United States. In one account the US Military Government in South Korea tried to prevent Rhee's return, forcing him to seek the aid of the Chiang Kai-shek.[34] At first Rhee was held under 'virtual house arrest',[35] but it soon became clear that he would be allowed to head a puppet government in South Korea. On 20 October Hodge staged a hero's welcome for Rhee who responded by praising the Americans and condemning Soviet policies. By now the Soviet Union was predictably hostile to American plans to instal a Rhee-headed government in the south. In fact Rhee was not at that time the only contender for the leadership of a new South Korean administration. Another independence activist, Kim Ku, was ambitious for power and prepared to dispute Rhee's claims. Kim initiated a series of strikes, demanded the recognition of a new government that he would head, and on 31 December staged a confrontation with Hodge. This proved to be Kim's undoing. Hodge, already convinced that Korea was not fit for independence, threatened to 'kill him [Kim] if he double-crossed me again'.[36] Now Rhee was able to develop his own political ambitions. In February 1946 – following the efforts of Hodge, Rhee and M. Preston Goodfellow, a leading US intelligence officer[37] – the Representative Democratic Council (RDC) was created as an embryo South Korean government.

The RDC had been established as a rightist coalition that would strengthen the American position in the forthcoming negotiations with the Soviets in the Joint Commission. At the same time the Democratic National Front (DNF), including the independence activists Yo Un-hyong and Pak Hon-yong, was formed as a coalition of moderate leftists and communists, 'an authentic voice of independent leftist opinion'.[38] But by now, with increasingly unambiguous US support, Syngman Rhee was securing his own political position. At the founding of the RDC in February he declared that the Council 'would get the approval of the US Military Government as the future South Korean government'. In fact the role of the RDC was largely supplanted by the Interim Legislature (the 'Interim Legislative Council of South Korea'), established in November 1946 as a puppet parliament.

In June 1947 the Interim Legislature was induced by the American authorities to pass a 'general election law' as a prelude to a South Korean election intended to legitimise Syngman Rhee's control of a pro-American administration. At the same time, against the background of the fruitless meetings of the US–Soviet Joint Commission, Washington decided to exploit its dominant position in the United Nations (see below). On 14 November 1947 the second plenary session of the UN General Assembly passed a resolution designed to create a 'UN Temporary Commission on Korea' (UNTCOK)*, to stage elections under UNTCOK control for the creation of a government, and thereafter to end the military occupation. The election was held on 10 May 1948 whereupon the UN Commission reported that the results, a resounding victory for Rhee and his fellow rightists, 'were a valid expression of the will of the electorate in those parts of Korea which were accessible to the Commission'. In fact, fielding only 30 observers, the Commission

---

*Later supplanted by UNCOK, set up to help Korea attain unification.

observed little of the election procedure; and soon the view spread that 'the elections were not in fact a free expression of the Korean will'.[39] On 12 December 1948 the UN General Assembly passed (by 41 to 6) a US-drafted resolution declaring the Rhee government to be 'lawful ... having effective control and jurisdiction over that part of Korea where the Temporary Commission was able to observe and consult ... based on elections which were a valid expression of the free will of the electorate'. The United States had predictably succeeded in securing international recognition for the puppet regime in South Korea, but now Syngman Rhee was so unpopular that the survival of his government seemed in doubt.

More than two millions Koreans – workers, peasants, students and others – had protested at the creation of the southern regime. At mass demonstrations there were shouts of 'UNCOK, get out:', 'We oppose the establishment of a separate government', and 'Leave the creation of a unified Korean government to us Korean people'. From the leftist perspective, those people allowed to vote (some groups, including the large number of illiterates, were banned) were coerced to visit the polling stations under the conditions of a police state. James Roper, the UP special correspondent (writing for the *Korean Central Yearbook*, 1949), describes the thugs 'armed with axe-handles, baseball bats and clubs' who were employed to ensure that the election went according to plan. Strikes were held throughout the south in protest at the election, and armed peasant/worker revolts were crushed by the US-backed military police. Some 46 polling stations and 73 police stations, despite protective barricades and machine-gun emplacements, were completely destroyed. This was the atmosphere in which the 30 UNCOK observers reported a free and fair election.

Syngman Rhee, like several other rightist politicians, declared himself 'automatically returned' since there was no other contestant, his original opponent, Choe Nung Jin, having withdrawn following terrorist threats. On 31 May 1948 General MacArthur flew to Seoul to congratulate Rhee on his success; and to hint at the possibility of a future reunification of the peninsula. Now Rhee was in a position to exploit the repressive administrative apparatus left by the Japanese, as had the US Military Government before him.[40] The left was ruthlessly suppressed, political appointments were corruptly contrived, and the police were used to check even the activities of Rhee's colleagues in the ruling party. In December the National Security Law was used to suppress leftist political activity and to remove radicals from their posts; soon afterwards a ban was placed on the South Korean Workers' Party (SKWP). In such a fashion Rhee's political opponents – even potential rivals in his own party – were variously intimidated or murdered; while specific anti-left organisations, such as the Anti-Communist Youth Corps, were similarly encouraged to use violence to crush their opponents.[41]

The United States was well pleased with the course of events. Washington quickly recognised the Seoul government, with John J. Muccio speedily despatched to serve as the US ambassador to Korea; China and the Philippines followed suit. The Soviet Union refused to recognise the new political regime in South Korea: *Pravda* (20 May 1947) had already charged that there were 12,000 political prisoners in South Korea and that the American authorities were supporting Japanese 'collaborationists' such as Syngman Rhee. There was now a pressing need for the Soviets to consolidate their position in the north.

THE ROLE OF KIM IL-SUNG

Kim Il-sung (1912–1994), originally Kim Sung Chu, was undeniably always the supreme survivor. Throughout the 1930s (as the 'General') he led a band of a few hundred Korean guerrillas against the Japanese occupation of the peninsula. With bases in Manchuria, Kim Il-sung attacked Japanese troops in that region and made forays into northern Korea – to such effect that the Japanese authorities created a special military squad to hunt him down. During the 1940s, with the Japanese launching intensive assaults against the Manchurian guerrillas, Kim Il-sung withdrew to south-eastern Siberia and culti-vated his ideological sympathies with the Soviet Union. At the same time there was a struggle for leadership among the Korean revolu-tionary groups in the Russian Maritime Provinces. Kim Il-sung was new to the region, liaising with the Soviet army for the first time, and did not speak Russian. In these circumstances his rise to the top of the revolutionary leadership, despite Russian tutelage, has been judged 'noteworthy', as was his prowess in securing his leadership position after the later Soviet withdrawal from North Korea.[42]

At the end of the Second World War, while Syngman Rhee was contemplating the situation from Washington, units of Kim Il-sung's Korean People's Revolutionary Army (KPRA) were contributing to the Japanese collapse in Korea. Some contingents advanced to the areas of Kyonghung and Kyongwon, usually in concert with Soviet troops, while other KPRA units landed at Unggi, Rajin, Chongjin and elsewhere. The Japanese surrender on 15 August 1945 did not bring to an end all the military operations in the Korean peninsula: some Japanese groups, unwilling to contemplate an ignoble end to Japanese imperial ambitions, continued to fight the Red Army and the KPRA units.

The Soviet authorities were happy to support Kim Il-sung's emergence as the leader of the Korean revolutionary factions, and his subsequent political rise to the pinnacle of the North Korean communist regime. Communist propaganda made much of the welcomes Kim Il-sung received when he returned home in triumph at the end of the war. Thus 'Committees Welcoming Kim Il-sung' were organised in Pyongyang, Seoul and many other regions; mass rallies welcomed 'the sun of the nation', 'the hero of Korea' (one Pyongyang rally numbered 400,000 people); wherever Kim Il-sung went – so we are told – he was greeted by the joyful masses in genuine celebration of their liberation from a brutal foreign occupation.

On 20 August 1945, addressing Korean and military cadres, Kim Il-sung urged the creation of a Marxist-Leninist party 'to steadily guide the Korean revolution to victory'; and a people's government 'to solve the question of power, the fundamental question in the revolution, and to build the people's armed forces which will defend our country, people and revolutionary gains'. At the same time the Soviet authorities moved to encourage the development of a strong indigenous Korean regime modelled on the Soviet political system.[43] In eschewing the creation of a Russian military government (that is, direct foreign control), the Soviets avoided many of the problems that the American military authorities created for themselves in the south.

On 5 October Kim Il-sung held a preliminary meeting in Pyongyang to consider the founding of a communist party; a sharp struggle was waged between the communists and what they dubbed the 'subversive sectarians' opposed to the creation of a true Marxist–Leninist party. An Inaugural Party Congress was held (10–13 October) to define particular principles and aims, including *the conversion of North Korea into a reliable base for the reunification of Korea and a nationwide revolution*. The Congress established the Central Organising Committee of the Communist Party of North Korea, while at the same time preparations were being made elsewhere for the creation of various people's organisations: on

30 November a General Federation of Trade Unions was formed to mobilise factory workers throughout the north; and on 31 January 1946 a Peasant Union was established. A Democratic Women's Union was created on 18 November 1945, and a Democratic Youth League – intended as a more broadly based organisation than the narrow Young Communist League (YCL) – on 17 January 1946. In addition, active federations were established for industrial technology, literature and the arts, Christians, Buddhists and many other social groups. A few non-communist parties also emerged, despite the growing Soviet character of the regime: for example, the Democratic Party (mostly small capitalists and Christians) and the Chondoist Chongu Party (peasant Chondo believers).

The North Korean Provisional People's Committee, later to become the highest administrative organ in North Korea, was established in February 1946 with Kim Il-sung as chairman and Kim Tu-bong as vice-chairman. A year later a people's assembly, comprising various ministries and bureaux, was created. In November 1947 a committee was established to draft a constitution for North Korea; the draft was accepted by the People's Assembly on 6 February 1948, with a decision on 9 July that the constitution would be implemented pending the stipulated election of the Supreme People's Assembly. At that time Kim Il-sung submitted a report in which he condemned the division of Korea, a deplorable act directly attributable to the manoeuvrings of the Americans.[44] The political developments in the South were observed with mounting resentment, until the election (10 May) that brought Syngman Rhee to power provoked a response from the North.

Few observers doubted that 'violence and repression rather than democratic freedom had determined the outcome' in the South (even the US Military Government had reported to the State Department that Rhee had few followers).[45] MacArthur, in Seoul on 15 August to congratulate Rhee, declared that the artificial barrier dividing Korea 'must and shall be torn down' – so fuelling Rhee's often expressed ambition to invade the North. Four days after the election, the northern regime cut the electricity supply to the South, forcing the United States to begin coal shipments and to fund the building of power plants. In July the communist People's Assembly announced that the election (stipulated in the new constitution) for the Supreme People's Assembly would be held on 25 August. Kim Tu-bong was elected chairman of the new assembly, which on 8 September proclaimed the establishment of the Democratic People's

The Fruits of Partition

Republic of Korea (DPRK). Kim Il-sung was appointed premier of the new state.

Soon after the election, in a remarkable propaganda initiative, the North Korean radio announced that a concurrent election had been held secretly in the South to choose 360 representatives for the 572-seat national Supreme People's Assembly. It was claimed that while 99.97 per cent of voters in the North had voted, some 77.52 per cent of the 8,681,754 eligible voters in the South had also clandestinely participated in the election organised by the North.[46] If the report of a secret southern vote was mere propaganda then it convinced Syngman Rhee: he quickly arrested 1300 people on suspicion of having taken part.[47] There were also reports that the American military authorities, apparently aware that a clandestine election was taking place, embarked upon a wave of suppression: a state of emergency was declared and mobile military units were deployed throughout South Korea. Throughout the whole period of the election 'tens of thousands were arrested and imprisoned, and several thousands killed or wounded'.[48]

The northern authorities represented the election as a historic North–South event that had produced an all-Korea Supreme People's Assembly. Steps had been taken to overcome the predictable repressive moves in the South: a ballot was not cast but the voter's name was signed under a 'double suffrage' system (representatives were elected for a South Korean Conference of People's Representatives, which then elected deputies to the Supreme People's Assembly).* The first session of the newly elected assembly took place in Pyongyang (2–12 September 1948) with 360 delegates said to represent the South. *Now, claimed the North, the whole of Korea had a national elected assembly; the analogous assembly in the South, the seats reserved for the North remaining vacant, was in no position to make an equivalent claim.*

Now Kim Il-sung was premier of the new Democratic People's Republic of Korea. On 10 September his choice of cabinet was approved by the Supreme People's Assembly which purported to represent the entire Korean people. It is significant that some of the

---

*A convention of 1002 elected delegates, purporting to represent the South Korean people, met in Haeju just north of the 38th parallel on 22–24 August to select the 360 of their number who would represent South Korea in the Supreme People's Assembly.

cabinet members already had established links with the South: for example, Pak Hon-yong, now Vice-Premier and Minister of Foreign Affairs, was the leader of the South Korean Workers' Party. With his own people installed in the cabinet, Kim Il-sung was now free to build a highly authoritarian regime which, in its intolerance of dissent, soon came to mirror the regime in the South. But there was one important difference: the government of North Korea, unlike the Rhee regime, was highly committed to reform (see below). This is the principal reason why, when the Soviet and American troops departed from the peninsula, the government of Kim Il-sung was relatively popular and secure whereas the regime in the South was continuously racked by disaffection, protest and armed revolt.

DEVELOPMENTS IN THE SOUTH

The US Military Government began by imposing an authoritarian regime that was similar in many ways to the Japanese administration it had nominally supplanted. At the same time, though with little commitment, the Military Government made a few hesitant moves in the direction of reform. These were severely hampered by the extant Japanese legal framework and by the predictable opposition from Syngman Rhee and his followers. On 5 October 1945 the Military Government announced (via the mechanism of Ordinance No. 9) that henceforth rents on farmers were to be restricted to $33\frac{1}{3}$ per cent of the annual crop instead of the former average of 50 per cent. This move encouraged people to think that real land reform might be on the agenda, not simply for reasons of common justice but because long-standing contention over land ownership continued to cause political disruption.

The question of land reform was discussed, proposals were made, but at that time no action was taken. It was suggested that the allocation to tenants of the 500,00 acres of paddy and 150,000 acres of dry fields formerly owned by the Japanese could constitute the first phase of a substantial land reform programme; to be followed by the disposition to the peasants of land owned by Korean absentee landlords.[49] In February 1946 an ordinance ('The Homestead Act') was proposed to allocate to peasants the land they occupied, but only after they had paid a sum 3.75 times the value of their annual production. No action was taken at that time but in early 1948 the

Military Government issued a decree allowing some 700,000 former Japanese holdings to be sold to 600,000 Korean tenant families. The various landlord factions had opposed reform at every stage and the Military Government had been largely sympathetic to their appeals. Thus in December 1946 Brigadier-General Charles G. Helmick, then the acting Military Governor, announced that 'If a land reform law is enacted by a Korean legislative assembly while Military Government is in power, land owners will receive adequate compensation.'[50] This meant that the US authorities were determined to protect the Korean landlords, widely perceived as a parasitic class that had helped to sustain the Japanese occupation. Moreover, the landlords' title to their land was often highly questionable. Thus Yong-jeung Kim, the President of the Korean Affairs Institute in Washington, commented that with a few exceptions the landlords had 'acquired their possession by usury or by other fraudulent means'.[51]

The Military Government continued to suggest modest land reform measures: for example, that a National Land Reform Administration (NLRA) be established as a state agency to acquire land with full compensation and thereafter to sell it to approved tenant families. Critics of the scheme charged that the terms of such a scheme – payment of 20 per cent of the annual crop value for fifteen years, plus additional tax obligations and upkeep costs would place a heavier burden on peasants than already existed under the landlord system; and that to end the feudal system it was necessary to distribute the land to the peasants without imposing further financial burdens. But the Interim Legislative Assembly, mainly concerned to represent landlord interests, had no interest in disturbing the traditional landlord–peasant relationship: even the modest (and questionable) reforms suggested by the Military Government were routinely blocked by the Assembly and the American authorities had always been reluctant to push for real change.

When the Military Government eventually promulgated the ordinance to sanction the sale of former Japanese holdings to Korean peasant families, the initiative was welcomed in the farming communities: despite left-wing opposition to the land sales 85 per cent of more than 1.4 million plots of land were sold over a five-month period. The scheme, leaving untouched the Korean landlord system, was sufficiently popular to cause candidates in the subsequent election (10 May 1948) to campaign for the further distribution of privately owned lands. But the Rhee government, already alarmed at the changes that had taken place, had no interest in promoting more reforms. When, on 15 August 1948, the US control of South Korea norminally ended, peasant families were being coerced into paying exorbitant prices for plots of land on threat of eviction. Liberal land reform bills were routinely blocked by Rhee and his supporters; and when Cho Pong-am, the Minister of Agriculture and Forestry, continued to urge reform that would benefit the farmers he was finally dismissed from office on 22 February 1949. Eventually a reform bill, much less radical than Cho Pongam had demanded, was promulgated (22 June). The new law entitled the government to purchase unfarmed land under generous compensation terms and thereafter to sell plots to peasant families. But even when the law had been passed, there was no evidence that it would be applied: as late as October 1949 the new Land Reform Law was not being enforced at all, and landlords were still fixing their own terms for land sales and forcing the peasant families to buy or be evicted.[52]

The South's tardy approach to reform derived solely from the character of the US Military Government and the subsequent Rhee regime. At the time of the Japanese surrender (15 August 1945), South Korea had a bigger proportion of working assets than did the North, simply because the fighting between the Soviet forces and the Japanese army only took place in the North, where the Japanese also carried out massive sabotage.[53] In such circumstances the South was in a better position to implement liberal reform schemes, had the political will existed; but the Rhee administration 'moved much more slowly and much less decisively to tackle the landholding and food supply situations'.[54] Food problems were exacerbated by the hoarding of rice in conditions of shortage and by the rapacious posture of the traditional landlords that served to demoralise and terrorise the farming communities. The economic gains in the South, where such could be discerned, derived mainly from US aid designed to prop up an ideologically useful but unenlightened regime. Much of the aid was dissipated in supplying consumer goods rather than in providing long-term investment, and by 1950 American voices were being raised against the provision of further aid to a dissolute and repressive regime: a bill for the supply of more aid to South Korea was voted down by the US House of Representatives in January 1950 and only reinstated (passed in March 1950) when Secretary of State Dean Acheson argued that the Republic of Korea (ROK) would collapse in two or three months without US aid (another $100 million was then provided).

In November 1948 John J. Muccio, the first US ambassador in Seoul, reported on the disturbing economic situation in South Korea. With massive expenditure on the armed forces and security, inflation was rising and the political situation was increasingly contentious. Corruption was endemic and Rhee had failed to tackle the mounting domestic problems, a manifest ineptitude that perhaps 'revealed incipient senility'.[55] In a similar vein a Central Intelligence Agency (CIA) analysis in 1948 acknowledged that the right-wing leadership in South Korea:

is provided by that numerically small class which virtually monopolises the native wealth and education of the country... Since this class could not have acquired and maintained its favoured position under Japanese rule without a certain minimum of 'collaboration', it has experienced difficulty in finding acceptable candidates for political office and has been forced to support imported expatriate politicians such as Syngman Rhee and Kim Ku. These . . . are essentially demagogues bent on autocratic rule'.[56]

The autocratic rightists were contrasted with the left-wing 'grassroots independence movement which found expression in the establishment of the people's committees throughout Korea in August 1945'.[57] Few observers doubted that South Korea had been converted into a police state to protect the interests of the landlord élite and the US strategic posture. One of the principal shaping factors in the origins of the Korean War was the deep unpopularity of the Rhee regime.

DEVELOPMENTS IN THE NORTH

As the Japanese forces in North Korea collapsed at the end of the Second World War they resorted to 'scorched earth' tactics, just as the German forces did in their retreat from the Soviet Union. The scale of sabotage in the North was on a scale far greater than anything known in the South. Thus 64 mines were totally flooded, 178 partially flooded, and six major industrial enterprises (including the Pyongyang Aircraft Factory) completely destroyed and 47 enterprises partially destroyed.[58] For this reason and because of the burden of the war 'North Korean industry was in a state of chaos and disrepair'.[59] Western observers have tended to emphasise the north's advantage in inheriting much of Korea's heavy industry (Table 5.1), but this was a mixed blessing: the costs of repairing the war damage were probably not much less than building the factories from scratch.[60] At the same time the Soviet Union made an immense contribution to the reconstruction of the North, just as the United States was to save the Rhee regime from collapse. Thus the Soviet authorities, wanting to present North Korea as a model Third World development, rapidly created the conditions for the effective confiscation of Japanese property and the rebuilding of the North Korean economy while allowing the emerging Korean regime a high degree of local autonomy. Between 1946 and 1949 the national income of North Korea more than doubled, with the gross value of industrial production increasing more than three-fold (the production of consumer goods almost trebled and agricultural production increased by 50 per cent).[61] Such developments – all to be catastrophically affected by the Korean War (1949–1953) – were accompanied by a radical land reform programme that far outstripped anything contemplated in the South.

On 9 February 1946 the North Korean regime adopted a Ten-Point Programme for agrarian reform based on the confiscation of all estates belonging to Japanese and pro-Japanese elements, and the nationalisation of all the estates owned by the big Korean landlords. The Soviet authorities supported this radical scheme, recognising the need to abolish the 'parasitical landownership' of the traditional Korean landlord class. The measures were popular among the peasant families but supporters of the dispossessed landlords created

Table 5.1   Distribution of resources at partition, 1945

Sector	North Korea (%)	South Korea (%)
Heavy industry	65	35
Light industry	31	69
Agriculture	37	63
Commerce	18	82

Source: Halliday, in J. Sullivan and R. Foss (eds), *Two Koreas – One Future*, 1987.

a wave of unrest. On 1 March, at a commemorative meeting (attended by Kim Il-sung) in Pyongyang in honour of a 1919 uprising, a hand-grenade was thrown from the crowd: Lieutenant T. Novichenko intercepted the device, saving the lives of the Soviet and Korean leaders, but was severely wounded himself.[62] Other terrorist attacks involved an arson attack on the house of Colonel General Chistiakov, and an attack on the house of Kang Ryang-uk, the Methodist Chief Secretary of the Provisional Government in the North and a relative of Kim Il-sung (Kang survived but his son, daughter and a visiting priest were killed). Such events did not delay the implementation of the radical agrarian reform measures: on 5 March the final decree was promulgated and before the end of the month all the confiscated land had been distributed among the peasant families. It is of interest that various Western sources, including intelligence reports, acknowledge that the process was essentially a peaceful one.[63] Other sources tell a different story: giving details of student demonstrations, arson attacks on schools and the buildings of the people's committees, and underground resistance from various factions.[64]

The poor peasants had benefited from the reforms, as had many of the industrial workers in the towns; and at the same time efforts were being made to establish the lineaments of a 'people's democracy' (the first in Asia, apart from Soviet Asia and Mongolia). A monolithic Soviet state was now emerging in North Korea in which a single communist party would be in control (two non-communist parties were allowed but controlled in various ways). Elections (officially free, fair and secret) were held to establish the municipalities and provincial and county people's committees. In November 1947 no less than 97 per cent of electors voted for the candidates of the Democratic National United Front, comprising a bloc of the three parties plus all the non-party candidates. Despite official claims, observers were quick to point out shortcomings in the election procedure ('some people were threatened'; some non-voters 'were taken away at gunpoint'). According to the Soviet newspaper *Izvestiia* (16 November 1946), 50.7 per cent of the elected candidates were non-party, 31.9 per cent members of the Workers' Party, and 17.4 per cent members of the Korean Democratic Party and the Chondogyo Party: it was reported that 'extraordinarily high patriotic enthusiasm and political activity' had been shown. The People's Assembly of North Korea, the highest organ of power, was elected when representatives of the newly elected people's committees met

(17–20 February 1947) in a congress; at the same time a dutiful letter was sent to Joseph Stalin in appreciation for the Soviet contribution to the liberation of the country. In February and March 1947 elections were held to establish the village and township people's committees. The final bricks in the structure of Kim Il-sung's 'people's democracy' were now in place.

After the liberation of North Korea in 1945 the number of Soviet troops was soon sharply reduced (to 10,000 by mid-1946), with a progressively diminishing military presence thereafter. At the same time a Soviet Civil Administration remained intact, and there were Soviet advisors in many industrial, agrarian and military sectors. In cities such as Pyongyang, Hungnam and Chongjin the Russians developed their own communities, served by their own hospitals, stores and schools staffed with Soviet personnel.[65] The North Korean Society for Cultural Relations with the Soviet Union had more than 1.3 million members; so there was abundant evidence that the Soviet influence on North Korea, albeit in the absence of direct military government, remained ubiquitous and deep-seated in the years after the liberation. Soviet engineers had progressively filled the gaps left by the departing Japanese, so further contributing, in an atmosphere of extensive propaganda, to the sovietisation of the North. There is no doubt that the Soviet Union contributed immensely to the rebuilding of the North Korean economy, and to the development of the North Korean armed forces. At the same time it would be foolish to imagine that the Soviet policy was any more disinterested than the American policy in the South: the Soviets had seized an opportunity to encourage the creation of a pro-Soviet regime in the North – an essentially ideological matter, but one with significant economic benefits as commercial ties with the Soviet Union replaced those that over decades had been built up with Japan.

By the beginning of 1948 communism had been securely established in North Korea: there were still factional disputes and dissident protests that were routinely suppressed by the authoritarian state. At the same time it should be acknowledged that the radical agrarian (and other) reforms had made the Kim Il-sung regime immensely popular among substantial sections of the North Korean population. More than 1,000,000 hectares of land had been confiscated and distributed free to more than 720,000 peasant households. Before the liberation around 20 per cent of the peasant families operated on an independent basis; under Kim Il-sung, during the period after liberation, virtually all the North Korean peasants became independent farmers. On 10 August 1946 a nationalisation law stated:

All enterprises, mines, power stations, railways, transport, communications, banking, trading and cultural establishments formerly owned by the Japanese state, juridical and private persons or by traitors to the Korean nation shall be confiscated without compensation and transferred to the ownership of the Korean people, namely, to the state.

On 4 October a 'resolution on measures to protect the right to private ownership and give play to the initiative of individuals in industrial and trading activities' was enacted: small free-enterprise initiatives were to be allowed in order to maximise the role of individual business effort in the rehabilitation of the national economy. Other laws were enacted to protect the rights of workers in employment; and on 30 July 1946 a Law on the Equality of the Sexes was announced: 'in all branches of state, economic, cultural, social and political life women have equal rights with men' (now women had the same rights to work, rest, education and social insurance, with the traditional system of polygamy banned). The repressive Japanese legal system, preserved in the South, was abolished in the North.

The North Korean peasants had at last realised their centuries-old dream of owning their own land; workers' rights had been enshrined in new legislation as never before; a new structure for popular democracy had been erected; and important steps had been taken for the emancipation of women. The regime of Kim Il-sung remained intolerant of political minorities and was highly authoritarian (increasingly so in the post-Second World War period), but it would be a mistake to assume a simple parity between suppression of political dissidents in the North and the mounting repression in the South. In the heady days of the immediate post-liberation period the northern regime worked to build a society in the interests of the majority of the people, whereas the southern regime was irredeemably committed to the fortunes of the landlord and capitalist class above all else. In the North there were factional disputes and subversive efforts that sometimes erupted into violence; in the South there was ongoing guerrilla activity, waves of peasant unrest, revolts in the armed forces and increasing repression. It was this very lack of parity between North and South that was to inflame the tensions between the two halves of the peninsula; and ultimately lead to war.

THE STRUGGLE FOR UNIFICATION

It is clear that the United States was the main architect of the Korean partition: most of 'the initiatives for division came from the US occupation and its conservative Korean allies, who faced a strong left in both North and South'.[66] Thus, despite the constant Western propaganda, 'the United States bears the major share of responsibility for the national division'.[67] We now know that substantial sections of the South Korean population, bitterly resentful of the US-imposed partition, were prepared to support an armed uprising against the southern regime in an effort to unify the country.

In the immediate post-liberation period the regime in the south embarked upon a massive campaign of repression to suppress the widespread leftist infrastructure that had been built up during the years of Japanese occupation. The first period of repression ran until the autumn of 1946 when a 'massive uprising'[68] occurred in the four southernmost provinces where most of the South Korean population lived. In August 1946 the US Military Government suppressed a peasant uprising in Haui Island, South Cholla Province; and at the same time mobilised aircraft and tanks to suppress a worker demonstration at the Hwasun Colliery. These events were accompanied by a US takeover of Japanese and Korean property in the south: railways, ships, communications facilities, banks, irrigation facilities, houses, warehouses, shops and land. According to US figures the seizure included 24 factories and more than 320,000 hectares of land (in total more than 80 per cent of the total property in South Korea). In September 1948 the United States concluded an agreement to transfer the property to the puppet Rhee regime, with the provision that 'the right of acquisition and ownership of that property can be removed according to the demand of the US government'. The agreement also allowed for substantial tracts of land, buildings, roads, and houses to remain the property of the US army.

In September 1946 more than 40,000 railway workers staged a general strike to demand improved living conditions, an end to the repressive tactics of the US Military Government, the implementation of democratic reforms, and the reopening of the US–Soviet Joint Commission talks on reunification and independence. The US authorities responded with the army, the police, various terrorist groups and even tanks to crush the strike. Before the protest had been crushed some 300,000 office workers, industrial workers and students had joined the strike. Demonstrators demanded an end to 'colonial enslavement', unification with the north, a transfer of power to the people's committees, and reforms similar to those being implemented in North Korea. The unrest spread through much of the South, at its peak embracing around 2,300,000 people.[69] The US-organised repression left 'hundreds dead and thousands in jail'[70] – though the resistance was never wholly crushed.[71]

On 3 April 1948 a major rebellion against the US-sustained puppet regime erupted on the volcanic island of Cheju, off the southern coast of Korea. Until early 1948 the political leadership on Cheju was rooted in the resilient people's committees that had first sprung up with the Japanese collapse in August 1945. Even General Hodge had once commented that Cheju was 'a truly communal area that is peacefully controlled by the people's committee without much Comintern [i.e. Soviet] influence'. The islanders had demonstrated on 1 March about the (plainly bogus) scheduled election on the mainland, whereupon the police had promptly arrested 2500 students and tortured one of them to death. This followed what even the American intelligence services were admitting was a 'widespread campaign of terrorism' being waged by pro-Rhee factions against the Cheju people's committees. In particular, the fascist Northwest Youth organisation was said (in a subsequent Korean press report) to have 'exercised police power more than the police itself and their cruel behaviour has invited the deep resentment of the inhabitants'.[72]

The Cheju guerrillas (the *Inmin-gun*, People's Army), numbering 3000 to 4000, were soon confronted by extra police and military groups from the mainland, and also by US air and naval units. One estimate suggests that the Cheju rebellion involved 30,000 deaths, about 10 per cent of the population.[73] There had been more than 100 battles, 6000 islanders were put in jail, and by April 1949 more than 20,000 homes had been destroyed. The South Korean authorities then transferred a third of the Cheju population (about 100,000 people) into protected enclaves, virtual concentration camps, along the coast. The US embassy reported: 'The all-out guerrilla extermination campaign ... came to a virtual end in April with order restored and most rebels and sympathizers killed, captured, or converted.'

A secondary rebellion broke out at Yosu in October 1948, and spread to other areas, when South Korean troops refused to embark for a mission against the Cheju rebels. On 20 October some 2000 recalcitrant troops had seized Yosu and begun spreading out to nearby towns; people paraded in the streets, waving red flags and shouting slogans, and then began trying before the people's courts an assortment of policemen, government officials, landlords and other rightists. The rebellion had spread to five towns, the insurgents had declared their own version of martial law, and hundreds of people were executed as 'reactionary elements'.[74] The rebellion was met with heavily armed mechanised units commanded by US officers, supported by naval guns and aircraft. Some 3000 people were killed. It is significant that although the United States now had no ostensible mandate to intervene in South Korean internal affairs secret protocols had placed the South Korean armed forces under US control. American C-47 transports had been used to transport South Korean troops and their equipment, and the US intelligence services worked closely with the South Korean forces. On 2 November another revolt broke out, this time among troops in the city of Taegu. This rebellion was quickly suppressed but the surviving rebels moved to join active guerrilla forces elsewhere in the region.

In 1949 a quarter of the South Korean army (two out of eight divisions), with substantial American support, had been assigned to combat the guerrillas; and (in most accounts) by the end of that year the guerrilla war had 'markedly subsided'.[75] Now the military effort was running in conjunction with Rhee's characteristic policies of harsh repression, intense security measures, and frequent purges of the police and the armed forces. The various sources suggest that at its peak in September 1949 the guerrilla army numbered around 3000[76]; and that by April 1950 there were only about 400 to 600 active guerrillas in South Korea. But if this were so, it was difficult to explain the tenuous grip that the Rhee regime had on much of the country. In early 1949 two US embassy vice-consuls, after a tour of the provinces, reported that in South Cholla the South Korean government had lost control 'outside of the cities and larger towns'; another American account noted how 'small attacks and ambushes punctuated by larger attacks' were common in much of North Kyongsang province; and in early 1950 Walter Sullivan of *The New York Times* wrote that large parts of South Korea 'are darkened today by a cloud of terror that is probably unparalleled in the world' and that in the 'hundreds of villages across the guerrilla areas' the local village guards endure nights that 'are a long, cold vigil of listening'.[77]

This meant that through 1949 and into 1950 substantial areas of South Korea were outside the control of the Rhee government. At that time the United States had no reason to feel comfortable about the success and security of its puppet dictatorship; just as Rhee himself had little reason to think he would stay long in power without some dramatic transformation in his fortunes. This is the context that should be borne in mind when considering the origins of the Korean War.

6 The Korean War

If I were in charge I would withdraw the United Nations troops to the coast and leave Syngman Rhee to the Chinese ... Korea does not really matter now. I'd never heard of the bloody place till I was seventy-four.

Winston Churchill[1]

Whatever might be the technical advantages of not 'getting bogged down' in Korea, I am sure that a moral defeat would mean the end of the white man's position in the East ...

Harold Macmillan[2]

Finally, to keep the attack from becoming overly costly, it was clear that we would have to use atomic weapons.

Dwight D. Eisenhower[3]

PRELUDE TO WAR

Few independent observers doubted that in the late 1940s the regime of Syngman Rhee in South Korea was an undemocratic tyranny, sustained solely by repression and US aid. The Republic of Korea (ROK) was constantly shaken by peasant uprisings and there were frequent clashes with the North Korean People's Army (NKPA) along the 38th parallel. The mounting tensions, revolts, crises and dislocation merely served to intensify the scale of the repression: the US-promoted South Korean regime was emerging as a 'fundamentally corrupt society';[4] despite massive American economic and military support, 'an unstable creation'.[5]

The peasant uprisings throughout the South were largely an indigenous response to a deeply unpopular regime. There were few signs of Soviet or North Korean support for the southern rebels. In April 1950 the Americans discovered that guerrillas in Kangwon and along the upper coast of North Kyongsang had received weapons and other supplies from the North Koreans but acknowledged that 'almost 100 per cent of the guerrillas in the Cholla and Kyongsang provinces have been recruited locally'.[6] In another American report it was conceded that the southern rebels 'apparently receive little more than moral support from North Korea'.[7] It is useful to remember that with few exceptions the only instances of external involvement in the southern guerrilla war were those where US officials, troops and military advisors were active in defence of Syngman Rhee's repressive regime. One estimate suggests that in South Korea about 100,000 people were killed in the late 1940s by the security forces that had been installed by the United States and which continued to be directed by American officers.[8]

The Rhee regime, despite the intense repression, had not managed to establish a secure political environment. During 1949 about 60 per cent of the national budget of South Korea was being spent in a vain attempt to stabilise the political situation; but there were frequent peasant and labour disturbances, and the security forces found it impossible to crush the widespread guerrilla activity throughout the southern provinces. The scale of the repression is indicated by the magnitude of the human casualties and destruction for April 1950 alone: 36,000 people killed; 11,000 people wounded; 45,000 homes burned completely, 4000 homes partly burned; 61,000 families, involving 316,000 people, sustaining damages; and 78,000 families, comprising 432,000 people, displaced.[9] The radical land reforms for which the peasants yearned never materialised and the massively exploitative landlord–peasant relationships were vigorously upheld by the US-directed security forces. Because security requirements swallowed up so much of the national budget there was no opportunity for substantial industrial investment, had there been the political will: in 1948 industrial production in South Korea declined to 20 per cent of that in 1940 under the Japanese occupation. The regime was barely kept afloat by the continuous repression and American aid, which had amounted to $550 million by 1950.

Throughout this period North Korea made repeated overtures to the southern regime for the peaceful reunification of the country. Some southern political figures (notably Kim Ku and Kim Kyu-sik) were responsive to the overtures from the North and signalled their willingness to enter into discussions; but Syngman Rhee, fearful that reunification would sweep away his unpopular regime, rejected all the North Korean proposals, refused to talk, and branded as 'traitors' all those who urged an end to partition. In June 1949 seven members of the southern National Assembly were jailed for talking to North Koreans; and Kim Ku, widely respected for his lifetime's work in the independence movement, was assassinated.

On 30 May 1950 the southern regime staged its second general election in order to demonstrate the democratic credentials of Syngman Rhee's government. The usual tactics were employed: ballot rigging, intimidation, financial corruption, the exclusion of certain groups from the franchise – but this time all the terror and political manipulation failed to deliver the goods. The Rhee faction lost heavily: of the 210 seats in the National Assembly, the government won a mere 56. Some 130 of the newly elected members were independents, among them men who had connections with North Korea and were keen to promote the cause of unification. By now Syngman Rhee had been totally discredited. His regime was repressive and corrupt, having demonstrated, even to right-wing sources, its indifference 'to the concept of popular freedom, representative only of ambition for power and wealth'.[10] At the same time the US protectors of Syngman Rhee were eager to advertise his unique virtues. Thus John Foster Dulles, then a consultant in the State Department, commented in Seoul on 14 June 1950 that Syngman Rhee (a fellow member of the World Council of Churches) and Nationalist China's (equally corrupt) Chiang Kai-shek ('those two gentlemen') were the moral equivalent of the founders of the Christian Church: 'They are Christian gentlemen who have suffered for their faith. They have been steadfast and have upheld the faith in a manner that puts them in the category of the leaders of the early Church.' On 19 June, Dulles addressed the South Korean parliament and offered further reassurance to the client dictator: 'I say to you: You are not alone. You will never be alone so long as you continue to play worthily your part in the great design of human freedom.'[11] However, there was ambiguity at that time about the degree of support that the United States would be willing to give South Korea in the event of a war with the North.

On 12 January 1950 the US Secretary of State Dean Acheson – in a speech approved by President Truman and the Joint Chiefs, and delivered at the National Press Club – drew what he termed the American 'defense perimeter' in the Pacific: *Korea was clearly left outside*. Acheson emphasized later that his words about the 'defense perimeter' echoed a speech delivered by General Douglas MacArthur on 1 March 1949.[12] Kim Il-sung was therefore encouraged to believe that in the event of war between North and South Korea the United States would not intervene.*

WHO STARTED IT?

The generally acknowledged start of the Korean War in June 1950 seems to have been a sudden dramatic escalation of fighting that was already taking place: the decisive factor was the overwhelming incursion of North Korean forces into South Korea, a circumstance that led to the massive participation of US and other allied forces and the increased involvement of the United Nations (see below) in the crisis. It is important to remember the scale of the pre-war fighting and the prevailing political atmosphere at the time.

On 4 May 1949 the South Korean forces launched an engagement at Kaesong in the region of the 38th parallel. Six infantry companies and several battalions were ordered into action against North Korean troops; in the ensuing series of battles over a four-day period, 400 North Korean and 22 South Korean soldiers were killed, and two of the six South Korean companies defected to the North. Subsequent engagements were investigated by the UN Commission on Korea (UNCOK), its delegation directed by South Korean army personnel, and blamed on the 'northern invaders'. No effort was made by the UN observers to report on the battles started by the South. In early August 1949 North Korean forces attacked South Korean army units occupying mountainous terrain just north of the 38th parallel. In two lengthy memoranda after this fighting the American ambassador in Seoul, John J. Muccio, reported that the South Korean forces on the Ongjin peninsula (just below the 38th parallel to the west) had been 'completely routed', and that 'the military were insistent that the only way to relieve pressure on Ongjin would be to drive north'. He noted that Captain Shin, the South Korean commander in the field, had decided against an immediate

---

*The apparent 'green light' shown by MacArthur and Acheson to Kim Il-sung in his contemplation of an invasion of South Korea may be compared to the analogous 'green light' offered by Glaspie and Kelly for Saddam Hussein's invasion of Kuwait on 2 August 1990 (see Geoff Simons, *Iraq: From Sumer to Saddam* (London: Macmillan 1994), pp. 311–17).

attack into the north towards Charwon, but that Prime Minister Yi Pom-sok, after a meeting with Rhee and Chiang Kai-skek, had criticised Shin for not attacking the North. The following day, Rhee told Shin that he should have attacked Charwon. There was no doubt that Syngman Rhee was enthusiastic about invading the North, fully supportive of his army commanders whose heads were 'full of ideas of recovering the North by conquest'.[13] Muccio took steps to discourage Rhee from attacking the North, but commented in early August 1949:

An aggressive, offensive spirit is emerging ... A good portion of the army is eager to get going. More and more people feel that the only way unification can be brought about is by moving north by force. I have it from Dick Johnston [a *New York Times* reporter] that Chiang Kai-shek told Rhee that the Nationalist air force could support a move north ... [14]

On 23 August South Korean naval patrol boats sailed up the Taedong river and sank four North Korean ships, and a week later Rhee again confirmed that he wanted to invade the North. On 30 September 1949 he wrote a letter to Dr Robert Oliver, his principal US advisor, in which he declared:

I feel strongly that now is the most psychological moment when we should take an aggressive measure ... We will drive some of Kim Il-sung's men to the mountain region and there we will gradually starve them out. Then our line of defense must be strengthened along the Tuman and Yalu rivers [i.e. the Sino-Korean border].[15]

In early 1950, Rhee announced that he was prepared 'to unify our territory by ourselves', even if this meant 'bloodshed and civil strife'. In March he made a radio broadcast to North Korea that the hour of their liberation had arrived; and after Rhee's decisive defeat in the May election he declared that he was ready to 'take Pyongyang within a few days'.[16] Through this period the South Korean forces had started more battles than had the North, according to Brigadier-General William Roberts, the chief of the US Korean Military Advisory Group (KMAG); and, according to MacArthur's intelligence chief, Charles A. Willoughby, at the time of the start of the Korean War 'the entire ROK army had been alerted for weeks and was in position along the 38th parallel'.[17] Rhee's wish to unite North and South Korea by force is well documented, as is his constant urging of the UN forces to march north during the war so that the whole of the peninsula could be united under his rule.[18]

In the prelude to the outbreak of war, there had been considerable military build-up in South Korea (as indeed in the North), a circumstance that is often ignored in Western sources. In the spring of 1948 the United States increased the level of military aid; and in August 1948 a conscription law was introduced to swell the ranks of the army. Military aircraft and other equipment were acquired from Canada, the United States and elsewhere, while the US expanded the air bases in Kimbo, Suwon, Kwangju, Taegu and Cheju Island. South Korean army officers were trained by US army personnel; and the entire South Korean forces were developed and supervised by US officers attached to KMAG (MacArthur dubbed the South Korean forces the 'best army in Asia'). On 30 December 1949 Syngman Rhee announced at a press conference that 'in the coming year we will strive as one to regain our lost territory ... We must remember that next year we should unify north and south Korea by our own strength'. At the same time there was growing talk among the officers of the South Korean army about the forthcoming 'northward expedition'.[19] In one pro-communist account MacArthur called Syngman Rhee to Tokyo in February 1950 to issue him with an eleven-point plan for the launching of the war against the North; a principal feature was to be the involvement of Japan as a base and supplier of munitions for the war. To this end, MacArthur advised Rhee to consult with the Japanese Prime Minister Yoshida about the 'normalisation of the ROK–Japan relations'.[20] (In fact there was very substantial Japanese involvement in the Korean War. The US military occupation of Japan after the Second World War had set about rebuilding the munitions industries for its own purposes; Japanese mercenaries fought in Korea; and Yoshida could be relied upon to support the growing military posture of the United States.[21])

In April 1950 a US State Department official, the Ambassador-at-large Philip C. Jessup, reported the 'constant fighting between the South Korean Army and bands that infiltrate the country from the North'. These were 'very real battles, involving perhaps one or two thousand men'; at the boundary 'you see troop movements, fortifications, and prisoners of war'.[22] In this context the question of who started the Korean War takes on a new meaning: there were continuous hostilities with aggressive initiatives launched from both sides (i.e. there was no sudden outbreak of war). In the North Korean version of events, the overwhelming invasion of the South was provoked by two days of artillery bombardment from the South Korean army as a prelude to a sudden surprise attack against the North Korean town of Haeju and other northern locations. It is useful to quote a North Korean source (not with any assumption of its veracity but to indicate an alternative version to that taken as axiomatic in most Western sources):

The US imperialists and the Syngman Rhee clique eventually provoked an aggressive war against the DPRK [the Democratic People's Republic of Korea] on June 25, 1950. The puppet army launched an attack at dawn all along the 38th parallel, intruding one–two kilometres deep in the territory of the northern half in the direction of Haeju, Kumchon and Cholwen [Charwon].

In the western sector of the front the 17th Regiment of the puppet Metropolitan Division came attacking in the directions of Taetan and Pyoksong, the First Infantry Division in three directions from the Kaesong area, and the 7th Infantry Division in the direction of the Ryonchon area.

In the eastern sector of the front the 6th Infantry Division of the puppet army came rushing in the directions of Hwachon and Yanggu, and the 8th Infantry Division from three directions towards Yangyang on the east coast.[23]

In fact there are some pro-Western sources that go some way to confirming this version of the outbreak of full-scale war. Thus at MacArthur's headquarters in Tokyo 'one of the important members of the occupation was called unexpectedly to the telephone. He came back and whispered. "A big story has just broken. The South Koreans have just attacked North Korea!"'[24] And Secretary of State Acheson 'never was quite sure that Rhee did not provoke the Red attack of 1950'.[25] It is of interest also that on 26 June the South Korean Office of Public Information announced that South Korean forces had in fact captured the northern town of Haeju, an event that the South Korean government later denied had ever taken place. Despite what the West has always claimed was a devastating surprise invasion, various reports did in fact confirm that the South Korean forces had taken Haeju at the start of the war.[26] Reports from US military intelligence suggested that it was South Korean forces that had attacked first.[27]

The aggressive intentions of Syngman Rhee towards North Korea were well known, copiously documented, and often an embarrassment to the United States government and the US military authorities in South Korea. The North too was equally interested in the possibility of reunification, though necessarily its interpretation of events was somewhat different to those emanating from Washington or Seoul. It would however be a mistake to assume a simple parity of pro-war rhetoric in the South and the North: even the usual anti-communist sources cite few rantings from Kim Il-sung to match those of Syngman Rhee and his bellicose supporters. Statements emanating from Pyongyang allow for the possibility of a militant (or military) reunification, but the temper is different to that of Rhee; and emphasis is sometimes given to the need for a *peaceful* reunification.

On 28 June 1949 the Democratic Front for the Attainment of the Unification of the Fatherland was established at Pyongyang, its aim being to lead the 'southern strategy'. The main points included: to struggle for the immediate withdrawal of American troops from southern Korea, and for the departure of the UN Commission; and to mobilise all forces of the people to struggle for the speedy unification of the country.[28] This is not an unambiguous recipe for military intervention from the North: the people whose forces are to be organised are essentially those of the South. Thus on 30 June 1949 the Democratic Front proposed that a 'peaceful unification must be effected by the Korean people themselves' via the mechanism of simultaneous elections in South and North Korea to a single supreme legislature for the whole country: 'This legislative organ is to adopt the constitution of the Korean Republic and form a constitution on the basis of that constitution. The government would dissolve the regimes existing in South and North Korea after taking over their functions.'[29] Reunification would be on Kim Il-sung's terms but there was no overt talk here of a military conquest of South Korea.

The escalation of conflict that grew into the Korean War derived essentially from two competing ideologies in the peninsula; but, as with Vietnam in the years that followed, the war was not simply a case of North versus South. Kim Il-sung, through an authoritarian implementation of policies that were guaranteed to win a substantial measure of popular support, had secured his regime in the North;

the ubiquitous Soviet influence was not the principal factor contributing to the stability of the communist regime. By contrast, Syngman Rhee, having lived for nearly 40 years in the United States, had by 1950 alienated the bulk of the South Korean population. At the outbreak of war in June there were many people in the North who would have welcomed the collapse of the Kim Il-sung regime; a far greater proportion in the South wanted to see an end to Syngman Rhee. Before the nominal start of the Korean War there was already widespread conflict in the South.

The American aims in Korea varied between repelling 'aggression' (in what was essentially a civil war), unifying the peninsula to roll back communism from the North, protecting an unpopular but virulently anti-communist client, and securing the emergence of South Korea as an independent capitalist state. The US-created division of the peninsula – *America's Parallel* – was a response to the burgeoning Cold War and served to exacerbate its tensions thereafter. The Soviet Union was cast as the principal culprit behind the communist invasion of the south (perhaps as a prelude to a massive incursion into Western Europe). Truman, Foster Dulles, Eisenhower and others inevitably saw the escalating Korean conflict as a phase in the global strategy of monolithic communism. But, like Winston Churchill, some American observers did not think Korea was important: thus on 2 May 1950 Senator Tom Connally, Chairman of the Senate Foreign Relations Committee, said that he did not think Korea was 'very greatly important' and that it had been said before 'that Japan, Okinawa, and the Philippines make the chain of defense which is absolutely necessary'.[30] And some Americans admitted the essentially domestic character of the Korean conflict. In November 1950, despite the ideological witch-hunts in the United States and the increasingly violent American Cold War propaganda, General MacArthur was prepared to admit that he had found 'no evidence of any close connection between the Soviet Union and the North Korean aggression'.[31]

The artificial US-originated division of Korea, the repressive tyranny in the south, the US-aided suppression of legitimate southern dissent, the authoritarian northern regime, the calculations of global strategy in the burgeoning Cold War – all contributed to the Korean War. It is simplistic to suggest, as do most unreflective Western sources, that the war was caused solely by a communist invasion of South Korea.

THE CHRONOLOGY OF CONFLICT

There is an abundant literature on the Korean War (against which all other periods of Korean History appear comparatively neglected), and so there is no need to rehearse the detail here. However, it is useful to remember the broad chronology of events and the scale of the international participation in what some observers have seen as a 'small world war'.

The course of the war is generally regarded as having four broad phases (shown in Figure 6.1). In most pro-Western sources (and some anti-US accounts) the Korean War started on 25 June 1950 with the North Korean invasion of the South.* This offensive resulted in the US-led United Nations forces being pushed back to the small area around the southern port of Pusan (the so-called 'Pusan perimeter') by early September. The audacious American landings at Inchon, just south of the 38th parallel, on 15 September 1950 were entirely successful in forcing the North Korean armies into retreat and in facilitating a UN breakout from the Pusan perimeter. In November the rapid advance of the UN forces towards the Yalu river provoked a massive Chinese intervention, causing a UN retreat on all fronts and hasty UN evacuations by sea from Hungnam and Wonsan in North Korea. By 24 January 1951 the UN retreat halted north of Taejon in South Korea, whereupon UN forces commanded by General Matthew B. Ridgway began a three-month counter-offensive (25 January–21 April) until the situation stabilised around the region of the 38th parallel. Fighting continued, but now with no dramatic swings of fortune for either side, until an armistice line was agreed on 27 July 1953. A broad chronology of the war is given in Table 6.1.[32]

THE FACE OF WAR

General S. L. A. Marshall, soldier and war historian, dubbed the Korean War – in the years before Vietnam – 'the century's nastiest little war'. Marshall's 'little' war directly or indirectly involved dozens of nations, with the active participation of personnel from the world's

---

*Characteristically, Kim Il-sung led his soldiers at the front: he was wounded at the battle of Hamhung.

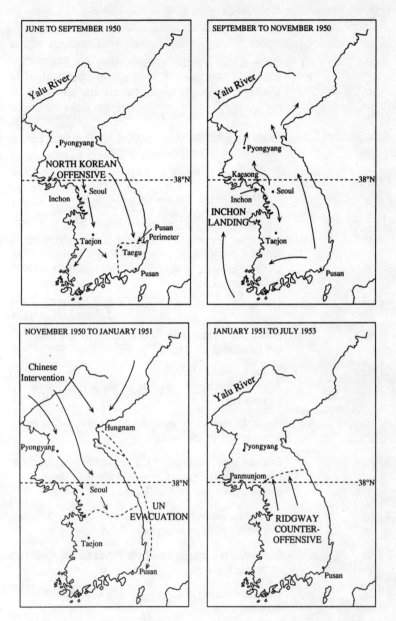

Figure 6.1　The four main phases (1950–1953) of the Korean War

Table 6.1   Chronology of the Korean War (1949–1953)

1949

4 May	South Korea launches military engagement at Kaesong; 4000 North Korean soldiers, 22 South Korean soldiers and about 100 civilians killed
June	North Korea launches attack on Ongjin peninsula
30 September	Syngman Rhee urges invasion of North Korea ('to clear up the rest of them in Pyongyang')

1950

25 June	North Korean forces (223,000-strong) under Choe Yong Gun invade South Korea; South Korean forces take Haeju and initiate other military attacks; disagreement about who first launched major assaults; North Korean forces sweep into South Korea; the United States takes various military initiatives prior to UN authorisation
25–30 June	UN Security Council, boycotted by Soviet Union (hence no veto), passes resolutions to underwrite US policy and to authorise further 'UN' actions under US command
27 June	Truman orders MacArthur to blockade North Korean coast and to provide air support to South Korean forces.
29 June	North Korean army seizes Seoul. Britain orders Far Eastern fleet to take action
30 June	Truman authorises use of US ground troops. US 24th Division under Major-General William F. Dean moves by sea and air into Korea
4 July	US troops under Lieutenant-Colonel Charles B. Smith join South Korean forces near Osan
5 July	South Korean troops and Task Force Smith routed by North Koreans
7 July	General Douglas MacArthur made Supreme UN Commander
7–21 July	More US troops (1st Cavalry and 25th Division) rushed to Korea from Japan

Table 6.1—continued

13 July	Lieutenant-General Walton H. Walker, commander of Eighth Army, given command of ground forces in Korea
18 July	Canadian Chiefs of Staff say UN Secretary General Trygve Lie, in requesting that troops be supplied for UN service in Korea, is making an appeal that is 'not authoritative'; Canadian support is later given
1 August	2nd US Infantry Division reaches Korea; Yakov Malik, Soviet delegate to the UN, ends Moscow's boycott to Security Council and takes over presidency
5 August–15 September	Lieutenant-General Walton H. Walker stabilises 'Pusan perimeter' after massive US retreat through South Korea; US 7th Fleet harasses North Korean forces along the coast; Choe's 14 infantry divisions launch unco-ordinated attacks against the perimeter; UN forces break out of Pusan area and push towards the 38th parallel
15–25 September	Major-General Edward M. Almond, under MacArthur, commands landing at Inchon 150 miles north of battlefront and west of Seoul – very successful military initiative
17 September	US forces capture Kimbo airport; cut railway and highway supplying North Koreans in the South; surround Seoul
26 September	US forces take Seoul; capture 125,000 North Korean troops
29 September	MacArthur and Syngman Rhee enter Seoul
October–December	Japanese volunteers accepted for UN combat duty; 46 Japanese vessels with 1200 former Imperial Navy personnel on combat duty in the Korean ports of Wonsan, Kunsan, Inchon, Haeju and Chinanpo; a few Japanese casualties; ships ordered home (15 December)
1 October–24 November	US forces advance to Yalu river; Mao Tse Tung orders Chinese 'Volunteers' to resist 'US imperialism'; Pyongyang falls to US troops; US divisions now incorporate other token UN forces (Turkish, Canadian, Australian, Philippine, Dutch, Thai)

Table 6.1—continued

15 October	Truman and MacArthur meet at Wake Island – later an issue in the Senate enquiry into the subsequent sacking of MacArthur
16–26 October	US forces move to east coast (Wonsan); delay while mines (sown by Soviet experts) are removed
25 October	Chinese troops fight UN forces less than 40 miles south of Yalu river
27 October	US Eighth Army advance halted by Chinese
November	Truman authorises an expansion of covert activities in the region; approves an OPC/CIA plan for the invasion of southern China using Chiang Kai-shek's remnant forces in Burma
3 November	US 25th Division pushed back from Yalu area
6 November	MacArthur condemns Chinese for 'aggression'; US troop reinforcements despatched to Korea
24 November	MacArthur launches fresh offensive (so-called 'reconnaissance in force')
25–26 November	Start of Chinese counter-offensive; 180,000 Chinese troops in 18 divisions sweep into North Korea; heavy US and Turkish losses; Eighth Army offensive halted
27 November–9 December	A force of 120,000 Chinese troops pushes south; US and South Korean forces in heavy retreat; Major-General Oliver Smith's 1st Marine Division surrounded by 8 communist divisions: decides not to retreat but 'to attack in another direction'
9 December	Relief column (3rd Division) meets marine vanguard outside Hungnam perimeter
5–15 December	Evacuation from Hungnam and Wonsan by air and by sea of 105,000 US and South Korean troops, 98,000 civilians, 350,000 tons of cargo and 17,500 vehicles; once at Pusan the evacuated X Corps becomes a strategic reserve for the Eighth Army
23 December	Walker killed in jeep accident; replaced by Lieutenant-General Matthew B. Ridgway
25 December	Chinese enter South Korea

Table 6.1—continued

1951

1–15 January	New communist offensive; 500,000 Chinese and North Korean troops push 200,000-strong US Eighth Army almost to Seoul
4 January	US forces organise hasty evacuation of Seoul; Seoul falls to communist forces – so changing hands for the third time; UN position stabilised 50 miles south of the 38th parallel
25 January– 10 February	Ridgway slowly drives north
1 February	US-drafted Security Council resolution declares China to be guilty of 'aggression'
10 February	Eighth Army retakes Inchon and Kimbo Airfield
18 February	UN troops reach outskirts of Seoul; prepare to launch 'Operation Killer'
7–31 March	UN 'Operation Ripper' relieves pressure on Seoul
15 March	US forces retake Seoul
3 April	US divisions cross 38th parallel
11 April	Truman sacks MacArthur; Ridgway takes over; General James A. Fleet rushes from United States to command Eighth Army
22–31 May	Communist spring offensive produces 70,000 communist and 7000 Eighth Army losses; UN forces advance on all fronts; approval for comprehensive 'hot pursuit' denied by US Joint Chiefs concerned by Soviet threats and mounting Free World anxieties
1–15 June	Consolidation of UN position; gains made in 'Iron Triangle' (Chorwan/Kumhwa/Pyongyang) and 'Punchbowl' (hill circle north-west of Sohwa)
23 June	Soviet ceasefire proposal; communist losses estimated at 200,000
10 July	Armistice talks start at Kaesong

Table 6.1—continued

August–November	Communists suspend negotiations after UN violation of neutral zone at Kaesong; UN attacks resume; Chinese driven from Iron Triangle and Punchbowl; communists propose fresh talks
25 October	Fresh peace talks begin at Panmunjom (village at 38th parallel)
November–December	US proposes demarcation line, provided other truce issues are settled within 30 days; US ground actions continue; 30-day limit expires on 27 November, so agreed line is invalidated

1952

January–April	Screening of PoWs; disorder erupts in prison camps; minor actions flare up along the front during protracted Panmunjom negotiations; communists and UN build up their forces; now estimated 800,000 communist troops (three quarters of them Chinese) in Korea
2 May	UN proposals on voluntary repatriation of prisoners rejected by communists
7–11 May	PoWs at Joje-do hold General Dodd hostage; UN and communists both announce stalemate over PoW issue
12 May	Ridgway succeeded by General Mark Clark
23 June	US bombers attack Yalu river power installations
29 August	Massive bombing attack, the heaviest of the war, launched against Pyongyang.
8 October	Panmunjom talks break down on the PoW issue; indefinite recess announced; 'Korean question' becomes a political football in the US presidential election
24 October	Eisenhower promises an honourable end to the Korean conflict if he is elected
4 November	Eisenhower elected President
10 November	Two new divisions and six regiments mobilised in South Korea
5–7 December	Eisenhower visits US forces in Korea

Table 6.1—continued

1953 February	General Maxwell D. Taylor takes command of Eighth Army; Clark proposes exchange of sick and wounded prisoners
28 March	Kim Il-sung and Peng Teh-huai (now commanding Chinese 'volunteers') agree Clark's proposals; continuing uncertainty in the communist world following the death of Stalin (5 March)
20 April	Beginning of 'Operation Little Switch': exchange of 5800 communists for 471 South Koreans, 149 Americans and 64 other UN personnel
26 April	Restart of peace talks
20 May	South Korean government threatens extension of air and ground operations to China, and intensification of military activity in Korea; Syngman Rhee refuses to agree any settlement that leaves Korea divided; urges resumption of military offensive against the North
28 May	Chinese launch attacks against US 25th Division outposts
8–17 June	PoW question resolved; Syngman Rhee releases 27,000 North Korean PoWs 'unwilling to be repatriated'
10–31 June	New Chinese offensive against South Korean troops – intended to bring US pressure on intransigent Rhee; US introduces reinforcements to buttress South Korea; 70,000 Chinese losses
10 July	Talks resume after US assures communists that Rhee will not be allowed to block progress; armistice finally agreed
27 July	Armistice signed at Panmunjom: confirms the existing battle line as a *de facto* boundary, and the exchange of prisoners – 77,000 communists against 12,700 UN personnel, including 3597 Americans and 945 Britons

most powerful states (the US, the Soviet Union, China, Britain, Japan and others), rendering the Korean conflict one of the few truly international conflagrations, a world war. Moreover, the Korean War produced perhaps four million dead with countless more men, women and children mutilated, starved and traumatised. Most of the sources offer token figures for troop and civilian casualties but there is rarely any attempt to convey what the Korean War signified in human terms.

The conflict escalated into a genocidal enterprise because of the arrogance of power, the 'impetuous desire to extend the universal relevance of the American way of life ... it was assumed that Koreans would welcome the opportunity to be tutored by Americans'.[33] And if the slaughter extended, as a necessary condition for such tutoring, to around two million North Korean civilians then such hapless victims would not be overly concerned. For, as General Curtis LeMay was keen to explain in his autobiography, the prodigious US bombardments of Asians in Korea sometimes failed because 'Human attrition means nothing to such people'; their earthly Asian lives are so miserable that they look forward to a death which promises them 'everything from tea-parties with long dead grandfathers down to their pick of all the golden little dancing girls in Paradise'. No matter that LeMay, with monumental cultural ignorance, confuses Confucianism or Buddhism with Islam; it is almost a favour to exterminate people in their own country by means of napalm or fire-storms. Nor of course does Western cultural arrogance stop with the American tutors of the world. In one source there is a remarkable collocation of British views on Asiatics in general and Koreans in particular. Here we learn that the Korean character is 'feckless and irresponsible', that hatred is 'endemic in the Koreans as in all Asiatics of Mongol stock', that Koreans are a 'sorry, contemptible and dishonest' bunch, that cruelty was an essential part of the Korean tradition, that the citizens of Seoul were willing to accept any government that would allow them to 'continue their socially anarchical lives', that 'Koreans are the thievingest people ... of all time', and that it is 'hard to believe ... that they will ever be able successfully to govern themselves'.[34] In such a culturally purblind atmosphere, with all the implied racist overtones, there were few restraints on the range of methods used by the world's most powerful state to prosecute a virtuous war.

Many different types of weapons were employed but none attracted such odium as napalm, widely used as an improved incendiary device. The first napalm patent, an American invention, was applied for on 1 November 1943; and the weapon was thereafter

used against the Germans to support the D-Day invasion, and in
massive quantities against the Japanese. The Korean War provided a
fresh opportunity to test napalm and related products on a sustained
and widespread basis. The effects of napalm are well known. The
substance is spread in clumps of burning jelly at temperatures ex-
ceeding 800°C, and in its 'improved' versions it cannot easily be
removed from human flesh. The results include deep burning, local
thrombosis, necrosis, pulmonary damage, heatstroke, oxygen starvation, carbon monoxide poisoning and infection–with varying
degrees of scarring and disability in survivors.[35] Napalm and white
phosphorus weapons (particles of the latter burn in human flesh for
hours or even days) were extensively used by the American forces in
Korea against both military and civilian targets.

Area bombing was used against towns and cities throughout North
Korea to the point that in whole provinces scarcely a building remained standing. Pyongyang itself was almost entirely destroyed by
incendiaries: tens of thousands of civilians were immolated in fire-
storms reminiscent of the fire-bombing of Japanese cities in the
Second World War. In early May 1953, American bombers attacked
hydroelectric power plants and dams on the Yalu river, creating
floods that swamped 27 miles of farmland. A subsequent analysis
published in the American journal *Air University Quarterly Review*
commented: 'to the Communists the smashing of the dams meant primarily the destruction of their chief sustenance – rice. The Westerner
can little conceive the awesome meaning which the loss of this staple
food commodity has for the Asian – starvation and slow death.'[36]
According to Seymour Hersh (*Kissinger*, 1983, p. 52), this was the
first deliberate bombing of irrigation targets since Hitler's Luftwaffe
destroyed dikes and dams in Holland in the Second World War.*

By the middle of 1952, American bombers were attacking power
plants, factories, bridges and roads throughout the north. On 23–24
June a dozen power plants were hit, with major industrial complexes
subsequently destroyed in the regions of Sindok, Kilchu and
Pyongyang. In September, aircraft flying from the carriers *Essex,
Princeton* and *Boxer* completely destroyed the major oil refinery at
Aoji. And despite the massive impact of 'conventional' weapons on

---

*The RAF 'dambuster' raids (17 May 1943) on the Moehne and Eder
dams were intended as a strike against German industrial potential: the
raids caused widespread agricultural damage.

a relatively small country, serious consideration was given to the possible use of atomic bombs. MacArthur had urged Eisenhower, while still President-elect, to adopt this option, and Eisenhower later acknowledged that 'to keep the attack from becoming overly costly, it was clear that we would have to use atomic weapons'.[37] However, there were problems with the allies. When President Truman had revealed in December 1950 that the US was considering the use of nuclear weapons, the British premier, Clement Attlee, had rushed to Washington to dissuade him. But to Eisenhower such difficulties were not insuperable:

> American views have always differed somewhat from those of some of our allies. For the British, for example, the use of atomic weapons in war at that time would have been a decision of the gravest kind ... an American decision to use them at that time would have created some disrupting feelings between ourselves and our allies. However, if an all-out offensive should be highly successful, I felt that the rifts so caused could, in time, be repaired.[38]

There were considerations of a weightier kind: the then small stockpile of American nuclear weapons was earmarked entirely for the European theatre, especially the Soviet Union, and perhaps atomic bombs were strategic rather than tactical weapons.[39] (In September 1966, Eisenhower commented on television: 'We'd have won the war in a week if we had used them.' Atomic bombs should not be used against Russia, since Russia could hit back, but that does not mean that 'in sticky situations you couldn't use a proper kind of nuclear weapon sometime'. He did not 'see any difference between gas warfare and this kind of warfare' and urged the Free World not to fear using atomic bombs 'in some outlying place where people or life seems to be cheap, and they want to have their way'.[40])

Atomic weapons were not used in Korea but there were ample horrors without them. Western reporters witnessed atrocities committed against North Korean prisoners of war, and filed graphic accounts that sometimes led to censorship problems back home. Reginald Thompson of the British *Daily Telegraph*, critical of MacArthur's 'assumption of a kind of divinity', became increasingly sceptical of the motives of the allied high command; as indeed did such other British journalists as Ian Morrison (*The Times*), James Cameron (*Picture Post*) and Rene Cutforth (BBC). Such men witnessed and reported the beating up of suspects, the torture of prisoners of war, the taping of thumbs to the terminals of field telephones, the execution of unarmed civilians by South Korean marines. At the village of Boopyung near Seoul, 290 men, women and children were crammed into six police cells, each measuring eight feet by sixteen, and left there for three weeks; on another occasion a North Korean soldier was crucified. The response of the UN high command, seemingly indifferent to the horrors being committed in its name, was to intensify the level of censorship and news control.[41] The French journalist Jean Larteguy, in the same spirit of independent witness, reported the results of an American napalm attack: 'The Chinese had not had time to dig any foxholes ... their charred bodies lay strewn upon the ground by the thousands and thousands ... bodies hideously twisted and commencing to decompose, the stink of rotting flesh.'[42] And there was the inevitable impact of the dollar in the hands of American soldiers far from home: 'In that city of Seoul, three-quarters destroyed, everything was up for sale. The GIs came in from the front and threw themselves with their dollars upon everything alcoholic or female,* placing a premium on the market in schoolgirls . . . .'[43]

In the terrible equation of war, the allied prisoners in North Korea and elsewhere were similarly brutalised, tortured and starved. American prisoners of war, it later emerged, had been surprisingly willing to collaborate with their communist jailors: some 70 per cent of the 7190 US prisoners held captive in China either made confessions or signed petitions demanding an end to the war.[44] The behaviour of the American soldiers contrasted poorly with that of the British, Australian, Turkish and other UN troops who do not appear to have been treated any more kindly that the US prisoners. Only 5 per cent of the American prisoners steadfastly resisted

---

*The American debauching of Korean women and girls began before the Korean War and has continued up to the present. Thus Saundra Sturdevant and Brenda Stoltzfus (*Let the Good Times Roll: Prostitution and the US military in Asia*, The New Press, New York, 1992) declare: 'one element in the Korean–American relationship has been constant: the continuous subordination of one generation after another to the sexual servicing of American males ... If someone dares call attention to the ceaseless orgy, all the usual bromides pour forth to drown out the faint cries of peasant girls yanked off a train in Seoul and thrown into a brothel, a thousand little justifications for the debasement of a thousand little girls at American hands ... Kidnapped, gang-raped and beaten by pimps while learning their few necessary words of English, they were ready for the street in a week.'

Chinese pressure, and – even more surprising – many stuck by their confessions when they returned to the United States. The official US explanation was that somehow the American troops had been 'brainwashed'. Only this, it was argued, could explain the extent of the collaboration, the persistence of the anti-West feelings, and the bizarre character of some of the allegations made by US troops against their own country: for example, that the American forces in Korea had resorted to bacteriological warfare, a charge later investigated by the UN General Assembly (see below).

The greatest number of casualties in the Korean War were suffered by the Chinese and the North Koreans. The estimates vary. It has been suggested that more than two million North Korean civilians died and about 500,000 North Korean soldiers. The lowest estimates for the number of Chinese dead are around half a million, with the highest putting the figure at three million. About a million South Korean civilians were killed; 415,000 South Korean troops died; and 429,000 were wounded. American deaths have been reckoned at 54,246, of which 33,629 were 'battle deaths'; a further 105,785 US soldiers were wounded. Of 10,218 American troops who were captured, only 3746 returned home: 21 refused repatriation and the rest died. The British Commonwealth – Britain, Canada, Australia and New Zealand – suffered 1263 killed and 4817 wounded. Belgium, France, Greece, Holland, Turkey, Columbia, Ethiopia, the Philippines and Thailand together suffered 1800 killed and 7000 wounded; half these casualties were Turks. There were also a few Japanese and Soviet casualties.

The war had produced perhaps ten million dead and wounded; and massive damage to the civil infrastructure of the entire peninsula. Nothing had been accomplished: the eventually agreed *de facto* border between North and South Korea was little different to the original partition drawn by the United States. But the fires of the Cold War had been stoked, the US was now back on a war footing, and the French colonialists were having problems in Indochina. Vietnam would be next.

THE UN ROLE

The decision to involve the United Nations in the affairs of Korea was not a UN initiative; it was a decision of the United States. The

United Nations Organisation, substantially funded by Rockefeller money, had been created a mere two years before as a successor to the now defunct League of Nations. American officials – among them the later defamed Alger Hiss – had drafted the UN Charter; the site of the UN headquarters had been established in New York, the new centre of world power in the pivotal shift from Europe; and US dominance of the United Nations, in both the Security Council and the General Assembly, was unchallenged. Washington calculated that UN involvement in the 'Korea question' would be helpful to American strategic interests. Trygve Lie, the first UN Secretary General, acknowledged that it was the United States that brought the Korean problem to the United Nations.[45]

A principal US interest was the reunification of Korea under a government that was broadly sympathetic to the West. Having provided Moscow with a route into North Korea as a tactical gambit in the Second World War, the Soviet presence in the Korean peninsula was now an embarrassment to Washington. Talks with Moscow had accomplished nothing, and so on 17 September 1947 the US State Department informed the Soviet government that it intended to refer the Korean question to the UN General Assembly (in which the United States was guaranteed overwhelming support). Despite Soviet opposition, the General Assembly voted 41 to 6 (with 7 abstentions) to refer the Korean question for committee consideration and report. Moscow countered by proposing that all foreign troops be withdrawn from the Korean peninsula to enable the Korean people to settle their own affairs. The Soviet proposal embarrassed both Washington and the Korean rightists: they had both recommended that foreign troops withdraw, but now knew that without the protection of US forces the repressive southern regime would quickly collapse – and so the Soviet proposal, one that would have prevented the Korean War, was blocked by Washington.

On 14 November 1947 the General Assembly predictably adopted an American resolution (43 to 9, with 6 abstentions) for the creation of a UN Temporary Commission on Korea (UNTCOK) for the supervision of nationwide elections and the guidance of the elected representatives. Without Soviet support, there was no prospect that UNTCOK would be able to involve North Korea in the plan. Washington therefore decided that UNTCOK would proceed with its programme for elections, but that these would unavoidably take place only in South Korea – a decision that induced the North to set up its own government and so to consolidate the division of the peninsula. The Korean communists branded UNTCOK 'a puppet consisting of the henchmen of American imperialism whose object is to make a colony of Korea',[46] opposed the rigged elections (10 May 1948) in the South, ran their own nationwide elections in parallel, and created a northern government that included a substantial number of southern representatives (see Chapter 5). UNTCOK predictably concluded – on the basis of reports from a handful of observers directed by the US military and the South Korean army – that the elections were free and fair, a reasonable reflection of the democratic will. The UN General Assembly voted to accept UNTCOK's conclusion and the tyrant Rhee was duly installed in South Korea as an American puppet. On 9 September 1948, Kim Il-sung was formally installed as the Prime Minister of the newly-formed Democratic People's Republic of Korea; on 12 October the Soviet Union recognised the new North Korean regime. The US-contrived division of the peninsula was now consolidated: Washington had succeeded in preventing the unification of the Korean people under popular rule.

What should properly be seen as the sudden escalation (rather than the outbreak) of the Korean War on 25 June 1950, with the over-whelming sweep of Kim Il-sung's armies into South Korea, brought an immediate American response. The first thought was how to offer military resistance to what was assumed to be a Soviet-inspired aggression.[47] It is now generally conceded that the United States took military action *before* UN authorisation had been given; and that, with or without UN support, Washington was determined to act in support of its perceived strategic interests. Thus Roy Jenkins (now Lord Jenkins of Hillhead) acknowledges that Truman 'authorized United States naval and air action sixteen hours in advance of the second UN resolution which gave him the authority of international legality'.[48] In a similar vein, Bernard Brodie, a former professor of international relations at Yale University and later a professor of political science at the University of California, points out that Truman 'committed the United States to air and naval intervention *before* the UN Security Council was able to take any action'[49] (original italics). Brodie points out that some writers have been confused by the fact that 25 June in Washington and New York is about a day later than 25 June in Korea: 'Thus, the UN Security Council meeting of June 25 occurred the day after the attack.'[50]

It is important also to remember that the first Security Council resolution, Resolution 82 (25 June 1950), in response to the North

Korean 'aggression' made no reference to UN military action (see Appendix 6). By the time Resolution 83 (27 June 1950) called for 'urgent military measures', Truman had already implemented the military recommendations presented to him by Dean Acheson on behalf of the State and Defense Departments.[51] This means that Truman took military action without UN authorisation; indeed, considering Brodie (above), in the absence of *any* Security Council resolution (even 82, in which 'every assistance' cannot be taken to mean *military* assistance, or there would have been no need for 83). By the time Resolution 84 (7 July 1950) requested the United States 'to designate the commander' of the UN forces, the Security Council was merely underwriting military initiatives already taken by Washington. Throughout the period of the UN's involvement in Korea the international organisation was manipulated by the United States in the interests of American foreign policy (see 'The Korean Paradigm', below).

Such considerations are important because they show the extent to which the UN involvement in the Korean war was a legitimate 'police action', and the extent to which the United Nations was suborned to serve Washington's strategic calculations. In fact it is clear that the United States used the UN as a tool of American foreign policy where the containment of communism in the burgeoning Cold War was the primary consideration. From a Western perspective such a ploy may or may not have been legitimate but it was clearly not motivated primarily by any general unacceptability of aggression in violation of the UN Charter. Then, as now, Washington was keen to discriminate between aggressions that were acceptable and those that were not. That the United States was interested more in the containment of communism than in the UN Charter is shown by the fact that Washington would have waged the Korean War whether or not the United Nations had sanctioned American policy. Thus Truman declared in a memorandum (19 July 1950) to Dean Acheson that had he [Acheson] 'not acted promptly' in involving the United Nations, 'we would have had to go into Korea alone'.[52] Then, as now, Washington considered American obligations under the UN Charter a secondary consideration. The primary concern was that 'the United States might invoke the moral support of the United Nations for such resorts to force as it might find necessary and desirable in the course of its cold war struggles'.[53]

As with more recent conflicts (Somalia, Iraq, Haiti, and so on) in which American forces have acted with nominal UN sanction, in Korea there were no UN constraints on American military initiatives.

The 'UN' war in Korea was run by the United States, and when General MacArthur exceeded his nominal UN remit he was disciplined not by UN Secretary General Trygve Lie or any other UN official but by Truman. The United Nations *per se* had nothing to do with the conduct of the Korean War. The General Assembly did however concern itself briefly with allegations that the UN (i.e. US) forces had used bacterial warfare in prosecuting their military aims. Thus in a letter (20 October 1952) addressed to the UN Secretary General the United States requested that the item 'Question of impartial investigation of charges of use by United Nations forces of bacteriological warfare' be placed on the agenda of the Seventh Session of the General Assembly. The United States denied the charges, made by the Soviet bloc, while the Soviet Union vetoed the offer of the International Committee of the Red Cross and the World Health Organization to assist in investigating the charges.

The item was considered in the second part of the Seventh Session of the General Assembly (between 27 March and 8 April 1953). Various documents were circulated to the examining committee: a cablegram (24 October 1952) from the DPRK Minister of Foreign Affairs to the President of the General Assembly, alleging the use of 'bacterial weapons' by 'the American interventionists' in North Korea; a cablegram (27 October 1952) from China's Foreign Minister, requesting participation in the debate; a letter (5 March 1953) from the Soviet delegation, forwarding statements by captured US Air Force officers (including Colonel F. H. Schwable and Major Roy H. Bley), describing the American use of bacterial weapons in Korea; and a note (27 March 1953) from the US representative, transmitting denial by members of the US armed forces in Korea of the confessions of Schwable and Bley. In the event the Assembly deliberations were inconclusive. The various participants predictably divided along bloc lines: the Soviet case was damaged by its veto of an independent enquiry, while the Schwable and Bley 'confessions' were widely discounted as resulting from coercion or 'brainwashing'. However, the status and efficacy of brainwashing have never been conclusively established. A US army report (that commented in passing that 'communists live like animals all their lives') declared: 'The prisoners, as far as Army psychiatrists have been able to discover, were not subjected to anything that could properly be called brainwashing. Indeed, the Communist treatment of prisoners, while it came nowhere near fulfilling the requirements of the Geneva Convention, rarely involved outright cruelty ... .'[54] At the same time the report claimed that a few American airmen were physically abused in an attempt to extract 'confessions' about germ warfare. The efforts of the UN General Assembly to establish the truth of the matter were inevitably hampered by the predictable bloc loyalties of all the interested members.

The United Nations was involved also in the protracted armistice talks; and with the question – raised several times between 1949 and 1991 – of UN membership being granted to North and South Korea as independent sovereign states. The armistice talks, conducted between the United Nations Command (essentially a US delegation) and the Chinese/North Korean representatives, dealt with such matters as the exchange of sick and wounded, the repatriation of all prisoners of war, peace safeguards, and economic and relief assistance to the war-ravaged regions. The United Nations Commission for the Unification and Rehabilitation of Korea (UNCURK) submitted various reports and recommendations, though by now it was clear to everyone that North and South Korea were consolidated as separate independent states with unambiguous loyalties and allegiances in the Cold War. The United Nations Korean Reconstruction Agency (UNKRA) submitted reports to the Economic and Social Council on the question of relief and rehabilitation; and associated schemes were initiated by such UN bodies as the World Health Organization (WHO), the Food and Agriculture Organization (FAO), and the United Nations Educational, Scientific and Cultural Organization (UNESCO). In its 462nd to 467th plenary meetings (30 November–3 December 1953), the General Assembly considered a US charge (letter, 30 October) of North Korean and Chinese atrocities committed against UN prisoners of war. On 3 December 1953 a joint draft resolution (A/L. 169), adopted by roll-call vote of 42 to 5 with 10 abstentions, expressed the Assembly's 'grave concern at reports and information' that the communist forces had 'employed inhuman practices against the heroic soldiers' of the UN forces 'and against the civilian population of Korea'; and condemned such acts as a violation of international law and the basic standards of morality. The charges, probably soundly based, were devalued by the partisan interests of the accusers; as with the accusations that the American forces had used germ warfare.

The question of the UN membership of either of the two Koreas was first brought to the United Nations when Nationalist China submitted a draft resolution (S/1305) for the admission of South Korea. Since the Republic of Korea was 'a peace-loving State' which was 'able and willing to carry out obligations contained in the Charter', the resolution recommended to the General Assembly that the Republic of Korea be admitted to membership of the United Nations. The Soviet Union vetoed the resolution on the ground that the Korean People's Democratic Republic (North Korea) had a government 'set up on the basis of all-Korean elections in August 1948 elections that had been based on equal universal and direct ballots'. A Soviet proposal for the admission of the Korean People's Democratic Republic was blocked by the United States with support from Britain and other countries. The Soviet Union again vetoed the admission of South Korea on 13 December 1955 and on 9 September 1957.

Now the Soviet Union was prepared to agree to the admission of South Korea, provided that North Korea was admitted at the same time. When the United States and its Western allies blocked this suggestion, the Soviet Union again used its veto on 9 December 1958 to prevent the admission of South Korea. The Soviet representative argued that the admission of both Koreas would help to promote contacts between the two, and so prepare the way for 'reunification on a peaceful and democratic basis'. When the West rejected this idea, the admission of South Korea was again blocked by the Soviet Union.

North Korea for a time suggested that both Koreas join the United Nations as a single entity, so overcoming the Korean division at a single stroke. South Korea predictably opposed this unworkable idea, and in 1991 made a unilateral bid for admission. When it emerged that neither China nor Russia was now prepared to veto the Seoul application, North Korea announced that it too would now apply for membership on the assumption that Washington would not use its veto. In Autumn 1991 both the Korean states were granted UN membership. The Korean division, hateful to most Koreans, had been further consolidated.

THE KOREAN PARADIGM

The American success in securing the three war resolutions (Resolutions 82, 83 and 84; see Appendix 6) as a means of reinforcing US foreign policy in the Cold War was achieved only because the Soviet Union, angry that Communist China was not allowed to take its proper seat in the Security Council, was temporarily boycotting the Council. This circumstance (dubbed 'adventitious' by Brodie, *War and Politics*, p. 60) meant that there was no chance of a Soviet veto in the Security Council at the outbreak of the Korean War: Yakov Malik, the Soviet UN ambassador, had been instructed to stay away and so, with rare freedom of action, Washington was able to draft resolutions and guarantee their passage through the Council.

Hence what the outbreak of the Korean War had in common with the 1990s disputes over Iraq, Libya, Somalia, Haiti and others was the absence of a veto threat to American initiatives in the Security Council. The Council, as the virtual executive of the United Nations, has always enshrined immense potential power, constrained only by the threat of the veto. Today – with Russia reluctant to veto the United States – the absence of a veto threat (as in June–July 1950) puts vast power in the hands of the dominant states in the Council: that is, in the hands of the United States. This is why the Korean example serves as an effective paradigm for the interpretation of US foreign policy initiatives in the 1990s. From the 'Korean Paradigm' it is possible to extract a broad multiphase agenda that has shaped American policy-making in the so-called New World Order:

1. Washington becomes aware of a significant event in the world. The event may be well publicised and known to the world community; or it may only be known to the recipients of intelligence information derived from human assets, satellite systems or other sources.

2. Washington estimates the strategic importance of the event. The analysis will only rarely have to begin from scratch; in most cases the new information will be injected into an established policy assessment framework.

3. Depending on the results of the rapid strategic analysis, Washington moves into action on whatever fronts are appropriate. There will almost certainly be propaganda initiatives to massage the information for wider consumption by both domestic and foreign audiences. Allies will be contacted 'to keep them on board'; and military forces may be mobilised. At the same time various approaches will be made to the United Nations, with focus on both the rotating and permanent members of the Security Council.

4. The United Nations (primarily the Council) is activated, but only in circumstances where its conclusions and decisions can be suitably manipulated. If the Security Council cannot be relied upon, then Washington will act anyway. It acted on Korea *before* it had UN authorisation; and it invaded Grenada and Panama, without the smokescreen of UN approval because it could not rely on a Security Council vote on those issues.

5. The UN, following the manipulated vote of affirmation, is enlisted for sanctions initiatives, military intervention or other measures judged helpful to American foreign policy interests. The UN is, however, always kept in its place. Inconvenient Articles of the UN Charter (for example, Articles 2(7), 19, 45, 47 and others) are ignored; any deployed US forces under nominal UN authorisation are kept under American command; and the UN Secretary General is either enlisted or side-stepped.

6. The political, military and strategic gains for the US are consolidated. Military bases may be established and puppet regimes reinforced. Commercial contractors are given fresh opportunities. The propaganda continues. When US spokespersons describe the events for the benefit of domestic audiences they talk about the 'American victory', of the 'US successes'; when they intend their comments to have an international flavour they talk about 'UN forces', 'the international community' and 'UN peacekeeping'.

This does not mean that each phase of the agenda is always given the same emphasis, or that the necessary activities and operations are invariably conducted with skill. Indeed, some American critics have argued that the Korean War itself was a massive failure for the United States: aiding the consolidation of communism, showing that the 'paper tiger' US could not even defeat North Korea, sacrificing tens of thousands of American lives and billions of dollars, and demonstrating that even in the temporary absence of the Soviet Union from the Security Council the United States could not achieve victory in its UN enterprise.[55] But from another perspective, the US secured an unpopular capitalist state on the Korean peninsula, boosted the American arms industry (so pleasing the industrial/military friends of government), rebuilt the industrial power of capitalist Japan to aid the containment of communism, and gave notice that US military intervention would threaten further popular revolutions in the Third World.

The significance of the 'Korean Paradigm' is not that the American performance in Korea was an undiluted success, the triumphant implementation of a precise strategic programme. What is important is that the Paradigm illuminates many New World Order conflicts in which Washington has acted to defend national interest. The plan that the United States developed to confront what was essentially a Third World civil war has been used to deal with events of interest to Washington following the collapse of the Soviet Union.[56]

7 The Aftermath

THE AFTERMATH OF WAR

The Korean people, little favoured by their geographical situation, have too often been forced to live in anticipation of war, with war itself, and in the fearful desolation of its aftermath. Throughout history the great powers of the time, with overweening imperial ambition and scant regard for indigenous communities, have contested the Korean peninsula, much as many other accessible states throughout the world have been trampled by giants. For the last 40 years, Korea, in the shape of two increasingly sovereign states, has managed to build a measure of independence; though half the peninsula still harbours a substantial foreign military presence, and national sovereignty *per se* is never a sufficient guarantee of domestic human rights. Today the two Koreas, like all states, are shaped by history and the current strategic perceptions of external powers.

The Korean War gave fresh scope for the consolidation of ideological divisions set to endure over subsequent decades, and for a scale of repression lubricated mainly by American intervention. Thus in retaking Seoul and restoring Syngman Rhee to power by September 1950, the United States set the scene for a fresh wave of repression: a US embassy official reported that 'probably more than 100,000 people' were killed when the Rhee regime was re-established by MacArthur, many more than the maximum US claim for the number of people murdered by the communists in the whole of Korea for the entire war.[1] After this spate of Rhee-inspired massacres, the killings continued in the months and years that followed. One particular mass execution, typical of many, was widely reported in the Western press and universally accepted as having been carried out by the US-protected Rhee forces: in February 1951 in Kochang in South Korea some 600 men, women and children were driven into a ditch and mown down by machine-gun fire.[2] It is facts such as these that helped to shape the subsequent tyrannies in the South, the authoritarianism of the North, and the solid ideological divide between the two.

The war had other consequences, some rarely advertised. For example, the United States, already reluctant to punish Nazi war criminals from the Second World War, now found fresh reasons to ignore crimes against humanity committed by torturers and mass murderers who were reliably anti-communist. Thus following the outbreak of the Korean War, John McCloy, the US High Commissioner for Germany, moved to secure the release of 79 major Nazi war criminals already tried and found guilty of the murder of at least two million people. The Nazi beneficiaries of US policy included all the concentration camp doctors, the top judges who had administered the 'special courts', *Einsatzgruppen* murderers, and convicted slave-labour criminals. Fritz Ter Meer, the convicted I. G. Farben criminal, commented upon his early release from the Landsberg prison near Munich: 'Now that they have Korea on their hands, the Americans are a lot more friendly.'[3]

The ideological significance of the Korean War was never in doubt: it was essentially a Cold War eruption fuelled by an American intervention designed to prevent a popular revolution. But the extent of the ideological conflict was not widely known at the time. In order to achieve the required Security Council resolutions (Appendix 6) for the underwriting of US policy, the Americans had frightened other Council members with propaganda about tanks manned by Russians invading South Korea. Because of this 'quite erroneous'[4] information, France and Egypt changed their views and then supported the United States in the Security Council: Washington had lied about Russian involvement in order to muster the necessary Council majority. However, during the later phases of the war there *was* Russian involvement; for example, when American and Soviet aircraft fought each other over Korea in a sustained conflict that cost some 1700 lives.[5] The then superpowers kept this element of the confrontation secret to prevent an escalation to world-war proportions. At the same time the scale of this ideological investment made it plain that a post-war reunification of the peninsula on either communist or US terms was the least likely outcome.

There were also suspicions in the West that American prisoners of war had been held in the Soviet Union, despite the terms of the 1953 armistice; and that even as late as the 1990s some of the PoWs may still have been alive.[6] It was reported also that Washington 'wrote off' more than 1000 American PoWs during the Korean War and left them to die in Soviet camps. Thus Lieutenant Colonel Philip Corso, a one-time national security official in the Eisenhower White House, testified before a Senate hearing in 1992 that he advised the President in 1955 to declare dead two trainload of US prisoners transported through China into Siberia.[7] Such details are part of the bitter legacy of the first major conflict of the Cold War period.

In March 1991 North Korea announced that it would not attend further meetings of the Korean truce body after the US-dominated United Nations Command named Hwang Won Tak, a South Korean general, as head of the UN delegation. After nearly 40 years the residual tensions remained. On 22 May 1992 South Korean border troops killed three North Korean soldiers who had reportedly crossed the heavily fortified frontier, and it was announced that the UN Command would protest to the North over the incident. On 15 June the United States brought the issue to the UN Security Council to protest at what it dubbed a serious violation of the armistice. The Democratic People's Republic of Korea (DPRK) responded on 28 September by characterising the two American reports as extremely distorted, by denouncing the appointment of Hwang Won Tak, and by depicting the incident as a drama concocted by the Republic of Korea (ROK) to impede the developing dialogue between the two states. On 12 July 1993 North Korea returned the remains of seventeen American servicemen killed in the Korean War, describing the handover of the remains, accepted by US Colonel Edward O'Dowd at a ceremony at Panmunjom, as a humanitarian gesture. It seemed unlikely that the act would do much to improve the worsening atmosphere between the US and North Korea over the nuclear question (Chapter 1). The tensions and differences that had shaped Korean attitudes for four decades seemed set to continue.

THE POLITICAL CHRONOLOGY (ROK)

The political culture that Syngman Rhee had developed in the Republic of Korea (South Korea) with US support was to sustain a sequence of tyrannies broadly sympathetic to American strategic aims and business interests. There have been seven South Korean Presidents (Table 7.1) since the founding of the Republic of Korea in 1948. All have been characterised by repressive security services, the suppression of popular revolts, and abuses of human rights. Today there are suggestions that the regime of Kim Young Sam is considerably more democratic than its predecessors, though the tensions within the political framework are usually simply ignored by Western powers more interested in bringing a recalcitrant North Korea within the broad hegemony of the so-called New World Order. The success of Kim Young Sam in building what he has dubbed a 'new Korea'

Table 7.1   *Presidents of South Korea (1948–1995)*

Syngman Rhee	1948–1960
Yun Po-son	August 1960–May 1961
Park Chung Hee	1961–October 1979
Choi Kyu-hah	October 1979–August 1980
Chun Doo Hwan	August 1980–February 1988
Roh Tae Woo	February 1988–February 1993
Kim Young Sam	February 1993–

through reform and change will hinge on the extent to which he can control the traditional cliques rooted in the military, the landlord class and the powerful business interests (see below).

Syngman Rhee had survived solely by means of US-aided repression. In 1949 members of the National Assembly, constitutional lawmakers, were arrested when they began passing laws unwelcome to Rhee; and when Rhee suffered his devastating defeat in the May 1950 elections he was saved only by the outbreak of the Korean War (Syngman Rhee, more than any other Korean politician, had an interest in a North–South conflict as a route to personal political salvation). Throughout the war, using the need for national security as a readily available excuse, he intensified the scale of the repression, ordering massacres of anyone and any group thought likely to be unsympathetic to his regime. By the end of the war Rhee had created a repressive force of more than 700,000 armed men, the basis of a powerful military faction soon to rule in its own name. Rhee had progressively abolished any residual constraints on his own authority: there was no discretion for local government; autocracy was extended; and through the late 1950s the press became increasingly controlled, by then substantially a voice of government. In 1952 to counter National Assembly opposition Rhee organised youth gangs to stir up demonstrations which he then used as an excuse for martial law. When Assembly members attempted to block the martial law declaration, Rhee used the police and intimidation to secure the necessary legislation. Two years later, using the same terrorist methods, he forced the Assembly to lift the two-term presidential constraint and to allow him to run again. In 1956 the 'opposition' elected a vice-president but by now there were no ideological differences between the various permitted political groupings: 'The political spectrum came to be painted in different yet still vivid tints of right.'[8]

In 1958, with some signs of stirring among genuine opposition factions, Rhee had Cho Pong-am arrested (in 1956 Cho had received two million votes for what one scholar described as 'a program of socialist democracy, a planned economy, and peaceful unification'[9]). Cho was quickly accused of sympathies with North Korea and was executed, his Progressive Party forcibly disbanded the following year. When the National Assembly tried to block a new law enabling Rhee to appoint all local officials, he sent police skilled in martial arts to remove opposition members from the Assembly building. Rhee's legislators then passed 22 bills without opposition.[10] In the 1960 elections Rhee used ballot rigging and terrorism to defeat Chang Myon, scarcely a liberal but a perceived threat to Rhee's personal autocracy. Student demonstrations broke out in protest at the ballot-box stuffing and naked intimidation of voters, whereupon the police fired into the crowds of demonstrators, killing more than 100. The massacre served to inflame popular feeling throughout South Korea, and by now even Rhee's hired thugs could no longer hold down the lid on national unrest. Washington, forced to accept that their chosen son was a political liability, encouraged Rhee to resign; he went into exile in Hawaii and died, a broken and disillusioned man, in 1965. Now the United States was casting around for another right-wing autocrat to run its strategic client state. After toying with the brief and inconsequential premiership of Chang Myong – during which over a ten-month period 2000 street demonstrations involving one million people took place (nearly 4000 people demonstrating each day in Seoul alone[11]) – Washington was happy to welcome a military coup.

The student protests were continuing, and on 5 May 1961 the National Student League for Unification passed a resolution calling for a North–South student conference to be held at Panmunjom on 20 May, a proposal eagerly supported by North Korean students. The South Korean army, by now the principal organ of state security, was becoming increasingly alarmed at these developments: it had fought a war to prevent a popular unification, and it was not prepared to tolerate a fresh wave of student and worker agitation designed to link North and South. For the army this was the last straw. On 16 May, four days before the scheduled meeting of students from the two Koreas, Major General Park Chung Hee led a military *coup d'etat* to overthrow the civilian government. The new phase of popular political agitation was over. The virulently anticommunist army, buttressed by the United States, was in total political control. Park declared martial law, dissolved the National

Assembly, and prohibited all semblance of democratic politics: parties were banned, demonstrations made illegal, and the vestigial freedoms of the press removed. New laws were passed to extend the power of the state to arrest and convict political opponents. Within a month of the coup Park had created the Korean Central Intelligence Agency (KCIA; on 1 January 1981 renamed the National Security Planning Agency), a body that was to have a dominant role in South Korea. New facilities for state surveillance were established to protect the newly created autocracy. Now the new administration, unchecked by countervailing political or judicial powers, was implicitly modelled on Japan's last decade (1936–1945) of repressive rule in Korea.[12]

On the morning of the coup the Park administration declared itself committed to strong anti-communism, respect for the UN Charter, closer relations with the United States, eradication of corruption, the creation of a self-supporting economy, national reunification, and the transfer of the government to civilian rule at the proper time. Of these, the US link was of crucial importance: the power of the army depended upon continued American support, as did the effectiveness of the newly created KCIA. And the United States had its own interest in supporting the military regime in South Korea, an effective bulwark against communism and a safeguard for American commercial interests. Moreover, with Washington's growing commitment to the repression of another Asian people, the Vietnamese, there were practical ways in which the military regime of South Korea could be exploited; namely, as a useful supplier of mercenary troops.

The idea that Western puppets in Asia could be deployed to suppress other Asians was not new. In the early 1950s, with the Korean War in progress and Washington helping to fund the French colonial war in Indochina, Eisenhower ordered the Defense Department and the National Security Council Planning Board to examine an offer by Syngman Rhee to send South Korean troops to help the French forces in Laos. The proposal was rejected 'because US public opinion would not support the maintenance of US forces in Korea while ROK forces were withdrawn from Korea for action elsewhere'; and because Rhee was demanding as a *quid pro quo* that his own US-funded army be increased from 20 to 35 divisions. In early June 1954, after the conclusion of the armistice in Korea, Admiral Arthur Radford, chairman of the Joint Chiefs of Staff, recommended that three South Korean divisions plus support troops be sent to Laos and Vietnam; but this time the plan was rejected by the

French who were, according to John Foster Dulles, 'insulted at the very idea'.[13] Washington continued to toy with the scheme and it was eventually implemented when Park Chung Hee had established his military regime in South Korea and at a time when the United States was working hard – via its 'Many Flags Program' – to win international support for its war against Vietnam.

By June 1965 only three US allies (South Korea, Australia and New Zealand) had responded to Washington's call for troops to be sent to Vietnam; and over the next year and a half just two more allies (Thailand and the Philippines) had joined them. The South Korean contribution was substantial. In early 1965 Park Chung Hee sent an infantry task force of 2200 men with ten karate instructors, soon to be augmented by an infantry division and a combat brigade. In 1966 a second infantry division, a regimental combat team and about 3000 additional troops were despatched, bringing the total number of South Korean soldiers in Vietnam to around 50,000.[14] This was a mercenary force paid a special bonus by Washington, a fact kept secret from both the US Congress and from America's other Asian allies in Vietnam.[15]

The size of the US financial contribution to its mercenary South Korean force was enormous. In 1969 a South Korean private normally earned $1.60 a month, but with the US bonus paid for service in Vietnam his monthly earnings amounted to $37.50. Over the period 1965–1973 South Korean troops remitted $185.3 million to South Korea.[16] And over broadly the same period the United States supported South Korean business to the tune of around $540 million by procuring war supplies in South Korea and by offering South Korean contractors lucrative construction and service deals in Vietnam. Korean firms were exporting military uniforms, boots, cement and corrugated metal roofing to Vietnam: 'In the construction and service field, at one point more than eighty South Korean companies held contracts with the US government in Vietnam. Their activities included construction and engineering, transportation of goods, and operating service facilities such as laundry shops and entertainment clubs.'[17] Over the entire period South Korea earned in excess of $2 billion for its support for the American aggression. Just as the Korean War had been a commercial godsend for Japan, so the Vietnam War brought immense trading benefits to the South Korean commercial community.

Washington also pledged to develop the armed forces in South Korea, a consideration dear to the heart of the military regime.

Thus, in addition to funding the specific South Korean troops sent to Vietnam, the United States, undertook to 'provide substantial items for modernizing ROK forces in Korea ... equip, train, and finance replacement forces for those going to Vietnam; improve the ROK anti-infiltration capability; improve the ROK arsenal for ammunition production; improve the living quarters for ROK forces in Korea'; and there would be 'more economic assistance loans'.[18]

In 1971 about a quarter of the South Korean troops in Vietnam were withdrawn, but the remainder stayed until early 1973, when they outnumbered US ground troops.[19] The autocratic regime in South Korea had derived immense commercial and military benefits from its support for the American war in Vietnam, but these had failed to stabilise the domestic political situation. Despite Park Chung Hee's internal repression, his comprehensive abrogation of human rights, the expansion of the army, and the copious flow of US funds, he was unable to crush the dissenting political factions. Soon Park would yet again be forced to declare martial law.

In the late 1960s there was growing worker discontent, forcing the government into further acts of suppression and new legislation. When women from the US-owned electronics company Oak Electronics went on strike for better wages and improved working conditions, a senior official from the US home office was despatched to South Korea to settle the dispute; after desultory talks he announced that because of the unreasonable demands of the women the factory would be closed. Further strikes were staged by textile workers at sixteen firms, by metal workers at Chosun Shipbuilding Company, and by auto workers at the Shaehan Motor Company, known to have links with General Motors. Chemical workers at the American subsidiary, Korea Pfizer Company, went on hunger strike; and on 13 November 1970 Chun Tae-il, a worker at the Seoul Peace Market, set himself on fire in protest at the brutal treatment of many employees. Park Chung Hee responded to such events by sending in the police and the army, and by introducing new anti-worker laws. Thus Article 18 of legislation introduced in January 1970 established free trade zones in which trade unions and strikes were illegal; here all disputes would be settled by compulsory arbitration controlled by the government and foreign corporations. A subsequent law extended such controls to all South Korean companies with foreign investments, whether or not the firms operated in a free trade zone.

At one level South Korea had witnessed spectacular economic development, but the society was increasingly stratified: the commercial and military elite were massively enriched while the workers and peasants were struggling for survival. A government report (May 1970) admitted that the unequal distribution of income was now causing serious social problems ('Most troublesome was the conspicuous consumption of the new elite'). In these circumstances, with the regime increasingly unpopular, Park used ballot rigging and terrorism to defeat his opponent, Kim Dae Jung, in the April 1971 presidential election. When the protests continued, Park declared a national emergency on 6 December, and three weeks later forced the National Assembly in illegal secret session to pass further repressive legislation. Now Park had enlarged powers to ban public protests, to determine rents and prices, to freeze wages, and to 'mobilize any material or human resources' for any required purpose. But even these new measures, adding substantially to the existing corpus of repressive law, were not thought sufficient.

On 17 October 1972 Park declared martial law, suspended the constitution, and then took steps to concentrate all political power in his hands and to maintain it without challenge. The new political framework, a manifest dictatorship, became known as the Yushin ('revitalising reform') system that prevailed through the second phase of Park's rule.[20] On 13 December, with the Yushin constitution in place, Park lifted martial law and ten days later had himself elected President of the newly created National Congress for Unification (a political ploy to attract those Koreans eager to see expanded links between North and South). Even now, Park failed to discourage opposition to his dictatorial rule. Under the terms of Emergency Decree No. 1 (January 1974), making it illegal to criticise the new constitution, scores of students, intellectuals and religious leaders were arrested, jailed and tortured. Other Emergency Decrees followed in quick succession: for example, one (No. 4, April 1974) prohibited membership of the National Democratic Youth and Student Federation or any affiliated organisation, while another (No. 9, May 1975) made any criticism of Park or his government illegal (the universal scope of this latter decree made further enactments unnecessary).

Throughout this period the United States was content to allow events to take their course: Park remained committed to the vigorous suppression of popular worker and peasant movements, and with the US-buttressed army intact there seemed no real threats to American business interests. In January 1973 President Richard Nixon had commented to Prime Minister Kim Jong Pil: 'I do not intend to interfere in the internal affairs of your country' (as though there was not already massive US involvement in South Korean commercial and military affairs). Washington was not prepared to comment on Park's suppression of dissident groups that clearly showed little sympathy for the delicate feelings of American investors in South Korea. It may also have been significant that certain well-placed South Koreans were spending millions of dollars buying support amongst US policy-makers in Congress. On 5 June 1977 Kim Hyung Wook, a former Director of the Korean Central Intelligence Agency (KCIA), identified Tongsun Park as a former KCIA agent who had spent vast sums bribing members of the US Congress. Moreover, the American CIA, the FBI, the Defense Department, the Department of Agriculture, the Internal Revenue Service and the US embassy in Seoul had known for years what was going on.[21]

By the late 1970s there was mounting turmoil throughout South Korea. Students and workers were protesting in most of the country's major cities, variously demanding unification with the North, a new democratic constitution, better wages and improved living conditions. Park resounded in the usual way, deploying the police and the army, resorting to the harsh legislation that he had forced onto the statute book. The KCIA became increasingly active, kidnapping labour organisers, beating some and taking others to court. In August 1979 workers congregating at the offices of the opposition New Democratic Party (NDP) were beaten and arrested; one was killed. The next day the KCIA removed Kim Young Sam, the NDP head, from the National Assembly; and then massive uprisings, involving thousands of workers and students, erupted in the industrial cities of Pusan and Masan. Park deployed troops in both cities but street battles continued despite large numbers of casualties. He then began planning a major military offensive against the protesting workers and students; but on 26 October 1979, before Park could issue fresh orders to his troops, he was shot and killed by Kim Chae-gyu, the Director of the KCIA and one of Park's closest aides. Now the triumphant students marched for reunification, a democratic constitution, and the dismissal of government hard-liners; soon they were joined by workers demanding higher wages and improved working conditions.

In conditions of mounting turmoil the army moved to fill the political vacuum; in particular, to block any movement towards political democracy. On 12 December 1979 Major General Chun Doo Hwan, head of the Defence Security Command, emerged victorious from the brief power struggle, and South Korea was set for another period of military government. Protests continued, with workers rushing to join the technically illegal labour organisations. A four-day miners' strike against rapacious employers, an overpriced company store and a corrupt union involved more than 3500 miners seizing rifles and dynamite to fight off attacks by combat police. Chun, still head of the Defence Security Command, now named himself head of the KCIA and expanded martial law to all the major cities: political activities were banned, the media were taken under direct government control, all colleges and universities were closed, and labour strikes were prohibited. The KCIA and the army began rounding up political leaders in an attempt to prevent the forming of organised opposition groups, but there were still widespread demonstrations against the new military coup. On 18 May 1980 one of the largest demonstrations – in the south-western city of Kwangju – was suppressed by combat paratroopers with merciless brutality. An *Asia Watch* report describes what happened:

> They repeated the same actions of the day before, beating, stabbing, and mutilating unarmed civilians, including children, young girls, and aged grandmothers. They forced both men and women to strip naked, made others lie flat on the ground and kicked them. Several sources tell of soldiers stabbing or cutting off the breasts of naked girls; one murdered student was found disemboweled, another with an X carved in his back. About twenty high school girls were reported killed at Central High School. The paratroopers carried out searches in side streets, fired randomly into crowds, carted off the bodies in trucks, and piled them in the bus terminal. They even took the wounded out of hospitals.[22]

The entire city mobilised against the military repression. Government buildings were set on fire; students erected barricades and set up machine-gun posts on campuses; TV and radio stations that refused to report the truth were destroyed. On 22 May the soldiers were forced to withdraw from the city, only to return with massive reinforcements five days later. Tens of thousands of troops attacked Kwangju, killing an estimated 2000 civilians, wounding 15,000, and finally ending all resistance.[23] The US General John Wickham, commander of the joint US–South Korea military command, personally approved General Chun's request to use South Korean forces in the attack on Kwangju.[24]

Chun had retained power by means of naked terror. Demonstrating students were arrested, sent to jail and tortured; a number of students were beaten to death while in custody. Members of the KCIA were installed on campuses to spy on dissident students and their lecturers; some students were expelled from college and forced to join the army, and many professors were made to resign. The churches were persecuted, the media censored (800 journalists fired, 170 publications banned), and the trade unions (where permitted to operate) tightly controlled. This scale of repression was highly congenial to corporate enterprise, particularly to the many companies that relied upon American investment. On 27 August 1980 Chun, having 'retired' from the military (which he still controlled), was elected President by the so-called National Conference for Unification. A rigged national referendum staged under martial law approved a new constitution; the KCIA was renamed the National Security Planning Agency; and the efforts persisted to drive down wages and cripple worker power in the interest of high corporate profits. A US corporate executive commented in 1982: 'It is in our own selfish interest to have a strong government [in South Korea] that controls the students and labor so that everything will blossom and grow and we can continue to make profits.'[25]

Washington was content to bolster Chun's military dictatorship and the terrorism that sustained it. The US State Department had supported the Kwangju massacre ('Korea is a treaty ally and the United States has a very strong security interest in that part of the world'), and President Jimmy Carter had signalled his approval by immediately agreeing $600 million worth of import credits; at the same time David Rockefeller, head of Chase Manhatten Bank, and William Spenser, head of First National Bank, took the trouble to visit Seoul to reassure the South Korean dictator of their continued financial support.[26] But even in this environment Chun found it impossible entirely to crush popular resistance. In 1980 and 1982 various demonstrations took place against the Kwangju and Pusan offices of the US Information and Service Center (USIS); on 23 May 1985 dozens of students took over the USIS library in Seoul; farmers marched on the US embassy and students occupied the office of the American Chamber of Commerce in protest at 'market terrorism'. At the same time the capacity of the joint US–South Korean military command to mobilise up to 200,000 troops (in, for example, the annual 'Team Spirit' war games) has always seemed to Washington an adequate hedge against popular revolution.

Throughout the 1980s there was mounting opposition to the Chun regime. Kim Dae Jung and Kim Young Sam led liberal opposition to the government, but were often outflanked by the efforts of the United Minjung People's Movement for Democracy and Unification (UMDU), a broad-front organisation calling for a 'people's constitution', and by the persistent effort of the radical student groups (in 1986 *Jamintu*, the Struggle Committee for Anti-Imperialism, and *Minmintu*, the National Democratic Struggle Committee for Anti-Fascism). Protests escalated through 1986 and 1987, with millions of people demonstrating over a three-week period following Chun's announcement on 10 June 1987 that his crony, the former general Roh Tae Woo, would be the ruling party's next presidential candidate. In one co-ordinated demonstration affecting some 34 cities, more than two million people paraded to demand the release of all political prisoners, an end to the use of tear gas by the authorities, and democratic reform. In the event the scale of the political rallies proved irresistible. Roh Tae Woo agreed a number of reforms (sanctioned by Chun a few days later), several thousand political prisoners were released, and Kim Dae Jung emerged from house arrest (in January 1981 his death sentence, passed by military tribunal in September 1980, was commuted to life imprisonment). In December 1987, following constitutional changes to allow direct election of the President, Roh was elected with 36.6 per cent of the popular vote; but the Roh–Chun ruling party (the so-called Democratic Justice Party) failed to win a majority in the Assembly. The scene was set for further change.

Now the opposition groups were in a position to put pressure on the government and to influence legislation. Various groupings had survived the bloody years of repression: Kim Dae Jung headed the Party for Peace and Democracy (PPD); Kim Young Sam the Reunification Democratic Party (RDP); and the former premier Kim Jong-pil the New Democratic Republican Party (NDRP). In 1990 the ruling Democratic Justice Party (DJP) negotiated a merger with the RDP and the NDRP to form the Democratic Liberal Party (DLP). Now it seemed that the traditional power of the military had finally been tamed.

The DJP, now forced to share power, was no longer able to guarantee its legislative plans; and with the prospect of another presidential election in December 1992 Roh was driven to contemplate compromise with his erstwhile political opponents. In October 1992 he declared war on corruption and sacked a number of central figures in the government: Lee Sahng, the head of the National

Security Planning Agency; Lee Tong Ho, the Interior Minister; Kim Ki Choon, the Justice Minister; and Son Chu Whan, the Information Minister. Two weeks before the election, Chung Ju Yung, a 77-year-old businessman running a vigorous campaign, complained that executives of his massive Hyundai conglomerate had been arrested by the police. At the same time his United People's Party (UPP) complained that Kim Young Sam's supporters were handing out men's underwear and initialled watches to influence the voters. The charges seemed unlikely to deflect attention from the main feature of the election: the contending political claims of the three principal candidates (Chung, Kim Young Sam and Kim Dae Jung).

On 19 December 1992, with 93 per cent of all votes counted, Kim Young Sam claimed victory with 42.1 per cent of the poll (Kim Dae Jung, 33.9; Chung Ju Yung, 16.1). It was clear that the election, the first of its kind in South Korean history, had not been entirely free of corruption (for example, Kim Young Sam supporters had bribed journalists to write favourable articles), but the incidence of corruption was manifestly less than under earlier regimes. Kim Young Sam now headed the first South Korean government that could reasonably claim a democratic mandate. Soon he was urging steps to improve the South's faltering economy and pledging that he would work for reunification with North Korea. At his swearing-in ceremony on 25 February 1993 Kim Young Sam acknowledged that 'misconduct and corruption are the most terrifying enemies attacking the foundations of our society'; and he declared that 'immediate reform will start at the very top'. He also challenged Kim Il-sung to discuss the reunification of the peninsula but was promptly denounced by North Korea for calling for international inspection of North Korea's nuclear facilities (see Chapter 1). On 6 March Kim Young Sam granted an amnesty to 40,000 political prisoners, the broadest such measure in South Korean history.

Significant steps were also taken to combat South Korea's endemic corruption. On 10 September 1993 the Chief Justice, Kim Duck-joo, resigned after an anti-corruption audit exposed illegal speculations in land. He commented, as the third corruption casualty in as many days: 'I am very sorry for causing worries to the people.' On 1 November the flamboyant presidential candidate Chung Ju Yung was convicted of diverting company funds to his campaign and then sentenced to three years in jail. Senior Judge Yang Sam Sung announced that because Chung had 'refused to show repentance or acknowledge his guilt' the sentence would not be suspended. Now light was also being thrown on other aspects of South Korea's shady history: for example, regarding the brutal treatment of Kim Dae Jung in the 1970s, with the possibility of new revelations that might embarrass Seoul, Tokyo and Washington.[27]

It was not long before the new regime of Kim Young Sam was facing problems. Soon three of his ministers were forced to resign on corruption charges and there were signs in Seoul of a campaign to block his reform plans.[28] On 16 December 1993 the government was shaken by demonstrations against the opening of the country's rice market as part of the GATT (General Agreement on Tariffs and Trade) deal: Lee Hoi Chang was appointed to succeed premier Hwang In Sung, and the entire cabinet was dismissed pending the appointment of new ministers. A week later Kim Young Sam appointed US-educated former professors to replace the deputy prime ministers in control of the economy and national unification. In addition, there was the mounting tension being fomented by Washington over North Korea's nuclear developments. Through 1993–4 the future of South Korea, still constrained by traditional power elites and the country's status as a resource in American strategic calculations, seemed increasingly uncertain.

THE POLITICAL CHRONOLOGY (DPRK)

The post-Korean War chronology of North Korea was largely shaped – as was that in the South – by the impact of the war; but whereas the South had suffered heavy damage for less than one year the North was relentlessly pounded from both air and sea for most of a three-year period. In proportionate terms the Democratic People's Republic of Korea (DPRK) was more comprehensively devastated than any country (including Germany and the Soviet Union) in the Second World War, and more than North Vietnam would be in the Vietnam War. Virtually 'every town and village was completely destroyed',[29] bombed or burned down from the air or destroyed in scorched-earth tactics as the US and other 'UN' troops retreated from the Yalu river at the end of 1950. General O'Donnell later testified to the Senate hearings on MacArthur: 'Everything is destroyed. There is nothing standing worthy of the name. Just before the Chinese came in we were grounded. There were no more targets in Korea.'[30] By the end of the first year of conflict the US

Air Force had dropped some 7.8 million gallons of napalm and 97,000 tons of bombs on North Korea. In two years, according to the DPRK, North Korea received 15 million napalm bombs, with Pyongyang receiving 1000 bombs per square kilometre. At the end of the bombing, Pyongyang, once a thriving city of nearly half a million people, had only two buildings intact. In late summer 1953 a British navy officer, Lieutenant Dennis Lankford, commented after travelling through the North Korean capital that Pyongyang 'has ceased to exist'.[31]

By the end of the war much of the surviving population of North Korea was living in caves or holes in the ground. Every possible target – factories, power stations, communication facilities, oil refineries, dams – had been hit. With a collapsed economy the DPRK was forced to cope with hundreds of thousands of orphans, the blind and the limbless, with countless thousands of victims disabled or traumatised by napalm. This is the background against which the post-war chronology of the DPRK should be considered.

In 1954 Kim Il-sung launched a Three-Year Plan to organise the people for reconstruction. Here he could rely on the coherent structure of the command economy; and on prodigious Soviet aid. There is a general consensus in the sources that the DPRK made a remarkable recovery.[32] Kim Il-sung also took the opportunity to concentrate power in his own hands, eliminating dissidents and fellow communists seen as a danger to his position, and establishing what many people saw as a 'cult of personality'. In the immediate post-war years Kim moved to crush the communist followers of Pak Hon Yong whom he blamed for the Korean War disasters; and in 1955–6 was criticised by other DPRK activists for economic mismanagement and for creating an authoritarian Kim cult. He responded by denouncing and removing the critics, and by increasing the pressures on activists to follow his political orthodoxy. By the late 1950s Kim Il-sung had removed all the barriers to the development of his own power. Now he alone, so the legend ran, could save a nation struggling for regeneration after receiving a greater tonnage of bombs than everything dropped on Europe during the entire period of World War Two.

In April 1956 the Third Congress of the Workers' Party of Korea (WPK) considered the launching of a new Five-Year Plan for the building of a socialist framework in North Korea. The plan, starting in 1957, was designed to establish agricultural co-operatives and to begin the socialist transformation of private trade and industry. The following year saw the launch of the Chollima Movement,* intended to accelerate the social and industrial progress of the Korean people. A principal aim of the Chollima Movement, modelled on China's Great Leap Forward, was to achieve economic self-sufficiency, at the same time developing North Korea's military strength after the withdrawal of the Chinese forces. With substantial American forces remaining in the South, the DPRK entered into a mutual defence treaty with China and the Soviet Union.

It was inevitable that North Korea continued to regard the United States as the greatest threat to its survival; in some estimates the US had virtually destroyed the DPRK during the horrendous years of the Korean War. Thus a resolution of the WPK Central Committee in 1960 declared:

> The ringleader of the imperialist forces is US imperialism. US imperialism is the greatest international exploiter, the architect of the reactionary forces of the world, an international military police, the citadel of modern-day bourgeois democracy, and the arch-enemy of the peoples of the entire world.

In 1964 the WPK Central Committee adopted the doctrine of three revolutionary tenets: to build North Korea as a revolutionary base, to support the revolutionary forces in South Korea, and to gain international support. It was hoped that Asian, African and Latin American countries would join the struggle, but the meeting of 29 Asian and African countries at the Bandung Conference (1955) had not been encouraging: it seemed that there was more interest in national independence and peace than in any fight against US imperialism.

With little international support outside China and the Soviet Union, the DPRK emphasised its *juche* (self-reliance) policy as both a domestic scheme and an independent foreign policy opposed to any kind of imperialism. At the same time Kim Il-sung continued to stress the importance of the international struggle against US hegemony: 'The Korean people support the peoples of all countries fighting against US imperialists. I regard their anti-US struggle as the support of my struggle for liberation of the Korean people.' He also attacked both China and the Soviet Union for giving too little

---

* *Chollima* traditionally signifies a horse galloping 1000 *ri* (1 *ri* = about 1 mile) a day.

material support to the struggle against US imperialism throughout the world. In the late 1960s, in an effort to garner more international support, North Korea launched various diplomatic initiatives, inviting cultural missions from other countries and establishing 'friendship associations' (in seven countries, only one of which had diplomatic relations with the DPRK).[33] During this period North Korea also began giving aid to Third World countries, developing its trade links, and expanding its contacts with Asian and African countries. At the DPRK's Independence Day celebrations in 1968, 71 delegations (34 from Africa) represented governments, parties, front organisations, social organisations and liberation movements.[34] But various international developments were working against North Korea's attempts to build a global anti-US consensus. Through the 1970s, despite the Vietnam War (by 1973 in its final phase), there were growing signs of *détente* between the Soviet Union and China on the one hand and the United States on the other. Moreover the Soviet invasion of Czechoslovakia in 1968 had led many Third World leaders to believe that there were few differences between Soviet aggression and American imperialism. By the 1980s, with the Soviet Union witnessing the progressive collapse of the East European political/military alliance, there was little international appetite for an anti-US crusade. Increasingly the DPRK was forced to rely on its policy of *juche* self-reliance, a posture that would come under mounting pressure in the so-called New World Order of the 1990s.

Throughout this entire period Kim Il-sung had managed to out-manoeuvre every faction that had emerged to challenge his authority. His position seemed secure. He had founded the Korean People's Revolutionary Army in 1932 and proclaimed the DPRK in 1948, serving as effective head of state thereafter.* Kim Il-sung became the President of North Korea in 1972 under the terms of his new 'socialist constitution',[35] a position he held until his death (July 1994). Through the 1970s he gave increasing thought to the question of the succession, and was re-elected President in 1982, having named his son Jong Il as his eventual political successor.

In October 1980 the Sixth Congress of the Korean Workers' Party officially confirmed that Kim Jong Il would succeed his father, Kim

---

* Kim Il-sung was often officially referred to as 'The Great Wise Leader President-for-Life Kim Il-sung, Dearly Beloved and Sagacious Leader'.

Il-sung, the supreme leader who had dominated North Korea for three and a half decades. Opposition to the decision continued until 1983 when more than 1000 political and military leaders were reported to have been purged, but by 1984, heavily exploiting the authority of his father, Kim Jong Il had emerged as the established heir apparent and effective ruler of the DPRK. The rationale behind Kim Il-sung's decision has been discussed at length.[36] It was obvious that the choice of Kim Jong Il would raise many questions; in particular, how could a great revolutionary leader contemplate creating what would obviously be seen as a feudalistic dynasty? One possible answer is that Kim Il-sung was struggling to confront the problem that Mao Tse-tung had also faced: how could a new generation, untried in revolution and war, be trusted to maintain the impetus of continuous revolution? (Mao had worried that youth might 'negate the Revolution and give a poor performance: make peace with imperialism'.) Kim Il-sung's answer seems to have been that the dynamic of the revolution could best be maintained by a leader from a great revolutionary family (Kim: 'families of revolutionaries are better in thoughts'). Thus in 1945, immediately after liberation, the Korean communists created the Mangyongdae School to train the heirs of revolutionaries as future leaders of the country.

At one time Kim Il-sung favoured his younger brother, Jong-ju, as his political successor. Kim Jong-ju had become co-chairman of the North–South Co-ordination Committee in July 1972 and served on the DPRK Political Committee (since 1980, the Politburo); but in October 1980, for reasons that can only be surmised, he was removed from both the Politburo and the 248-member Central Committee.* It was alleged that Kim Jong-ju was suffering from mental depression, but other men in poor health have been allowed to serve at the highest levels of state power.[37] In the mid-1970s South Korean sources began citing Kim Jong Il as Kim Il-sung's successor; and at the Sixth Party Congress (October 1980) Kim Jong Il was extolled as 'endlessly loyal to the great leader, perfectly embodying the ideas, outstanding leadership, and noble traits of the leader, and brilliantly upholding the grand plan and intention of the leader at the highest level;' and as possessing 'bright wisdom, deep

---

* Kim Il-sung's second wife, Song Ae, has worked to advance her five children within the Party and diplomatic hierarchy, but to uncertain effect.

insight, [a] strong sense of revolutionary principles and [a] strong will'.[38]

Kim Jong Il has long held senior positions in the Politburo, the Party Secretariat and the National Defence Commission, so signalling his grip on the main organs of state power. On 9 April 1993 he was elected to the top military post in the DPRK, taking over from his father the chairmanship of the National Defence Commission and so further consolidating his authority. It remains to be seen whether he will be able to retain power after Kim Il-sung's death; Kim Jong Il has not been tempered, like his father, by long decades of violent struggle and political manoeuvring in a hazardous environment. Moreover, the trend today is towards pluralism, with 'great leaders' (of whatever ilk) more likely to be viewed with cautious circumspection. In the modern political climate it is increasingly thought to be imprudent to tie the security of the state to the fortunes of a single man, however illustrious his ancestry. In February 1994 such thoughts were reinforced by the news that Kim Jong Il had been seriously injured, perhaps in a shooting accident. Soon afterwards the reports were toned down, with South Korean defence sources saying that there were no grounds to support the rumour.[39]

For the West it was easy to characterise the dominant Pyongyang political family as a 'dynasty from hell'. In such propaganda, Kim Il-sung was not merely geriatric and paranoid, but 'the most absolute dictator' on earth, with a mad and debauched son who has a speech handicap and 'a taste for terrorism and a lust for power'.[40] The 'sinister Asian Pinochio, an inveterate liar who began life as a wooden puppet ... continues to twitch' long after the puppet masters 'have been thrown out of the theatre'.[41] In fact Kim Il-sung, then aged 82, appeared to be alert, charismatic and very knowledgeable. Thus the British analyst Aidan Foster-Carter has referred to Kim's 'affable, joky and charming' conversation; Dr Bill Taylor, a retired US Army colonel who had met Kim twice, said that he 'knows everything; Bosnia, Somalia, the Gulf, the lot' (*The Observer*, 19 June 1994); and ex-President Jimmy Carter, himself trained as a nuclear engineer, declared during his visit (June 1994) to Pyongyang that he was impressed with Kim Il-sung's detailed knowledge of reactor design. Few such observers imagined that within weeks Kim would be dead.

At the same time there are obvious dangers in concentrating power in the hands of one man over a period of decades. Even the official Chinese publication *Hongqi* (Red Flag) commented in 1980,

soon after the DPRK announcement that Jong Il would succeed his
father, that bad effects flow from one man holding too many important posts for too long; and that concentrating political power in one
man's hands is incompatible with a healthy communist party.[42]

Today North Korea is seen largely by Western commentators as a
failed command economy with a collapsing industrial sector,
inefficient agriculture and a disgruntled but impotent population
(much in the way that the successive South Korean terrorist dictators
were depicted as resolute democrats helping to protect Christian civilisation and the Free World). There is evidence (though much of it
tentative and necessarily congenial to Western propaganda) of
purges, worker protests, student demonstrations, assassination attempts and food riots in North Korea. One authority gives examples
of 'rumoured unrest', though he is constrained to comment that none
'have been fully confirmed'.[43] Defectors have reported food riots, and
Amnesty International has frequently commented on the DPRK's
poor human rights record, just as it castigates the South (see below).

It is ironic that US policy towards the DPRK makes it possible
for the North Korean leadership to blame the regime's failures and
repression on the machinations of evil foreign powers (in particular,
on US imperialism). If Washington had relaxed its pressure on
North Korea, a possibly paranoid Kim Il-sung would have had
fewer excuses to persist with the authoritarian constraints on his
latter-day hermit kingdom. Internal pressure for liberalisation would
mount, the DPRK would be prised open, and the character of the
North Korean regime would be exposed.

THE SHAPE OF DEVELOPMENT

At one level there is a singular parity between the historical circumstances of South Korea (ROK) and North Korea (DPRK). Both
owed their inception to powerful foreign powers, as did the early
leadership of the two states: Syngman Rhee, even from the US point
of view a far from ideal favourite son, was installed in the South as
a strategic Western asset; and it cannot be assumed that Kim Il-
sung, despite his closer proximity to the Korean struggle over
decades, would have gained power in the North without Soviet
sponsorship. At another level the parity breaks down. The Russian
forces left North Korea after the Second World War, as did the

Chinese forces after the Korean War, but in the South the American forces have maintained a continuous but fluctuating presence since 1945. Even today, half a century after the US-imposed partition, Washington keeps almost 40,000 troops in the Republic of Korea as protection against the event of popular insurrection and against what is routinely depicted as the threat from the North. Moreover, competing ideologies have worked to shape very different societies: the totalitarian North, 'a tight weave of mass organizations',[44] has emphasised the political role of the people, albeit within the confines of an authoritarian framework; the South, traditionally hostile to mass organizations, has relied on strong security services (aided by US intelligence and the promise of US military protection) to keep the Republic of Korea safe for capitalism and Washington's strategic game plans. In this environment neither North nor South, equally concerned with the primary requirement of survival, has been overly concerned to protect the human rights of individuals thought to threaten the security of the state.

Human rights organisations have long charted the lamentable records of both North and South Korea. Thus cases in the files of Amnesty International include (for South Korea):

Kang Ki-hun, a dissident activist sentenced to three years in prison for aiding the protest suicide of Kim Ki-sol in 1991. Kang was wrongly convicted after an unfair trial failed to find him guilty.

Suh Kyung-Won and Pang Yang-Kyun, ill-treated in detention and wrongly sentenced to fifteen years in prison on charges of spying for North Korea.

Hwang Suk-yong, Chang Ki-pyo and Kim Nak-jung, dissidents imprisoned for long terms; Choi Il-bung imprisoned for publishing socialist books and articles.

Kim Nak-jung, Chun Hee-sik, Song Hae-suk and Noh Jung-song, all allegedly tortured while in custody; Pae Choon-il, Kim Sang-chol and Lee Jong-chon allegedly tortured by police; 25 prisoners (including Ham Ju-myong, Hwang Tae-kwon and Park Dong-oon) sentenced to long prison terms after confessions allegedly made under torture.

Kim Nak-jung, 61-year-old writer and activist, arrested and beaten by the security police; in November 1992 sentenced to life imprisonment under the Security Law.

Aged prisoners in poor health held without charge or trial under renewable preventive detention orders.

Yu Won-ho, Moon Ik-hwan, Lee Bu-yong, Lee Yong-hee, Lee Chang-bok, Lee Jae-oh and Koh Eun imprisoned for making contact with North Korea; National Assembly member Suh Kyung-won imprisoned for visiting North Korea; others imprisoned for attending a Youth Festival in Pyongyang.

In January 1994 Amnesty International called for the immediate and unconditional release of Lee Kun-hee, a Democratic Party worker serving a three year prison term under the Security Law.[45] Here it is suggested that the arrest was made to damage the credibility of Kim Dae Jung in the 1992 presidential election. Lee Kun-hee was one of 67 people arrested for alleged links with a North Korean spy ring (Amnesty suggests that 'there is no evidence that many of them, including Lee Kun-hee, had any connection with spying activities'). At the same time Amnesty protested at the arrest of Son Pyong-son on 26 September 1992 by six or seven officials of the National Security Planning Agency without a warrant of arrest. Son was tortured over several days and told to admit his alleged contacts with North Korea. In February 1993 he was sentenced to life imprisonment.

In February 1994 Amnesty issued a comprehensive report providing evidence that human rights violations were continuing under the government of President Kim Young Sam.[46] The South Korean government had decided to abandon proposed amendments to the repressive National Security Law (NSL) and the Labour Dispute Mediation Act, laws that limit freedom of expression and association. It had failed to introduce measures to protect prisoners from torture and to live up to its promise to ratify the UN Convention against Torture. Throughout 1993 dozens of people were arrested for exercising their rights to freedom of expression and association, and new incidents of torture were reported.

The Amnesty report explores the repressive character of the National Security Law, highlights the arrests of trade union leaders, considers the operation of the Social Surveillance Law (enacted in 1989), highlights the use of torture and other coercive methods to force prisoners to change their political allegiances, indicates the regime's failure to rectify past human rights violations (some political prisoners held for more than 40 years), and highlights the continuing use of torture (beatings, sleep deprivation, sexual assault) to extract confessions and the continuing resort to the death penalty (where neither the relatives of prisoners, nor their lawyers, are told of impending executions; and where the prisoners themselves are told only a few hours before the execution takes place). In early 1994 the Amnesty International Journal emphasised that the Amnesty research mission had 'found evidence of hundreds of political prisoners, torture and new arrests of prisoners of conscience'.[47]

Other reports suggested that South Korea was maintaining its reputation as a 'baby exporter', witnessing extensive wife-beating (10 per cent of wives beaten almost every day), seeing fresh incidents of corruption (causing Buddhist monks to fight pitched battles with riot police), and failing to safeguard the welfare of mental patients (psychiatric patients shackled to their beds killed when fire destroyed a hospital in Nonsan).[48] In February 1994 there were mass protests in Seoul at the government's decision to open South Korea's rice market to foreign imports as part of the GATT deal at the end of the Uruguay Round of trade talks. Some 15,000 police confronted around 20,000 demonstrators chanting 'Down with Kim Young Sam! USA, go away!'. Kim had earlier pledged: 'I am going to stop the rice imports at the cost of my presidency'; but on 9 December 1994, as a prelude to the GATT deal, he declared: 'I had no choice but to seek competition and co-operation inside the system rather than to seek isolation in international society. I apologise to the public, feeling keenly the responsibilities of not keeping my promises.'[49]

It seems clear that South Korea has not yet emerged from the culture of its brutal past: excessive police powers, repression, indifference to human rights, naked economic exploitation – all seem set to continue in an economic environment shaped essentially by the profit needs of powerful corporations. South Korea has achieved significant economic successes,[50] but here as elsewhere the fruits of development have not been justly spread. Many of the tensions that racked the Republic of Korea in the post-war decades have not been removed, and there is a further hazard on the horizon: the ambiguous shadow of North Korea. It may be that the real threat is not of military confrontation or nuclear development, but that in a post-reunification world (see below) South Korea may be saddled with the burden of rebuilding a bankrupt North. Such an eventuality, as Germany has found, would do little for human rights.

North Korea, through the period during which the South was run by military dictatorships, was developing its own form of authoritarian regime. By any token the DPRK has evolved as a totalitarian state, exhibiting the classical features of this type of political system. One source usefully sets forth the characteristics of the totalitarian state: (a) the existence of an official ideology; (b) the maintenance of a single mass party dedicated to the official doctrine; (c) the reliance on systematic terror and a police surveillance system; (d) the control of mass media for official indoctrination; (e) the complete monopoly of violence under the close supervision of the party; and (f) a centralised planned economy.[51] Each of these criteria has been exemplified to a large degree throughout the history of the DPRK. The party has progressively strengthened its grip on all aspects of society, defining the character of the social institutions and extending its control over every element of the planned economy.

As with South Korea, the North's economic achievements have been significant, though accompanied by unfulfilled plans, unpaid loans and frequent worker protests. At the same time genuine progress has been made in the areas of women's rights, health care, nursery provision, education and other social sectors. In such fields every opportunity is taken to create 'a new communist type of personality' (that is, to extend the scope of indoctrination). Thus when a meal was served at a state nursery, even the youngest children were taught to say 'thank you, Father Kim Il-sung'; the day began with a pledge of allegiance to Kim Il-sung and all the pupils were taught to believe that it was to him that they owed food, clothing, shelter, and life itself.[52] They were encouraged to esteem Kim Il-sung more highly than their parents; but at the same time great emphasis is placed on the importance of the family (Article 63 of the constitution states: 'Marriage and the family are protected by the state. The state pays great attention to consolidating the family, the cell of society').[53]

Over the decades the DPRK economy had been sustained largely by Soviet aid and by Soviet trade on favourable terms. The rapid rebuilding of North Korea after World War Two and the Korean War was accomplished mainly through Soviet economic assistance in one form or another, a strategic ploy that was to change radically when the Soviet Union moved into its own deep crisis. Through 1989 and 1990 there was a sharp decline in Soviet–North Korean trade, with a further deterioration in 1991. Now the DPRK, having lost its favoured trading status, was forced to pay for goods and services in hard currency at world market prices. At the same time there was a significant reduction in the amount of China–North

Korean trade, despite the relatively warm political climate between the two countries. Paradoxically, North Korea was by now deriving useful benefits from trade with Japan and South Korea, a sign that the long envisioned reunification might at last be on the agenda and that North Korea – despite all its instincts – might eventually be sucked into the world financial system. None of this seemed helpful in the short term to a regime seemingly facing bankruptcy and economic collapse.

Through 1992 there were growing signs that North Korea was in economic trouble. In August a Western diplomat in the country reported that riots had broken out when citizens were ordered by the government to exchange old banknotes for new, with a limit on how many could be exchanged, so cutting the amount of money in circulation and reducing the standard of living. Here a key problem was that people were increasingly forced to rely on the black market for food, and so were forced to accept higher prices than those charged by the state. The Public Security Ministry had already warned that any protests against food rationing policy and any stealers of food would be severely punished.[54] In August 1993 there were further reports of food riots, caused in part by the poor 1992 harvest. Korean-Japanese who had been allowed to visit North Korea were told by relatives of food riots and other uprisings by a desperate population struggling to cope with a collapse of basic services such as water, sewerage systems and electricity. On billboards a new slogan had appeared: 'Let's Eat Two Meals a Day, Not Three!' Now, it was said, there was virtually no support for Kim Jong Il (the 'Dear Leader'), set to assume full power on the death of his father. At the same time anyone suggesting that conditions were deteriorating was likely to end up in prison.[55] On 24 August a North Korean army defector painted a similarly grim picture of food riots: 'soldiers have raided government food supplies that were supposed to be for the people ... well-connected businessmen and merchants have stolen food, using the support of the army'. A thwarted coup attempt had led to the execution of ten generals.[56]

The growing economic crisis had its inevitable impact on human rights: because of agricultural failure and mismanagement the regime was increasingly forced to rely on terror. In October 1993 Amnesty International submitted a detailed report condemning North Korea's human rights record. Since the 1960s tens of thousands of people have been imprisoned under various forms of arbitrary detention; thousands have been tortured, with the death penalty widely used. Political prisoners have been held in camps in appalling conditions, sometimes receiving virtually no food and forced to subsist on what they could produce themselves; many have died in these detention camps. Cases listed in the Amnesty report include:

Shin Sook Ja, aged 50, and her two daughters, Oh Hae Won (aged 17) and Oh Kyu Won (aged 14), reportedly detained in November 1986 after Shin Sook Ja's husband Oh Kil Nam requested political asylum in Denmark. Shin Sook Ja and her daughters are reportedly still held in detention.

Shibata Kozo, aged 62, a political prisoner since October 1964; in late 1990 still reportedly held in a 're-education' camp.

Various North Koreans reportedly held in unacknowledged detention, a particularly vulnerable condition; disappearances – for example, Kim Myong-se, unable since mid-1992 to contact his wife and other family members after he requested political asylum in Russia.

Summary executions for various offence, including political crimes; North Korea has told Amnesty that the death penalty is used only in rare circumstances, but refuses to give statistics. In November 1992, according to foreign students in North Korea, an unknown man accused of 'hooliganism' and 'ideological divergence' was publicly executed before a large crowd in Hamhung.

Thousands of people, including children, held at the Yodok detention centre; clothing issued only once in three years; insufficient food and virtually non-existent medical facilities; some prisoners have died of cold and hunger; 'punishment cells', too low for standing upright and too narrow for lying down flat, used to detain prisoners for weeks at a time (Amnesty: 'conditions that amounted to torture or cruel, inhuman or degrading treatment or punishment prohibited under international rights standards').[57]

On 14 October 1993 the DPRK authorities issued a reply to the Amnesty report, stating that they 'categorically reject' the information as 'either utterly groundless or far from the fact'. At the same time they confirmed the use of public executions and failed to address Amnesty's detailed charges. They acknowledged that in 1992 a man had been publicly executed 'at the request of the crowd'. Furthermore, North Korea, granted prior sight of the Amnesty report, recommended that Amnesty 'stop the publication of the document'.

The report also highlighted the detention of 20,000 North Koreans currently forced to work in the Khabarovsk Territory and Amur Region of the Russian Federation, under the direction of North Korean officials and according to a DPRK–Russian agreement. North Korean workers had been detained in the camps for 're-education' for periods ranging from six days to six months; and many human rights abuses had been alleged. At least fifteen inmates who escaped from the camps in 1992 requested political asylum in South Korea.[58] In their response to the Amnesty report the DPRK authorities acknowledged the North Korean-run logging camps in the Russian Far East, commenting that 'there is no "prison" but only education rooms' which are 'intended to give knowledge about the Russian laws to those workers who were taken on charges of violation of the laws and handed over to our side'; there is no criminal punishment 'inflicted on the violators' but 'security' personnel 'educate workers to properly observe the Russian laws'. Amnesty remained concerned that places of detention existed in the logging camps and that violations of human rights continued.

On 9 December 1993 North Korea issued an official communiqué following an emergency meeting of the Communist Party's Central Committee. It declared that the seven-year economic plan was to be suspended, noting that industrial output, energy supplies and agricultural production were below target. With rare frankness the communiqué admitted what many observers had suspected: that the North Korean economy was in a 'grave situation', now suffering 'grim trials'. The Central Committee meeting also saw the surprise rehabilitation of Kim Il-sung's younger brother, Kim Jong-ju, after eighteen years of political obscurity. In conditions of mounting economic difficulty there was still a discernable jostling for power at the highest levels of the North Korean state. On 1 May 1994 the South Korean Yonhap news agency quoted a diplomatic source as saying that Kim Il-sung himself was soon to visit China. A principal reason for the visit was to find ways of rescuing North Korea's ailing economy.

THE ROUTE TO UNIFICATION?

The United States created the artificial partition of Korea as a long-term strategic ploy. Thus President Truman commented: 'The 38th parallel as a dividing line in Korea was never the subject of international discussions. It was proposed by us as a practicable solution when the sudden collapse of the Japanese war machine created a vacuum in Korea.'[59] Any suggestion – by General Hodge and others – that it might be prudent to consider a total withdrawal of US and Soviet forces, linked to a removal of the demarcation line 'so as to unify Korea' was quickly rejected when Washington realised the likely complexion of the nationwide Korean government that would emerge. Hodge himself soon appreciated the dangers of an American withdrawal from Korea. In a post Second World War communication (22 June 1946) he expressed concern about the effects of Soviet propaganda on the Koreans ('They have little knowledge of national or international economic affairs, and are easily swayed by golden tongues and promises'), still believing that the Koreans were not ready for independence. Hodge noted:

> Communism in Korea could get off to a better start than practically anywhere else in the world. The Japanese owned the railroads, all of the public utilities including power and light, as well as all of the major industries and natural resources. Therefore, if these are suddenly found to be owned by 'The People's Committee' (The Communist Party), they will have acquired them without any struggle of any kind or any work in developing them. *This is one of the reasons why the United States should not waive its title or claim to Japanese external assets located in Korea until a democratic (capitalistic) form of government is assured.* (My italics)[60]

This was the reality behind all the Western talk of Korean independence. If the puppet Syngman Rhee proved able to establish a secure South Korea for the benefit of American capitalism then Washington may have been prepared to contemplate a military withdrawal. In the event this never happened. By the late 1940s substantial numbers of American troops had departed from South Korea but only after a joint US–south Korean military command had been imposed.

The consolidation of the division did little to erode the Korean appetite for unification: in the years that followed, both North and South – albeit with different and characteristic political analyses and solutions – addressed the problems created by partition.[61] The ROK approach was to advocate free elections supervised by the pliant US-dominated United Nations, a formula that had successfully installed the undemocratic Rhee in the South; unsurprisingly, the North rejected this approach. Just as Washington was reluctant to withdraw from the South until the region could be made secure for capitalism, so the Soviets were well prepared to defer unification until conditions were ripe for the communisation of the whole country. Thus at a KWP Central Committee meeting on 3 October 1954, Kim Il-sung admitted that until American imperialism could be effectively isolated by the revolutionary forces there would be 'a long, difficult, and hard road' to unification.

In the years immediately following the Korean War, Kim Il-sung's primary concern was the problem of economic development, a consideration not unrelated to the question of unification. In 1958 he emphasised that the successful completion of the Five-Year Plan (1957–1961) was 'the most important guarantee for national unification'; the struggle 'to carry out the Five-Year Plan is the very struggle to accelerate the peaceful unification of our Fatherland'. Kim Il-sung hoped that via this route the people in South Korea would 'see with their own eyes the superiority of our socialist system'. Kim, a principal architect of the military invasion of the South, now seemed highly committed to *peaceful* unification. By contrast, Syngman Rhee's official slogan was 'March north!', an exhortation not abandoned until the collapse of the Rhee government in April 1960.[62]

The North continued to urge the isolation of American imperialism, while the South continued to advocate a UN approach to unification. In the South, progressive activists created groups to accelerate the movement towards unification. Thus the influential Federation for National Unification, founded by students at Seoul National University, was dedicated to 'the ideas of achieving national unification and the removal of foreign influence in both South and North Korea'. The Federation's first resolution (1 November 1960) demanded that the older generation assume moral responsibility for the South–North division, that political parties in South Korea prepare for nationwide elections in which they would have to compete with the Communist Party, that premier Chang visit the United States and the Soviet Union to explore the Korean unification question, and that negotiations begin on the right of free correspondence between the South and the North. The North approved the progressive unification efforts, but the South was hostile. The southern regime had no confidence in its ability to win a democratic contest with communism at that time. Thus the ruling Democratic Party proposed that North–South contact 'should be taken up only when our political stability and internal security have been achieved'.[63]

With little effective progress made towards unification, the existence of the two Koreas increasingly appeared to be a permanent feature of the political landscape. The South, suffering under military dictatorships, seemed primarily concerned with domestic security; the North, frustrated by the failure of its peaceful approach to unification, moved towards a more militant posture. At the same time both regimes worked to garner foreign support and to increase their influence in the United Nations (while rejecting the competence and authority of the US-dominated United Nations, the North Korean regime used the international forum to give publicity to its cause). Washington now seemed interested in consolidating a 'two Koreas' policy, content to maintain a permanent military presence in the South and to tolerate the ossification of the division.

In the early 1970s North Korea redoubled its efforts to win international support. Between 1972 and 1975 the DPRK established diplomatic relations with 53 states, including seven Western European nations (Sweden, Finland, Norway, Denmark, Iceland, Austria and Switzerland). In May 1973 North Korea was admitted to the World Health Organization (WHO) by a vote of 66 to 41, a diplomatic triumph that gave the DPRK observer status in the United Nations. Two years later North Korea achieved a further important diplomatic victory: the UN General Assembly passed a resolution calling for the dissolution of the UN Command, the withdrawal of all foreign troops from South Korea, and a peace agreement to replace the Armistice Agreement. There was no prospect of Washington observing the General Assembly resolution;* had it done so, the way would have been open to Korean unification. The DPRK hailed the resolution as a 'signal victory' for itself and an 'ignominious defeat' for the United States and South Korea (notwithstanding the passing of a pro-ROK resolution in the same session of the Assembly). For the first time the United Nations had voted to evict the US forces from South Korea.

---

* Washington characteristically picks and choose which UN resolutions it will observe. It has, for example, always ignored General Assembly resolutions 47/19, 48/16 and 49/24 that demand an end to the illegal US economic blockade in Cuba.

The DPRK worked also to build up links with South Korea; suggesting, for example, that it co-host the Olympic Games scheduled to take place in Seoul in 1988. South Korea predictably opposed the suggestion but Juan Antonio Samaranch, the President of the International Olympic Committee (IOC), gave serious thought to the idea. It was suggested that teams from South and North Korea would be integrated, would walk side by side behind their two flags (headed by an Olympic flag), that the marathon and road cycling races would pass through both territories, and that the preliminary rounds of team sports would be held in the North. The suggestions aroused predictable Western hostility, even *The Guardian*, a normally progressive London newspaper, commenting that Samaranch had 'perhaps dangerously, agreed ... to join in the charade of meetings, at all levels, between North and South Korea'.[64]

The meetings were held, but came to nothing. North Korea wanted to co-host the 'Pyongyang–Seoul Games', a proposal that the IOC refused to agree. At the second meeting (January 1986), South Korea suggested that some events be held in the North though dispute about their number continued to divide the negotiators. The fourth and final talks (14–15 July 1987, at Lausanne) broke down when the differences between the representatives of North and South could not be bridged: the North was now insisting on hosting eight sports with their associated television rights, with Seoul prepared to give up six.[65] The dispute had threatened the allocation of the games to Seoul, a situation thrown into further turmoil when a South Korean aircraft carrying 115 people was blown up, apparently by North Korean terrorists, in November 1987. In the event the 1988 Seoul games were held,* and duly boycotted by North Korea. Another avenue to at least a partial and temporary unification had been blocked.

However, the collapse of the Olympic talks was not allowed to prevent the development of other forms of contact between North and South. Late 1988 saw a small volume of inter-Korean trade, a trickle that expanded in subsequent years ($22 million in 1989, $190 million in 1991). Now it seemed that South Korea was set to

---

* The West gave little attention to the mass eviction of working people to 'beautify' Seoul for the games (see *Disposable People: Forced evictions in South Korea*, Catholic Institute for International Relations (CIIR), 1989).

become 'a major trading partner, export destination and source of hard currency for North Korea'.[66] Some progress towards unification has been made in sport, despite the Olympic fiasco, with discussions on the formation of a joint team for the 1990 Asian Games in Beijing; and via unprecedented meetings held in late 1990 between leading politicians from the North and South (the North Korean Yon Hyong Muk visited Seoul to meet Roh Tae Woo, and Kang Young Hoon later travelled to Pyongyang to meet Kim Il-sung). Subsequent meetings were cancelled in protest at the provocative US–South Korean 'Team Spirit' war games, though resurrected after a suitable interval. There have also been musical exchanges across the demilitarised zone (DMZ) and a greater access in the South to information about North Korean life.[67]

On 12 December 1991 Lee Dong Bok, a South Korean spokesman, emerged from a hotel function-room in Seoul to announce agreement with North Korean officials on a draft non-aggression pact for the Korean peninsula. He declared the accord a 'historic milestone'; and later that day the elated South Korean premier, Chung Won Shik, dubbed the agreement 'a New Year present for the Korean people'. Now there was speculation that summit talks would be held between Kim Il-sung and the South Korean President, Roh Tae Woo. The accord commits the two sides not to take up arms against each other, lays the basis for arms reductions, and calls for increased economic and social contacts between North and South. North Korea reportedly made several important concessions, including dropping its insistence that it would talk only with the United States; in turn, Seoul dropped its demand that the accord would not affect any other international treaty to which it is a party.[68] No firm steps were taken in the direction of unification, but there were growing signs that Pyongyang was considering the creation of special economic zones, similar to those in southern China, to enable the DPRK to increase its trade with the capitalist South.[69]

Further talks were held in 1992 with the aim of expanding the cultural and trade links. On 7 September agreement was announced on a 70-article accord on cross-border economic exchanges, a spokesman for the South–North Dialogue Office in Seoul declaring: 'Both Koreas have reached agreement on a supplementary accord on economic and other exchanges.' There was now scope for direct transport links, cross-border mail services, and various trade and economic exchanges. A week later agreement was reached in Pyongyang on the establishment of commissions to deal with a range of projects in the military, economic, political, social and cultural spheres. Chung Won Shik applauded this 'giant step towards opening an era of reconciliation and co-operation', but regretted that agreement had not been reached on nuclear inspections and on the reuniting of families divided since the Korean War. On 22 November 1993 South Korea's President Kim Young Sam, unaware of an impending demise, said that he was optimistic that he would meet Kim Il-sung, and that he expected to see a North–South 'commonwealth' within five years.

There were now clear signs that the policy of peaceful unification was gaining momentum. In his inaugural address (25 February 1993) President Kim Young Sam urged the need for 'a reasoned national consensus on achieving this crucial goal [of unification]'. 'Genuine unification', he stressed, would guarantee political and economic freedom, and respect for human rights. In words designed for the North Korean President he declared: 'If, President Kim, you really care about the Korean people and desire genuine reconciliation and unification between our brethren in the South and North, we can meet at any time and in any place to discuss this dream ... I truly believe that we, as one people, will be able to resolve the issues that divide us.'

The new South Korean government was now shaping a three-phased unification formula to achieve a peaceful and orderly transition. First there would be reconciliation and co-operation, followed by the creation of a Korean commonwealth, and finally the establishment of a single, unified state. The policy takes into account the simultaneous entry of the ROK and the DPRK into the United Nations, and the agreements already concluded between the North and the South. The existing agreements would help to foster the requisite atmosphere of reconciliation, while exchanges and other measures would aid the establishment of trust and facilitate the reduction of military tension. During the commonwealth phase both sides would continue to exercise sovereignty in domestic administration, defence policy and foreign relations; but common social, cultural and economic communities would be developed, while joint institutions would discuss the practical task of unification. Finally, members of the South and North Korean legislative bodies would draft a new unified constitution to allow political integration to be achieved through democratic elections.[70]

It is easy to speculate on the immense problems in this unification scenario, not least the fact that North and South Korea are not the only players in the game. In any reckoning the history of Korea is one in which a national people have constantly been buffeted and exploited by powerful foreign powers, either through manifest colonial occupation or via the harsh mechanism of puppet regimes. It remains to be seen whether the Korean people will at last achieve a genuine national sovereignty, despite the pressures and threats of powerful foreign states working to a different agenda. Thus the researchers Saundra Sturdevant and Brenda Stoltzfus, noting how 18,000 South Korean women are organised as prostitutes to service American soldiers, comment that the task of the US military is to 'make it difficult to achieve reunification except under terms favourable to South Korea and the United States'.[71] North and South Korea will be reunited only when Washington approves.

Appendix 1
Treaty on the Non-Proliferation of Nuclear Weapons (1968)

The States concluding this *Treaty*, hereinafter referred to as the 'Parties to the Treaty'.

Considering the devastation that would be visited upon all mankind by a nuclear war and the consequent need to make every effort to avert the danger of such a war and to take measures to safeguard the security of peoples,

Believing that the proliferation of nuclear weapons would seriously enhance the danger of nuclear war,

In conformity with resolutions of the United Nations General Assembly calling for the conclusion of an agreement on the prevention of wider dissemination of nuclear weapons,

Undertaking to co-operate in facilitating the application of International Atomic Energy Agency safeguards on peaceful nuclear activities,

Expressing their support for research, development and other efforts to further the application, within the framework of the International Atomic Energy Agency safeguards system, of the principle of safeguarding effectively the flow of source and special fissionable materials by use of instruments and other techniques at certain strategic points.

Affirming the principle that the benefits of peaceful applications of nuclear technology, including any technological by-products which may be derived by nuclear-weapon States from the development of nuclear explosive devices, should be available for peaceful purposes to all Parties to the Treaty, whether nuclear-weapon or non-nuclear-weapon States,

Convinced that, in furtherance of this principle, all Parties to the Treaty are entitled to participate in the fullest possible exchange of scientific information for, and to contribute alone or in co-operation with other States to, the further development of the applications of atomic energy for peaceful purposes,

Declaring their intention to achieve at the earliest possible date the cessation of the nuclear arms race and to undertake effective measures in the direction of nuclear disarmament,

251

Urging the co-operation of all States in the attainment of this objective,

Recalling the determination expressed by the Parties to the 1963 Treaty banning nuclear weapon tests in the atmosphere, in outer space and under water[1] in its Preamble to seek to achieve the discontinuance of all test explosions of nuclear weapons for all time and to continue negotiations to this end.

Desiring to further the easing of international tension and the strengthening of trust between States in order to facilitate the cessation of the manufacture of nuclear weapons, the liquidation of all their existing stockpiles, and the elimination from national arsenals of nuclear weapons and the means of their delivery pursuant to a Treaty on general and complete disarmament under strict and effective international control.

Recalling that, in accordance with the Charter for the United Nations,[2] States must refrain in their international relations from the threat or use of force against the territorial integrity or political independence of any State, or in any other manner inconsistent with the Purposes of the United Nations, and that the establishment and maintenance of international peace and security are to be promoted with the least diversion for armaments of the world's human and economic resources.

Have agreed as follows:

ARTICLE I

Each nuclear-weapon State Party to the Treaty undertakes not to transfer to any recipient whatsoever nuclear weapons or other nuclear explosive devices or control over such weapons or explosive devices directly, or indirectly; and not in any way to assist, encourage, or induce any non-nuclear-weapon State to manufacture or otherwise acquire nuclear weapons or other nuclear explosive devices, or control over such weapons or explosive devices.

ARTICLE II

Each non-nuclear-weapon State Party to the Treaty undertakes not to receive the transfer from any transferor whatsoever of nuclear weapons or other nuclear explosive devices or of control over such weapons or explosive devices directly, or indirectly; not to manufacture or otherwise acquire nuclear weapons or other nuclear explosive devices; and not to seek or

---

(1) Treaty Series No. 3 (1964), Cmnd. 2245.
(2) Treaty Series No. 67 (1946), Cmd. 7015.

receive any assistance in the manufacture of nuclear weapons or other nuclear explosive devices.

ARTICLE III

1. Each non-nuclear-weapon State Party to the Treaty undertakes to accept safeguards, as set forth in an agreement to the negotiated and concluded with the International Atomic Energy Agency in accordance with the Statute of the International Atomic Energy Agency[3] and the Agency's safeguards system, for the exclusive purpose of verification of the of its obligations assumed under this Treaty with a view to preventing diversion of nuclear energy from peaceful uses to nuclear weapons or other nuclear explosive devices. Procedures for the safeguards required by this Article shall be followed with respect to source or special fissionable material whether it is being produced, processed or used in any principal nuclear facility or is outside any such facility. The safeguards required by this Article shall be applied on all source or special fissionable material in all peaceful nuclear activities within the territory of such State, under its jurisdiction, or carried out under its control anywhere.

2. Each State Party to the Treaty undertakes not to provide: (*a*) source or special fissionable material, or (*b*) equipment or material especially designed or prepared for the processing, use or production of special fissionable material, to any non-nuclear-weapon State for peaceful purposes, unless the source or special fissionable material shall be subject to the safeguards required by this Article.

3. The safeguards required by this Article shall be implemented in a manner designed to comply with Article IV of this Treaty, and to avoid hampering the economic or technological development of the Parties or international co-operation in the field of peaceful nuclear activities, including the international exchange of nuclear material and equipment for the processing, use or production of nuclear material for peaceful purposes in accordance with the provisions of this Article and the principle of safeguarding set forth in the Preamble of the Treaty.

4. Non-nuclear-weapon States Party to the Treaty shall conclude agreements with the International Atomic Energy Agency to meet the requirements of this Article either individually or together with other States in accordance with the Statute of the International Atomic Energy Agency. Negotiation of such agreements shall commence within 180 days from the original entry into force of this Treaty. For States depositing their instruments of ratification or accession after the 180-day period, negotiation of such agreements shall commence not later than the date of such deposit. Such agreements shall enter into force not later than eighteen months after the date of initiation of negotiations.

---

(3) Treaty Series No. 19 (1958), Cmnd. 450.

ARTICLE IV

1. Nothing in this Treaty shall be interpreted as affecting the inalienable right of all the Parties to the Treaty to develop research, production and use of nuclear energy for peaceful purposes without discrimination and in conformity with Articles I and II of this Treaty.

2. All the Parties to the Treaty undertake to facilitate, and have the right to participate in, the fullest possible exchange of equipment, materials and scientific and technological information for the peaceful uses of nuclear energy. Parties to the Treaty in a position to do so shall also co-operate in contributing alone or together with other States or international organizations to the further development of the applications of nuclear energy for peaceful purposes, especially in the territories of non-nuclear-weapon States Party to the Treaty, with due consideration for the needs of the developing areas to the world.

ARTICLE V

Each Party to the Treaty undertakes to take appropriate measures to ensure that, in accordance with this Treaty, under appropriate international observation and through appropriate international procedures, potential benefits from any peaceful applications of nuclear explosions will be made available to non-nuclear-weapon States Party to the Treaty on a non-discriminatory basis and that the charge to such Parties for the explosive devices used will be as low as possible and exclude any charge for research and development. Non-nuclear-weapon States Party to the Treaty shall be able to obtain such benefits, pursuant to a special international agreement or agreements, through an appropriate international body with adequate representation of non-nuclear-weapon States. Negotiations on this subject shall commence as soon as possible after the Treaty enters into force. Non-nuclear-weapon States Party to the Treaty so desiring may also obtain such benefits pursuant to bilateral agreements.

ARTICLE VI

Each of the Parties to the Treaty undertakes to pursue negotiations in good faith on effective measures relating to cessation of the nuclear arms race at an early date and to nuclear disarmament, and on a treaty on general and complete disarmament under strict and effective international control.

ARTICLE VII

Nothing in this Treaty affects the right of any group of States to conclude regional treaties in order to assure the total absence of nuclear weapons in their respective territories.

ARTICLE VIII

1. Any Party to the Treaty may propose amendments to this Treaty. The text of any proposed amendment shall be submitted to the Depositary Governments which shall circulate it to all Parties to the Treaty. Thereupon, if requested to do so by one-third or more of the Parties to the Treaty, the Depositary Governments shall convene a conference, to which they shall invite all the Parties to the Treaty, to consider such an amendment.

2. Any amendment to this Treaty must be approved by a majority of the votes of all the Parties to the Treaty, including the votes of all nuclear-weapon States Party to the Treaty and all other Parties which, on the date the amendment is circulated, are members of the Board of Governors of the International Atomic Energy Agency. The amendment shall enter into force for each Party that deposits its instrument of ratification of the amendment upon the deposit of such instruments of ratification by a majority of all the Parties, including the instruments of ratification of all nuclear-weapon States Party to the Treaty and all other Parties which, on the date the amendment is circulated are members of the Board of Governors of the International Atomic Energy Agency. Thereafter, it shall enter into force for any other Party upon the deposit of its instrument of ratification of the amendment.

3. Five years after the entry into force of this Treaty, a conference of Parties to the Treaty shall be held in Geneva, Switzerland, in order to review the operation of this Treaty with a view to assuring that the purposes of the Preamble and the provisions of the Treaty are being realised. At intervals of five years thereafter, a majority of the Parties to the Treaty may obtain, by submitting a proposal to this effect to the Depositary Governments, the convening of further conferences with the same objective of reviewing the operation of the Treaty.

ARTICLE IX

1. This Treaty shall be open to all States for signature. Any State which does not sign the Treaty before its entry into force in accordance with paragraph 3 of this Article may accede to it at any time.

2. This Treaty shall be subject to ratification by signatory States. Instruments of ratification and instruments of accession shall be deposited with the Governments of the United Kingdom of Great Britain and Northern Ireland, the Union of Soviet Socialist Republics and the United States of America, which are hereby designated the Depositary Governments.

3. This Treaty shall enter into force after its ratification by the States, the Governments of which are designated Depositaries of the Treaty, and forty other States signatory to this Treaty and the deposit of their instruments of ratification. For the purposes of this Treaty, a nuclear-weapon State is one which has manufactured and exploded a nuclear weapon or other nuclear explosive device prior to 1 January 1967.

4. For States whose instruments of ratification or accession are deposited subsequent to the entry into force of this Treaty, it shall enter into force on the date of the deposit of their instruments of ratification or accession.

5. The Depositary Governments shall promptly inform all signatory and acceding States of the date of each signature, the date of deposit of each instrument of ratification or of accession, the date of the entry into force of this Treaty, and the date of receipt of any requests for convening a conference or other notices.

6. This Treaty shall be registered by the Depositary Governments pursuant to Article 102 of the Charter of the United Nations.

ARTICLE X

1. Each Party shall in exercising its national sovereignty have the right to withdraw from the Treaty if it decides that extraordinary events, related to the subject matter of this Treaty, have jeopardized the supreme interests of its country. It shall give notice of such withdrawal to all other Parties to the Treaty and to the United Nations Security Council three months in advance. Such notice shall include a statement of the extraordinary events it regards as having jeopardized its supreme interests.

2. Twenty-five years after the entry into force of the Treaty, a conference shall be convened to decide whether the Treaty shall continue in force indefinitely, or shall be extended for an additional fixed period or periods. This decision shall be taken by a majority of the Parties to the Treaty.

ARTICLE XI

This Treaty, the English, Russian, French, Spanish and Chinese texts of which are equally authentic, shall be deposited in the archives of the Depositary Governments. Duly certified copies of this Treaty shall be transmitted by the Depositary Governments to the Governments of the signatory and acceding States.

Appendix 2
UN Security Council Statement on IAEA Inspection Issue, S/1994/ PRST/13, 31 March 1994

The Security Council this evening called upon the Democratic People's Republic of Korea to allow the inspectors of the International Atomic Energy Agency (IAEA) to complete the inspection activities agreed between the People's Republic and the Agency on 15 February, as a step in fulfilling its obligations under the Treaty on the Non-Proliferation of Nuclear Weapons.

In a statement read out by its President, Jean-Bernard Merimee (France), on behalf of its members, the Council, taking note of the IAEA Director-General's report to it on 22 March, expressed its concern that the Agency had been unable to draw conclusions as to whether there had been either diversion of nuclear material or reprocessing or other operations in the People's Republic. It invited him to report further on the question of completion of the inspection activities, including the follow-on inspections required to verify that there had been no diversion of nuclear material required to be safeguarded.

The Council requested the People's Republic and the Republic of Korea to renew discussions on the implementation of the Joint Declaration on the Denuclearization of the Korean Peninsula and appealed to those Member States engaged in dialogue with the People's Republic to continue that dialogue. It decided that if necessary it would further consider the matter in order to achieve full implementation of the IAEA-Democratic People's Republic of Korea safeguards agreement.

The statement, which will be issued as document S/1994/PRST/13, read as follows:

'The Security Council recalls the statement made by the President of the Council on 8 April 1993 (S/25562) and its relevant resolution.

'The Council reaffirms the critical importance of International Atomic Energy Agency (IAEA) safeguards in the implementation of the Treaty on the Non-Proliferation of Nuclear Weapons (the Treaty) and the contribution which progress in non-proliferation makes to the maintenance of international peace and security.

'The Council notes with appreciation the efforts of the Director-General of the IAEA and the Agency to implement the IAEA-Democratic People's Republic of Korea safeguards agreement (INFCIRC/403).

'The Council reaffirms the importance of the joint declaration by the Democratic People's Republic of Korea and the Republic of Korea on the denuclearization of the Korean Peninsula, and of the parties to the declaration addressing the nuclear issue in their continuing dialogue.

'The Council welcomes the joint statement of the Democratic People's Republic of Korea and the United States of 11 June 1993, which included the decision of the Democratic People's Republic of Korea to suspend the effectuation of its withdrawal from the Treaty, and the understanding reached between the Democratic People's Republic of Korea and United States in Geneva in July 1993, and the progress achieved on that basis.

'The Council welcomes also the agreements reached in February 1994 between the IAEA and the Democratic People's Republic of Korea, and between the Democratic People's Republic of Korea and the United States.

'The Council takes note that the Democratic People's Republic of Korea has accepted in principle IAEA inspections at its seven declared sites, following its decision to suspend its withdrawal from the Treaty on 11 June 1993, and of the Statement by the General Department of Atomic Energy of the Democratic People's Republic of Korea (S/1994/319).

'The Council takes note also of the IAEA Board of Governors' findings concerning the matter of compliance and the IAEA Director-General's report to the Security Council of 22 March 1994 (S/1994/322), and expresses its concern that the IAEA is, therefore, unable to draw conclusions as to whether there has been either diversion of nuclear material or reprocessing or other operations.

'The Council calls upon the Democratic People's Republic of Korea to allow the IAEA inspectors to complete the inspection activities agreed between the IAEA and the Democratic People's Republic of Korea on 15 February 1994, as a step in fulfilling its obligations under the IAEA-Democratic People's Republic of Korea safeguards agreement and in honouring non-proliferation obligations of the Treaty.

'The Council invites the Director-General of the IAEA to report further to the Security Council on the question of completion of the inspection activities agreed between the IAEA and the Democratic People's Republic of Korea on 15 February 1994 when the Director-General is scheduled to report on the follow-on inspections required to maintain continuity of safeguards and to verify that there has been no diversion of nuclear material required to be safeguarded, as noted in the Director-General's report to the Council (S/1994/322).

'The Council requests the Democratic People's Republic of Korea and the Republic of Korea to renew discussions whose purpose is implementation of the Joint Declaration on the Denuclearization of the Korean Peninsula.

'The Council appeals to those Member States engaged in dialogue with the Democratic People's Republic of Korea to continue that dialogue in accordance with the agreement reached on February 25 1994.

'The Council decides to remain actively seized of the matter and that further Security Council consideration will take place if necessary in order to achieve full implementation of the IAEA-Democratic People's Republic of Korea safeguards agreement.'

The meeting was convened at 7:52 p.m. and adjourned at 8:02 p.m

Appendix 3
Agreement (24 July 1907) confirming Japanese Annexation of Korea

I. The Government of Korea shall act under the guidance of the Resident General in respect to reforms in administration.

II. The Government of Korea engage not to enact any laws, ordinances or regulations, or to take any important measures of administration without the previous assent of the Resident General.

III. The judicial affairs in Korea shall be set apart from the affairs of ordinary administration.

IV. The appointment and dismissal of all high officials in Korea shall be made upon the concurrence of the Resident General.

V. The Government of Korea shall appoint as Korean officials the Japanese subjects recommended by the Resident General.

VI. The Government of Korea shall not engage any foreigner without the concurrence of the Resident General.

VII. Art. I of the Protocol between Japan and Korea signed on the 22nd of August, 1905, shall hereafter cease to be binding.*

Annual Report, 1907, App. G. This agreement was that in which Korea agreed to accept a Japanese financial adviser, now no longer necessary with the increased Japanese control.

Appendix 4
Programme, Statutes and Inaugural Declaration of the Association for the Restoration of the Fatherland (ARF)

THE PROGRAMME

1. To mobilize the entire Korean nation and realize a broad-base anti-Japanese united front in order to overthrow the piratical Japanese imperialist rule and establish a genuine people's government in Korea;

2. To defeat Japan and overthrow its puppet state 'Manchukuo' by the Koreans resident in Manchuria through a close alliance between the Korean and Chinese people, and to effect full autonomy for the Korean people residing in Chinese territory;

3. To disarm the Japanese armed forces, gendarmes, police and their agents and organize a revolutionary army truly fighting for the independence of Korea;

4. To confiscate all enterprises, railways, banks, shipping, farms and irrigation systems owned by Japan and Japanese and all property and estates owned by pro-Japanese traitors, to raise funds for the independence movement, and to use part of these funds for the relief of the poor;

5. To cancel all loans made to people by Japan and its agents and abolish all taxes and monopoly systems; to improve the living conditions of the masses and promote the smooth development of national industries, agriculture and commerce;

6. To win the freedom of the press, publications, assembly and association, oppose terrorist rule and the fostering of feudal ideas by the Japanese imperialists, and to release all political prisoners;

7. To abolish the caste system which divides the *ryangban* (nobles) and the common people, and other inequalities; to ensure equality based on humanity irrespective of sex, nationality or religion; to improve the social position of women and respect their personalities;

8. To abolish slave labour and slavish education; to oppose forced military service and military training of young people; to educate people in our national language, and to enforce free compulsory education;

9. To enforce an eight-hour day, improve working conditions and raise wages; to formulate labour laws; to enforce state insurance laws for the workers, and to extend state relief to the unemployed;

10. To form a close alliance with nations and states which treat the Koreans as equals and to maintain comradely relations of friendship with states and nations which express goodwill and maintain neutrality toward our national-liberation movement.

THE STATUTES

The Statutes of the ARF comprise eight chapters and 14 articles plus three supplementary articles. These together define the requirements for membership, admission procedure, regulations for members' activities, the organisational principles, the responsibilities of branches, and other details. The Statutes were framed to unite as many patriotic forces as possible and to mobilise them in the anti-Japanese struggle.

INAUGURAL DECLARATION

Preamble: 'Our nation is indeed in an unprecedentedly pitiable situation. Deprived of the land and the hope for the future, which road should it take? It has no alternative but to fight the Japanese imperial robbers. Only then can it see the dawn of national liberation.'

The Declaration then emphasises the importance of unity and how the ARF was built to unite all the anti-Japanese forces at home and abroad, according to its ten-point programme (above):

1. The entire Korean nation, irrespective of classes, sex, position, party affiliation, age, and difference of religion, will unite as one, fight the enemy Japanese imperialist aggressors, liberate the country and establish a genuine people's government of Korea .... .

2. The Koreans in Manchuria will fight in close alliance with the Chinese to overthrow the aggressive setup of Japanese imperialism and its vassal state 'Manchukuo' and effect genuine national autonomy of the Koreans residing in the Chinese territory .... .

3. We will expand and strengthen the revolutionary armed ranks to achieve the cause of national liberation .... .

4. In order to build an independent and sovereign state, rich and powerful, we will follow genuinely popular and democratic policies in the economic and cultural domains .... .

5. We will maintain a close alliance with nations and states which express goodwill and observe neutrality to the Korean national-liberation movement and form a joint front against the Japanese imperialist aggressors, the enemy.

The Declaration then appeals for ARF groups to be formed at once in factories, mines, railways, schools, offices, army barracks, shops and elsewhere to help wage a vigorous liberation struggle.

Appendix 5
Moscow Agreement (27 December 1945), extract relating to Korea

III. KOREA

1. With a view to the re-establishment of Korea as an independent state, the creation of conditions for developing the country on democratic principles and the earliest possible liquidation of the disastrous results of the protracted Japanese domination in Korea, there shall be set up a provisional Korean democratic government which shall take all the necessary steps for developing the industry, transport and agriculture of Korea and the national culture of the Korean people.

2. In order to assist the formation of a provisional Korean government and with a view to the preliminary elaboration of the appropriate measures, there shall be established a Joint Commission consisting of representatives of the United States command in southern Korea and the Soviet command in northern Korea. In preparing their proposals the Commission shall consult with the Korean democratic parties and social organizations. The recommendations worked out by the Commission shall be presented for the consideration of the Governments of the Union of Soviet Socialist Republics, China, the United Kingdom and the United States prior to final decision by the two Governments represented on the Joint Commission.

3. It shall be the task of the Joint Commission, with the participation of the provisional Korean democratic government and of the Korean democratic organizations to work out measures also for helping and assisting (trusteeship) the political, economic and social progress of the Korean people, the development of democratic self-government and the establishment of the national independence of Korea.

The proposals of the Joint Commission shall be submitted, following consultation with the provisional Korean Government for the joint consideration of the Governments of the United States, Union of Soviet Socialist Republics, United Kingdom and China for the working out of an agreement concerning a four-power trusteeship of Korea for a period of up to five years.

4. For the consideration of urgent problems affecting both southern and northern Korea and for the elaboration of measures establishing permanent coordination in administrative-economic matters between the United States command in southern Korea and the Soviet command in northern Korea, a conference of the representatives of the United States and Soviet commands in Korea shall be convened within a period of two weeks.

Appendix 6
Security Council Resolutions 82, 83 and 84 (June–July 1950) authorising UN intervention in Korean civil war

82 (1950). Resolution of 25 June 1950
[S/150]

The Security Council,

Recalling the finding of the General Assembly in its resolution 293 (IV) of 21 October 1949 that the Government of the Republic of Korea is a lawfully established government having effective control and jurisdiction over that part of Korea where the United Nations Temporary Commission on Korea was able to observe and consult and in which the great majority of the people of Korea reside; that this Government is based on elections which were a valid expression of the free will of the electorate of that part of Korea and which were observed by the Temporary Commission; and that this is the only such Government in Korea,

Mindful of the concern expressed by the General Assembly in its resolutions 195 (III) of 12 December 1948 and 293 (IV) of 21 October 1949 about the consequences which might follow unless Member States refrained from acts derogatory to the results sought to be achieved by the United Nations in bringing about the complete independence and unity of Korea; and the concern expressed that the situation described by the United Nations Commission in Korea in its report menaces the safety and well-being of the Republic of Korea and of the people of Korea and might lead to open military conflict there,

Noting with grave concern the armed attack on the Republic of Korea by forces from North Korea,

Determines that this action constitutes a breach of the peace; and

I

Calls for the immediate cessation of hostilities;
Calls upon the authorities in North Korea to withdraw forthwith their armed forces to the 38th parallel;

II

Requests the United Nations Commission on Korea:
  (a) To communicate its fully considered recommendations on the situation with the least possible delay;
  (b) To observe the withdrawal of North Korean forces to the 38th parallel;
  (c) To keep the Security Council informed on the execution of this resolution;

III

Calls upon all Member States to render every assistance to the United Nations in the execution of this resolution and to refrain from giving assistance to the North Korean authorities.

> *Adopted at the 473rd meeting*
> *by 9 votes to none, with 1*
> *abstention (Yugoslavia).*

83 (1950). Resolution of 27 June 1950
[S/1511]

The Security Council
Having determined that the armed attack upon the Republic of Korea by forces from North Korea constitutes a breach of the peace,

Having called for an immediate cessation of hostilities,

Having called upon the authorities in North Korea to withdraw forthwith their armed forces to the 38th parallel,

Having noted from the report of the United Nations Commission on Korea that the authorities in North Korea have neither ceased hostilities nor withdrawn their armed forces to the 38th parallel, and that urgent military measures are required to restore international peace and security,

Having noted the appeal from the Republic of Korea to the United Nations for immediate and effective steps to secure peace and security,

Recommends that the Members of the United Nations furnish such assistance to the Republic of Korea as may be necessary to repel the armed attack and to restore international peace and security in the area.

Adopted at the 474th meeting
by 7 votes to 1 (Yugoslavia).

84 (1950). Resolution of 7 July 1950
[S/1588]

The Security Council,
Having determined that the armed attack upon the Republic of Korea by forces from North Korea constitutes a breach of the peace,

Having recommended that Members of the United Nations furnish such assistance to the Republic of Korea as may be necessary to repel the armed attack and to restore international peace and security in the area,

1. *Welcomes* the prompt and vigorous support which Governments and peoples of the United Nations have given to its resolution 82 (1950) and 83 (1950) of 25 and 27 June 1950 to assist the Republic of Korea in defending itself against armed attack and thus to restore international peace and security in the area;

2. *Notes* that Members of the United Nations have transmitted to the United Nations offers of assistance for the Republic of Korea;

3. *Recommends* that all Members providing military forces and other assistance pursuant to the aforesaid Security Council resolutions make such forces and other assistance available to a unified command under the United States of America;

4. *Requests* the United States to designate the commander of such forces;

5. *Authorizes* the unified command at its discretion to use the United Nations flag in the course of operations against North Korean forces concurrently with the flags of the various nations participating;

6. *Requests* the United States to provide the Security Council with reports as appropriate on the course of action taken under the unified command.

Adopted at the 476th meeting
by 7 votes to none, with 3
abstentions (Egypt, India,
Yugoslavia).

Notes

Notes to the Introduction

1. Paul Bracken, professor of political science at Yale University, observed that 'North Korea is in a crisis that threatens its existence', a crisis in which the nuclear weapons dispute had to be set in the context of North Korea's 'social revolution – a basic transformation in the internal ordering of state and society' ('Nuclear weapons and state survival in North Korea', *Survival*, Vol. 35, no. 3 (Autumn 1993), pp. 137–53).

2. The pundits were now describing the mounting tensions in North and South Korea, the (alleged or actual) mobilisation of forces, and the relative strengths of the contending factions; and speculating on the likely outcomes of various military scenarios. See, for example, Mark Frankland, 'The web that is weaving Korea into a war zone', *The Observer*, London, 27 March 1994; Edward W. Desmond, 'If the shooting starts, who will win?', *Time*, 4 April 1994, pp. 19–21; Rupert Cornwell, 'Pundits ponder the arithmetic of another war', *The Independent*, London, 11 June 1994.

3. Lord Acton's nineteenth-century observation ('Power tends to corrupt and absolute power corrupts absolutely') is much quoted, but commentators generally have little impulse to quote what follows: 'Great men are also always bad men, even when they exercise influence and not authority' (*Life and Letters of Mandel Crighton*, London, 1904). Compare Anthony Trollope (*Prime Minister IV*, viii, 1876): 'We know that power does corrupt, and that we cannot trusts kings to have loving hearts'; and William Pitt, Earl of Chatham (House of Lords, 9 January 1770): 'Unlimited power is apt to corrupt the minds of those who possess it.'

4. The most blatant examples of such cynical US manipulation relate to Iraq (see Geoff Simons, *Iraq: From Sumer to Saddam* (London: Macmillan 1994) pp. 319–25) and Libya (see Marc Weller, 'The Lockerbie Case: a premature end to the 'New World Order'?', *African Journal of International and Comparative Law*, no. 4, 1992.

5. 'Gatt ready to take in Chinese', *The Guardian*, London, 4 June 1994.

6. It was not immediately clear whether such attempts at jury tampering (i.e. US diplomacy) would succeed.

7. Various UN-linked agencies were reporting the catastrophic impact of sanctions on the ordinary Iraqi people. See, for example, *Special Alert*, FAO/WFP Crop and Food Supply Assessment Mission to Iraq, joint publication by Food and Agriculture Organization and World Food Programme, no. 237, July 1993.

8. *News Summary*, United Nations Information Centre (18 Buckingham Gate, London SW1E 6LB), NS/13/94, 14 April 1994.

9. Marc Weller (reader in international law, St Catharine's College, University of Cambridge, England), 'The Lockerbie case', p. 14.

10. John Sullivan and Roberta Foss (eds), *Two Koreas – One Future?* (Lanham, Md: 1987) University Press of America, p. 164.
11. This is not intended to imply that North Korean violations are legitimate, only that the law should be equally binding on all parties.
12. Quoted by Seymour M. Hersh, *The Samson Option* (London: Faber & Faber, 1991) pp. 209–10.
13. Ibid., pp. 210–11.
14. Ibid., p. 213; just as American nuclear-linked products would be channelled to Iraq to support Saddam Hussein's nuclear weapons development programme (see Kenneth R. Timmerman, *The Death Lobby: How the West armed Iraq* (London: Fourth Estate, 1992).
15. James Adams, *The Unnatural Alliance: Israel and South Africa* (London: Quartet Books, 1984), p. 38.
16. John Carlin, 'Pretoria came close to dropping nuclear bomb on Luanda', *The Independent*, London, 30 March 1993.
17. Terry McCarthy, 'Tokyo soothes fears over its nuclear aims', *The Independent*, London, 9 February 1994.
18. Kevin Rafferty, 'Japan agonises over N. Korean sanctions', *The Guardian*, London, 6 June 1994.
19. When Israel complained that such inspections were an infringement of national sovereignty, the Americans quietly abandoned any pressure for nuclear inspections at Dimona.
20. Rafferty, 'Japan agonises'.
21. See, for example, Chung Kyungmo who describes (in Sullivan and Foss (eds), *Two Koreas*, pp. 142–5) how 'An increasing number of South Koreans have come to realise that the UN Flag that flutters in the skies of their country is legally fraudulent and morally indefensible'.
22. Gordon Thomas, *Journey into Madness: Medical torture and the mind controllers* (London: Corgi Books, 1989) pp. 159, 162; John Marks, *The Search for the 'Manchurian Candidate'* (London: Allen Lane, Penguin Books, 1979) p. 23.
23. Robert Jay Lifton, *The Nazi Doctors: A study in the psychology of evil* (London: Macmillan, 1986) p. xii.
24. This was during the Vietnam war when, for example, Lieutenant William Calley and his troops rounded up 347 civilians at My Lai and raped, mutilated and murdered them; and when American B-52 aircraft were 'terror bombing' (*The Washington Post*) Hanoi and Haiphong to the point that, apart from the dead and maimed, 30,000 children were made permanently deaf at Christmas 1972.
25. Quoted by James Pringle, 'Neighbours fear Kim Jr's finger on nuclear button', *The Times*, London, 23 October 1993.

Notes to Chapter 1: The Mounting Tensions

1. Martin Walker, Simon Tisdall and Paul Webster, 'Hurd says Saddam must go', *The Guardian*, London, 2 March 1991.

2. Noam Chomsky, 'The weak shall inherit nothing', *The Guardian*, London, 25 March 1991.

3. There are many examples of US violations of international law and the UN Charter. Here we need only cite the US repudiation of the 1971 Montreal Convention over the Lockerbie outrage, the unilateral imposition of a no-fly zone over southern Iraq, the use of civilian starvation as a war-time and peace-time political weapon (Haiti, Iraq, Cuba) in violation of the Geneva Convention, the protection of Israel's decision to ignore many Security Council resolutions (most recently, SC 799), the repudiation of the World Court ruling (1986) condemning US terrorist acts against Nicaragua, the refusal to comply with General Assembly resolutions (47/19 and 48/16) condemning the US blockade of Cuba, etc.

4. A prime example of such a parallel operation, designed to protect US global strategic and commercial interests, is the pressure that was applied on states to conclude the Uruguay GATT round (end-1993), despite the drastic consequences that this would have for many countries (primarily those in the Third World). By mid-1994 the GATT deal had led to massive public protests in India, the collapse of the South Korean cabinet, and a new US trade war with Japan.

5. William Neikirk,'We are the world's guardian angels', *Chicago Tribune*, business section, 9 September 1990, quoted by Noam Chomsky, *Deterring Democracy* (London: Verso, 1991) p. 5.

6. Patrick Buchanan, 'Have the neocons thought this through?', in Micah L. Sifry and Christopher Cerf (eds), *The Gulf War Reader* (New York: Times Books, Random House, 1991), pp. 213–15.

7. Henry Kissinger, 'The delicate balance', *Los Angeles Times*, 24 February 1991, reprinted as 'A false dream', in Sifry and Cerf (eds), ibid, pp. 461–5.

8. John Lichfield, 'Pentagon lists "the next seven wars"', *The Independent*, London, 18 February 1992; Patrick Tyler, 'Pentagon pleads case for "regional war" firepower', *The Guardian*, London, 18 February 1992.

9. Quoted in Patrick Cockburn, 'Post Cold War world defeats Clinton', *The Independent*, London, 30 May 1994.

10. This of course is the perennial problem: *quis custodiet ipsos custodes?* (who will guard the guardians?).

11. The shortcomings of the NPT (and other related considerations) are well discussed in Alva Myrdal, *The Game of Disarmament: How the United States and Russia ran the arms race* (Manchester: Manchester University Press 1977) Chs. 6 and 7.

12. A decision bitterly resented by Britain, eager to continue using the Nevada test site for the development of warheads for the Trident missile and for the development of a new tactical 'gravity bomb' for use in various roles (Rupert Cornwell, 'Clinton to extend ban on nuclear testing', *The Independent*, London, 1 July 1993); see also David Fairhall, 'Britain cautious as nuclear test ban talks begin in Geneva', *The Guardian*, London, 3 February 1994.

13. Martin Walker, 'US admits to "losing" nuclear material', *The Guardian*, London, 21 May 1994.

14. Martin Walker, 'Pentagon aims to repair crumbling bridges in the Pacific', *The Guardian*, London, 19 November 1991.
15. 'Safeguards inspections to DPRK', *IAEA Newsbriefs*, Vol. 7, no. 3(55), June/July 1992.
16. Matthew Campbell, 'Russians storm jet to stop Korean bomb', *The Sunday Times*, London, 20 December 1992.
17. Simon Tisdall, 'Rush to stop Korea A-bomb', *The Guardian*, London, 27 February 1993.
18. Raymond Whitaker and Peter Pringle, 'North Korea steps up war preparations', *The Independent*, London, 16 March 1993.
19. Reuter report, 'War at hand, says N. Korea', *The Guardian*, London, 16 March 1993.
20. Simon Tisdall, 'West poised for sanctions on N. Korea', *The Guardian*, London, 17 March 1993.
21. 'Pyongyang's ambitions', *International Herald Tribune*, 28 June 1993.
22. Paul F. Horvitz, 'US gives warning to North Koreans on nuclear bomb', *International Herald Tribune*, 5 July 1993.
23. Donna Smith, 'Clinton tells N. Korea not to develop bomb', *The Guardian*, London, 12 July 1993; Stephen Robinson, 'Clinton woos troops with retaliation threat to N. Korea', *The Daily Telegraph*, London, 12 July 1993.
24. James Adams and Jon Swain, 'US targets cruise missiles at Korea', *The Sunday Times*, London, 7 November 1993; Ambrose Evans-Pritchard, 'Clinton Korea missile crisis risks all-out war', *The Sunday Telegraph*, London, 7 November 1993.
25. David E. Sanger, 'Nuclear agency sounds alarm over North Korea', *International Herald Tribune*, 3 December 1993.
26. Ibid.,
27. S/26456/Add. 2, United Nations, 7 December 1993, p. 3.
28. Ibid., pp. 4–8.
29. James Adams, 'America prepares for war with North Korea', *The Sunday Times*, London, 12 December 1993; J. F. McAllister, 'Frightening face-off' ('Washington considers hard-line options ... '), *Time*, 13 December 1993.
30. Teresa Poole, 'Korea needs "patience"', *The Independent*, London, 28 December 1993.
31. Patrick Cockburn, 'White House attacked over nuclear deal', *The Independent*, London, 6 January 1994; 'Nuclear bluff', *The Economist*, London, 8 January 1994.
32. David E. Sanger, 'North Koreans buy 40 old Soviet subs', *International Herald Tribune*, 20 January 1994.
33. John D. Morrocco and David Hughes, 'Korean impasse spurs Patriot plans', *Aviation Week and Space Technology*, 31 January 1994.
34. Raymond Whitaker, 'N. Korea raises nuclear stakes', *The Independent*, London, 22 February 1994.
35. James Adams, 'N. Korea warns of war over its nuclear secrets', *The Sunday Times*, London, 20 March 1994.
36. Stephen Robinson, 'US threats of reprisals as heat rises in nuclear row', *The Daily Telegraph*, London, 21 March 1994.

37. 'Rift between IAEA and North Korea deepens', *News Summary*, NS/10/94 (London: United Nations Information Centre, 24 March 1994).

38. 'Moscow presses for summit to prevent Korean war', *The Times*, London, 25 March 1994; Simon Tisdall, 'Russia moves to defuse tension over N. Korea', *The Guardian*, London, 25 March 1994.

39. Simon Tisdall, 'Chinese veto hits US nuclear policy in Asia', *The Guardian*, London, 31 March 1994.

40. David Usborne, 'Pentagon talks war to N. Korea', *The Independent*, London, 1 April 1994.

41. Rupert Cornwell, 'US sends mixed signals to N. Korea', *The Independent*, London, 4 April 1994.

42. 'New Korea nuclear row', *The Daily Telegraph*, London, 30 April 1994.

43. Shim Jae Hoon, 'Nuclear two-step', *Far Eastern Economic Review*, 28 April 1994.

44. 'N-plant fears', *The Observer*, London, 15 May 1994; 'North Korea violating nuclear rules', *The Daily Telegraph*, London, 21 March 1994; Raymond Whitaker, 'N. Korea sets off nuclear alarm', *The Independent*, London, 21 May 1994.

45. Reuter report, 'N. Korea cleared of diverting nuclear fuel to produce arms', *The Guardian*, London, 21 May 1994.

46. 'North Korea thought to have separated Pu in the 1970s with Soviet help', *NuclearFuel*, 22 June 1992, p. 15.

47. 'The Yongbyon puzzle', *Asiaweek*, 9 March 1990, pp. 17–19.

48. Joseph S. Bermudez Jr, 'North Korea's nuclear programme', *Jane's Intelligence Review*, September 1991, pp. 404–11.

49. *IAEA Newsbriefs*, Vol. 7, no. 3(55), June/July 1992, p. 3; D. Albright and M. Hibbs, 'North Korea's plutonium puzzle', *The Bulletin of the Atomic Scientists*, November 1992, pp. 36–40.

50. Mark Hibbs, 'Isotopics show three North Korean reprocessing campaigns since 1975', *NuclearFuel*, 1 March 1993, pp. 8–9.

51. Terry McCarthy, 'Koreas agree on nuclear arms ban', *The Independent*, London, 2 January 1992; Tae-Hwan Kwak and Seung-Ho Joo, 'The denuclearisation of the Korean peninsula: problems and prospects', *Arms Control*, Vol. 14, no. 2, August 1993, pp. 65–92; D. Albright and M. Hibbs, 'North Korea's plutonium puzzle', *The Bulletin of the Atomic Scientists*, November 1992, pp. 36–40.

52. Nick Rufford, David Leppard and Ian Burrell, 'Koreans build A-bomb complex', *The Sunday Times*, London, 4 April 1993.

53. R. Jeffrey Smith, 'N. Korea and the bomb: high-tech hide-and-seek', *The Washington Post*, 27 April 1993.

54. James Adams, 'CIA falls out over Korea's "bogus" bomb', *The Sunday Times*, London, 24 October 1993; Stephen Engelberg and Michael R. Gordon, 'North Korea likely to have developed own atomic bomb, CIA tells president', *International Herald Tribune*, 27 December 1993.

55. Bruce W. Nelan, 'Playing a game of nuclear roulette', *Time*, 10 January 1994.

56. Leonard Doyle, 'Satellite adds to evidence of N. Korean bomb plans', *The Independent*, London, 25 March 1994.
57. Kevin Rafferty, 'Korean student demonstration highlights US dilemma', *The Guardian*, London, 30 May 1994.
58. Martin Walker, 'North Korea "has crossed red line"', *The Guardian*, London, 1 June 1994.
59. Martin Fletcher, 'US to press for punitive sanctions on North Korea', *The Times*, London, 3 June 1994; Martin Walker, 'North Korea brings world to crisis point', *The Guardian*, London, 3 June 1994.
60. Patrick E. Tyler, 'Beijing cautions against escalating North Korea rift', *International Herald Tribune*, 3 June 1994; Steven Erlanger, 'Yeltsin to insist on a conference prior to embargo', *International Herald Tribune*, 3 June 1994.
61. Patrick Cockburn, 'US pushed ahead on N. Korea sanctions', *The Independent*, London, 4 June 1994; 'Containing North Korea' (editorial), *The Daily Telegraph*, London, 4 June 1994.
62. James Adams, 'Clinton sends in fleet to put pressure on Korea', *The Sunday Times*, London, 5 June 1994.
63. William Arkin and Richard Fieldhouse, *Nuclear Battlefields* (Cambridge, Mass: Ballinger 1985), pp. 120, 121, 231.
64. Stephen Goose, 'The Military situation on the Korean peninsula', in John Sullivan and Roberta Foss (eds), *Two Koreas – One Future?* (Lanham, Md: University Press of America, 1987) pp. 80–2.
65. Martin Hart-Landsberg, *The Rush to Development: Economic change and political struggle in South Korea* (New York: Monthly Review Press, 1993) p. 287.
66. Leonard Doyle, 'West finds riches in deadly mine trade', *The Independent*, London, 6 June 1994.
67. See, for example, Kenneth R. Timmerman, *The Death Lobby: How the West armed Iraq* (London: Fourth Estate, 1992).
68. Douglas Jehl, 'Iran "close to North Korean missile deal"', *The Guardian*, London, 9 April 1993; Rupert Cornwell, 'Iran "seeks missile deal" with N. Korea',*The Independent*, London, 9 April 1993.
69. Martin Walker, 'US concealed North Korean missile deal', *The Guardian*, London, 13 December 1993.
70. Simon Tisdall, 'Asia's nuclear reaction', *The Guardian*, London, 2 April 1993.
71. Rupert Guest, 'BAe wins £39m Seoul arms deal', *The Daily Telegraph*, London, 14 May 1994; Leslie Yazel, 'BAe consortium will ship combat system to Korea', *Computing*, London, 26 May 1994.
72. *ROK-PRC Relations* (Seoul, Korea: Korean Overseas Information Service, March 1994).
73. William Walker and Frans Berkhout, 'Japan's plutonium problem – and Europe's', *Arms Control Today*, September 1992, p. 6, table 1.
74. Ibid., p. 7, table 2.
75. *Choson Ilbo*, Seoul, 23 January 1992.
76. Naoaki Usui and George Leopold, 'N. Korean launch may spur Japan missile defence upgrade', *Defence News*, 21 June 1993.

77. Annika Savill, 'Japanese win right to nuclear weapons', *The Independent*, London, 9 July 1993; Kevin Rafferty, 'Nuclear rethink forced on Japan', *The Guardian*, London, 18 August 1993.
78. Selig S. Harrison, 'The three-cornered nuclear suspense in Northeast Asia', *International Herald Tribune*, 2 November 1993.
79. Jon Swain, 'Japan dares not cut N. Korea's nuclear lifeline', *The Sunday Times*, London, 14 November 1993; David E. Sanger, 'North Korea exiles help regime to build threat', *International Herald Tribune*, 2 November 1993; Hugo Gurdon, 'Japan bankrolls Kim's timebomb', *The Sunday Telegraph*, London, 15 January 1994.
80. Terry McCarthy, 'Japanese hi-tech in N. Korean missiles', *The Independent*, London, 15 January 1994.
81. *ROK-Japan Relations* (Seoul, Korea: Korean Overseas Information Service, March 1994).
82. Raymond Whitaker and Rupert Cornwell, 'Pressure on N. Korea alarms its neighbours', *The Independent*, London, 8 November 1993; Nick Cumming-Bruce, 'Crisis? The world thinks there's a crisis?' ('South Koreans are more worried by American reactions than by an attack from the North'), *The Observer*, London, 3 April 1994; Edward W. Desmond, 'We'd like to help but ... ' ('Japan reluctantly prepares for a Pyongyang–Washington showdown'), *Time*, 16 May 1994.
83. *Unification Policy* (Seoul, Korea: Korean Overseas Information Service, March 1994).
84. 'Planning for a Boomsday Scenario' (*Korea Countdown*, published by Merit Communications, Seoul), *Time*, 6 June 1994.
85. Ibid.,
86. A principal current role for the CIA is economic espionage, not only against foreign commercial competitors of the US but also against GATT and related conferences. In December 1990, a CIA official declared that the CIA had been 'involved in GATT and every trade negotiation. We take tasks from US negotiators to find out about the [the other countries'] positions. We usually have someone who's right there, or within cable reach ... We tell our negotiators "Here's what the other side left out or is holding back"' (*The Independent*, London, 14 November 1990); *The Guardian*, London, 29 December 1990; *The Daily Telegraph*, 24 January 1992.
87. GATT was designed as a principal tool for the purpose, a main pillar of the IMF/World Bank/GATT/TNC nexus.
88. 'Koreans trade nuclear insults', *The Observer*, London, 5 June 1994.
89. A commentary in the *Ta Kung Pao* newspaper declared that the problem 'now lies in North Korea's obstinate attitude'. This followed a report from the Chinese news agency Xinhua that China's UN ambassador, Li Zhaoxing, had 'openly delivered a message of strong warning to the North Korean side'. One commentator (Simon Long, *The Guardian*, London, 7 June 1994) suggested that China's opposition to sanctions was 'tactical rather than political'.
90. Raymond Whitaker, 'N. Korea offers nuclear inspection too late', *The Independent*, London, 9 June 1994.

91. Raymond Whitaker, 'UN nuclear agency takes first crack at N. Korea', *The Independent*, London, 11 June 1994.

92. Rupert Cornwell, 'Pundits ponder the arithmetic of death of another war', *The Independent*, London, 11 June 1994.

93. Graham Hutchings, 'Defiant China sets off nuclear blast', *The Daily Telegraph*, London, 11 June 1994; Teresa Poole, 'Relief at Chinese nuclear explosion', *The Independent*, London, 11 June 1994.

94. Hugo Gurdon, 'N. Korea risks UN embargo "thumbscrew"', *The Daily Telegraph*, London, 13 June 1994.

95. Diane B. Kunz, 'Sanctions never work and Kim Il-sung knows it', *The Daily Telegraph*, London, 13 June 1994.

96. Kevin Rafferty, 'Southerners brave out hot war alert in shadow of North Korea's guns', *The Guardian*, London, 14 June 1994.

97. Martin Walker, Mark Tran and Kevin Rafferty, 'Clinton may send troops to S. Korea', *The Independent*, London, 17 June 1994.

98. Patrick Cockburn and Teresa Poole, 'N. Korea and US narrow differences', *The Independent*, London, 17 June 1994.

99. Kevin Rafferty and David Hearst, 'North Korea "reverses ban on monitors" ', *The Guardian*, London, 17 June 1994.

100. Nick Rufford, 'Carter arranges first North-South summit as US keeps its powder dry', *The Sunday Times*, London, 19 June 1994; Catherine Field, 'Divided Korean leaders to meet', *The Observer*, London, 19 June 1994.

101. Maurice Weaver and Hugo Gurdon, 'Clinton at odds with Carter over stand on Korea', *The Daily Telegraph*, London, 18 June 1994.

102. Martin Walker, 'Clinton opts to wait and see after Carter visit', *The Guardian*, London, 18 June 1994; Jonathan Freedland, 'US and allies offer to ease N. Korea in from the cold', *The Guardian*, London, 20 June 1994; 'Seoul wary as it prepares for summit with North Korea', *The Independent*, London, 21 June 1994.

103. Martin Walker, 'Korea nuclear deal hangs on pledge of "no first use"', *The Guardian*, London, 22 June 1994.

104. Martin Walker, 'Mad as hell over what they've done to America', *The Guardian*, London, 25 June 1994.

105. Nick Rufford, 'Korea on alert as suspicions grows after the mystery death of Kim Il-sung', *The Sunday Times*, London, 10 July 1994; Hugo Gurdon, 'Korea balanced on edge of hope and fear', *The Daily Telegraph*, London, 11 July 1994.

106. Nick Rufford and James Adams, 'North Korea mourns the monster', *The Sunday Times*, London, 10 July 1994.

107. Nick Rufford, 'Defiant Korea marches on towards Armageddon', *The Sunday Times*, London, 12 June 1994.

108. Hugo Gurdon and Robert Guest, 'Seoul senses softer line as Kim Jong-il takes power', *The Daily Telegraph*, London, 12 July 1994; Robert Guest, 'Seoul is seeking to build bridges with Kim Jong-il', *The Daily Telegraph*, London, 13 July 1994.

109. Robert Guest, 'Pyongyang's new leader tightens grip on military', *The Daily Telegraph*, London, 15 July 1994.

110. Nick Rufford, 'Korean funeral delay fuels fear', *The Sunday Times*, London, 17 July 1994; Donald Kirk, 'Funeral delay fuels fears of purges in Korea', *The Observer*, London, 17 July 1994; Kevin Rafferty, 'Vanishing act by "Baby" Kim's rivals', *The Guardian*, London, 18 July 1994.
111. 'North furious as Seoul says Kim started the war', *The Daily Telegraph*, London, 22 July 1994.
112. Edward W. Desmond, 'Will the Dear Leader be great?', *Time*, 25 July 1994.
113. *Patterns of Global Terrorism 1993*, Department of State Publication 10136, Washington, released April 1994, p. 25.
114. David Watt, 'How we see the Americans', in Lawrence Freedman (ed.), *The Troubled Alliance* (London: Heinemann, 1983), pp. 28–43.
115. Anna Tomforde, 'Weapon-grade plutonium smuggled into Germany', *The Guardian*, London, 18 July 1994.
116. James O. Jackson, 'Nightmare in a vial of dust', *Time*, 1 August 1994, pp. 22–3.
117. Marie Colvin, 'Britain's Gulf war ally helped Saddam build nuclear bomb', *The Sunday Times*, London, 24 July 1994, pp. 1–2.
118. Seymour M. Hersh, *The Samson Option* (London: Faber & Faber 1991) pp. 318–19.
119. Kenneth R. Timmerman, *The Death Lobby: How the West armed Iraq* (London: Fourth Estate, 1992).
120. Robert Guest, 'Defector says N. Korea has five atomic bombs', *The Daily Telegraph*, London, 28 July 1994.

Notes to Chapter 2: Beginnings

1. William E. Henthorn, *A History of Korea* (New York: The Free Press 1971) pp. 8–9.
2. Ki-baik Lee, *A New History of Korea* (Cambridge, Mass.: Harvard University Press 1984) p. 3.
3. Henthorn, *History of Korea*, p. 11.
4. Kim Choljun, 'Primitive culture and the beginning of the tribal states', in *Korea, its Land, People and Culture of All Ages* (Seoul, Korea: Hakwon-Sa 1960) p. 21.
5. Lee, *New History of Korea*, p. 8.
6. Edwin O. Reischauer and John K. Fairbank, *A History of East Asian Civilization*, Vol. I: *East Asia: The Great Tradition* (Boston, Mass.: Houghton Mifflin 1960) pp. 402–3.
7. Reischauer and Fairbank (ibid., p. 403) argue for 'some historical substance in that it [the legend] relates to the definitely Sinicized kingdom of Choson'. Against this, M. Frederick Nelson (*Korea and the Old Orders in Eastern Asia*, (Baton Rouge, La: Louisiana State University Press, 1946, p. 21) comments that the Shang books in the Chinese *Book of History*, the only source of the tale, are 'fabrications written in Chou times as propaganda to justify the overthrown of the

Shang by the Chou. The migration of Chi-tzu' has 'no historical value'.

8. Takashi Hatada, *A History of Korea*, trans. and ed. Warren W. Smith and Benjamin H. Hazard (Santa Barbara, Cal.: ABC-Clio 1969) pp. 4–5.
9. Lee, *New History of Korea*, pp. 21–2
10. Ibid., p. 23.
11. Nelson, *Korea and the Old Orders*, p. 20.
12. G. Nye Steiger, *A History of the Far East* (New York: Ginn 1944), p. 203.
13. Lee, *New History of Korea*, p. 37.
14. Hatada, *History of Korea*, p. 21.
15. Lee, *New History of Korea*, pp. 49–51; Henthorn, *History of Korea*, pp. 40–2; Hatada, *History of Korea*, pp. 21–2.
16. Henthorn, *History of Korea*, p. 53.

Notes to Chapter 3: The Unified State

1. Takashi Hatada, *A History of Korea* (Santa Barbara, Cal.: ABC-Clio, 1969) p. 25.
2. William E. Henthorn, *A History of Korea* (New York: The Free Press, 1971) pp. 61–4, 68–77.
3. Ibid., pp. 68–73; Edwin O. Reischauer and John K. Fairbank, *A History of East Asian Civilization*, vol. I: *East Asia: The Great Tradition* (Boston, Mass.: Houghton Mifflin, 1960), pp. 412–14.
4. Henthorn, *History of Korea*, p. 79.
5. Hatada, *History of Korea*, p. 32–6.
6. John K. Fairbank, Edwin O. Reischauer and Albert M. Craig, *East Asia, Tradition and Transformation* (London: George Allen & Unwin, 1973), pp. 292–7; Reischauer and Fairbank, History of East Asian Civilisation, vol I, pp. 416–23; Pyon Taesop, 'Koryo Dynasty', in, *Korea, its Land, People and Culture of All Ages* (Seoul, Korea: Hakwon-Sa, 1960), pp. 28–36.
7. Fairbank *et al.*, *East Asia*, p. 293.
8. Hatada, *History of Korea*, pp. 47–8.
9. Ibid., p. 52.
10. Ibid., pp. 53–4.
11. Reischauer and Fairbank, *History of East Asian Civilization*, vol. I, p. 426.
12. Ki-baik Lee, *A New History of Korea* (Cambridge Mass.: Harvard University Press, 1984), pp. 165–71.
13. Kim Yongdok, 'Yi Chosun', in *Korea, its Land, People and Culture of All Ages*, pp. 40–5; Reischauer and Fairbank, *History of East Asian Civilization, vol. I, pp. 427–9, 431–2*.
14. Henthorn, *History of Korea*, p. 141.
15. Reischauer and Fairbank, *History of East Asian Civilization*, vol. I, p. 434.

16. Hatada, *History of Korea*, p. 81.
17. Richard Storry, *A History of Modern Japan* (Harmondsworth, Middx: Penguin Books, 1963) p. 49.
18. Quoted in ibid., p. 50.
19. Quoted in Yoshi S. Kuno, *Japanese Expansion in the Asiatic Continent* (Berkeley, Cal., 1937–40) vol. I, pp. 303–4.
20. Hatada, *History of Korea*, p. 78.
21. M. Frederick Nelson, *Korea and the Old Orders in Eastern Asia* (Baton Rouge, La: Louisiana State University Press, 1946) p. 78.
22. Ibid.,
23. Lee, *New History of Korea*, p. 216.
24. Quoted by Nelson, *Korea and the Old Orders* p. 82.
25. Ibid., p. 85.
26. Ibid., p. 110.
27. J. H. Longford, *The Story of Korea*, (London, 1911) pp. 226–7.
28. *United States House Exceecutive Documents*, 28 Cong., 2 Sess., no. 138, 'Extensions of American Commerce – Proposed Mission to Japan and Corea' (Washington, D.C.: 1845).
29. Ivan Morris, *The Nobility of Failure: Tragic Heroes in the History of Japan* (London: Secker & Warburg, 1975), pp. 217–75.
30. Hatada, *History of Korea*, p. 97.
31. Nelson, *Korea and the Old Orders*, pp. 139–41.
32. David Bergamini, *Japan's Imperial Conspiracy* (London: Panther Books, 1972), pp. 265–6.
33. Ibid., p. 266.
34. W. G. Beasley, *The Modern History of Japan*, (London: Weidenfeld & Nicolson, 1973) p. 170.
35. Storry, *History of Modern Japan*, p. 140.

Notes to Chapter 4: The Japanese Colony

1. *Lytton Report*, League of Nations document, 1932, vii, 12, p. 13.
2. Quoted in Tyler Dennett, *Roosevelt and the Russo-Japanese War* (New York, 1925) pp. 97–101.
3. The terms of the Taft–Katsura agreement, encouraging the Japanese annexation of Korea (1910), were not made public until 1922.
4. The support of Britain for Japanese imperialism brought minor dividends in the First World War. Japan demanded that Germany remove her warships from the Far East and relinquish Kiau-Chau, her much-valued leased territory in China. When Germany ignored Japan's ultimatum, Japanese warships shelled Tsing-tau and bombed it using sea-planes. On 7 November 1914, Tsing-tau fell to British and Japanese troops.
5. M. Frederick Nelson, *Korea and the Old Orders in Eastern Asia* (Baton Rouge, La: Louisiana State University, 1946) p. 260.
6. Robert T. Oliver, *Syngman Rhee: The Man Behind the Mask* (London: Robert Hall, 1955), pp. 71–2.

7. Michael Montgomery, *Imperialist Japan: The Yen to Dominate* (London: Christopher Helm, 1987), p. 206.

8. T. F. Millard, *America and the Far Eastern Question* (New York, 1909), p. 131.

9. Nelson, *Korea and the Old Orders*, p. 279.

10. Ibid., p. 281.

11. Montgomery, *Imperialist Japan*, p. 209.

12. An Joong Keun became enshrined as a national patriot. Thus the twelve-year-old Kim Il-sung, later to become communist leader and the President of North Korea, introduced a play, performed at Baiksan School at Fusung, to celebrate how An Joong Keun killed Ito Hirobumi: 'This is revenge taken by those deprived of their fatherland against those criminals who have taken our fatherland from us. But An Joong Keun was murdered by the pirates ... Who could not sympathise with An Joong Keun who loved his fatherland at the risk of his life?' In the play that followed, Kim Il-sung played the part of An Joong Keun, so, we are told, inspiring the audience 'with anti-Japanese patriotic thoughts' (Baik Bong, *Kim Il Sung*, (Beirut, Lebanon: Dar Al-Talia, 1973), p. 66.

13. Nelson, *Korea and the Old Orders*, pp. 282–3.

14. Ibid., p. 283.

15. Quoted by Nelson, ibid.,

16. Hong Isop, 'The Modern Period', in *Korea, its Land, People and Culture of All Ages*, (Seoul, Korea: Hakwon-Sa, 1960), p. 89.

17. Janet E. Hunter, *The Emergence of Modern Japan* (London: Longman, 1989), pp. 50–1.

18. Hong Isop, 'The Modern Period', p. 97.

19. Kim Han Gil, *Modern History of Korea* (Pyongyang, Korea: Foreign Languages Publishing House, 1979) pp. 10–11.

20. Oliver, *Syngman Rhee*, p. 118.

21. Quoted by Oliver, *Ibid*, p. 119.

22. Ki-baik Lee, *A New History of Korea*, trans. Edward W. Wagner and Edward J. Shultz (Cambridge, Mass.: Harvard University Press, 1984, pp. 347–8).

23. Ibid., p. 352.

24. Ibid., p. 353.

25. Ibid., p. 357.

26. Donald A. Jordan *Chinese Boycotts versus Japanese Bombs* (Ann Arbor, Mich.: University of Michigan Press, 1991) pp. 23–5, 36–7, 42–3.

27. Ibid., p. 24.

28. Cited by Montgomery, *Imperialist Japan*, p. vii.

29. *The Economist*, London, 17 August 1991, p. 44.

30. This translation, made shortly after the event, is given in Lee, *New History of Korea*, p. 342; an alternative translation, with the rest of the Declaration, is given in Oliver, *Syngman Rhee*, pp. 136–8.

31. Quoted in Oliver, *Syngman Rhee*, p. 138.

32. Takashi Hatada, *A History of Korea*, trans. and ed. Warren W. Smith Jr and Benjamin H. Hazard (Santa Barbara, Cal.: ABC-Clio, 1969), p. 115.

33. Lee, *New History of Korea*, p. 344.
34. Oliver, *Syngman Rhee*, pp. 140–1.
35. Chong-sik Lee, *The Politics of Korean Nationalism* (Berkeley Cal.: University of California Press, 1965); quoted in Michael C. Sandusky, *America's Parallel* (Alexandria, Va: Old Dominion Press, 1983), p. 57.
36. Philip Jaishon (ed.), *Korean Review*, vol. 1, no. 5 (July 1919), pp. 9–10; cited by Sandusky, *America's Parallel*, p. 61.
37. Sandusky, *America's Parallel*, p. 62.
38. Kim Han Gil, *Modern History of Korea*, p. 20.
39. Quoted by Kim Han Gil, ibid., p. 21.
40. Chosa Jiho, Investigation Section, General Affairs Department, South Manchurian Railway Company, 25 November 1928, p 49; quoted by Kim Han Gil, ibid, p. 29.
41. European colonialism in Africa and Asia was no less racist than Japanese colonialism in Asia. Moreover, at a time when Japan was expanding its Asian hegemony the US Congress was extending the scope of the racist Exclusion Act to ban immigration of Asians. A document produced by the US Asiatic Exclusion League noted in 1907 how the 'racial incompatibility as between the people of the Orient and the United States represents a problem of race preservation which it is our imperative duty to solve in our own favor'; and a 1906 Senate Document (Number 147, 1906, 59:2:3) declared that 'our children should not be placed in any position where their youthful impressions may be affected by association with pupils of the Mongolian race' (taken to include all Asians) (quoted in Benjamin B. Ringer, *'We the Peoples' and Others; Duality and America's Treatment of Its Racial Minorities* (New York and London: Tavistock Publications, 1983 pp. 687–8, 689).
42. Edward Behr, *Hirohito: Behind the Myth* (Harmondsworth, Middx: Penguin Books, 1990) p. 70.
43. Oliver, *Syngman Rhee*, p. 168.
44. Rentaro Mizuno, when a minister in Seoul in 1919, was wounded in a bomb-throwing incident, an event said to have exacerbated his intense dislike of the Koreans. The fourth anniversary of the incident fell on 2 September 1923 (Leonard Mosley, *Hirohito, Emperor of Japan* (London: Weidenfeld & Nicolson, 1966) pp. 81–2).
45. Noel F. Busch, *Two Minutes to Noon* (New York: Simon & Schuster, 1962); Mosley, *Hirohito*, pp. 83–5.
46. See, for example, John Dower, *War Without Mercy: Race and Power in the Pacific War.* (London, Faber & Faber, 1986).
47. Ibid., pp. 282–5.
48. Edward S. Miller, *War Plan Orange: The US Strategy to Defeat Japan, 1897–1945* (Annapolis, Md: Naval Institute Press, 1991).
49. Ibid., p. 361.
50. Lee *New History of Korea* pp. 353–4.
51. Quoted by Lord Russell of Liverpool, *The Knights of Bushido* (London: Corgi, 1976) p. 58.
52. Quoted by Russell, ibid.
53. Ibid., p. 59.

54. Terry McCarthy, 'Japan voices remorse for wartime use of sex slaves', *The Independent*, London, 5 August 1993. In December 1991, 35 Korean women filed a 700 million yen (£3 million) suit against the Japanese government claiming compensation for their wartime suffering as 'comfort women' (Terry McCarthy, 'Japanese army forced girls into sex slavery'. *The Independent on Sunday*, London, 15 December 1991). On 31 August 1993 the South Korean government announced that it would pay a lump sum of £4500 and £120 a month for life to each of the 121 surviving women used as sex slaves by Japan's Second World War army (AP report, *The Guardian*, London, 1 September 1993).
55. Dower, *War Without Mercy*, pp. 47, 363n.
56. Quoted by Sandusky, *America's Parallel*, p. 82.

Notes to Chapter 5: The Divided Nation

1. Francis L. Loewenheim, Harold D. Langley and Manfred Jonas (eds), *Roosevelt and Churchill: Their Secret Wartime Correspondence* (London: Barrie & Jenkins, 1975) p. 43.
2. Robert T. Oliver, *Korea, Forgotten Nation* (Washington, D. C.: Public Affairs Press, 1944).
3. Anthony Eden, *The memoirs of Anthony Eden: The Reckoning* (Boston, Mass.: Houghton Mifflin, 1965) p. 438.
4. US Department of State, *Foreign Relations of the United States: Diplomatic Papers, Conferences at Cairo and Teheran* (Washington, D.C.: US Government Printing Office, 1961) pp. 399–404.
5. Robert E. Sherwood, *Roosevelt and Hopkins: An Intimate History* (New York: Harper, 1948) p. 777.
6. Jim Bishop, *FDR's Last Year, April 1944–April 1945* (London: Hart-Davis, MacGibbon, 1975) p. 370.
7. Bruce Cumings, 'The Division of Korea', in John Sullivan and Roberta Foss (eds), *Two Koreas – One Future?* (Lanham, Md and London: University Press of America, 1987) pp. 7–10; Jon Halliday and Bruce Cumings, *Korea: The Unknown War* (London: Viking, 1988) pp. 16–17.
8. Cumings, 'Division of Korea', p. 7.
9. Peter Lowe, *The Origins of the Korean War* (London: Longman, 1986) p. 19.
10. Ki-baik Lee, *A New Histoy of Korea*, trans. Edward W. Wagner and Edward J. Shultz (Cambridge, Mass.: Harvard University Press, 1984) p. 374.
11. Oswald Garrison Villard, 'We must free Korea now', November 1945, p 521, quoted by Michael C. Sandusky, *America's Parallel* (Alexandria, Va: Old Dominion Press, 1983) p. 26.
12. Quoted by Kim Han Gil, *Modern History of Korea* (Pyongyang, Korea: Foreign Languages Publishing House, 1979) p. 187.
13. Alfred Crofts [member of USAMIGIK], 'Our Falling Ramparts – the Case of Korea', *The Nation*, 25 June 1960, p. 545.

14. E. Grant Meade [member of USAMIGIK], *American Military Government in Korea* (London: Oxford University Press, 1951) pp. 59–62.
15. John Gunther, *The Riddle of MacArthur* (London: Hamish Hamilton, 1951).
16. Meade, *American Military Government*, pp. 59–62.
17. A. Wigfall Green [member of USAMIGIK], *Epic of Korea* (Washington, D.C.: Public Affairs Press, 1950) p. 95.
18. Ibid., p. 97.
19. Hak-Joon Kim, *The Unification Policy of South and North Korea* (Seoul, Korea: Seoul National University Press, 1977) p. 39.
20. US Department of State, *Bulletin*, 21 October 1945, p. 646.
21. Halliday and Cumings, *Korea*, p. 29.
22. Kim Chang-sun, *Fifteen-year History of North Korea* (Washington, D.C. 1965).
23. Bruce Cumings, *The Origins of the Korean War: Liberation and the Emergence of Separate Regimes, 1945–1947* (Princeton, N.J. 1981) pp. 388–9.
24. Anna Louise Strong, *Inside North Korea* (Montrose, Cal., 1951) p. 8.
25. Eric Van Ree, *Socialism in One Zone: Stalin's Policy in Korea, 1945–1947* (Oxford: Berg Publishers, 1989) p. 86.
26. Quoted by Ree, ibid., p. 87.
27. Quoted by Ree, ibid., p. 89.
28. Kim Chang-sun, *Fifteen-year History*, p. 126.
29. Hak-Joon Kim, *Unification Policy*, p. 42.
30. Robert A. Scalapino and Chong-sik Lee, *Communism in Korea*, Part 1 (Berkeley and Los Angeles, Cal.: University of California Press, 1972) pp. 314–24.
31. Ibid., pp. 332–3.
32. George M. McCune, with the collaboration of Arthur L. Grey Jr, *Korea Today*, (Cambridge, Mass.: Harvard University Press, 1950) pp. 243–4.
33. Sandusky, *America's Parallel*, p. 39.
34. Kim Youngwon A., *Divided Korea: The Politics of Development, 1945–1972* (Cambridge, Mass.: Harvard University Press, 1976) p. 73; cited by Ree, *Socialism in One Zone*, p. 236.
35. Kim, *Divided Korea*, pp. 74–5.
36. Quoted by Lowe, *Origins of the Korean War*, p. 25.
37. Deputy Director of the Office of Strategic Services (OSS), the forerunner of the CIA, Cumings, *Origins of the Korean War*, p. 188.
38. Lowe, *Origins the Korean War* p. 26.
39. D. F. Fleming, *The Cold War and its Origins, 1917–1960* (New York: Doubleday, 1961), p. 592; W. Douglas Reeve, *The Republic of Korea* (London: Oxford University Press, 1963) pp. 26–7.
40. Hak-Kyu Sohn, *Authoritarianism and Opposition in South Korea* (London: Routledge, 1989) p. 16.
41. Sungjoo Han, *The Failure of Democracy in Korea* (Berkeley, Cal.: University of California Press, 1974) pp. 26–31.

42. Dae-Sook Suh, 'Kim Il-song: his personality and politics', in Robert A. Scalapino and Jun-Yop Kim (eds), *North Korea Today: Strategic and Domestic Issues* (Berkeley, Cal.: University of California Press, 1983) p. 49.

43. US Department of State, *North Korea: A Case Study in the Techniques of Takeover*, (Washington, D.C: Department of State Publication, 7119, Far Eastern Series, no. 103 US Government Printing Office, p. 103.

44. Even observers believing that partition was not entirely an American ploy conceded the confused atmosphere surrounding the division of Korea. Thus Richard Whelan (*Drawing the Line* (London: Faber & Faber, 1990) p. 48): 'Korea was thus divided into two hostile states – not really by American design, but by confusion, drift, misunderstanding, resentment, expedience, incompetence, good intentions, intransigence, failed bluffs, dashed hope, and fear.'

45. Ibid., pp. 46–7.

46. Hak-Joon Kim, *Unification Policy*, p. 65.

47. Whelan, *Drawing the Line*, p. 47.

48. *Korean Central Yearbook*, 1950, p. 220, quoted by Kim Han Gil, *Modern History of Korea*, p. 259.

49. US Department of State Economic Mission, *Land Reform in Korea*, Seoul, 13 September 1947, p. 1, cited by McCune, *Korea today*, p. 129.

50. *Chukan Digest*, Department of Public Information, Seoul, no. 60, 14 December 1946, quoted by McCune, *Korea Today*, p. 130.

51. Yong-jeung Kim, *Voice of Korea*, 17 January 1948, quoted by McCune, *Korea Today* p. 131.

52. McCune, *Korea Today*, pp. 132–8.

53. Jon Halliday, 'The Economics of North and South Korea', in Sullivan and Foss (eds), *Two Koreas – One Future?*, p. 23.

54. Ibid.

55. Lowe, *Origins of the Korean War*, p. 57.

56. Quoted by Halliday and Cumings, *Korea*, p. 23.

57. Ibid.

58. Halliday, in Sullivan and Foss, *Two Koreas – One Future*, p. 21.

60. Joseph Sanghoon Chung, *The North Korean Economy: Structure and Development* (Stanford, Cal.: Hoover Institution Press 1974) p. 57 (citing Japanese source).

61. Halliday, 'Economics of North and South Korea', p. 23.

62. Ree, *Socialism in One Zone*, pp. 151–2.

63. Sources cited in ibid., p. 152.

64. Ibid., p. 153.

65. Ibid., p. 165.

66. Cumings, 'Division of Korea', p. 10.

67. Ibid., p. 11; even official South Korean publications, manifestly pro-American, acknowledge that the 'US in the South' was one of the reasons for the frustrations of the efforts of the Koreans to establish an independent government (see, for example, *Facts About Korea* (Seoul, Korea: Korean Overseas Information Service, 1993) p. 26).

68. Cumings, *Origins of the Korea War*, pp. 351–79.

69. Kim Han Gil, *Modern History of Korea*, pp. 244–5.
70. Cumings 'Division of Korea', p. 14.
71. Even as late as 1954, after the end of the Korean War, there was residual guerrilla activity in the South – finally extinguished by the US-sponsored 'Operation Ratkiller'.
72. Quoted by Halliday and Cumings, *Korea*, p. 36.
73. Cited by Lowe, *Origins of the Korean War*, p. 57.
74. Hak-Joon Kim, *Unification Policy*, p. 78.
75. Soviet specialist, cited by Glenn D. Paige, 'Korea', in Cyril E. Black and Thomas P. Thornton (eds), *Communism and Revolution* (Princeton, N.J.: Princeton University Press, 1964) pp. 215–42.
76. One CIA estimate (cited by Halliday and Cumings, *Korea*, p. 43) suggests there may have been as many as 6000 guerrillas in South Korea in early 1949.
77. Quoted by Halliday and Cumings, ibid., pp. 46–7.

Notes to Chapter 6: The Korean War

1. Quoted by Lord Moran, *Winston Churchill: The Struggle for Survival, 1940–1965* (London: Sphere Books, 1968) p. 446.
2. Harold Macmillan's diaries (13 December 1950), unpublished, in Harold Macmillan's Archives, quoted in Alisdair Horne, *Macmillan, 1894–1956*, vol. I (London: Macmillan, 1988) p. 329.
3. Dwight D. Eisenhower, *The White House Years: Mandate for change, 1953–1956* (London: Heinemann, 1963) p. 180.
4. Max Hastings, *The Korean War* (London: Michael Joseph, 1987) pp. 31–2.
5. Callum MacDonald, *Britain and the Korean War* (Oxford: Basil Blackwell, 1990) p. 10.
6. Quoted by Jon Halliday and Bruce Cumings, *Korea, the Unknown War* (London: Viking, 1988) p. 47.
7. Ibid.
8. Noam Chomsky, *Deterring Democracy* (London: Verson, 1991) p. 335.
9. Takashi Hatada, *A History of Korea*, trans. and ed. Warren W. Smith Jr and Benjamin H. Hazard (Santa Barbara, ABC-Clio, 1969) p. 140.
10. Hastings, *Korean War*, p. 32.
11. Leonard Mosley, *Dulles: A biography of Eleanor, Allen and John Foster Dulles and their family network* (London: Hodder & Stoughton, 1978) p. 256.
12. Acheson quotes relevant sections of his own speech and MacArthur's in Dean Acheson, *Present at the Creation: My Years in the State Department* (New York: W. W. Norton 1969) pp. 355–7.
13. British sources, quoted by Halliday and Cumings, *Korea, The Unknown War*, p. 53.
14. Ibid.
15. Ibid., p. 54.
16. Quoted in D. F. Fleming, *The Cold War and its Origins, 1917–1960* (New York: Doubleday, 1961) vol. II, p. 654.

17. Ibid., p. 599.
18. Edwin P. Hoyt, *Pacific Destiny* (New York: W. W. Norton, 1981) p. 259.
19. Kim Han Gil, *Modern History of Korea* (Pyongyang, Korea: Foreign Languages Publishing House, 1979) pp. 279–84.
20. Ibid., p. 287.
21. Reinhard Drifte, 'Japan's Involvement in the Korean War', in James Cotton and Ian Neary (eds), *The Korean War in History* (Manchester: Manchester University Press, 1989) pp. 120–34.
22. Radio address, 13 April 1950, reprinted in *Department of State Bulletin*, 24 April 1950, p. 627, quoted in William Blum, *The CIA: A Forgotten Story* (London: Zed Books, 1986).
23. Kim Han Gil, *Modern History of Korea*, p. 306.
24. John Gunther *The Riddle of MacArthur* (London: Hamish Hamilton, 1951) p. 166.
25. Fleming, *Cold War*, p. 654; see also the account in John Quigley, *The Ruses for War: American Interventionism since World War Two* (New York: Prometheus Books, 1992) pp. 35–48.
26. *Daily Herald*, London, 26 June 1950; *The Guardian*, London, 26 June 1950; *New York Herald Tribune*, 26 June 1950.
27. Harry S. Truman, 'The Korean Situation, Its Significance to the People of the United States', 19 July 1950, *Department of State Bulletin*, vol. 23, p. 165.
28. *Izvestiia*, 1 July 1949, in *The Current Digest of the Soviet Press*, vol. I, no. 27 (2 August 1949) pp. 22–3, quoted in Hak-Joon Kim, *The Unification Policy of North and South Korea* (Seoul: Seoul National University Press, 1977) p. 82.
29. Hak-Joon Kim, *Unification Policy*, p. 83.
30. Quoted by Stephen E. Ambrose, *Rise to Globalism: American foreign policy since 1938* (Harmondsworth, Middx: Penguin Books, 1988) p. 117.
31. MacArthur conversation with James Plimsoll, in Gavan McCormack, 'The Korean War: Comments on "Review Article"', 1986; cited in John Pilger, *A Secret Country* (London: Jonathan Cape, 1989) p. 124.
32. Compiled from a dozen sources; useful chronologies of the Korean War are given in Hastings, *Korean War*, pp. 438–42; and R. Ernest Dupuy and Trevor N. Dupuy, *The Collins Encyclopedia of Military History*, 4th edn. (London: HarperCollins, 1993) pp. 1354–67.
33. Michael C. Sandusky, *America's Parallel* (Alexandria, Va: Old Dominion Press, 1983) p. 333.
34. All sources in Ra Jong-yil, 'Political Settlement in Korea: British Views and Policies, Autumn 1950', in Cotton and Neary, *Korean War in History*, pp. 53–5.
35. *Incendiary Weapons*, a SITPRO (Stockholm International Peace Research Institute) monograph (Stockholm: Almqvist & Wiksell, 1975) pp. 153–4.
36. Quoted by Seymour Hersh, *Kissinger, The Price of Power* (New York: Simon & Schuster, 1983) p. 52.
37. Eisenhower, *White House Years*, p. 180.

38. Ibid.
39. Bernard Brodie, *War and Politics* (London: Cassell, 1973) pp. 64–5.
40. Quoted by I. F. Stone, *In a Time of Torment* (London: Jonathan Cape, 1968) p. 240.
41. Trevor Royle, *War Report* (London: Grafton Books, 1987) pp. 236–49.
42. Jean Larteguy, *The Face of War: Reflections on Men and Combat*, trans. Beth de Bilio, extract in Paul Fussell (ed.), *The Bloody Game: An anthology of war* (London: Scribners, 1991) p. 668.
43. Ibid., p. 669.
44. Eugene Kinkead, *Why They Collaborated* (London: Longman, 1960); John Marks, *The Search for the 'Manchurian Candidate'* (London: Allen Lane, Penguin Books, 1979) pp. 125–6.
45. Trygve Lie, *In the Cause of Peace* (New York: Macmillan, 1954) p. 324.
46. FBIS, *Daily Report*, 21 November 1947, Korea, quoted in Hak-Joon Kim, *Unification Policy* p. 62.
47. Nikita Khrushchev in the much-quoted *Khrushchev Remembers, The Glasnost Tapes* (Boston, Mass.: Little, Brown, 1990) pp. 144–7, declares that Kim Il-sung started the Korean War with Stalin's support.
48. Roy Jenkins (now Lord Jenkins of Hillhead), *Truman* (London: Collins, 1986) p. 169; for Jenkins, however, this violation of the UN Charter was 'a very minor fault and one on the right side'.
49. Brodie, *War and Politics*, p. 60.
50. Ibid.
51. Harry S. Truman, *The Truman Memoirs*, vol. II: *Years of Trial and Hope, 1946–1953* (London: Hodder & Stoughton, 1956) pp. 352–3.
52. Quoted by Merle Miller, *Plain Speaking: an oral biography of Harry S. Truman* (New York: Berkeley Publishing Corporation, 1974) p. 265.
53. Inis L. Claude Jr, *Swords into Plowshares: The problems and progress of international organisation* (London: University of London Press, 1964) p. 246.
54. Cited, with other reports, by Kinkead, *Why They Collaborated*, pp. 17, 34.
55. See, for example, G. Edward Griffin, *The Fearful Master: A second look at the United Nations* (Belmont, Mass. Western Islands, 1972) p. 178.
56. See Geoff Simons, *The United Nations: A Chronology of Conflict* (London: Macmillan, 1994) ch. 7; Geoff Simons, *UN Malaise: Power, Problems and Realpolitik*, (London: Macmillan, 1995), ch. 3.

Notes to Chapter 7: The Aftermath

1. Jon Halliday and Bruce Cumings, *Korea, the Unknown War* (London: Viking, Penguin Books, 1988) p. 146.
2. Ibid.
3. Tom Bower, *Blind Eye to Murder* (London: Paladin-Granada, 1983) p. 418; see also Christopher Simpson, *Blowback: America's recruitment of Nazis and its effects on the Cold War* (London: Weidenfeld & Nicolson, 1988) pp. 190–2.

4. John Quigley, *The Ruses for War: American Interventionism since World War II* (Buffalo, N.Y.: Prometheus, 1992) p. 38.
5. Jon Halliday, 'Secret war of the top guns', *The Observer*, London, 5 July 1992.
6. In June 1992 President Yeltsin wrote to Senator Kerry's Senate select committee on Pow/MIA (missing in action) cases, admitting that American PoWs from The Second World War and Korea had been held in the Soviet Union, some of whom may still be alive. Senate investigators had given the names of British PoWs captured in Korea and held in Siberia and China (Nigel Cawthorne, 'Security agency "traced 200 senior air crew to gulags"', *The Guardian*, London, 17 June 1992); see also Matthew Campbell and Ian Glover-James, 'Hidden American raises Gulag hopes', *The Sunday Times*, London, 21 June 1992.
7. Ben Fenton, 'Eisenhower "let PoWs die in Siberia"', *The Daily Telegraph*, London, 11 November 1992.
8. Gregory Henderson, 'The politics of Korea', in John Sullivan and Roberta Foss (eds), *Two Koreas – One Future?* (Lanham, Md: University Press of America, 1987) p. 103.
9. James B. Palais, ' "Democracy" in South Korea, 1948–72', in Frank Baldwin (ed.), *The American–Korean Relationship Since 1945* (New York: Pantheon Books, 1974) p. 326.
10. Martin Hart-Landsberg, *The Rush to Development: Economic change and political struggle in South Korea* (New York: Monthly Review Press, 1993) pp. 133–4.
11. Youngwan Alexander Kim, *Divided Korea: The politics of development, 1945–1972* (Cambridge, Mass.: Harvard University Press, 1976) p. 209.
12. Henderson, 'Politics of Korea', p. 104.
13. George McT. Kahin, *Intervention: How America became involved in Vietnam* (New York: Anchor Books, Doubleday, 1987) p. 42.
14. Ibid., pp. 333–4.
15. Hart-Landsberg, *Rush to Development*, p. 147.
16. James Stentzel, 'Seoul's second bonanza', *Far Eastern Economic Review*, 30 July 1973, p. 43.
17. Frank Baldwin, 'America's rented troops: South Koreans in Vietnam', *Bulletin of Concerned Asian Scholars*, October–December 1975, p. 39.
18. Roland A. Paul, *American Military Commitments Abroad* (New Brunswick, N.J.: Rutgers University Press, 1973) pp. 103–4.
19. Kahin, *Intervention*, p. 336.
20. The Yushin phase (1972–1979) is considered in detail in Hak-Kyu Sohn, *Authoritarianism and Opposition in South Korea* (London: Routledge, 1989).
21. Lew Perdue and Ken Cummins, 'The Korean Connection', in Robin Moore, Lew Perdue and Nick Rowe, *The Washington Connection* (New York: Condor, 1977) pp. 3–74.
22. Asia Watch Committee, *Human Rights in Korea* (Washington D.C., Asia Watch, 1985) p. 37.
23. Hart-Landsberg, *Rush to Development*, pp. 217–18.
24. Ibid., pp. 222–3.

25. Quoted in 'Buying time for change', *Far Eastern Economic Review*, 12 November 1982, p. 40.
26. Hart-Landsberg, *Rush to Development*, p. 223.
27. Terry McCarthy, 'Spotlight turns on dissident's ordeal on the high seas', *The Independent*, London, 2 September 1993.
28. Terry McCarthy, 'Kim reforms run into opposition from old cliques', *The Independent*, London, 12 March 1993.
29. Jon Halliday, 'The economics of North and South Korea', in Sullivan and Foss (eds), *The Koreas – One Future?*, p. 26.
30. *Military Situation in the Far East*, Hearings before the Commitee on Armed Services and the Committee on Foreign Relations, US Senate, 82nd Congress, 1st Session, p. 3075, cited by Halliday, ibid.
31. Dennis Lankford, *I Defy: The Story of Dennis Lankford* (London: Wingate, 1954) p. 156.
32. See, for example, the highly partisan account in Kim Han Gil, *Modern History of Korea* (Pyongyang, North Korea: Foreign Languages Publishing House, 1973) pp. 387–489.
33. Sang-Seek Park, 'North Korea's policy towards the Third World', in Robert A. Scalapino and Jun-Yop Kim (eds), *North Korea Today: Strategic and Domestic Issues* (Berkeley, Cal.: University of California Press, 1983) pp. 319–22.
34. Ibid.
35. A discussion of the 1972 constitution is given in Chin-wee chung, 'The evolution of a constitutional structure in North Korea', in ibid., pp. 19–42.
36. See, for example, Chong-Sik Lee, 'Evolution of the Korean Workers' Party and the rise of Kim Chong-il', in ibid., pp. 65–80.
37. Ibid., p. 75.
38. Quoted by Chong-Sik Lee, ibid., p. 76.
39. 'North Korean heir "critically injured"', *The Guardian*, London, 18 February 1994; 'N. Korean heir-apparent "hurt in shooting accident"', *The Independent*, London, 18 February 1994. In 1987 the South Korean Defence Minister announced on television the death of Kim Il-sung, a few days before the 'Great Leader' was filmed greeting foreign dignitaries in Pyongyang.
40. 'Macabre dance of a dynasty from hell', *The Sunday Times*, London, 14 November 1993.
41. Ibid.
42. Cited by Chong-Sik Lee, 'Evolution of the Korean Workers' Party', p. 80.
43. Aidan Foster-Carter, *Korea's Coming Reunification: Another East Asian Superpower?* (London: Economist Intelligence Unit, April 1992) p. 90.
44. Chong-Wook Chung, 'Mass organisations and campaigns in North Korea', in Scalapino and Kim (eds), *North Korea Today* p. 81.
45. Amnesty International index: ASA 25/06/94, January 1994.
46. *South Korea: Human Rights Violations Continue Under the New Government*, Amnesty International index: ASA 25/08/94, February 1994.
47. 'New evidence of violations', *Amnesty International (British Section) Journal*, January–February 1994, p. 5.

48. Reuter and AFP reports; see *The Guardian*, London, 14 March 1994; *The Guardian*, London, 4 April 1994; *The Independent*, London, 11 April 1994; *The Guardian*, London, 20 April 1993.

49. Kevin Rafferty, 'Rice farmers prove country still rooted in soil', *The Guardian*, London, 25 February 1994.

50. See, for example, Kevin Rafferty, 'Growth and export figures confound gloomy forecasts', *The Guardian*, London, 25 February 1994; Aidan Foster-Carter, 'Confident dolphin no longer in fear of whale-sized neighbours', *The Guardian*, London, 25 February 1994.

51. Carl Friedrich (ed), *Totalitarianism* (New York: The University Library, 1964) pp. 52–3.

52. Changsoo Lee, 'Social policy and development in North Korea', in Scalapino and Kim (eds), *North Korea Today*, p. 126.

53. Ibid., p. 127.

54. Terry McCarthy, 'Looking for trouble in North Korea', *The Independent*, London, 12 September 1992.

55. T. R. Reid, 'N. Korea "shaken by riots"', *The Guardian*, London, 20 August 1993.

56. Kevin Rafferty, 'N. Korean defector tells of food riots', *The Guardian*, London, 25 August 1993; Jon Swain, 'Crisis in the land of fear', *The Sunday Times*, London, 5 September 1993.

57. *North Korea, Summary of Amnesty International's Concerns*, Amnesty International index: ASA 24/03/93, October 1993.

58. See also the report by Claudia Rosett (of *The Wall Street Journal*), '*Korean "slaves" die in hidden Russian gulags*', *The Sunday Times*, London, 17 April 1994.

59. Harry S. Truman, *The Truman Memoirs* vol. II: *Years of Trial and Hope, 1946–1953* (London: Hodder & Stoughton, 1956) p. 334.

60. Ibid., p. 339.

61. A detailed examination of the partition is given in Hak-Joon Kim, *The Unification Policy of South and North Korea* (Seoul: Seoul National University Press, 1977).

62. Ibid., p. 166.

63. Quoted by Hak-Joon Kim, ibid., p. 184.

64. John Rodda, *The Guardian*, London, 7 June 1985.

65. Christopher R. Hill, *Olympic Politics* (Manchester, England: Manchester University Press, 1992) pp. 204–7.

66. Foster-Carter, *Korea's Coming Reunification*, p. 53.

67. Ibid., p. 57.

68. John McLean, 'North and South Korea agree to sign peace pact', *The Independent*, London, 13 December 1991.

69. Terry McCarthy, 'Koreas talk across a tense divide', *The Independent*, London, 27 December 1991.

70. *Unification Policy* (Seoul, Korea: Korean Overseas Information Service, March 1994.

71. Saundra Pollock Sturdevant and Brenda Stoltzfus, *Let The Good Times Roll: Prostitution and the US military in Asia* (New York: The New Press, 1992) p. 15.

Bibliography

Acheson, Dean, *Present at the Creation: My Years in the State Department* (New York: W. W. Norton, 1969).

Ambrose, Stephen E., *Rise to Globalism: American Foreign Policy since 1938* (Harmondsworth, Middx: Penguin Books, 1988).

Baik Bong, *Kim Il Sung*, 3 vols (Beirut, Lebanon: Dar al-Talia, 1973).

Beasley, W. G., *The Modern History of Japan* (London: Weidenfeld & Nicolson, 1973).

Behr, Edward, *Hirohito: Behind the Myth* (Harmondsworth Middx: Penguin Books, 1990).

Bergamini, David, *Japan's Imperial Conspiracy* (London: Panther Books, 1972).

Bishop, Jim, *FDR's Last Year, April 1944–April 1945* (London: Hart Davis, MacGibbon, 1975).

Black, Cyril E. and Thomas P. Thornton (eds), *Communism and Revolution* (Princeton, N.J.: Princeton University Press, 1964).

Blum, William, *The CIA: A Forgotten Story* (London: Zed Books, 1986).

Boyd, Andrew, *Fifteen Men on a Powder Keg: A History of the UN Security Council* (London: Methuen, 1971).

Brodie, Bernard, *War and Politics* (London: Cassell, 1973).

Busch, Noel F., *Two Minutes to Noon* (New York: Simon & Schuster, 1962).

Chomsky, Noam, *Deterring Democracy* (London: Verso, 1991).

Chung, Joseph Sanghoon, *The North Korean Economy: Structure and Development* (Stanford, Cal.: Hoover Institution Press, 1974).

Claude, Inis L. Jr, *Swords into Plowshares: The Problems and Progress of International Organization* (London: University of London Press, 1964).

Cotton, James and Ian Neary (eds), *The Korean War in History* (Manchester, England: Manchester University Press, 1989).

Cumings, Bruce, *The Origins of the Korean War: Liberation and the Emergence of Separate Regimes, 1945–1947* (Princeton, N.J.: Princeton University Press, 1981).

Dower, John, *War Without Mercy: Race and Power in the Pacific War* (London: Faber & Faber, 1986).

Eden, Anthony, *The Memoirs of Anthony Eden: The Reckoning* (Boston, Mass: Houghton Mifflin, 1965).

Eisenhower, Dwight D., *The White House Years: Mandate for Change, 1953–1956* (London: Heinemann, 1963).

Fairbank, John K., Edwin O. Reischauer and Albert M. Craig, *East Asia, Tradition and Transformation* (London: George Allen & Unwin, 1973).

Fleming, D. F., *The Cold War and its Origins, 1917–1960* (New York: Doubleday, 1961).

Foot, Rosemary, *A Substitute for Victory: The Politics of Peacemaking at the Korean Armistice Talks* (Ithaca, N.Y.: Cornell University Press, 1990).

Green, A. Wigfall, *Epic of Korea* (Washington, D.C.: Public Affairs Press, 1950).

Grey, Jeffrey, *The Commonwealth Armies and the Korean War* (Manchester, England: Manchester University Press, 1988).

Griffin, G. Edward, *The Fearful Master: A Second Look at the United Nations*, (Belmont, Mass.: Western Islands, 1972).

Gunther, John, *The Riddle of MacArthur* (London: Hamish Hamilton, 1951).

Halliday, Jon, and Bruce Cumings, *Korea: The Unknown War* (London: Viking, 1988).

Handbook of Korea (Seoul, Korea: Korean Overseas Information Service, Ministry of Culture and Information, 1978).

Han, Sungjoo, *The Failure of Democracy in Korea* (Berkeley, Cal.: University of California Press, 1974).

Hart-Landsberg, Martin, *The Rush to Development: Economic Change and Political Struggle in South Korea* (New York: Monthly Review Press, 1993).

Hastings, Max, *The Korean War* (London: Michael Joseph, 1987).

Hatada, Takashi, *A History of Korea*, trans. and ed. Warren W. Smith Jr and Benjamin H. Hazard (Santa Barbara, Cal.: ABC-Clio, 1969).

Henthorn, William E., *A History of Korea* (New York: The Free Press, 1971).

Hersh, Seymour M., *Kissinger: The Price of Power* (New York: Simon & Schuster, 1983).

—— *The Samson Option: Israel, America and the Bomb* (London: Faber & Faber, 1991).

Higham, Charles, *Trading with the Enemy* (London: Robert Hale, 1983).

Horowitz, David, *From Yalta to Vietnam: American Foreign Policy in the Cold War* (Harmondsworth, Middx: Penguin Books, 1967).

Hoyt, Edwin P., *Pacific Destiny* (New York: W. W. Norton, 1981).

Hunter, Janet E., *The Emergence of Modern Japan* (London: Longman, 1989).

Jordan, Donald A., *Chinese Boycotts Versus Japanese Bombs* (Ann Arbor, Mich.: University of Michigan Press, 1981).

Kahin, George McT., *Intervention: How America became involved in Vietnam* (New York: Anchor Books, Doubleday, 1987).

Kennedy, Malcolm D., *The Estrangement of Great Britain and Japan, 1917–35* (Manchester, England: Manchester University Press, 1969).

Khrushchev, Nikita, *Khrushchev Remembers: The Glasnost Tapes* (Boston, Mass.: Little, Brown, 1990).

Kim Chang-Sun, *Fifteen-year History of North Korea* (Washington, D. C. 1965).

Kim, Hak-Joon, *The Unification Policy of South and North Korea* (Seoul, Korea: Seoul National University Press, 1977).

Kim Han Gil, *Modern History of Korea* (Pyongyang, Korea: Foreign Languages Publishing House, 1979).

Kim, Key-Hiuk, *The Last Phase of the East Asian World Order* (Berkeley, Cal.: University of California Press, 1980).

Kim Youngwan A., *Divided Korea: The Politics of Development, 1945–1972* (Cambridge, Mass.: Harvard University Press, 1976).

Kinkead, Eugene, *Why They Collaborated* (London: Longman, 1960).

—— *Korea, Its Land, People and Culture of All Ages* (Seoul, Korea: Hakwon-sa, 1960).

Lee, Ki-baik, *A New History of Korea*, trans. Edward W. Wagner and Edward J. Shultz (Cambridge, Mass.: Harvard University Press, 1984).

Lie, Trygve, *In the Cause of Peace* (New York: Macmillan, 1954).

Loewenheim, Francis L., Harold D. Langley and Manfred Jonas (eds), *Roosevelt and Churchill: Their Secret Wartime Correspondence* (London: Barrie & Jenkins, 1975).

Longford, J. H., *The Story of Korea* (London, 1911).

Lowe, Peter, *The Origins of the Korean War* (London: Longman, 1986).

MacDonald, Callum, *Britain and the Korean War* (Oxford: Basil Blackwell, 1990).

Manchester, William, *American Caesar: Douglas MacArthur, 1880–1964* (London: Hutchinson, 1979).

Marks, John, *The Search for the 'Manchurian Candidate'* (London: Allen Lane, Penguin Books, 1979).

McCune, George M. (with collaboration of Arthur L. Grey Jr), *Korea Today* (Cambridge, Mass.: Harvard University Press, 1950).

Meade, E. Grant, *American Military Government in Korea* (London: Oxford University Press, 1951).

Miller, Edward S., *War Plan Orange: The US Strategy to Defeat Japan, 1897–1945* (Annapolis: Naval Institute Press, 1991).

Miller, Merle, *Plain Speaking: An Oral Biography of Harry S. Truman* (New York: Berkeley Publishing Corporation, 1974).

Montgomery, Michael, *Imperialist Japan: The Yen to Dominate* (London: Christopher Helm, 1987).

Moore, Robin, Lew Perdue and Nick Rowe, *The Washington Connection* (New York: Condor Publishing Company, 1977).

Morris, Ivan, *The Nobility of Failure: Tragic Heroes in the History of Japan* (London: Secker & Warburg, 1975).

Mosley, Leonard, *Dulles: A Biography of Eleanor, Allen and John Foster Dulles and their Family Network* (London: Hodder and Stoughton, 1978).

—— *Hirohito, Emperor of Japan* (London: Weidenfeld & Nicolson, 1966).

Myrdal, Alva, *The Game of Disarmament: How the United States and Russia ran the Arms Race* (Manchester, England: Manchester University Press, 1977).

Nelson, M. Frederick, *Korea and the Old Orders in Eastern Asia* (Baton Rouge, La.: Louisiana State University Press, 1946).

Oliver, Robert T., *Korea, Forgotten Nation* (Washington, D.C.: Public Affairs Press, 1944).

—— *Syngman Rhee: The Man Behind the Mask* (London: Robert Hall, 1955).

Pisani, Sallie, *The CIA and the Marshall Plan* (Edinburgh: Edinburgh University Press, 1991).

Quigley, John, *The Ruses for War: American Interventionism since World War II* (New York: Prometheus Books, 1992).

Ree, Erik Van, *Socialism in One Zone: Stalin's Policy in Korea, 1945–1947* (Oxford: Berg, 1989).

Reeve, W. Douglas, *The Republic of Korea* (London: Oxford University Press, 1963).

Reischauer, Edwin O., and John K. Fairbank, *A History of East Asian Civilization*, vol. I East Asia: the Great Tradition (Boston Mass.: Houghton Mifflin Company, 1960).

Ringer, Benjamin B., *'We the Peoples' and Others; Duality and America's Treatment of Its Racial Minorities* (New York and London: Tavistock Publications, 1983).

Royle, Trevor, *War Report* (London: Grafton Books, 1987).

Sandusky, Michael C., *America's Parallel* (Alexandria, Va: Old Dominion Press, 1983).

Scalapino, Robert A. and Chong-Sik Lee, *Communism in Korea* (Berkeley, Cal.: University of California Press, 1972).

Scalapino, Robert A. and Jun-Yop Kim (eds), *North Korea Today: Strategic and Domestic Issues* (Berkeley, Cal.: Centre for Korean Studies, Institute for East Asian Studies, University of California, Berkeley, 1983).

Sherwood, Robert E., *Roosevelt and Hopkins: An Intimate History* (New York: Harper, 1948).

Sifry Micah L., and Christopher Cerf (eds), *The Gulf War Reader* (New York: Times Books, Random House, 1991).

Simons, Geoff, *The United Nations: A Chronology of Conflict* (London: Macmillan, 1994).

—— *UN Malaise; Power, Problems and Realpolitik* (London: Macmillan, 1995).

Simpson, Christopher, *Blowback: America's Recruitment of Nazis and its effects on the Cold War* (London: Weidenfeld & Nicolson, 1988).

Sohn, Hak-kyu, *Authoritarianism and Opposition in South Korea* (London: Routledge 1989).

Steiger, G. Nye, *A History of the Far East* (New York: Ginn, 1944).

Storry, Richard, *A History of Modern Japan* (Harmondsworth, Middx: Penguin Books, 1963).

Strong, Anna Louise, *Inside North Korea* (Montrose, Cal. 1951).

Sturdevant, Saundra Pollock and Brenda Stoltzfus, *Let the Good Times Roll: Prostitution and the US Military in Asia* (New York: The New Press, 1992).

Sullivan, John, and Roberta Foss (eds), *Two Koreas – One Future?* (Lanham, Md: University Press of America, 1987).

Timmerman, Kenneth R., *The Death Lobby: How the West armed Iraq* (London: Fourth Estate, 1992).

Truman, Harry S., *The Truman Memoirs*, vol. I: *Year of Decisions, 1945* (London: Hodder & Stoughton, 1955).

—— *The Truman Memoirs*, vol.II: *Years of Trial and Hope, 1946–1953* (London: Hodder & Stoughton, 1956).

Whelan, Richard, *Drawing the Line: The Korean War, 1950–1953* (London: Faber & Faber, 1990).

Index